CW01261760

FEMINISM, TRADITION AND CHANGE IN CONTEMPORARY ISLAM

FEMINISM, TRADITION AND CHANGE IN CONTEMPORARY ISLAM

Negotiating Islamic Law and Gender

Shehnaz Haqqani

ONEWORLD
ACADEMIC

A Oneworld Academic Book

First published by Oneworld Publications Ltd in 2024

Copyright © Shehnaz Haqqani 2024

The moral right of Shehnaz Haqqani to be identified as the Author of this work has been asserted by her in accordance with the Copyright, Designs and Patents Act 1988

All rights reserved
Copyright under Berne Convention
A CIP record for this title is available from the British Library

ISBN 978-0-86154-840-8
eISBN 978-0-86154-841-5

Typeset by Geethik Technologies
Printed and bound in Great Britain by Clays Ltd, Elcograf S.p.A.

Oneworld Publications Ltd
10 Bloomsbury Street
London WC1B 3SR
England

Stay up to date with the latest books, special offers, and exclusive content from Oneworld with our newsletter

Sign up on our website
oneworld-publications.com

FSC
www.fsc.org
MIX
Paper | Supporting responsible forestry
FSC® C018072

This book is dedicated to Muslims and non-Muslims everywhere who struggle to reconcile any areas of their religious practice passed down through tradition with what they know intuitively to be right. Know that you have options, and those options are beautiful. Keep asking questions. Keep exploring. Your *jihad* is not in vain. May we live to see the world we are working towards building.

Table of Contents

List of Tables		ix
Introduction		1
Chapter 1:	A Rhizomatic Approach to the Islamic Tradition	29
SECTION 1:	**THE NEGOTIABLES**	67
Chapter 2:	Child Marriage	71
Chapter 3:	Sexual Slavery in Islam	111
Chapter 4:	Female Inheritance in Islam	143
	Conclusion to Section 1	167
SECTION 2:	**THE NON-NEGOTIABLES**	171
Chapter 5:	Muslim Women's Interfaith Marriage	173
Chapter 6:	Female-Led Mixed-Gender Prayer	241
	Conclusion to Section 2	299
	Conclusion: the Politics of Negotiation and Relevance	303
Acknowledgements		321
Bibliography		327
Notes		337
Index		373

List of Tables

Table 1: The *sharī'a* reflects God's will or intent.

Table 2: The consensus of the scholars is always binding.

Table 3: God intended gender equality.

Table 4: How old was Aisha when Muhammad married her?

Table 5: The Prophet's marriage to Aisha is *Sunnah*.

Table 6: Is there a minimum age for marriage in Islam? If so, what is it?

Table 7: The consensus of the scholars on child marriage is binding.

Table 8: Islamic law permits slavery.

Table 9: Islam outlawed slavery.

Table 10: Slavery in any form is morally wrong.

Table 11: Men can have sexual relations with women they enslave.

Table 12: Islamic law's position on slavery is binding on Muslims today.

Table 13: In Islamic law, a daughter's inheritance is half that of a son's.

Table 14: I think a daughter's inheritance should be half that of a son's.

Table 15: My children, both sons and daughters, will receive an equal share.

Table 16: The consensus on female inheritance is binding today.

Table 17: Islamic law's position on women's interfaith marriage is binding.

Table 18: Women's marriage to the People of the Book isn't allowed in Islam, and Muslims today must maintain the consensus.

Table 19: Women's marriage to People of the Book is not allowed in Islam, but it should be.

Table 20: Muslim women are allowed to marry People of the Book.

Table 21: General attitude towards female-led mixed-gender prayer.

Table 22: Muslims' attitudes towards female-led prayer.

Table 23: The consensus on female-led prayer is binding today.

Table 24: Is *ijmā'* (or scholarly consensus) binding on Muslims?

Introduction

There's a disconnect between modern and pre-modern understandings of Islam, but it remains unacknowledged in the mainstream. This book is a product of an ethnographic study of Muslim Americans' conceptions of and engagements with Islam and Islamic law, examining their evolving views and their appeals to religious authority. Lay Muslim Americans are inconsistent in how they interpret pre-modern (pre-nineteenth century) doctrines – accepting reforms to certain issues on the basis of human rights and social justice, while ruling out reforms of particular hierarchical gender laws and not perceiving them as related to human rights. For instance, while contemporary Muslim Americans reject slavery and child marriage, despite their permissibility in the historical legal Islamic tradition, they maintain male marital privileges in accordance with the Islamic past. They do not open up the historic construction of gender roles in the Islamic tradition to interpretation. I investigate Muslims' interpretive choices and their relationship with an Islamic past that is invoked and explained to maintain gender hierarchy as though it is inherent, fundamental to Islam, even when the historical tradition, when freshly examined, reveals a more multivalent picture.

In March 2005, amina wadud, a prominent female scholar of Islam, led a mixed-gender prayer in New York – an act prohibited by pre-modern Islamic consensus. She pointed out that there is no Qur'anic or prophetic evidence against female-led prayers of mixed congregations. Moreover, the reasons the prohibition exists are rooted in now-debunked patriarchal assumptions about male and female sexuality. As she argued, since the Prophet Muhammad sought to promote women's rights and gender equality and abolish injustices, the prohibition against female-led prayer is not Islamic. Muslims almost universally objected to the prayer, insisting that Islam forbade such an act and that any attempts to alter this were efforts to change Islam.[1] According to this response, 'Islam' offers a clear non-negotiable position on female-led prayer. The historical scholarly consensus cannot be reopened or subjected to new criticism.

However, the Islamic consensus can and has changed on some issues, such as slavery. In summer of 2015, when ISIS invoked Islam's past acceptance of slavery to enslave Yazidi women, Muslim scholars and lay Muslims from around the world were outraged.[2] Muslims pointed to the legal abolition of slavery across the globe; their claims were supported by the idea that slavery is inhumane and therefore forbidden. While the global Muslim population rejected this attempt by ISIS to revive slavery despite the historical permissibility of enslaving people, they opposed wadud's prayer leadership, claiming that it challenged the historical scholarly consensus. These different visions of Islam's (in)flexibility beg serious attention.

The relationship between the two above cases is significant. While historical scholars of Islam accepted slavery, contemporary scholars reject it as un-Islamic and even as prohibited, arguing that the practice is not acceptable today, and the permissibility of slavery in the past must be contextualised. Yet the idea that the (non-textual) prohibition on female-led prayer must still apply today is not questioned commonly. Modern Muslims contextualise and reject parts of the Islamic historical tradition, while asserting its non-negotiability in other areas.

The inconsistent approaches to the Islamic past guide the main question of this book: what do lay Muslim Americans understand to be the criteria for changing the scholarly consensus? That is, how do they decide when past Islamic legal precedents are open to renegotiations and when they must remain unaltered? And how do Muslims explain such choices, and how do they – if at all – think about the pre-modern doctrines with which they disagree? To examine lay Muslim Americans' evaluation of the legitimacy of historically established doctrine, I compare contemporary lay Muslim opinions on gender issues where change has occurred with those where change is resisted. I argue that the renegotiation with historical Islam is a complex process channelled by lived reality, gender, and generation. What I mean by 'change' is twofold: first, change in meaning, interpretation, and application of Qur'anic verses, prophetic practice, and scholarly opinion between pre-modern Islam and contemporary, twenty-first-century American Islam. Second, I look at changes in social practice – i.e. the ways Muslims negotiate tradition in how they live their lives.

The selective invoking of the historical past to support contemporary understandings of practices shows there is discontinuity between how modern Muslim Americans see Islam and the consensus of the Islamic tradition before the nineteenth century. Ideas about what is Islamically acceptable and unacceptable have shifted, but not consistently. To investigate this inconsistency, my study surveys five topics: child marriage, sexual slavery, female inheritance, female-led prayer, and women's interfaith marriage. I explore answers to my research questions through two methods: a textual analysis of historical and contemporary literature on the issues, and in-depth ethnographic interviews in Austin, Texas. The interviews took place with 40 Sunni Muslim Americans. An equal number of participants were married and unmarried.[3] All of them were over the age of 18, and they came from varied racial and ethnic backgrounds. All self-identified as American.

THE FIVE TOPICS

The five topics I've chosen demonstrate the inconsistencies in modern Muslim Americans' approach to the tradition. Both my respondents' views (as a sample of lay Muslim Americans today) and those of contemporary Muslim scholars' on child marriage and sexual slavery differ from those of the pre-modern legal tradition. Similarly, existing female inheritance laws are being widely renegotiated, or should be according to my respondents. While the dominant scholarly position is still that daughters must receive half of the inheritance that their brothers get, lay Muslims argue that the inheritance rules in the Qur'an no longer apply. I classify these three topics as 'negotiables' of Islamic law as a result of these shifts. In contrast, current opinions on female-led prayer and women's interfaith marriage are predominantly the same as those of the prevailing pre-modern positions in scholarly discourse, even if some of my respondents express more nuanced perspectives or desire for change. I nonetheless classify these two issues as 'non-negotiables' of

Islamic law because they are perceived as closed to change, according to contemporary scholars of Islam as well as many of my respondents.

I have selected these issues for several reasons. Beside the practical impacts on the lived realities of Muslim women, they also illustrate the tensions between the 'Islamic tradition' and the changes it has undergone already. These issues challenge assumptions about the inflexibility of 'tradition', and they reveal the complex ways in which negotiations within religious traditions occur. Further, traditionalist Muslim scholars appear at pains to explain or justify traditional or classical doctrines from Islamic jurisprudence (*fiqh*) on all these issues because of the stark discrepancies between the initial reasons for their existence and the contemporary context. The variety of modern Muslim viewpoints on these doctrines challenges the claim that Islamic law is unalterable and divine, or at least raises questions about how the negotiation process takes place to determine which doctrines, however established, are negotiable. Because traditionalist Muslim scholars refer to pre-modern scholarship on Islam to justify their teachings, it is worth exploring how contemporary Muslims negotiate the patriarchal assumptions embedded in these doctrines, whether as teachers or as practitioners of Islam.

It may be suggested that slavery and child marriage do not belong in the same category as female-led prayer and women's interfaith marriage because the former are general social practices, while the latter are prohibitions for practising Muslims. Some of my respondents observed the two categories are not comparable because the permissibility of the first category is rooted in sociohistorical and cultural contexts, whereas the second one was somehow rooted in unchanging Islamic truth. By contrast, I argue that these issues are parallel because the historical positions on all four of them, as permissions or prohibitions are all justified or renegotiated through 'contextualisation'. I am interrogating precisely why 'context' may be invoked to renegotiate some parts of the historical scholarly consensus but not others in mainstream Muslim thought.

DEFINING 'ISLAM' AND OTHER KEY TERMS

Investigating these issues requires exploring and clarifying, or complicating, the meanings of 'Islam', 'Islamic law', 'Islamic tradition', *sharīʿa* (popularly, Islamic law), and *fiqh* (Islamic jurisprudence). Lay Muslims often conflate and present these terms as though they were synonymous and clearly understood. In fact, when formulating the interview questions, one of the major struggles I encountered was in deciding which terms to use when referring to 'Islam'. Might a question such as 'Do you believe Islam permits the marriage of individuals who have not yet reached puberty?' evoke the same response as the question, 'Do you believe Islamic law' (or even 'Islamic tradition') permits the marriage of individuals who have not yet reached puberty?' Muslims do not invoke the term 'Islamic tradition' in their daily language of Islam. Lay Muslims tend to speak of 'Islam', 'God', and/or 'the *Sunnah*' (examples from the life of the Prophet Muhammad, or prophetic practice – we will see later that definitions of *Sunnah* vary). My respondents asked me what I meant by 'Islam', or even 'Islamic law', occasionally, and when this question appeared, I noticed that it did so only in the cases for which the contemporary opinions are largely incompatible with historical ones (e.g. slavery and child marriage). When I asked them what Islam's position on slavery is, for example, many of them asked, 'What do you mean by "Islam"?' At other moments, when I used the term 'Islamic law', as in 'Islamic law on gender roles' and my respondents appeared hesitant to answer or said, 'I don't know', I replaced 'Islamic law' with 'Islam' and they had clearer answers. I therefore decided to use both terms, 'Islamic law' and 'Islam', but not 'Islamic tradition', in the interviews. I asked specifically for participants' definitions of 'Islam' and 'Islamic law' at the beginning of each interview, or during it if I sensed any discrepancies in their opinions and definitions. I provide my respondents' definitions of these terms in the first chapter; however, I believe a summary is necessary here. While they offered different meanings of the terms, a fair assessment is that for most of them, *sharīʿa* refers to 'basic' rules and guidelines, while 'Islam' is 'a way of life' and 'submission to God'. 'Islam' is broader and encompasses the Qur'an, the *Sunnah*, the *sharīʿa*, and scholarly engagements with all of these, whereas the *sharīʿa* is derived strictly from the Qur'an and the *Sunnah*.

'Islam' in this study includes more than merely the Qur'an and the *Sunnah*. It encompasses the historical Islamic tradition and its contemporary manifestations. Islamic tradition encompasses the variety of sources of Islam – but highlights the human (and historically male) articulations of 'Islam' as an ideal. This articulation appears in the form of *fiqh*, or jurisprudence, and its sources include the various interpretations (*tafsīr*) of the Qur'an, the practice and teachings of the Prophet Muhammad (the *Sunnah*), and the customs (*ʿurf*) of scholars whose interpretations are eventually taken authoritatively, and in some cases become laws. I limit the term 'Islamic tradition' to the doctrinal contents of the four legal schools of Sunni Islam, namely, Ḥanafī, Mālikī, Shāfi'ī, and Ḥanbalī, each named after its founder. These schools are, among Sunnis, authoritative. The schools' positions on the various gender issues on which this study focuses are well-documented in historical texts, such as in a legal compendium by Ibn Rushd (d. 1198), an Andalusian scholar and jurist known as Averroes in the West, titled *Bidāyat al-Mujtahid* (*The Distinguished Jurist's Primer*), to which I refer along with several other pre-modern Islamic legal works.

SIGNIFICANCE OF THIS RESEARCH

I use the case study of one American city, Austin, Texas, to discuss the ways that change is negotiated, particularly in relation to gender. As such, I do not claim that my results apply to all Muslim Americans or to Muslims universally. I do, however, believe that my results and the patterns I am investigating are part of, and not isolated from, the larger Muslim American discourse on Islam, gender, and change, and they therefore contribute to our understanding of contemporary Islam in America and indeed the rest of the Western world. In part, this is because Texas has the fifth-largest Muslim population in the United States, with long-established communities of multiple generations.[4] Some of the authorities discussed in this book, like Yasir Qadhi and Nouman Ali Khan, are established in Texas, with Qadhi having been born in Houston. Moreover, my respondents' ideas of Islam are largely parallel to those shared by Muslim Americans generally according to my study of American Islam.

Previous scholarship seeking to understand this phenomenon of the evolution of practice and thought in Islam has focused on the scholarly elite, neglecting the perspectives of lay Muslims. To provide lay perspectives, I conducted in-depth, in-person interviews with 40 Sunni American Muslims in Austin where I established connections and networks with local individual Muslims, organisations, and community services during my graduate-school years. I interviewed participants about the five topics of my study, assessing their opinions and what they believe the Islamic positions on the topics are. The final question I asked was what criteria participants believe are necessary to modify historical legal positions for modern contexts. I wanted to understand when and why participants accept historical positions as relevant and applicable today, and when and why they believe those positions need change. This book provides field research on a set of overlooked questions and assumptions about the construction of the Islamic tradition, and of Islam, and it critically engages with traditionally established notions of gender in Islam.

This study is also timely. Muslim women's interfaith marriages are increasingly common, inheritance laws are being renegotiated, and the attempt by ISIS to revive slavery in 2014 sparked a new conversation about slavery in the Islamic tradition. Muslim women's quest for religious authority, such as the right to lead prayer, has gained attention over the past two decades, and the prohibition on leading prayers continues to reflect attitudes towards women's rights in other spheres of life as well.

Moreover, the study has three broad social implications. First, it speaks to wider issues in the sociology of religion, such as how a religious community consents to redefining and modifying its understanding of and commitment to the idea of tradition. Muslims maintain their spirituality and loyalty to Islam while simultaneously challenging the doctrines that hinder a more ethically grounded practice of religion. Second, this study addresses the question of religious communities' arguments for gender-based reforms that do not betray a tradition to which many are unconditionally committed. Contemporary academic scholars have already shown that early Muslim scholars' conceptions of gender widely influenced the ways that they approached gender relations in establishing rules and guidelines on, for example, marriage, female leadership, and inheritance.[5] My study brings these issues to the forefront and highlights the gendered nature of the production of knowledge and the establishment of gender roles and rights in religious communities. Third, the research contributes to existing literature that provides tools for Muslim women to question and challenge the gendered foundations of the Islamic tradition that have historically only allowed limited changes. Grasping the fluidity of the tradition may enable Muslim women to push for the advancement of their rights without feeling as though they are transgressing against an unassailable tradition.

THEORETICAL FRAMEWORK

What is a religious tradition, and how does it evolve while simultaneously being perceived as authentic by its adherents? Talal Asad proposes that viewing Islam as a discursive tradition may help us to understand it as a religion that relies on an authoritative discourse-based, historically established past while also being relevant to the future (where the tradition is headed) through the present.[6] He famously coins this term, 'discursive tradition', to refer to the diversity and localised manifestations of past and contemporary Islam. Asad's definition of Islam acknowledges Muslims' relationship to their past, the present, and to changes that Islam undergoes through modification, reinterpretations, and re-representations. Zareena Grewal studies Muslim Americans who travel to the Middle East to learn 'real' and 'authentic' Islam, which they imagine is non-existent in the United States. She critically discusses the ways that 'tradition' is conceptualised in the minds of the student-travelers she engages as they use it to claim authority in the Muslim American community.[7] In my discussions with respondents on criteria of authority and their definitions of 'scholars', I found that their ideas on tradition, scholars, and authority largely resemble the views espoused by the student-travelers in Grewal's study. My research relies on Asad's concept of Islam as a discursive tradition to understand how Muslims negotiate their contemporary understandings of gender as well as on Grewal's discussion of the mythical Islamic tradition that my discussants implicitly invoked to explain their opinions. I develop Asad's idea further through my proposal that the Islamic tradition be viewed as a rhizome, discussed in detail in chapter 1.

Another theory I draw from is that of tradition as stratigraphy, which helps explain the changes made to past interpretations and practices, primarily because of the positioning of the interpreter. Stratigraphy refers to 'the layering of meaning and interpretation: one story or interpretation can be retold in many different ways, with layers of detail added in subsequent generations'.[8] This story or interpretation can be of a text or a concept, with changed meaning, explanation, and detail interpolated by new generations of interpreters. Walid Saleh and Karen Bauer, among others, have shown that exegetes of the Qur'an have historically picked and chosen from previous works, rendering some interpretations as valid and others as invalid.[9] For instance, since gender hierarchy was taken as a matter of fact in pre-modern societies, it makes sense that Muslim scholars chose to present it as inherent to the Qur'an and, in turn, established legal rulings based on those assumptions. The interpreters of subsequent generations may add to those previous interpretations and traditions as their social realities evolve. I apply the theory of stratification to analyse the ways in which contemporary Muslims rely on stratified views of Islam and gender in their everyday life. Ayesha Chaudhry and Karen Bauer have observed that while the Islamic tradition is claimed to be diverse and nuanced, this does not always apply to gender, except in very subtle ways; this is true in my study where the dominant scholarly view tends to lean towards maintaining gender inequality (interfaith marriage, female inheritance, female-led prayers), but diversity of opinion is certainly present in my respondents' views, with important qualifiers. I argue that, because of the gendered nature of authority and knowledge in Islamic tradition, selective changes that take place within this tradition, including canonisation, are likewise gendered. This argument parallels recent scholarship in Islamic Studies, such as Nevin Reda and Yasmin Amin's *Islamic Interpretive Tradition and Gender Justice*, which critiques the notion of an accepted collection of authoritative texts, or a 'canon', and argues that since processes of canonisation are deeply human (male) endeavours and are constantly in flux, new egalitarian and ethical interpretations of the Islamic tradition are possible; they also argue for an interpretation of Islam that recognises and is in touch with Muslims' lived reality.[10] Significantly, this volume also challenges the claim that the Islamic tradition is based in a sound and consistently applied methodology, a claim commonly used to dismiss Muslim feminist arguments for change. Related to this discussion is the notion of a gendered authority in Islam. Many scholars have already shown that historical interpretations and other engagements with religious scriptures are gendered because they have thrived through a gendered paradigm.[11]

The social construction of knowledge is not limited to the humanities and social sciences. Scientific research has always been used to advance ideology, and is thus inseparable from politics. It is widely known that European scientists historically used biological and natural sciences to argue against racial equality – specifically, they used scientific knowledge and arguments to support existing societal claims about the superiority of certain races over others. All of these claims have since been debunked. Similarly, feminist approaches in the biological sciences have challenged previously established notions of sexuality and offered groundbreaking theories about the role of gender and social assumptions in promoting particular viewpoints.[12] Feminist scientists have studied in detail the gendering of scientific knowledge, including the role of the agent (male scientist) who pretends to be absent but is subconsciously always in command.[13] They have also shown how social and political concepts of sexuality and gender can and have influenced biological understandings.[14] Notable examples include nineteenth-century scientists and physicians using female biology (e.g. references to their anatomy, such as the uterus) to argue that women should not engage in intensive study because it would 'physically harm women by diverting energy from their uterus to their brain'.[15] Additionally,

Emily Martin, in her research on sociocultural anthropology, has explored 'the gender stereotypes hidden within the scientific language of biology', such as in biology textbooks' descriptions of menstruation and the reproductive cycle.[16] Descriptions of the biological processes in female bodies versus in male bodies are drastically different: male biological phenomena are marvelled at and treated as remarkable miracles while female processes are described as prone to death and loss.[17] Such descriptions reflect social and cultural attitudes towards women and men in broader society rather than being rooted in a careful, impartial description of the human body. I draw from these past studies on the gendered construction of knowledge and authority to support a part of my argument that the reluctance to engage feminist knowledge and feminist propositions plays a role in preventing change within the Islamic tradition.

Scholars of Islam and gender are thus ultimately, either implicitly or explicitly, asking the following questions: what is Islam, how is the Islamic tradition developed, and who is allowed to be part of its construction and development? For example, Kecia Ali's *Sexual Ethics and Islam* is devoted to exploring the question of what 'Islam' is through a focus on what makes sexual relations lawful in Islam. She examines the tension between what contemporary Muslims believe the Islamic tradition's stances on sex, marriage, divorce are, and what the texts actually indicate. My study is an exploration of what lay Muslims believe Islam says about the five issues under focus and how they explain any discrepancies that arise.

That Islamic law and interpretations of the Qur'an have undergone change is not the point of this study. Indeed, given the immense body of scholarship on the subject, that much should be obvious from the outset. Other scholars have already explored the changing nature over time of Islamic law and Qur'anic commentaries, and the role of humans in their construction, development, and advancement. Scholars in this category emphasise early and medieval Muslim scholarly and juristic creativity in simultaneously embracing and reforming Islamic law and interpretation as they deemed necessary.[18] Most academic studies of Islamic law and Qur'anic interpretation use sources written by jurists and other scholarly elites, rather than ordinary Muslims. Ziba Mir-Hosseini's *Islam and Gender: The Religious Debate in Contemporary Iran*, for example, groups the different perspectives that scholars of Islam hold on gender into those of traditionalists, neo-traditionalists, and modernists; she does this through a set of questions she asks jurists and scholars in Iran on issues related to gender, women, and marriage, noting the inconsistent ways many of them approach these issues.[19] Ayesha Chaudhry's *Domestic*

Violence and the Islamic Tradition offers an exploration of commentaries on the Qur'anic verse Q. 4:34, similarly categorising the different approaches and their evolution as traditionalist, neo-traditionalist, progressive, and reformist.[20] Karen Bauer's *Gender Hierarchy in the Qur'an: Medieval Interpretations, Modern Responses* surveys differences between pre-modern and modern interpretations of Qur'anic verses on creation, female testimony, and marital hierarchy, and examines the ways that each generation of interpreters negotiates with the previous generation in its attempt to make sense of Qur'anic verses in new contexts.[21] Hadia Mubarak's *Rebellious Wives and Neglectful Husbands* strives to capture the diverse attitudes towards marriage, divorce, and polygyny.[22] Highlighting the ways that modern male Sunni scholars depart from pre-modern ones in their engagement with these issues, she argues that phenomena such as colonialism, nationalism, modernity, and the commentator's own personal background are crucial to their conclusions.[23] Finally, Karen Bauer and Feras Hamza's *An Anthology of Qur'anic Commentaries* explores the various and competing perspectives on issues such as human creation, marital roles, Mary, mother of Jesus, women's legal testimony, and Qur'anic ideas of modesty.[24] They show that while Qur'anic commentaries are always in conversation with the cultural and political milieu of the commentator's time and place, commentators also honour and reference the commentaries of past generations as a way to demonstrate knowledge of and ground their authority in the historical male tradition.

Unlike this previous scholarship, my purpose is to document the lengths to which Muslims, both lay and scholarly, go to rationalise what they find as problematic aspects of the Islamic past and to Islamically justify social change. I show how contemporary lay Muslims exert their own pressures on the theory of the law.

LAW, CONTEXTS, AND INTERPRETATION

Appreciating the historical legal and exegetical traditions' approaches to these gender issues entails understanding the contexts in which Islamic law and Qur'anic interpretation were developed and in which their framers operated. Much scholarship exists on the origins of Islamic law, its development, and its influences. I apply the findings of these studies to Islamic law in this work by highlighting the role that sociohistorical contexts play in establishing consensus, consensus itself being a process of negotiation among various legal schools, individual scholars, and, as my research shows, lay practising Muslims.

The context(s) in which Islamic law originates and develops are ones that, at least to non-specialists of religion, are unimaginable because of the sorts of concerns that dominated the discourse of the time. In pre-nineteenth-century Islam, both slavery and gender hierarchy were unquestioned and wholly acceptable aspects of everyday social life – sanctioned by law and by morality.[25] A vertical paradigm of social relations that assumed gender hierarchy – with God above men and men above women, thus men superior to women – was understood not only as normative but as a part of the divine plan. Only in the modern period, the 1800s onwards, did scholars and lay Muslims begin to seriously question the underlying assumptions pre-modern Muslim scholars operated under to justify and explain their understanding of God, the Qur'an, and Islam. Given this context, one might imagine that it is fairly reasonable to question the validity of the prohibitions that resulted from particular social, legal, and moral assumptions about both gender and social hierarchy.

Thus, while this book explores in depth the rationales for the prohibitions on some gendered doctrines – such as female-led mixed-gender prayers and interfaith marriages for Muslim women – a key concern for me is the context in which these prohibitions emerged. Sociohistorical contexts are often acknowledged for cases like slavery but not for opinions on gender, such as in the cases on which this study centres; that is, doctrines regarding gender are treated ahistorically, as being fixed in immutable, natural realities. This explains the significance of the following question: when the rationale behind a particular prohibition no longer applies, how do Muslims explain its continuation, and what new reasons are attributed to the prohibition? As I will discuss particularly in chapter 4, on female-led prayer, Behnam Sadeghi illustrates that scholars – and I add lay Muslims – offer new justifications to pre-modern positions of juristic consensus to maintain them because they believe them to be 'Islamic'. The medieval context is not just one where slavery was a normal part of daily life: as Leila Ahmed shows, early Islamic texts were produced, interpreted, and later rendered into law in a context where, particularly for elite men, distinctions between concubine, woman for sexual use, and woman as object were inevitably blurred.[26] Left to the jurists, the law came to be a product of male interpretations and patriarchal assumptions and expectations. In such a context, then, one might find nothing outlandish about a prohibition on women marrying non-Muslim men.

Context does not always suffice in explaining the dominance of certain positions, however.[27] Certainly all the legal schools, despite the variations among them, were influenced by the patriarchal assumptions, biases, and realities of their contexts. But this would also assume that the same context necessarily results in the same conclusions, and the Islamic tradition is widely known for its tremendous diversity of thought. Indeed, these assumptions about the role of context mislead one into thinking that, first, it is even possible to know with certainty what the context was, and, second, that the context remained the same throughout the hundreds of years that Islamic law was developed. In reality, however, the social milieu of Muslim societies differed even from city to city. What, then, does it mean to fairly claim that any given practice or doctrine originated in a certain historical context when context alone is not a productive explanation? My argument is not that context explains doctrinal positions on which consensus has been reached. I'm interested in why context is mobilised as a legitimate explanation on some issues, while for others, contextualisation is seen as an invalid approach.

CHAPTER OUTLINE

In chapter 1, 'A Rhizomatic Approach to the Islamic Tradition', I argue that existing (scholarly and lay) understandings of the Islamic tradition can be best conceptualised through a rhizomatic model, a Deleuzian metaphor based on the rhizome plant (as opposed to a traditional root), which is characterised by complex and horizontal roots. The rhizome metaphor has been applied in many disciplines, such as sociology, economics, and education; I apply it to Islamic Studies because it aptly illustrates the nuances of the Islamic tradition. For instance, a rhizomatic model engages interconnectedness in such a way that selectively choosing from traditions appears natural to religious practitioners, as it allows for boundaries and categories to remain fluid.

Section 1 encompasses two chapters, which explore the 'negotiables' of the Islamic tradition: child marriage and sexual slavery. Both chapters emphasise the ways in which contemporary opinions on these two issues depart from historical scholarly consensus, which permitted child marriage and sexual slavery. Chapter 2, 'Child Marriage', investigates the issue of child marriage and the discrepancies between historical and contemporary Muslim views on it. Almost all my participants project onto Islam their modern ideals of agency and consent by arguing that Islam never supported child marriage – as historical scholars may be said to have projected their own ideas onto Islam as well. They insist that child marriages are fundamentally un-Islamic because Islam requires the consent of the marrying parties for a valid marriage. This discrepancy provides a case of negotiating the tradition that makes sense when analysed through the rhizomatic model I proposed in chapter 1. As I move on to analyse my respondents' attitudes toward child marriage, I discuss some of the major themes that emerged in our conversations, such as Aisha's marriage to Muhammad (believed to have occurred when she was six years old, with consummation at nine); the reliance on Hadiths (reports attributed to Muhammad) specifically in the case of child marriage to support the respondents' position that it is un-Islamic; and shifting ideas of what constitutes the *Sunnah*, or way of the Prophet Muhammad.[28]

In chapter 3, 'Sexual Slavery', I discuss historical views on men's right to sexual relations with enslaved women, and contemporary Muslims' understandings of slavery in Islam. First, I analyse Qur'anic verses that arguably support sexual relations with enslaved people, while also briefly addressing the argument that the Qur'anic verses about 'those whom your right hands possess' do not necessarily permit sexual contact with slaves. I then discuss attitudes towards slavery within the historical legal tradition. I highlight the case of Māriya the Copt, a Christian woman whom the earlier Islamic sources acknowledge as a concubine of the Prophet but whose status as a wife or concubine is ambiguous. The implications of Māriya's being a wife or a concubine are significant: if Māriya was Muhammad's concubine, then sexual relations with slaves are sanctioned in the *Sunnah* and not just in the legal tradition. Muhammad's relationship with Māriya and the permissibility of slavery in the historical Islamic tradition are instances where a clash occurs between the *Sunnah*, classical jurisprudence, and modern notions of sexuality. I then move on to my discussants' views towards slavery and their understandings of Islam's position on this subject. I conclude that contemporary Muslims' views on slavery and its contemporary impermissibility in Islam require distinguishing between 'Islam' and 'Islamic law'. While several of my discussants had initially told me that 'Islamic law' and 'Islam' are the same, they, too, eventually acknowledged the distinction between the two, arguing that Islamic law would not permit something that Islam prohibits or vice versa. My respondents assume that Islam is a system of principles guided fundamentally by equality, justice and compassion. Although a few of my respondents believed slavery is still acceptable in Islam, they qualified their positions with statements such as 'but only if the slaves are treated with respect and as equals'. Those who believed slavery was permissible in the past but not today also explained that slavery was permissible on the grounds that those enslaved would be treated with dignity and as equals. Others believed it was always and still is impermissible because it goes against the core of Islam, which is to treat others respectfully.

In chapter 4, 'Female Inheritance', I investigate the issue of female inheritance through an analysis of the relevant Qur'anic verses, contemporary debates, and my respondents' rationales for maintaining or modifying the historical ruling that daughters receive half the inheritance of sons. While the Qur'an tends to be ambiguous in most of its guidelines, its laws on inheritance for daughters and sons are more specific: 'to the male, a portion equal to that of two females' (Q. 4:11). I pay special attention to how contemporary Muslims are negotiating the traditional guidelines as they attempt to apply them to their lives in circumstances that are different from those in which the laws emerged. For instance, many scholars, and many lay Muslims including most of my respondents, contextualise the Qur'anic verses on inheritance to argue that when the inheritance rules were revealed, it was a great justice to women to receive a share in inheritance because women were not seen as entitled to inheritance at the time. Given this context, they argue, the verses indicate Islam's attempt to improve women's rights. Moreover, since men are required to take care of their female counterparts, the inheritance portions assigned to women suggest that they are in fact receiving a privilege, since their inheritance (theoretically) belongs solely to them, whereas men are required to spend theirs on their families. Since the context in which the verses were revealed originally radically differs from that of my discussants, most of them support equal inheritance for daughters and sons. An important conclusion from this discussion is that female inheritance laws *are* being renegotiated, and those individuals who have been or are negatively affected by the current laws oppose them. Besides the relevance of gender in these conversations, the respondents' generation is also important: for example, the fact that single (i.e. younger) men support equal inheritance laws for sons and daughters is significant because their support for equal distribution shows that current broader discourses about gender equality are creating an awareness of women's rights in the minds of younger generations of Muslims.

The second section focuses on the issues currently considered 'non-negotiable', at least by the majority of Muslim scholars: women's interfaith marriage and gender-mixed female-led prayer. The chapters in this section highlight the parallels between historical and contemporary ideas on the topics while discussing the ways in which contemporary explanations of the prohibitions depart from historical ones. Chapter 5, 'Muslim Women's Interfaith Marriage', deals with Muslim women's marriage to '*Ahl al-Kitāb* or *kitābīs*, or People of the Book (i.e. Jews and Christians). Since the Qur'an does not explicitly prohibit women's marriage to these *kitābī*s, I am interested in Muslims' contemporary justifications of this traditional prohibition that some of them still insist upon despite their willingness to discard other traditional doctrines given new contexts. For example, most of them follow the popular mainstream rejection of the idea of male superiority (although with qualifications). The chapter provides an analysis of the Qur'anic verses on interfaith marriage, along with their commentaries (*tafsīr*). Since the original contexts of the prohibition warrant an acknowledgment, I also discuss the historical contexts of the relationship between slavery and marriage to emphasise the point that my respondents made when explaining that legal stipulations must change in a changing sociohistorical context. The conclusion discusses some of the gaps in the rationales commonly given to support the prohibition.

Chapter 6, 'Female-Led Mixed-Gender Prayers', addresses current opinions regarding female-led prayers, highlighting scholarly debates and my participants' perceptions of the subject. I analyse the historical tradition's views on female-led prayers and the ways they shape contemporary scholarly ideas on the issue. I then present and analyse the responses of my research participants to questions related to female-led prayers. Looking for patterns in their responses that help answer my larger question of which positions of consensus are negotiable and which ones are non-negotiable, I discuss the three most common responses my respondents offered as explanations for the prohibition on female-led prayer: female modesty and male sexuality, a 'lack of precedent', and the notion that it is an unnecessary, irrelevant goal. I argue that the prohibition on female-led mixed-gender prayer remains and is supported by most of my respondents (men and women) because it is perceived as an irrelevant issue, not urgent or oppressive like child marriage and sexual slavery, as some of them said. As with the issue on women's interfaith marriage, which received more support from my discussants than female-led prayer did, many of my respondents support a re-evaluation of the prohibition on female-led prayer but feel bound by the prevailing scholarly opinion. What makes the issue non-negotiable is not my discussants' views towards it but the current dominant scholarly consensus. While my respondents are less hesitant to disagree with scholarly opinions on many other issues, on female-led prayers, they chose to defer to scholars. Few of my discussants who supported the prohibitions challenged their own assumptions embedded in these ideas. Some paused to comment that a certain claim or statement of theirs did not make any sense, but they maintained their position that they would defer to authorities on these matters and/or that there must be wisdom behind the prohibitions.

The conclusion, 'The Politics of Negotiation and Relevance' reflects primarily on my discussants' views on change and tradition. In all issues in this study, we learn that Muslims are negotiating their understandings of the tradition and of change. They seek to preserve the Islamic tradition as sincerely as possible, while also acknowledging the need to respond to contemporary struggles and realities. When asked what counts as a legitimate reason to modify or change historical positions of consensus, all respondents referenced a shift in context and time. They agreed that Islam and Islamic law are flexible, as illustrated by a question many of them asked: 'Which Islamic law?' (although specifically in questions regarding Islamic law's position on slavery and child marriage). Islamic law is flexible, clearly, because Islam – according to most participants – is a rational religion. They all agreed that a position, however much based in consensus, can change with time, context, or a shift in social norms. In other words, consensus is not necessarily binding. Since there appears to be a pattern that might explain or help scholars, or even lay practicing Muslims, predict when historical consensus is or was negotiable, the conclusion sets out to identify this pattern, highlighting the role of gender, generation, and lived reality. I theorise the idea of relevance, connecting lay Muslims' perception of some gendered issues, such as female-led prayers, as 'irrelevant' to a recent academic conversation on the politics of citation and the dismissal of feminist and women's scholarship. The chapter also provides charts to illustrate how differences in gender and generation/marital status affect opinions on the different topics and to highlight the differences in how scholarly consensus is imagined generally versus for the specific topics.

METHODOLOGY

This book utilises a twofold methodology. It consists, first, of an analysis of historical legal texts and contemporary Muslim scholarship on the topics under study (child marriage, sexual slavery, female inheritance, women's interfaith marriage, and female-led prayer). Second, this study includes in-depth interviews with lay Muslim Americans in Austin. I describe these two methods in detail, giving more attention to the ethnographic interviews because of their complexity and critical role in reaching my conclusions. I also discuss my criteria for choosing participants, the process of finding and recruiting them, and details about where and how the interviews took place.

A. Textual Methodology

A major goal of the study is to note points of departure from historical views as they are represented in contemporary sources of Islam and in contemporary Muslims' perceptions of the pre-nineteenth-century sources. The nineteenth century is an important period in the study of Islam for several reasons, notably the reality and impact of colonialism that led to social, political, and religious reform movements and engagements with modernity. Colonialism led to an epistemological shift in the production of knowledge about Islam, prompting many scholars of Islam to use the nineteenth century as a significant point of demarcation. I compare historical and contemporary opinions on the five topics of the study. I use various texts, including *The Distinguished Jurist's Primer* by Ibn Rushd (d. 1198).[29] This book on comparative Islamic law presents the dominant opinions of Muslim jurists from five Islamic legal schools: Ḥanafī, Mālikī, Shāfi'ī, Ḥanbalī, and Ẓāhirī. Ibn Rushd, also known as Averroes, is regarded as one of the most influential and authoritative scholars of Islam. I also use the Qur'an, its interpretations, Hadiths, and legal texts as well as other authoritative sources that have shaped popular perceptions of Islam's positions on these matters. Other legal texts that I relied on include Ibn Taymiyya's (d. 1328) *Majmū' Fatāwā* and Ibn Qudāmah's (d. 1223) *Kitāb al-Mughnī*.[30] Both of these influential texts are compilations of legal opinions from different schools, although both authors were Ḥanbalī. Other sources include exegetical scholarship when necessary, such as in the case of women's interfaith marriage and female inheritance, and contemporary discussions of these issues by popular Muslim scholars on *YouTube* and Islamic websites. Throughout the study, when available, I reference the views of contemporary Western Muslim scholars whom my discussants viewed as authoritative, such as Yasmin Mogahed, Yasir Qadhi, and Nouman Ali Khan.[31] I also analyse feminist interpretations, relying on academic and occasionally, when useful, online popular material. Feminist scholars often oppose the traditional positions of consensus and offer alternative interpretations, which I draw upon in my conclusions.

Some participants were uncertain about the purpose of the study and my role in it. Many of them suggested to me that I ask 'proper scholars' the questions I was asking them, although some appreciated that I was interested in their opinions for this portion of the research. While many of my respondents referenced contemporary Muslim American preachers and scholars in some of their responses, the pre-modern sources I rely on in this research did not come up much during the course of the interviews, except in the discussion on female-led prayer. For example, only a few of them believed that Islam prohibits women from leading other women in prayer. When I asked whether women can lead other women in prayer and they agreed, some asked what the legal schools' positions were on this issue. Often, once the interview was over, we returned to some of the topics they had questions about, and if they wanted to know more, I directed them to the sources I was using. It was during the post-interview conversations I had with many of them that they asked me what 'Islam actually says' about the topics we had discussed; I shared with them that each of these topics had been heavily debated historically, and some scholarly opinions on female-led prayer, child marriage, and slavery were most shocking to them.

Through the textual methodology, I was able to substantively assess which of the five topics had undergone change. Using the interviews I conducted, I was able to explain why some issues have been understood differently over time, while interpretations of others seem more resistant to change, and what this reveals about the ways in which change is negotiated in religious traditions. Relying on social media content analysis when useful also allowed me to note disagreements between scholarly figures and lay Muslims' perspectives.

B. Ethnographic Methodology

Between May and December 2016, I conducted 40 open-ended, semi-structured, one-on-one interviews with Sunni Muslims in Austin. All interviews were confidential, and the discussants were assigned pseudonyms. Participants were promised confidentiality, and none of their real names are used in the study. To ensure that there is no identifiable information in the study about any of the participants, I used general geographic information when referring to respondents instead of the specifics they had given (e.g. instead of Malaysia, I use South-East Asian; instead of Egyptian, I use North African).

Most of these interviews took place in person, and some took place on the phone, in accordance with the discussant's preference and availability.

I chose Austin as the location of the study because I had established a rapport of trust with the Muslim community there, as a resident of the city for several years. The connections I made in Austin during my graduate years afforded me the necessary access to meet community members – and to have community leaders endorse the study – and to discuss issues with them that are often considered controversial and sensitive. I had previously conducted a pilot study of Austin Muslims' views on gender and Islam, such as homosexuality, polygamy, and women's interfaith marriage. This study introduced me to the Austin community, and some of the people who participated in the informal study also offered to participate in the current research. My connections with the community were essential to the successful undertaking of the current research.

My selection criteria were that my interviewees identify as Sunni Muslim and as American, live in Austin at the time of the study, and be over the age of eighteen. I limited my sample to Sunni Muslims because of the differences in Sunni and Shi'i Islam on questions of authority and on what each sect considers authoritative knowledge and sources. For instance, while Sunni Islam permits Muslim men to marry women from the People of the Book, the majority Shi'i view prohibits men's marriage to all non-Muslim women although permitting *mut'a* (temporary marriage) to them. Similarly, Shi'i and Sunni Muslims do not hold the same Hadiths to be authoritative, including some of the ones I highlight in this study; Sunnis and Shi'is moreover rely on separate Hadith collections and apply different standards of authenticity and reliability.[32]

Racial background and immigration status were not a part of the criteria, because my respondents identified themselves as American regardless of how long they had lived in the United States. Their identity as American was important to the study so that I was able to assess where their opinions may be influenced by contemporary trends in American Islam (e.g. the idea that certain common Muslim practices are 'cultural', not 'Islamic') and because the scholars they follow are Americans, such as Yasir Qadhi, who speak to their specific struggles and contexts.

I sought an equal number of married and unmarried individuals. Once I selected the primary group, I sub-categorised them as follows. Of the 40 individuals I selected, 20 were men and 20 women; 10 of each gender were married (at the time of the study or in the past), and 10 were unmarried (never previously married, although three respondents were engaged at the time of the study). These numbers were deliberately chosen to ensure an equal representation. The reason I chose not to categorise them by age, or any other marker, and instead by gender and marital status is that in the aforementioned pilot study I conducted in 2013, I discovered that the respondents' views on marriage, sexuality, and Islam differed significantly between married and unmarried individuals. The married individuals, for example, often invoked their experiences with marriage to explain their views. Similarly, in this study, marital status and gender played pivotal roles, as opposed to, for example, race.

The Recruitment and Interview Process

To solicit respondents, I relied on my own networks in the Austin community. Specifically, I used Facebook groups for the Austin Muslim Community, an Austin Muslim e-mailing list known as AMAANAH, the mosques I attend frequently, a private Islamic school, and informal invitations branching out from individuals I know personally. When recruiting participants for the study, I first created flyers and sought permission to distribute them from mosques and other Muslim-majority spaces, such as a private local Islamic school. On some Fridays, mosque administrations also made announcements that the study was taking place and urged prospective participants to contact me for details. Since the flyers included my e-mail address, many people responded via e-mail; others responded through my Austin Muslim friends' social networks, particularly Facebook, when people shared information about the study and the call for participants. At one point, I was struggling to find married men, which was resolved by my married women friends' help in encouraging their husbands and/or their husbands' friends to participate. The individuals I interviewed were not limited to my own personal network because they were recruited through various media and fora.

The interview process involved a discussion of the purpose of the research and my commitment to maintaining confidentiality. Each interview began with an introduction to myself and to the study and the respondents' permission for me to audio-record the entire interview. Most interviews took place in person, such as at a café. Once I had obtained their permission to record, I first asked general questions about their background – racial/ethnic, age, marital status, educational background, and whether they were converts to Islam or born Muslim. I invited them to share anything else they were comfortable sharing, such as how long they had been in the US if they had immigrated to the US from another country.

Since I focus on doctrinal positions and arguments, I asked my participants about their opinions on different statements and topics, and evaluated their responses to determine whether and when they align with traditional legal positions. I did not notify them of what the historical agreed-upon positions on any given issue were except when they asked, and I informed them only after the interview was over if they were still interested. In such cases, I observed their responses – and I analyse them in relevant chapters.

Challenges During the Interview Process

One of the major struggles I faced during the interviews was that many interviewees began to question their own knowledge of Islam as they realised I was interested, among other issues, in their perceptions. Several participants apologised for not knowing the 'Islamic' position on some of the issues, even when I informed them that everything they know and whatever they do not know is useful for my research. Explaining the purpose and significance of their opinions and current knowledge proved challenging because the method through which I appeared to be studying Islam was unfamiliar to many participants. Additionally, because the interviews often took place as a discussion between me and the respondents, and because I asked many follow-up questions based on the answers they gave, they began to express hesitance to share an opinion as we continued because they felt as though their lack of knowledge on an issue disqualified them from sharing their thoughts. To me, this demonstrates that they have internalised the idea that they are not entitled to an opinion on Islam unless they are scholars, that their experiences and interpretations are not worth studying. Some respondents noted the pattern of the questions – e.g. what their opinion on a certain topic/practice was, what they believed Islam's position on it was, and whether they believe the consensus on the matter was binding for today's Muslims – and this made them doubt their current knowledge. For instance, the following was a common comment: 'I mean, I don't know. Doesn't Islam prohibit X [e.g. the marriage of underaged children]? I thought it did…' I often struggled to respond to questions about Islam's position on a given issue because I did not want to influence participants' responses in any way; I wanted their knowledge and opinions. Some participants acknowledged my expertise (I introduced myself as a student of Islam and gender) and occasionally asked me, 'What does Islam say about this?' or 'What do the texts say?' In such cases, we would discuss what 'the texts' say after the interview was over.

As a researcher, I played a complex role in the study, as simultaneously an insider and outsider in the community whose perceptions I studied. I was an insider to the extent that I identify as a Sunni Muslim and am deeply familiar with the nuances that discussants often referenced, including Islamic terminology and common Western Muslim tropes, such as 'that's not Islam; that's culture'. I was also an outsider, however, because of my own personal (non-mainstream) positions on these issues as well as my position as the researcher and/or specialist on gender and Islam.

As a single Muslim woman, I often had difficulty reaching Muslim men and seeking their participation for the study. Many men, whether they were interested in participating or not, mostly those whom I met around the mosque, explained to me that I should not include men in the research because of Islam's prohibition on gender mixing. They pointed out that since I am not allowed to be alone with men, Muslim men were unlikely to agree to the interview unless I changed my method and either simply passed out surveys at the mosque or did group interviews. This also suggests that my sample of men, single or married, was affected: some such men with conservative opinions such as opposition to gender-mixing or any interaction between women and men who are not related to each other clearly declined to participate in the study. I did, however, interview a few such men, as can be seen in their conversations below, some on the phone and some in person.

Further, as a feminist Muslim American, I found this project – the sheer nature of the interviews, the issues under focus, some respondents' reactions and responses to the questions – overwhelming and, to an extent, emotionally and psychologically daunting. Some (male and female) respondents spoke with ease and casualness of the emotional, physical, intellectual inferiority of women; some (male and female) explained the uncontrollable sexual urges of men because of which women have to relinquish some level of power to them; some shared their expectations of proper Muslim behaviour and practice; some attributed their anti-LGBTQ+ opinions to God; and so on. Professional ethics enabled me to listen as these participants explained what Islam was, even in ways that were patronising and offensive to women, racial minorities, gender non-conforming Muslims, and other marginalised communities and groups. Listening to these interviews during the transcription and analysis stages was emotionally challenging.

My encounters with the majority of the participants, however, were not challenging. Most respondents were respectful and careful not to offend me, other women, or other Muslims. One married male participant, for example, when explaining his positions on female-led prayer repeatedly stated, 'Sister, I apologise. I do not want to hurt you, but you should hear the male perspective on this to understand better.' Because I had explained to them the purpose of the study and my interest in their personal opinions and their knowledge on Islam's positions on the topics in focus, they commonly said, 'Since you want my opinion, this is my opinion.'

One particular incident deserves to be highlighted in detail. This interview stands out as the most challenging I had to endure. My experience with Salim was not simply uncomfortable, but potentially dangerous, too. It also put me in a position that made me reflect on my status as a researcher and my relationship with my respondents. I had not anticipated the questions Salim asked me. I found it difficult to answer him in a way that would not invalidate my research, in his view, but that would also be a fair representation of my views so that I was not deceiving him. I was as open with him about the way I practise Islam as professionally necessary in order for him to decide if participating in this project was worth his time. As both this incident and many other encounters with my participants suggest, social scientific research is not always viewed as a legitimate method for understanding Islam.

In late October 2016, Salim e-mailed me to ask if I still needed participants for my study because he was interested in participating.[33] We scheduled a time to conduct the interview via phone because meeting in person would be difficult for him. When we first spoke, he said, 'For some reason, I thought you'd be a brother [male Muslim].' I asked if he was still willing to participate now that he knew I was a sister, and he said, yes, because 'it's for the good of the community and a fellow Muslim'.

As we spoke, he made comments about born-Muslims who do not practise Islam 'properly', one of which was about Muslim-identifying women who do not cover their hair but think they are still Muslim – or they cover their hair only in the parking lots of mosques as they prepare to enter the mosque; he called such women 'parking lot hijabis'. I appreciated these thoughts as a researcher, but I wondered if he would have agreed to participate in the study if he knew I did not cover my hair outside the mosque. When we were close to finishing the interview, he said that he had to leave, but we would continue once he was available again, and he suggested I come to the mosque he attends where he would introduce my study to more prospective participants. I agreed and planned to attend the mosque later.

I arrived at the mosque slightly after the *Maghrib* (evening) prayer and thus missed an opportunity to meet a larger group of people, but I stayed for *'Isha* prayer, the night (final) prayer until around nine o'clock. Salim introduced me to a few men and I collected a few contacts. When I saw a group of men slightly apart from us, I told Salim I would go speak with them as well in case they might be interested. He said he did not know them – he was introducing me primarily to Muslims of his race whom he knew – and he instructed me to stay back while he went to talk with them first. He had mentioned earlier that as a woman, I must not stand near the men's entrance to the mosque because it does not look good; it looks immodest. After about five minutes, he returned to give me permission to speak with them.

When I finished describing my project and its significance to the two men remaining in the group, one of them offered, 'You need to have some questions on a piece of paper to ask. You can't just go up to people and ask them for their opinions.' Confused, I asked, 'What do you mean? Yes, of course I have a set of questions. Do you mean a questionnaire?' He said, 'A questionnaire or not, you need to have actual proper questions.' After attempting to assure him that I did have written questions, he consistently interrupted me as I firmly stated that I knew what I was doing, I'd done this before, and I'd been doing this for a while – that this process of recruiting people for my project and of conducting interviews was not new to me. He reluctantly accepted that I might know what I am doing.

The attempts to explain to me what I should really be doing did not end there. This same individual insisted that I need to be talking with actual scholars of Islam about these kinds of issues because it does not matter what 'Muslims think' about anything. The men had other suggestions: had I considered how helpful it would be for me to give a presentation to the mosque congregants about my project and then 'ask them, for example, how many of you think this, how many of you think that, and then ask them why or why not?' I assured them that I had considered doing group interviews and focus groups, but that this was currently the method I had settled upon for confidentiality purposes. Salim then offered, 'And you must make sure that all of your participants are proper Muslims. You can't just interview anyone claiming to be Muslim.' I informed him that, yes, one of the criteria was that all my participants had to agree that Islam was important to them in a significant way – e.g. when they made major decisions about their lives, they took Islam into consideration.

Eventually, the other two individuals in the group said that they did not want to participate in the project. I thanked them for their time, and we all parted ways, Salim and I walking in the same direction. He had mentioned earlier that because it was dark and because I am female, I must not take the bus back because it was not safe. He offered to give me a ride back home with him and his wife. I thanked him for his offer and said I did not wish to trouble him, that I would gladly take the bus. He said that was not appropriate because he wanted me to be safe, and I accepted his offer. As we walked, he said, 'Sister, two advices. One, every good Muslim goes to the mosque. Don't interview anyone who does not go to the mosque.' I told him that that mosque-going was a complicated matter because a lot of good Muslims don't go to mosques for many different reasons. He asked, 'Like what?' I said, 'Well, many don't like the treatment of women in mosques, others don't live close to mosques, and praying at mosque, especially for women, is not considered obligatory anyway.' He said, 'And the second piece of advice. If I understand you correctly, you are a student of Islam. You must cover your hair properly.'

'Thank you for your advice. I appreciate it,' I replied.

'Do you cover your hair outside of the mosque?'

'No, I don't,' I responded, regretting it instantly, feeling uncertain about being honest about my practice of Islam.

'Why not?' he asked, almost aggressively.

Knowing that such a question is not personal according to many Muslims, I did not suggest otherwise to him, saying only: 'I have currently made an informed choice not to cover my head.' Instantly regretting my honesty again, I realised that the correct answer to his question would have been, 'I know that I'm obligated to, and I'm trying to gradually become a better Muslim. I will begin wearing the *hijab* right away, and I thank you for your reminder.' Because I did not stick to the 'script', he then asked if I wanted to be raped because women who did not cover their heads were more likely to be raped than those who did, and he asked how I felt disobeying 'God's clear commands'.

After nearly an hour of his interrogation and insistence that I study Islam properly, I decided that perhaps I should let him know that I have studied this issue in depth, and as a specialist in gender and Islam, I believe I have a right to my own interpretations of Islam, particularly given the male-dominated consensus on how Islam is understood. This escalated the situation, however, and he asked me why I hate men. I responded that I did not hate men, and eventually, he said it was late and he needed to get home. As he moved towards his car, forgetting to give me the ride he had promised at the beginning of our meeting because it was late and a sister should not be left alone at night, I asked him if he was willing to finish the last question of the interview the next time he was available. He answered, 'With all due respect, I've lost my appetite.' We said our goodbyes and parted ways.

As I walked the approximate mile to the bus stop, it occurred to me that he deemed me worthy of security and his male protection only so long as I was willing to cover my hair and not 'disobey God's clear commands' and to share his exact beliefs about Islam. When it was clear to him that I had made a deliberate choice not to cover my hair and I had thereby departed from what he considered correct Islam, I was no longer entitled to the security that all women deserve. Interestingly, he had initially seen me as a 'good' Muslim, from our interview and my initial meeting with him at the mosque, before he realised I do not cover my hair on a consistent and regular basis like a good Muslim woman should.

While not representative of my experiences during these interviews, this particular incident reflected my own experiences and those of many other Muslim women, especially those who study Islam. Our authority, identity and relationship with Islam are all judged by our outward manifestations of obedience to a larger system of rules.

Throughout the interviews, there were moments when some respondents began to express discomfort with the topics we were discussing. As we will see in the rest of this book, this discomfort is not isolated: it is connected to broader trends about what is perceived as relevant and urgent enough for Muslims, particularly Muslim women, to talk about and invest their energies in. Both my respondents' and mainstream Muslim preachers' perceptions of 'relevance' and 'urgency' reflect broader trends in change and resistance to change, and larger ideas about gender, privilege, and lived reality. But this book's approach to Islam as a rhizome offers Muslims plenty of reasons to be hopeful about the direction and development of Islam, and the possibility of positive change grounded within the tradition.

Chapter 1

A Rhizomatic Approach to the Islamic Tradition

This chapter offers a rhizomatic model for conceptualising Islam. I draw on the notion of the rhizome as developed by Gilles Deleuze and Félix Guattari in reference to the rhizomatic root structure of certain plants that lack a 'traditional root'.[1] I argue that the flexibility of the Islamic tradition, as shown through my ethnographic data and a comparison of past and present scholarly and lay opinions, is best explained by this rhizomatic conception.

A rhizomatic approach explains precisely why the tradition can adapt under new conditions and contexts. This is because, unlike 'the necessary hierarchy and strict categorisation of the tree metaphor, the rhizome concept allows, indeed requires, non-hierarchical linkages, made pragmatically as they are needed, horizontally or across any number of levels, and linking elements of disparate nature when appropriate, crossing categories'.[2] I show that existing ideas and constructions of the Islamic tradition – as understood by academic scholars of Islam, popular Muslim teachers of Islam, and lay Muslims – form a rhizome characterised by complexity, flexibility, and selectivity. My primary argument is that rhizomatic thinking addresses the complexities of a historical Islamic tradition, and challenges simplified representations of fixed boundaries, categories, and roots. A rhizomatic approach acknowledges that the Islamic tradition is neither a monolith nor a concrete reality. Instead, it is a fluid, flexible human construct that allows space for a multiplicity of opinions to exist simultaneously. These multiplicities are an essential part of the Islamic tradition's survival.

Throughout this chapter, I use the term 'the Islamic tradition' to mean the manifestation of Islam in accordance with my discussants' understandings of 'the religion of God' and its derivatives. As I discuss below, according to my respondents, the sources of Islam are the Qur'an, the *Sunnah*, the legal schools, their preferred individual scholars' opinions, a vague notion of consensus, context (time, place, situation), and common sense. This definition draws from Karen Bauer, who defines the tradition as:

> aspects of medieval social and intellectual heritage: the Qur'an and its interpretation, hadiths, historical narrations, law, and custom… 'Tradition' [also] partially consists of specific interpretations that are passed from generation to generation, and yet continually reinterpreted, appropriated, and repurposed through time as the *'ulama* [traditionally trained scholars of Islam] engage with their intellectual legacy in changing circumstances.[3]

While I will return to the various meanings and articulations of 'Islamic tradition' later, I want to highlight here that, for my discussants, what I call the 'Islamic tradition' and 'Islam' are synonymous both in this chapter and throughout this book, even though discussants do not use the former term.

The chapter is divided into three main sections. First, I describe the theory of the rhizome and the importance of conceptualising tradition as a rhizome. I show that a rhizomatic approach, as opposed to an arborescent one, best represents the Islamic tradition and particularly the selectivity that lay Muslims and scholars of Islam attribute to Islam. In the second section, I discuss the key components of a tradition: stratification, flexibility, political and historical contingencies, and imagination and nostalgia. I show that understanding the Islamic tradition therefore requires an appreciation of the process of its formation (e.g. through the layering of meanings and interpretations); its recognised diversity and flexibility in Islamic history and legal history in particular – albeit not on all issues; the role of colonialism in perceptions of Islam today; and nostalgic views of an idealised past. The third section deals with lay Muslim Americans' constructions of the Islamic tradition. Relying on the ethnographic research I conducted, I conclude that my discussants' understanding of Islam is an excellent example of the rhizomatic approach. The mainstream scholars whom my discussants invoke in their responses also seem to understand the tradition as a rhizome, although they do not explicitly identify it as such. Both groups' projections of the Islamic tradition prescribe a formula for how its flexibility works: that is, the flexibility does not apply in cases that threaten gender hierarchy. While not always consistent with each other or internally, both groups' approach to the Islamic tradition fits a rhizomatic model that helps explain how they perceive their selectivity as a simple projection of what 'Islam' teaches.

A RHIZOMATIC VIEW OF THE TRADITION: AN ALTERNATIVE APPROACH

Some of the existing definitions of 'tradition' in Islamic studies implicitly point towards the idea of tradition as a rhizome. For example, Talal Asad's concept of a discursive tradition acknowledges Muslims' relationship to their past, to their present, and to changes that the tradition undergoes. He proposes that Islam be approached as 'a discursive tradition that includes and relates itself to the founding texts of the Qur'an and the Hadith'.[4] He continues:

> A tradition consists essentially of discourses that seek to instruct practitioners regarding the correct form and purpose of a given practice that, precisely because it is established, has a history… An Islamic discursive tradition is simply a tradition of Muslim discourse that addresses itself to conceptions of the Islamic past and future, with reference to a particular Islamic practice in the present. Clearly, not everything Muslims say and do belongs to an Islamic discursive tradition. Nor is an Islamic tradition in this sense necessarily imitative of what was done in the past.[5]

This definition speaks to the dynamic nature of texts, practices, and ideas, and it allows for the reinterpretations of not only texts but concepts as well. While not explicit in Asad's analysis, this approach is general enough to implicitly allow for Muslim feminist discourse to be a part of the tradition – because Islam is a tradition of Muslim discourse, not necessarily of Muslim male or patriarchal or mainstream Muslim discourse. Nor is this discourse solely the monopoly or production of the elite: it involves the interpretation and application of both texts and practices.

Zareena Grewal also challenges portrayals of the Islamic tradition that suggest it is merely passed down, received, and accepted uncritically by authorities or custodians, such as the *'ulama* (scholars of Islam). In her discussion of Muslim Americans' construction of the Islamic tradition, she points out that students who travel overseas for religious knowledge 'often talk about their tradition in simple, static terms, as an object that can be found, excavated, and brought home'.[6] However, she notes, the actual 'process of studying, teaching, and arguing over what constitutes tradition are [sic] far more complex and challenging than the retrieval of a souvenir'.[7] She defines tradition as 'a process of debate over what links past, present, and future in a continuity that is meaningful and authoritative'.[8] Critiquing common understandings of tradition as 'a simple act of preservation', she argues that:

> elements of the past are mediated into the present by custodians, individuals in the present who decide which aspects of the past are nonessential to the tradition's future and, therefore, may be deleted or de-emphasized. Custodians also decide which elements should be emphasized, highlighted, even added in order to ensure the tradition's survival in the future.[9]

Grewal's study shows that it is not just reformist scholars who selectively preserve and modify parts of the tradition and add to it when they deem necessary; the *'ulama* approach tradition the same way. What is different about their approaches, however, is what the custodians in different groups of Muslims deem essential and non-essential.

Ayesha Chaudhry's articulation of the term 'Islamic tradition' and its use among various groups of Muslims is also worth reviewing here. She argues that Muslims speak of this term:

> as a vague and disembodied concept. For them, the 'Islamic tradition' is legendary. Being so mythologized, the 'Islamic tradition' has taken on an overblown and overbearing authoritative status. Its canonical powers are invoked to defend interpretations of the Qur'an that might not accord with modern values, including Q. 4:34 [the verse commonly believed to allow husbands to hit their wives], and also to assuage modern Muslim anxieties about the relevance of the text to the modern world. The 'Islamic tradition' is invoked as the solution to all modern problems, even if the content of those solutions is never clear.[10]

Thus, the Islamic tradition is treated as though it is a body of fixed values, guidelines, and rules that can answer any given question at any given time – even though in practice, its guidance on specific issues is often unclear.

In her discussion of Black Muslims, Su'ad Abdul Khabeer sees lay practitioners as 'progenitors of a discourse, an epistemology, an aesthetic, and an embodiment' that she calls Muslim Cool.[11] 'Muslim Cool', she asserts, is a way of being Muslim that lies at the intersection of Islam and hip hop and 'draws on Blackness to contest two overlapping systems of racial norms: the hegemonic ethnoreligious norms of Arab and South Asian U.S. American Muslim communities on the one hand, and White American normativity on the other'.[12] Her interlocutors, whom she calls her teachers, are engaged in hip-hop-based activism and are often 'rendered invisible' by hegemonic racial and religious norms, but they find affirmation and validation in spaces they have forged for themselves, such as IMAN (Inner-City Muslim Action Network), in Chicago. They contest meanings of Islam and the Islamic tradition that have been drawn by non-Black Muslims to determine the boundaries of the religion. In so doing, they expand the definition of Islam, so that it is inclusive and in intimate conversation with popular culture, race, and religion more broadly. Abdul Khabeer situates their conceptualisation of Islam as embedded in the Islamic tradition, 'diverse and dynamic in both textual and lived form'.[13] She highlights that Blackness remains and always has been central to Islam in the United States, whether through Muslim Americans' self-identification in relation to Blackness, or by determining the permissibles and impermissibles in Islam (e.g. the kind of instruments and music widely believed among non-Black Muslims to be permissible), or through the regulating of Black Muslims' practice of Islam by non-Black Muslims. She centres lay Muslims' understanding of Islam as a liberating force, an Islam they use to navigate a complex intersectional identity living between white supremacy and a South Asian and Arab-centric Islam in the US, defying a narrow idea of Islam that excludes Black Muslims.[14]

Other scholars, too, critique the narrow ways that the Islamic tradition is imagined, both by Muslim scholars and non-Black lay Muslims, and argue instead for a more expansive understanding of Islam. Sherman Jackson, for example, interrogates notions of an 'authentic Islam', typically understood by Muslims as stemming from an imagined 'Muslim world', referring to South Asia and the Middle East; he therefore critiques the Muslim immigrant monopoly of the Islamic tradition.[15] Jackson argues that Sunni orthodoxy's lack of reach to African American Muslims is a consequence of the fact that it is constructed and imagined without an acknowledgment of African American realities. Jamillah Karim also explores the ways that Muslim Americans negotiate an American identity through a case study of South Asian and Black Muslims. She pays particular attention to the ways that Black and South Asian Muslims engage – or do not engage – each other, exploring the ways in which Black women and South Asian women reinforce as well as resist ethnic boundaries and divisions.[16] In all of these studies, we see a challenge to the idea of one dominant form of Islam that marginalises and jeopardises other forms.

Given this history of the evolution of the Islamic tradition and the forces influencing it, as well as critiques of a narrow understanding of it, I argue that the construction of the Islamic tradition is a collective, discursive attempt to understand what Islam is and what it means for the present and the future of Muslims. This construction is connected to broader issues of imagination, identity, and memory. In her study of historical portrayals of new converts' attachment to Islam and the role of memory and its revision through time, Sara Savant discusses adherence to tradition as represented by memory – or rather, layers of memory and imagination – as integral to religious identity. Emphasising the relationship between tradition and memory, Savant describes the construction and accumulation of tradition as follows:

> Traditions, like objects, patterns of action, and ways of thinking, are reproduced and disseminated, and they frequently exhibit differences that suggest adaptation and therefore interpretation… The concept of memory, on the other hand, draws attention to the power of traditions to affect individuals and collectivities. As a tradition accumulates weight and authority, it shapes collective agreements about the past, thereby creating memories. These collective agreements are deeply held by groups and the individuals within them, but they can also be opposed, changed, and otherwise subjected to negotiation, especially by the people who consider them to represent 'their' past…[17]

The tradition is therefore connected to a collective sense of community, authority, and memory. It is guided by an imagined past that contributes to identity formation in the present and in the future.

While academic scholars and theorists such as Asad and Grewal have begun to think seriously about the connections between tradition and the past, present, and future, my research shows that the scholarly elite are not the only ones who participate in these conversations. Lay Muslims also engage tradition in meaningful ways that contribute to and shape their present and their future. New meanings are attached to the symbols of the past so that they make sense in the present and will remain relevant in the future.

THE ISLAMIC TRADITION AS A RHIZOME

The Deleuzian idea of a rhizome has been applied to many disciplines and fields, including Islamic Studies. For example, Alberto Fernández Carbajal applies it to queer Islam and sexuality, Daniel Tutt to the Iranian philosopher Mulla Sadra, and, most recently, Michael Muhammad Knight to Islam more broadly, including the Qur'an, Hadiths, Sufism, sacred sites, and Islamic theology.[18] Knight argues that 'Deleuzian Islamic theology…must confront orthodoxy as a social construction that privileges some voices and erases others'.[19] After all, 'Historical Islam reveals an abundance of ways that diverse thinkers and communities reproduce God and the Prophet as concepts; the lived reality of Islam is messier than the notion of a singular "Islamic theology" could accommodate.'[20] I agree with Knight about Deleuze's 'most fruitful contribution' to Islam: 'the way that he affirms multiplicity'.[21] In Deleuzian Islam, what Knight also terms 'Deleuzo-Islamic theology', Islam is:

> a dynamic, variegating rhizome defined by connections to its outside with multiple points of entry and exit. Islam-as-rhizome affirms positive relations to heterodoxy, which is to say a conception of Islamic theology as forever heterogenous, always in flux, never in its finished form or accessible in its original state, but always a plastic proto-Islam in development.[22]

Thus, in his chapter on the Qur'an, Knight argues that because 'the rhizome pursues connections with everything', 'different connections become possible, as specific verses enable linkages to diverse literatures and resources and the Qur'an expands its powers by hooking up to other books' or sources of knowledge.[23] This is precisely how scholars are able to incorporate updated knowledge of the world into the Qur'an, such as descriptions of the earth as flat or spherical depending on the latest scientific research. Similarly, by not providing details in its stories, the Qur'an allows its readers to fill in gaps because it 'opens its body for entry from outside'.[24] In his chapter on Sufism – typically understood as the mystical dimension of Islam – Knight challenges the assumption that *tariqa-based* Sufism (Sufism based on specific orders led by a teacher with disciples) is a 'purely aborescent assemblage with all the power located in the master at center', since there are in fact multiple lineages and trees, which destabilise an imagined centre.[25] Indeed, Knight argues that an Islamic atheism can be extracted from the Islamic tradition because of the rhizomatic tendencies of the various sources of Islam, depending on how one defines 'atheism' and 'Islamic', and by uncovering the 'rejected and forgotten archives and voices at the edge of orthodoxy-making power'.[26]

To be sure, the fact that Islam is dynamic and defined by multiplicities does not mean that it has to 'revel in absolute chaos and perpetual deconstruction all the time, but it still exhibits a release from the need for Islam to remain forever clear and unchanged'.[27] The data from my interviews with my respondents shows precisely this. At no point do my respondents begin to think Islam is random, sporadic, or chaotic. Every explanation they gave, every opinion they shared, was grounded in 'Islam', even as their definition of and sources for 'Islam' changed from topic to topic. Different groups of Muslims, between lay and scholarly as well as across sectarian and ideological differences, can prioritise different issues and sources at a given moment, and these priorities change with time and context. A majority view, a 'mainstream' view, appears to exist at all times, but the same view does not persist as the mainstream, dominant view in all contexts and times.

The lived-reality aspect of Islam is crucial to this book. As we will see in two chapters – namely, women's interfaith marriage and female inheritance – most of my respondents' opinions on the issue are informed by their lived reality. Scholars often distinguish between 'textual Islam' and 'oral' or 'lived' Islam: that of the male elite and women, respectively.[28] This is often expressed through interpretations of the Qur'an (*tafsīr*). Sa'diyya Shaikh's concept of 'the *tafsir* of praxis' and Juliane Hammer's 'embodied *tafsir*' remind us that women's engagement with Islam is profoundly shaped by their experiences, which for many women take precedence over traditional interpretations of the Qur'an.[29] This is clearest in the chapter on female inheritance, where most of my male and female, married and unmarried respondents argued in support of equal inheritance laws unequivocally, unconditionally – arguing that was the Qur'an's intention, despite seemingly clear Qur'anic texts to the effect that daughters receive half a share. Hammer and Shaikh argue that exegesis of the Qur'an is rooted in one's notion of justice and personal experiences, particularly those interpretations that result from an unjust reading of the text. Shaikh coins the phrase '*tafsir* through praxis' in the context of Muslim women's experiences of a violent interpretation of the Qur'anic verse 4:34, which is often read to allow a husband to physically discipline his wife. A '*tafsir* of praxis' explains interpretations of the Qur'an through lived reality, a religious-studies approach that distinguishes a practitioner's experience of religion from institutionally defined beliefs. In other words, one's experiences inform their interpretations of the Qur'an. Hammer's 'embodied *tafsir*', developed in the context of amina wadud's prayer leadership, extends Shaikh's argument to apply the textual interpretation to bodily engagements with religious practice. While it is commonly assumed that women's interpretations are unreliable because they are rooted in personal experience and therefore are biased, Scott Kugle proposes that all interpretive communities are communities of experience; it is simply the experience of the male elite, who have dominated religious tradition, that is accepted as 'normal' and 'authoritative'.[30] By contrast, marginalised communities' interpretations of scriptures are dismissed as mere experiences rather than based on the textual tradition. The textual tradition demonstrates that only 'the experiences of patriarchal, aristocratic, slave-owning men have been thoroughly textualized in the remote past'.[31]

Deleuze and Guattari developed the metaphor of the rhizome in contrast to what they describe as an arboreal model.[32] They describe the latter, which represents hierarchies, as follows:

> [It] stems originally from Aristotle's 'classic theory of categories', which in essence propounds that entities are placed into the same category, by rational division, according to objective assessment of shared characteristics. It has been the basis for scientific classification and taxonomy… This model is characterized by vertical and fixed linkages, and binary choices, and by the linking of elements only of the same general nature.[33]

This same model informs most historical understandings of the Islamic tradition and its relationship with feminist interpretations of Islam. That is, the declaring of feminist interpretations of Islam, such as prayer leadership of mixed-gender congregations, as deviant and even 'un-Islamic' implies that the Islamic tradition has been established and settled, and that Muslim feminists have little to nothing to contribute to its shaping.[34]

Deleuze and Guattari contrast the tree with a rhizome: 'A tree has particular roots that embed themselves in the soil at a particular place and give rise to branches and then leaves in a particular way. It is a system of derivation: first the roots, then the trunk, then the leaves. The roots are embedded here and not elsewhere. The branches are bound to the trunk, the leaves to the branches.'[35] Unlike a traditional tree, a rhizome can 'shoot out roots from any point, leaves and stems from any point'.[36] It has no beginning (roots), no middle (trunk), and no end (leaves). It is, as Todd May explains it, 'always in the middle, always in process. There is no particular shape it has to take and no particular territory to which it is bound. It can connect from any part of itself to a tree, to the ground, to a fence, to other plants, to itself.'[37] This difference between a tree and a rhizome is crucial to understanding the Islamic tradition: the rhizome easily connects one point to another in the same way that the tradition does.

The rhizome has several key characteristics that are especially helpful for the understanding of any given tradition: 1) The principle of connection indicates that 'any point of a rhizome can be connected to anything other, and must be'.[38] 2) Heterogeneity, because those connections are always heterogeneous. 3) Multiplicity, or 'dimensions that cannot increase in number without the multiplicity changing in nature',[39] signifying rupture, or the idea that a rhizome 'may be broken, shattered at a given spot, but it will start up again on one of its old lines or on new lines';[40] other names for this process include segmentarity and stratification.[41] 4) Cartography characterises rhizomes because 'unlike tracings, the rhizome pertains to a map that must be produced, constructed, a map that is always detachable, connectable, reversible, modifiable, and has multiple entryways and exits and its own lines of flight'.[42] 5) Rhizomes exhibit *decalcomania*, formations through 'continuous negotiation with their context, constantly adapting by experimentation, performing an active resistance against rigid organization and restriction'.[43] More simply, a rhizome defies binaries and is purely rooted in connectivity and multiplicities (e.g. feminist, contemporary, reformist, pre-modern, etc.). Each of these characteristics of a rhizome has parallels with the idea of a tradition: a tradition never forms on its own, in and of itself, in a vacuum. Instead, it develops through continuous negotiation with new contexts and constantly adapts itself through experimentation and change.

Todd May, explaining the significance and relevance of rhizome theory, applies it to the concept, construction, and development of cities as well as the need for diversity, not unification, in city planning and development: 'Cities are not matters of function; they are matters of connection. They are rhizomes, not trees. Only this is certain: it is the relationships among the diversity of aspects of urban life that create a vibrant street life, not their segregation into areas of uniformity. Diversity nourishes cities; uniformity strangles them.'[44] The description is remarkably pertinent to the Islamic tradition, particularly in the following:

> Cities are not organic and they are not mechanistic. They are machinic. It is not that no order emerges. An order, an actualization, does emerge. But its emergence has nothing to do with self-subsistent elements arranged according to a pre-given pattern. [Order does not emerge] from connections that are melded once and for all. [Instead,] it emerges from specific contexts of diversity in ways that both create and are created by the elements of that diversity.[45]

This concept of actualisation is essential because, for Deleuze and Guattari, a critical question is how people develop and actualise new, different possibilities, and how they form connections. Unlike the tree metaphor of a tradition, 'the rhizome concept allows, indeed requires, non-hierarchical linkages, made pragmatically as they are needed, horizontally or across any number of levels, and linking elements of disparate nature when appropriate, crossing categories. It represents a "decentered network...allowing immediate connections between any of its points".'[46] In other words, the rhizome, like a tradition, is inherently structured in such a way that linking seemingly disparate, disconnected parts of it makes sense. Rhizomatic thinking explains why 'picking and choosing' occurs. More importantly, it informs us that, in fact, what is happening is not picking and choosing but rather connecting the dots, or making connections, through a careful, deliberate and creative engagement with tradition. As Deleuze and Guattari write, 'Unlike trees or their roots, the rhizome connects any point to any other point, and its traits are not necessarily linked to traits of the same nature.'[47] 'Picking and choosing' illustrates different possibilities that exist, which are the results of interpretive choices, engagement and negotiations with traditions. The rhizomatic approach offers an interesting and complex theoretical metaphor for the interconnectedness of ongoing processes. Rhizomatic thinking is beneficial in addressing the complexities of the historical, discursive, and other traditions within Islam, challenging any simplified representations of fixed boundaries and categories.

Specific elements of the Islamic tradition, such as Islamic legal schools, also exhibit features of the rhizome. For instance, as David Vishanoff points out, the 'genius' of Islamic thought is that it 'can express new ways of thinking and relating to the world through a discourse that appears ancient and unchanging', an idea very much in line with many of the characteristics of the rhizome as described above.[48] Both the Islamic tradition as a whole, as well as specific parts of it, are rhizomatic.

Tradition and Stratigraphy

The concept of stratigraphy helps explain the changes that a tradition accrues gradually. As described earlier, Sara Savant applies the geological concept of stratigraphy to an Islamic past constructed in the memory of Iran's ninth- to eleventh-century Persians as they converted to the new faith. She demonstrates that these new adherents maintained loyalty and a sense of belonging to the new community, as the first large group of non-Arab converts to Islam, by writing themselves into the early Arabic and Islamic accounts of the past. Memory is integral to the construction of the past, of tradition, of faith. However, this construction of the past is not infinitely flexible: the past is 'reworked within certain boundaries', and these boundaries are drawn by shapers of tradition who seek creative ways to 'maintain, preserve, and value as "authentic" aspects of [the] past that [serve] their agendas while omitting, reformulating, maligning, and otherwise suppressing those that [trouble] them'.[49] Creating a tradition requires a morphing of the past in ways that serve the interests and commitments of those with the power to morph it, and lay practitioners play a significant role in this process.

Islam is a tradition because it grows through a process of stratigraphy. Karen Bauer, in her discussion of a stratigraphic approach to Islam, adds, 'the term stratigraphy can describe the continual accretion of meanings in the genre of *tafsīr* [commentaries on the Qur'an]. Through time, interpretations built up in layers, and the very process of building up could also impose new meanings on the text and on earlier interpretations.'[50] This layering allowed scholars to impose new meanings onto past interpretations that gradually became part of what later generations accepted as tradition. This layering of meanings and interpretations also explains how continuity and change are simultaneously crucial to traditions: the story (or 'spirit') remains at the crux of its interpretations and re-interpretations as the details added by subsequent generations are expanded with time. Specifically in the *tafsīr* tradition, 'authors would selectively pick and choose from previous works, usually without crediting the original author'.[51] Bauer provides several examples of this 'stratigraphic accretion' through which scholars – both contemporary and historical ones – are able to '[discard] the unsavory elements' of previous interpretations and Hadiths.[52] These examples include differences in interpretations of female testimony, different versions of Hadiths related to the creation story, debates on which Hadiths remain pertinent over time, and the meaning of Qur'anic verses on a husband's right to discipline his wife. As I will show, the Qur'an, or at least perceptions of the Qur'an's teachings on certain issues (such as women's interfaith marriage and female inheritance), play a crucial role in people's views of the negotiables and non-negotiables, of what is considered flexible in the tradition and what is considered static.

The Fluidity of the Historical Islamic Tradition

Medieval Muslim jurists developed a system that facilitated a multiplicity of opinions. They employed terms such as *takhayyur* (picking and choosing) and *tarjīḥ* (preponderance), among others, specifically to accommodate the fluidity and flexibility of past legal interpretations.[53] Wael Hallaq notes that jurists never questioned the idea of legal pluralism and expected it to endure, introducing a system that would allow for both scholars and lay people to pick the least stringent of the interpretations and rulings available to them.[54] Hallaq shows that pre-modern scholars, jurists and others, never claimed, let alone insisted, that their work, their theories, or the subject matter they were discussing (such as *usūl al-fiqh* ['principles of Islamic jurisprudence']) was fixed or well-defined.

In response to the argument that modern and contemporary scholars and reformers are operating outside the framework of the Islamic tradition, Ahmed Fekry Ibrahim argues that the pragmatism that underlies reformist methodology has precedent in pre-modern Islamic law. Ibrahim challenges the assumption that pragmatism is a by-product of modernity and shows, instead, that reformists' strategies are much more grounded in the historical Islamic tradition than some historians – and I add lay Muslims and Muslim preachers – give them credit for. Ibrahim argues that 'jurists resorted to these departures when a commitment to legal methodology could not achieve the desired legal outcome, to wit, the permission of pragmatic eclecticism'.[55] In other words, Muslim scholars have always departed from their predecessors when they deemed it necessary, such as when their desired outcome was not being accommodated by an adherence to past opinions and conclusions.

Some of the technical terms that demonstrate the flexibility of pre-modern Islamic law are as follows: *tarjīḥ* (preponderance), *tatabbu' al-rukhaṣ* (pursuing the dispensations), *takhayyur* (picking and choosing, i.e. selecting the best option of many), *ijtihād* (independent reasoning, legal reasoning), and *maṣlaḥa* (welfare of society).

Tarjīḥ, or preponderance, is determined by 'the strength of evidence or the number of authorities supporting a given view'.[56] In the pre-modern period, multiple juristic opinions were evaluated, and the opinion with the strongest evidence was chosen or established as the most correct option for any given situation. This doctrine often involved 'ad hoc reasoning designed to privilege the result that a given jurist desired'.[57] The explicit criteria on which *tarjīḥ* (preponderance) was based rarely included social needs, despite the possibility that, as Ibrahim notes, social needs must have motivated new interpretations.[58] Significantly, *tarjīḥ* was an option available not only to jurists but also to the laity.[59]

The term that did allow for social needs to be a legitimate reason for engendering new interpretations was *tatabbu' al-rukhaṣ*. Literally 'pursuing the dispensations' of the legal schools, the term refers to 'the conscious decision to pursue [revisit] the juristic opinion perceived to be most expedient from any of the four Sunni schools', or from within the same school.[60] Prior to the rise of the legal schools, however, the term referred to 'the selection of the less stringent juristic opinions of mujtahids [scholars of Islam trained in *ijtihād*, thus qualified to provide independent reasoning or re-interpret established legal rulings]'.[61] Because it was historically associated with the Qur'anic term *ittibā' al-hawā'* (or following one's whims) and some scholars even used the two terms interchangeably, Ibrahim infers that this negative connotation may explain 'the tendency among some modern reformers to opt for the use of the term *takhayyur* [selecting from among a variety of opinions]' instead.[62] Therefore, *takhayyur* and *tatabbu' al-rukhaṣ* are used synonymously in the modern period.[63] *Takhayyur* and *tarjīḥ* 'were mostly exercised within the same school', whereas '*tatabbu' al-rukhaṣ* is more often associated with crossing school boundaries'.[64]

Takhayyur is derived from the root word for 'selecting' and refers to the practice of picking and choosing legal rules from a variety of sources and legal schools in order for scholars to arrive at a conclusion that works best in a given context.[65] In the Ottoman Civil Code (1869–76), *takhayyur* was exercised to select opinions deemed most appropriate, not just among the Sunni legal schools but also among non-Sunni schools in order to 'accommodate the needs of modern Muslim nation states'.[66] Similarly, *talfīq*, which literally means 'to sew two pieces of cloth together', is a form of *tatabbu' al-rukhaṣ* and refers to the combining of two doctrines.[67] Ibrahim suggests that one instance of its use may be 'when a woman is married off with neither the permission of her guardian (*walī*) nor the presence of two witnesses... This person would be combining the Mālikī position (considering a marriage contract valid even without witnesses) with the Ḥanafī view (a woman of age and sound mind can marry without a guardian).'[68] Wael Hallaq notes that in some countries, like Egypt and Iraq, the use of *talfīq* has allowed for 'radical changes even in inheritance law, e.g., making lawful a bequest in favor of an heir (prohibited in Sunni but not in Shiʿi law), with the proviso that the total bulk of the bequeathed property not exceed one-third of the estate'.[69] Clearly, as Ibrahim's example of *talfīq* shows, these strategies were not intended for scholars alone but were and remain available to lay people also. Hallaq, however, states that 'traditional Islamic law made it forbidden for both the jurists and "state authorities" to resort to ...' *talfīq* and related devices.[70] Both scholars and lay people have nonetheless continued their application.

The terms *ijtihād* and *maṣlaḥa* are significant and not only do they demonstrate the flexibility of Islam but are recognised and popular concepts used to accommodate social change in Islam. *Ijtihād* exists as a tool for Muslims, usually scholars trained in Islamic sciences but practically available to lay Muslims as well, to offer new interpretations of a doctrine, practice, or teachings that are no longer applicable outside of the contexts in which they originated. *Ijtihād* is inherently rooted in reason, often defined as 'legal reasoning' or 'independent reasoning'. The prohibition or legal restrictions on polygyny in some Muslim-majority countries, such as in North Africa, occurred because of the application of *ijtihād*. *Maṣlaḥa*, too, has been used for social change, the most common example being that of the abolition of slavery: while the historical Islamic tradition accepted slavery as a reality and Islamic law takes its practice for granted, modern scholars argue that Islam today cannot accept slavery as morally permissible because it is a violation of the dignity of the individual person and because it has a harmful impact on society. *Maṣlaḥa*, often defined as public good, welfare, or public interest, is rooted in a desire for positive social change, the reduction of harm, and the genuine well-being of society; it thus allows Muslims to change a practice or teaching in the interest of a common, collective good.

Finally, several sources of the *sharīʿa* hint at the dynamic nature of Islam in accommodating change. *Maqāṣid al-sharīʿa* (objectives of the *sharīʿa*), a branch of Islamic knowledge concerned with figuring out the purpose of Islamic law, is especially useful because of its attempt to infer from divine sources God's intent. These *maqāṣid* include the preservation of life, lineage, health, property, religion, intellect, honour, among others, although five are typically listed: religion, life, intellect, lineage, and property.[71] This list is subjective, of course, in that it identifies some patriarchal interests as among these divine intents, such as the preservation of the male lineage. However, I propose that we can apply the larger message of such an endeavour to an ethical understanding of Islam, as the *maqāṣid* have been developed and continue to be developed in modern times. Muḥammad al-Ṭāhir ibn ʿĀshūr (d. 1973), for example, adds equality to the list of the *maqāṣid*, insisting in fact that '[human] equality is insured in Islamic legislation. To establish the equality of individuals or groups in Islamic legislation, we are not required to search for its underlying reasons; it is sufficient to insure that nothing contravenes equality.'[72] He uses Q. 4:135 to support his idea that equality is inherent to the Qur'an; the verse requires believers to uphold equality and justice even if it be against their own selves, parents, or kin. He also explicitly argues that the Qur'an does not distinguish between different categories of human because they are all children of God.[73]

Read collectively, all of the above terms demonstrate that a principle that was clearly important for medieval Muslim jurists was a multiplicity of viewpoints from which both scholars and the laity could choose. The purpose was to create ease and accommodate an individual's convenience, signalled by the definitions of some of these terms as the 'least' or less 'stringent opinion'. Pragmatic concerns motivate these doctrines, such that 'scholars engaging in picking rulings according to pragmatic concerns appeal[ed] to these principles and values [such as the aims of the *sharīʿa* (*maqāṣid*) and legal principles (*qawāʿid fiqhiyya*)] to justify their choices'.[74] As new issues and concerns arose, whichever past ideals no longer fit into the tradition were modified and replaced with better, more suitable ideas.

To be sure, the use of these tools was regulated. Not all opinions were considered or could be declared valid, and all opinions that one could select from were expected to fall within the boundaries of 'valid disagreement', or *khilāf*. Nor were these options all considered equally valid or equal in principle. For instance, *takhayyur* (picking and choosing among multiple sources and interpretations) was considered 'a last resort after *tarjīḥ* [failed] to yield a preference for one legal option'.[75] But which opinions were valid or invalid was always a matter of debate and continues to be so. My point is that the pre-modern legal scholars often (but not always) made attempts to ensure that what they perceived as the 'best' possible meaning or interpretation won. The idea is that a system has already been put in place that contemporary Muslims can draw upon to accommodate their evolving needs. There is no valid reason to associate the Islamic tradition exclusively with its patriarchal renditions; instead, the tools that pre-modern scholars developed may be utilised even to challenge the historical interpretations.

While what is 'best' or 'worst' may change with time and may be politically motivated – or be a conclusion derived solely by male scholars – the tools in the historical tradition can be and are utilised by contemporary Muslim scholars, particularly feminists, to arrive at new conclusions. One example is divorce, as Judith Tucker addresses. When obtaining divorce, Muslim women under Ottoman rule relied on legal pluralism, choosing a judge or a legal school based on the desired outcome rather than on their own school.[76] Tucker notes that Hanafī courts commonly accommodated 'the doctrines of other legal schools on divorce when such flexibility appeared to provide a woman with more options and protections'.[77] Yossef Rapoport, too, in his study of Mamluk society (1250–1517 in Egypt, Palestine, and Syria), shows the ways in which women used different forms of divorce allowed to them in Islamic law to end their marriages.[78] Thus, what I am suggesting is that Islamic feminism, as a part of the tradition, now plays a role in these debates about what constitute the 'best' and 'least stringent' interpretations. Clearly, with the absence of women's opinions among the juristic options available to Muslims historically, Muslim women's contributions today expand the existing multiple viewpoints and options from which one can choose.

Why, then, is the impression of the stagnant, fixed nature of the Islamic tradition on questions of gender so pervasive among mainstream Muslim scholars and lay Muslims? I suggest that a primary reason is the portrayal of Islam in the discourse of Western colonisers, which became hegemonic even in Muslim societies. In the next section, I discuss the role of colonialism and orientalism on current constructions of the Islamic tradition.

Tradition, Colonialism, and Nostalgia

European colonialism profoundly shaped Muslim, and orientalist, conceptualisations of the Islamic tradition in ways that contribute greatly to the now popular assumptions about what the Islamic tradition, or Islam, 'says' about any given issue. Muslim scholars internalised orientalist projections of Islam and Islamic law, leading to an ossified view of the Islamic tradition.[79] Arguably, the colonialist and orientalist projections onto the Islamic tradition, or at least Islamic law, are due to orientalist scholars' misreading of the doctrine of *taqlīd. Taqlīd* 'has been translated by influential European scholars in terms of blind adherence to established norms or tradition, as "imitation," "servile imitation," and "unquestioning acceptance," and the term became "associated with "intellectual timidity, and/or depletion of creative and interpretive energies."'[80] Of course, orientalist scholars have not been alone in this perception, and they adopted this attitude towards *taqlīd* from Muslim scholars such as Abd al-Wahhāb (d. 1792) and Shah Walī Ullah al-Dihlawī (d. 1762), 'both of whom criticised excessive reliance on *taqlīd*'.[81] For other Muslim scholars, however, *taqlīd* worked in conjunction with *ijtihād*. Humeira Iqtidar explains that Muslim scholars eventually internalised the colonialist and Enlightenment idea of tradition:

> From the late 18th century, relying on an Enlightenment conception of tradition as unchanging and regressive, a conflation of tradition as blind adherence and taqlīd as tradition was operationalized by colonial scholars/administrators in their policy decisions. In South Asia, such assumptions played a role in the homogenisation, codification and ultimately stagnation of sharī'a that the British administrators carried out under the rubric of Anglo-Mohammaden law with the aspiration to standardise. This codification led to the loss of precisely that internal diversity, even contradiction, that made sharī'a adaptable and alive…[82]

The colonialists' assumptions about what constitutes tradition and law were embedded into their administrations in ways that continue to influence Muslims' own understanding of their tradition. While this is certainly not the view that all Muslim scholars have adopted, my aim is to theorise the prevalent attitude towards the Islamic tradition, on issues of gender in particular, as ossified. Assumptions about the Islamic tradition being stagnant developed over time, first affecting Muslim scholars and eventually gaining their way into lay Muslim spaces where the idea was internalised.

The doctrine of *taqlīd* is rarely associated with change, but recent scholarship has shown the productive ways in which Muslim scholars utilised it to grant themselves the opportunity to add to existing interpretations. *Taqlīd* allowed, and continues to allow, for 'predictability and flexibility at the same time'.[83] Muhammad Qasim Zaman's study of the *'ulama* and the construction of authority in South Asia, particularly in British India, also provides evidence of choices to negotiate practices and understandings of Islam with changing times and circumstances, showing that, in fact, the doctrine of *taqlīd* facilitated a scholar's disagreement with past interpretations and conclusions.[84]

This tension between colonialism and the Islamic tradition exists because of the subjugation of Muslims by non-Muslims and the shifting of Islamic legal systems by colonialists. As Zaman asserts:

> In the colonial context, when Islam and the Muslims were politically subdued and the colonizers and the colonized viewed one another with serious misgivings, the Muslims could not be certain of how the British would implement the law even when they claimed to base their decisions on Islamic legal sources. The consequences of entrusting Islamic law to non-Muslims were thus unforeseen and potentially undesirable.[85]

Meanings of the term 'Islamic tradition' are now indelibly tied to the colonialist experience. Specifically, as Ayesha Chaudhry points out, 'colonial and post-colonial religious scholarship continues to be viewed – in some circles – with contempt as tainted, corrupt, and in all ways inferior to pre-colonial scholarship. The pinnacle of Islamic thought, therefore, is usually seen to lie in the pre-colonial age, when the scholars were able to curry God's favour and came to represent a pristine, spiritually ascendant "Islamic tradition".'[86] Thus, whether, when, and how modifications to the tradition may occur are deeply coloured by colonialism, the historical experience through which Muslims' relationship with Islam and an Islamic past was tainted. As a result, today much re-engagement with the Islamic past is a product of concerns that emerged exclusively because of colonialist disruptions of Muslim identity, imagination, and faith.

Still, the flexibility of the pre-modern Islamic tradition was not a simple matter and it was not afforded to all issues. Scholars and lay people continue to negotiate with it. For instance, as shown earlier, pre-modern Muslim jurists created a system in which flexibility was afforded to them and to lay Muslims through a diverse set of interpretations of most issues. After colonialism, however, this diversity and flexibility appears to have been stifled through orientalist projections of the Islamic tradition, an idea that subsequent generations of Muslims, including traditional scholars and lay Muslims, later internalised. Hallaq offers examples of academic scholars of Islam, such as John Esposito, who have accepted this claim to such an extent that they speak of the 'stifling' of the 'dynamism of legal development' as early as the eleventh century, leading to a 'static Muslim society and law in the medieval period'.[87] Hallaq argues that this is an inaccurate reflection of the Islamic past and is instead a product of orientalist projection onto Islam, Arabs, and Muslims. I will argue that this internalisation of orientalist attitudes appears in more subtle ways as well, such as through claims that 'Islam' forbids interfaith marriages for Muslim women or 'Islam' or 'the Islamic tradition' does not allow women to lead mixed-gender prayers.[88]

While the contemporary academic and mainstream scholars in this study acknowledge the fluidity of the Islamic tradition, many of them appear to limit modification to that tradition to its custodians alone. I argue, however, that the preservation and modification of, and addition to, the tradition is not the task of religious authorities and specialists alone. Lay Muslims are also an integral part of that mediation and negotiation process.

IDEAS ABOUT THE TRADITION AMONG CONTEMPORARY POPULAR AMERICAN MUSLIM SCHOLARS AND PREACHERS

I now turn to the views of three contemporary individuals whom my informants commonly invoked as authoritative scholars and whose knowledge of Islam they trust: Yasir Qadhi, Nouman Ali Khan, and – when specifically asked if they know any female scholars – Yasmin Mogahed. I characterise them as 'popular' preachers, by which I mean accessible preachers of Islam whose teachings are perceived to be consistent with the status quo and consensus positions, and who appeal to the lay Muslim community. While some of these scholars, such as Yasir Qadhi, have academic training as well as traditional training in Muslim seminaries, their audience remains the broader Muslim community, and they all preach a form of Islam that relies heavily on gender hierarchy. These preachers' presence on the internet and their accessibility to lay Muslims help tremendously with Muslims' perceptions of them as scholarly or religious authorities, whether or not they have the training to be considered as such – in fact, Mogahed does not. They are, essentially, what we call influencers, social media personalities with significant followings who are able to affect the behaviour and beliefs of their audiences.[89] Other such contemporary popular Muslim American preachers include Omar Suleiman, Tamara Gray, Hamza Yusuf, Khalid Latif, and many others.[90] Only Qadhi and Khan figured frequently in my respondents' views, however, and Mogahed much less so.

These three scholars' conceptualisations of the 'Islamic tradition' is like that of much academic engagement with the concept insofar as the flexibility, diversity, and nuance of the tradition are acknowledged. However, it is also significantly different because popular preachers and scholars imagine a collective agreement on the temporal boundaries of the tradition – for example, when it begins, when it ends, and when it necessitates (re)negotiations.[91]

Yasir Qadhi, a graduate of Islamic University of Madinah and Yale University, is an instructor at Al-Maghrib Institute, an Islamic seminary in North America and Europe. Qadhi is based in the United States and is one of the most influential teachers and scholars of Islam in the West. While searching for Qadhi's views on change, tradition, and Islam, I found a *YouTube* lecture of his titled 'Looking Back as We Look Forward: Change & Modernity', presented in Detroit in December 2013.[92] As of March 2023, the video has received over 87,000 views. In this talk, Qadhi seeks to show that Islam is a flexible religion that recognises the need for change when necessary. He discusses the scholarly debates on the impermissibility of coffee in the sixteenth century (because it was declared an intoxicant) and on the use of the printing press (because it might allow non-specialists to exploit the knowledge available in the classical texts). His point is that while these two were declared forbidden for centuries in the past, their impermissibility was never valid in the first place because there was 'always a dissenting opinion' around these issues.[93] He incorrectly claims that for consensus to be legitimate, there must be no dissenting opinions, no challenges to the established position, a claim to which I will return.

Important for our purpose here is Qadhi's observation that, presumably in the West, Islam has been 'solidified' and the point of reference for it is 'a group of people' who do not understand the needs of Muslims in the West. He states that 'modern scholars are grappling with modern issues of a very different nature, of a nature that you cannot open up Ibn Taymiyya and Ibn Kathir…and find a simple cut-and-paste *fatwa* [for a modern issue]… So the Deobandis [a nineteenth-century revivalist Sunni group originating in South Asia] look up to India, Pakistan, the Salafis [a nineteenth-century revivalist Sunni group originating in Saudi Arabia] to Saudi Arabia… But the fact of the matter is that our Islam from them cannot be unconditional because they don't live our lives, they don't understand our situation and scenario.'[94] Clearly, Islam is not the same for all Muslims and is subject to change depending on context and circumstance. In fact, Qadhi explicitly says, 'You know there's a cliché, and we were taught this: There's only one Islam, and that is the Islam of the Prophet. My dear brothers and sisters, it sounds very nice, but what do you mean there's only one Islam?'[95]

However, he continues, not all of Islam is subject to change: there are some fixed, basic principles of Islam that must never be changed under any circumstances. This is where Qadhi's construction of Islam becomes relevant for our discussion on change and tradition. According to him, the foundations of Islam are those that God has revealed, and these are: 'belief in Allah, belief in the Prophet, names and attributes of Allah, *qadr* [predestination], the Qur'an being the uncreated speech of Allah – all of this is rock solid; we cannot and should not, can never alter this.'[96] How does one know what cannot be changed? he asks. 'The easiest way to know this is when the scholarly body of the entire *ummah* [universal Muslim community] agrees that something is *ḥarām* [forbidden].'[97] This, he explains, is why the prohibitions on the printing press and coffee were never legitimate: there were always scholars who disagreed. Significantly, he offers the examples of same-sex relations and female-led mixed-gender prayers as cases in which the historically established position can never change because, he claims, no scholar has ever disagreed with these prohibitions:

> One of the biggest controversies in our time is about same-sex relationships. This is a very, very, very difficult problem. People have been banned, people have lost their jobs, people have stopped travelling because of this issue. They might have said statements that were harsh or whatnot. We *cannot* change the fundamental point that we can never accept it to be morally permissible for two people of the same gender to have sexual relations. This is a fundamental. We agree upon this

> point. There's *nothing* that can change this fundamental. What *can* change? Our language of addressing the problem…[98]

What is unclear from this statement is how these 'fundamentals' of Islam, the non-negotiable teachings, practices, and doctrines of Islam, are defined since earlier he argued that the six articles of faith are the fundamentals of Islam. Further, who is this 'we' that 'agree upon this point' that same-sex relations are 'morally' impermissible? He continues this notion of the non-negotiables in Islam, giving the example of mixed-gender female-led prayers:

> Another example [is] the issue of female-led *ṣalāh* [prayer]. By and large, there is *ijmā'* [consensus] on this point. There is unanimous consensus that a woman *cannot* lead a mixed congregation *ṣalāh*. This is an evidence in our *sharī'a*, *ijmā'*. You know what *ijmā'* means? It means *all* the scholars have agreed on this issue. When all the scholars agree, *khalāṣ, sami'na wa ata'na* ['that's it; we hear and we obey', a reference to Qur'anic verse 24:51]. So when there is *ijmā* ', we respect that *ijmā'* because *ijmā'* is a source of Sunni law.[99]

Here, he claims, again incorrectly, that 'all the scholars' of the universal Muslim community have agreed that women cannot lead prayers: as I discuss later in this book, among the many pre-modern scholars who permitted women to lead mixed-gender prayers were Abu Thawr and al-Ṭabarī, and many today permit it as well.[100] For Qadhi, then, 'tradition' is limited to the consensus of what he imagines was established by the unanimous agreement of past scholars – but he does not address which scholars and from what time period. He even adds that these are among the 'basic principles' of Islam.[101] While he had not mentioned the prohibitions on same-sex relations and female-led prayers in Islam in the basic principles he outlined earlier in the lecture, he adds them later as examples of 'basic principles' because of the historical consensus on these two topics. It appears, then, that for him, the six articles of faith and the hetero-sexism established by earlier Muslim scholars through consensus are the basic principles of Islam. In other words, Islam, at its core, is gendered in a patriarchal and hierarchical way that leaves no room for egalitarianism once a group of Muslim (male) scholars agree for it to be the case, even if newer generations of scholars disagree with the previous generations.

It is noteworthy that in cases of gender, he adopts the very method that he critiques by not including in his definition of consensus (the agreement of 'the scholarly body of the entire *ummah*') the contemporary *ummah* and scholarly body, just as it excludes those medieval scholars who approved of mixed-gender female-led prayer. If the 'scholarly body of the entire *ummah*' must agree on an issue in order for it to be a valid position, then the prohibition on female-led prayer is invalid because not all scholars agreed on it and certainly not all of the *ummah* agrees to it, either, unless those disagreeing with Qadhi on this issue do not count as part of his imagined *ummah*.

The other individuals whom my participants (and other Muslims in the United States) follow and trust are Yasmin Mogahed and Nouman Ali Khan. A trained psychologist and the only female instructor at Al-Maghrib Institute in the United States in 2017 and now one of two, Mogahed has a following among Muslims on college campuses across North America. She appeals particularly to her followers for her work on spiritual and personal development and for 'her gift of captivating an entire audience with her thoughts and insightful reflections'.[102] Only one participant named her without my asking if there were any female scholars whom they trusted, followed, or deemed authoritative. Most referenced her as the only female scholar they knew. Thus, while Mogahed did not come to their minds automatically, she is well known as a spiritual, motivational speaker who presents herself and is accepted as an authority on Islam, although some did point out that they were not sure whether she is a scholar.

Nouman Ali Khan, another preacher who figures prominently in the research, is another influential teacher of Islam in the United States. He studied Arabic formally in Pakistan and taught the language at Nassau Community College in New York.[103] He lectures regularly on Arabic grammar, Qur'anic exegesis, and other topics related to Islam. In 2006, Khan founded Bayyinah, an institute dedicated to training students in Arabic in Dallas, Texas.[104]

While almost all participants named Khan in response to a question about their favourite scholars, some also said, 'I used to listen to him [Nouman Ali Khan], but now I don't.' When I asked why, those who felt comfortable explaining said that they no longer trust him because he 'left his wife and seven kids for his secretary': respondents who answered along these lines included Lema (57) and Pamir (65), a married couple of South Asian background. Lema and Pamir also added, 'How can we trust him now if he can't follow Islam properly himself?' For these individuals, a person's authoritative position is not determined solely by their knowledge and training but also by whether and how their ethical treatment of others meet the standards of those seeking knowledge from them. Significantly, for those of my respondents who no longer support or follow Nouman Ali Khan, a person's authority is linked to their treatment of their children and wife; to be respected, they must treat their family well; they must have integrity.

While Nouman Ali Khan and Yasmin Mogahed do not speak about the tradition, or change and Islam, in the general way that Yasir Qadhi does, they do reinforce and preach a fossilised vision of the Islamic tradition implicitly. In their teachings on isolated topics, such as female-led prayer in Mogahed's case (she does not support this) and sexual slavery in Khan's case (he supports sexual slavery), the tradition is not open to change where consensus has been established.[105] These preachers' ideas about the tradition are best summarised by Grewal in *Islam is a Foreign Country*. She shows that 'those who are in the role of custodians too often seek to...reduce tradition to a fossilized body of (Eastern) knowledge and practices'.[106] However, as Zaman demonstrates, 'the multiplicity of the actions and discourses of the 'ulama...suggests a far more flexible understanding of the world, and of Islam, than is often acknowledged – and not just by observers or critics of the 'ulama but often also by themselves'.[107] That they do not recognise this flexibility – on questions of gender, as with Qadhi – despite offering alternative interpretations where they deem necessary and thus clearly partaking in shaping the tradition, suggests that they believe that gender issues are ordained by God as inflexible and immutable.

LAY MUSLIMS' CONSTRUCTION OF THE ISLAMIC TRADITION

I now discuss my respondents' views of the Islamic tradition, Islamic law or *sharīʻa*, and also of Islam generally, specifically as these terms pertain to gender and change. I want to analyse their understandings of *sharīʻa* and 'consensus' as well as their use of the words 'Islam' and 'tradition'. Most of the discussants used the words 'Islam', 'Islamic law', 'the scholars', '*ijmāʻ*/ consensus', and 'the *madhhab*s' (legal schools) synonymously, if they used these terms at all. I conclude from my conversations with them three major points. According to my respondents, 1) Islam – whether as manifested in the Islamic tradition, the legal schools, the scholars, or the Qur'an and *Sunnah* – has already given women all imaginable rights and privileges there are, and to seek more rights is a deviation from proper Islam and interrupts the balance that Islam guarantees; 2) established consensus can change with time if the existing consensus contradicts 'common sense' or 'social norms' and/or when a new group of scholars collectively decide that a change is necessary;

and 3) 'Islam' and 'the Islamic tradition' may be used interchangeably, in my participants' view, because for them, the 'Islamic tradition' encompasses the Qur'an and *Sunnah*, the *madhhab*s, tradition, and *sharī'a*.

Sharī'a is commonly translated as 'Islamic law', although this is misleading because it encompasses non-legal dimensions of Islam as well, such as ethical, moral and ritual. Moreover, it is often conflated with *fiqh*, or Islamic jurisprudence. Many scholars have instead highlighted the difference between *sharī'a* and *fiqh*, finding the distinction to be not only liberating but also essential to social change from within the Islamic tradition. Ziba Mir-Hosseini, for example, discusses the two terms extensively in her book *Journeys Toward Gender Equality in Islam*, where she includes interviews with contemporary Muslim scholars on *sharī'a* and *fiqh*.[108] Muslim scholars have historically understood the *sharī'a* to be an abstract set of divine laws, immutable and infallible because they underlie broad concepts such as justice, kindness, piety; much of *sharī'a*, they believe, is unattainable and inaccessible. *Fiqh*, however, is the implementable human articulation and understanding of *sharī'a* that does change with time and context. The term *fiqh* derives from the Arabic word 'to understand' and refers to 'the process of human endeavour to discern and extract legal rules from the sacred sources of Islam: that is, the Qur'an and the Sunna (the practice of the Prophet, as contained in hadith, Traditions)'.[109] Mir-Hosseini has argued in favour of relying on this distinction for the purposes of extracting from Islam's sacred sources an ethical, egalitarian practice of Islam:

> It is essential to stress this distinction and its epistemological and political ramifications. *Fiqh* is often mistakenly equated with Shari'a, not only in popular Muslim discourses but also by specialists and politicians, and often with ideological intent: that is, what Islamists and others commonly assert to be a 'Shari'a mandate' (hence divine and infallible), is in fact the result of *fiqh*, juristic speculation and extrapolation (hence human and fallible). In other words, while the Shari'a is sacred, eternal and universal, *fiqh* is human and – like any other system of jurisprudence – mundane, temporal and local.[110]

Khaled Abou El Fadl concurs that 'While Shari'ah is divine, fiqh (the human understanding of Shari'ah) was recognised to be only potentially so, and it is the distinction between Shari'ah and fiqh that fueled and legitimated the practice of legal pluralism in Islamic history.'[111] This is why there is only one *sharī'a* but historically dozens or even hundreds of *fiqh*s, legal schools.[112] Since not all of *sharī'a* is inaccessible, however, the debate around which specific issues are negotiable and non-negotiable persists.[113] For example, as Marwa Sharfeldin discusses in the context of efforts by Egyptian women's rights NGOs to reform the personal status law from a religious perspective, activists distinguish between *sharī'a* and *fiqh*: the basic principles of the *sharī'a*, for them, are anti-patriarchal, but 'it is the *fiqh* (jurisprudence) produced by scholars in the classical era that contains patriarchal elements, echoing the social context of its production'.[114] They distinguish between the *sharī'a* as 'the work of God, the eternal divine message contained in the Qur'an, which does not change with time and space' and *fiqh* as 'the work of man, which encompasses the changeable human attempts at understanding this message'.[115] Through this distinction, they are able to 'advance a new fiqh, which reinterprets the main sources of Shari'a'.[116]

Like many Muslims, my respondents were largely unaware of this distinction. I asked them how they might define the term *sharī'a* or what *sharī'a* meant to them. I used the term 'Islamic law', and some of them would correct me and say '*sharī'a*' because, they pointed out, 'Islamic law' does not encompass the nuances of what '*sharī'a*' entails. Several participants asked me what I meant by '*sharī'a*' – was I talking about the Islamic law of the past or today? Their question to me often led to productive conversations about the evolution of laws and the necessity of change in new circumstances. That today's Islamic law would differ from that of the past was a common idea, specifically in conversations on child marriage, sexual slavery, and female inheritance. Many stated that the *sharī'a* was developed in a different context, in which the scholars may not have imagined a world like the one Muslims, and particularly Muslim Americans, live in today. The question of what the *sharī'a* even means came up specifically during our conversations on child marriage and sexual slavery, as I will discuss.

Many agreed that the Qur'an and the *Sunnah* (prophetic practice) should be the source of the *sharī'a* and of Islam, thus suggesting that 'Islam' and '*sharī'a*' were synonymous. According to Aisyah (20, unmarried, of South-East Asian origin), for example, the *sharī'a* 'is interpretations of the Hadith and the Qur'an that go into legal processes… The core of it is the Qur'an and *Sunnah*.' This was also her response to 'what is Islam': the Qur'an and the Sunnah primarily, 'and then the scholars' interpretations wherever there is a lack of clarity in the Qur'an and the *Sunnah*'. Naghma (23, single, South Asian background) was not sure if 'all of the *sharī'a* is in the Qur'an' but 'the *sharī'a* should stem from the Qur'an and the *Sunnah*, and change should be acceptable whenever there are contradictions between what scholars say or have said and what the Qur'an and the *Sunnah* teach'.

For others, 'Islam' and '*sharīʿa*' are different. Islam is broader than the *sharīʿa*, encompassing the Qur'an, the *Sunnah*, the *sharīʿa*, and scholarly engagements with all of these. Orzala (33, married female, white) said, 'Islam to me means the path upon which we walk to Allah based on living the principles of *sharīʿa*, Qur'an, revelation. *Sharīʿa* to me is God's law. The distinction is that *sharīʿa* guides one in how to walk the path of peace. Islam is a way to live, *sharīʿa* is the guide for how to live that.' For her, the two concepts are not synonymous or interchangeable, but certainly interdependent.

According to Michael (56, married, white, convert), 'The *sharīʿa* is a set of laws that Allah has; our job is to navigate that river of knowledge.' These rules are established in the Qur'an, the *Sunnah*, and scholarly interpretations of the Qur'an and *Sunnah*. Because the *sharīʿa* has already delineated for Muslims what is permissible and impermissible, Muslims today cannot change established rulings, since 'the *sharīʿa* is the perfect law of Allah that we do our best to roll our way towards'. For him, therefore, *sharīʿa* is a set of unchanging established laws of God.

Some participants stated that the *sharīʿa* is 'not set in stone'. Sandara (20, unmarried, of South Asian origin), for instance, said that for her, *sharīʿa* is 'more of a moral way of life, like it's not set in stone, but, like, these are sort of guidelines and you take it and interpret it for yourself, or you read what the scholars say about it and you follow. It's not like how we think of Western law, but sort of an interpretation and how you want to believe and live your life.' For her, then, *sharīʿa* is both scholarly and lay, individual, personal interpretations of Islam, an attempt at a moral way of life.

Others suggested that 'Islam' and 'Islamic law' were not the same: Travis (25, unmarried male, white, convert) translated the *sharīʿa* as 'sacred law' and defined it as 'the system for interpreting God's decrees, commands, prohibitions as relates to physical practice, as relates to actions'. Rana (67, married female, of South Asian background) believes that the *sharīʿa* does reflect God's will but 'only if it's clear in the Qur'an'. Significantly, the difference between the *sharīʿa* and Islam, then, is that the former is a system that is potentially fallible and not necessarily complete, some suggested, whereas Islam is infallible and complete and therefore not open to change.

Thus, the majority appeared to envision the *sharīʿa* as the 'basic rules' of Islam as outlined in the Qur'an and the *Sunnah*. However, 'Islam' too, for them, is the culmination of everything that is in the Qur'an and the *Sunnah*. When asked what the difference between the *sharīʿa* and 'Islam' is, many stated that the *sharīʿa* is more specific whereas Islam is more general. The '*sharīʿa*', some explained, is God's law, God's rules, or 'God's guidelines', whereas 'Islam' is 'a way of life' and *sharīʿa* is a part of it. Nonetheless, some insisted, it is Islam that forbids female-led communal prayers and women's interfaith marriage, in this case using 'Islam' and '*sharīʿa*' synonymously. On these questions relating to gender, Islam therefore becomes an unchanging set of tenets, an idea that was expressed implicitly by some respondents. Only a few explicitly said that 'Islam' and '*sharīʿa*' are the same. One married couple of South Asian origin, interviewed together (Lema, 57; Pamir, 65), explicitly said that 'Islamic law' and 'Islam' are the 'same thing' and both mean 'the Qur'an and the *Sunnah*'.

ISLAM

As shown above, there is little clarity among lay Muslims on what the *sharīʿa* is and its relationship with and place in Islam. With most participants using the terms 'Islam', 'Islamic law', 'our tradition', 'the Qur'an and *Sunnah*' interchangeably, I decided to ask them what they meant by their use of 'Islam' (such as in their statements 'Islam says X about female-led prayer' or 'Islam prohibits Y'). This was particularly informative in discussions on the distinction between *sharīʿa* and Islam, which, as shown above, some of them suggested were the same. Michael (56, married male, white, convert) simply defined 'Islam' as 'the name of our religion'. When I asked him about the difference between *sharīʿa* and Islam, he said, 'The question seems strange. It is like asking, "Elaborate the differences between mind and body." They are different by definition.' Zigar (21, single male, of South Asian origin) said, 'This might seem fairly generic, but Islam to me might mean something more along the lines of a way of living life whereas *sharīʿa* is more of a legalistic or juristic aspect of Islam within the confines of the tradition.' A practice's status as 'Islamic' or 'un-Islamic', then, is more about the *sharīʿa*'s position on the matter than it is about Islam's. According to Wadaan (21, unmarried male, of South Asian origin), the difference between the two terms is that *sharīʿa* has a more human layer to it than 'actual Islam' and is based to some extent on social constructs:

> I would say that *sharīʿa* is Islamic law. And what separates Islam from *sharīʿa* is that *sharīʿa* is also based on…*fiqh* [and] Hadiths… So it's more man-made than actual Islam. But there are parts of the *sharīʿa* that are one hundred percent from the Qur'an. But…some of it is also, like, social constructs.

Gahez (77, married male, South Asian background), similarly stated:

> Islam...literally means submission and peace. It is a framework and a set of guidelines for life, defined in Qur'an, so *all* human beings can be peaceful with each other if they truly followed [Islam] and have a healthy society. The basic beliefs are the Oneness of Allah as the creator and master of the universe, who created all human beings, who are ultimately accountable to Him on a Day of Judgement, so the humans can self-police their own conduct and behaviour in this life.

Ultimately, the distinction or relationship between 'Islam' and '*sharī'a*' is worth emphasising. My respondents do not share the same understanding of these terms.[117] What made our conversations even richer and more fascinating is that their definition of 'Islam' also changed in accordance with the issue at hand. Overall, however, 'Islam' appears to be a clear set of guidelines, not a social construct, whereas '*sharī'a*' is 'man-made' and only parts of it are derived from 'Islam'. There is not only disagreement, however; there is also a lack of clarity. This lack of clarity carries practical implications such as influencing Muslims' opinions and beliefs about what is permissible and impermissible in Islam – for example, the claim that women cannot lead communal prayers because the *sharī'a* does not allow it. Table 1 shows the respondents' answers, on a scale of 1 to 5 (5 being 'completely agree' and 1 being 'completely disagree') to the statement 'The *sharī'a*' reflects God's will or intent.'

Ijmā' (Consensus)

One of the most unclear sources of Islam and Islamic law is *ijmā'*, typically translated as 'consensus'. There is no consensus on the meaning of 'consensus'. For some, it means the majority scholarly view; for others, it is the majority view of only the first three generations of Muslims; yet others include the opinions of lay Muslims, the entire Muslim *ummah* (community), as we shall see throughout this book. Many scholarly and lay critiques have been offered relying on *ijmā'* as a source of prohibition. For example, in their introduction to the translation of Malik b. Anas's (d. 795) *Muwaṭṭa'*, one of the earliest collections of Hadiths and Islamic law, Mohammad Fadel and Connel Mone-

Table 1: The *sharīʿa* reflects God's will or intent.

Scale	Single Women (10 total)	Single Men (10 total)	Married Women (10 total)	Married Men (10 total)	Total
1 (completely disagree)	0	1	1	0	2
2	1	1	1	1	4
3 (I'm not sure)	2	3	0	1	6
4	5	3	6	0	14
5 (completely agree)	2	2	2	8	14

tte discuss other jurists influenced by Malik, such as al-Shāfiʿī, founder of the Shāfiʿī school of law. The two had different approaches to Islamic law and its sources, such as disagreements over 'what constituted evidence of prophetic law, or the *Sunnah*'.[118] Specifically on *ijmāʿ*, Fadel and Monette note that while many other jurists understood consensus to refer to the agreement of the majority of scholars, al-Shāfiʿī understood it as 'requiring the agreement of *all* Muslims, not just the agreement of the learned'.[119] He thus eliminated *ijmāʿ* as a source of law, since that would simply be unattainable. Fadel and Monette explain that:

> In most cases, claims of agreement or consensus indicated that a majority of jurists agreed on a particular principle of law, and not that *all of* them agree. Furthermore, even these majoritarian agremeents were not universal, but instead often reflected only local majorities of scholars. Accordingly, a claim of consensus or agreement often boiled down to the agreement of a majority of scholars in a particular location, such as the scholars of the Hijaz (Mecca and Medina), those of Iraq (Kufa and Basra), or the Levant.[120]

I return to this idea of consensus in chapter 2 when discussing Carolyn Baugh's findings on the ways that *ijmāʿ* is constructed in the debate on child marriage.[121]

Most of my respondents were familiar with the idea of *ijmāʿ*, that there was such a notion in Islam as a collective scholarly opinion. When and whether they agreed with what they assumed the *ijmāʿ* to be, however, depended on the issue we were discussing. Table 2 below documents their response to my statement about whether consensus is binding.

Table 2: The consensus of the scholars is always binding.

Scale	Single Women (10 total)	Single Men (10 total)	Married Women (10 total)	Married Men (10 total)	Total
1 (completely disagree)	3	2	3	3	11
2	1	6	2	3	12
3 (I'm not sure)	2	0	1	2	5
4	1	0	3	0	4
5 (completely agree)	3	2	1	2	8

As table 2 shows, of the 40 participants, only 12 agreed or completely agreed that following the consensus was obligatory upon Muslims, i.e. that dissent with the scholarly consensus is not permitted in Islam. During the discussion, however, when individual topics were being discussed, some changed their answers to, 'Actually, it depends', because 'well, some issues are just clearly stated in the Qur'an.'

While most of the respondents clearly did not agree that consensus is always binding, invoking the idea of a 'historical context' to explain why not, the following chapters show that there are some cases in which the discussants believe that consensus is binding. This is a significant departure from the more common idea, posited by scholars and preachers, that change is not the norm: it is an exception. My participants suggest that departing from the consensus is in fact the norm, with exceptions when change is 'not necessary'. Their positions on consensus on the individual topics are discussed in the conclusion of this book.

Traditional Islam

Almost none of my participants used the word 'Islamic tradition', and hence asking what they thought Islamic tradition was would be conceptualising their opinions in categories they did not use themselves. Since many used 'traditional Islam' throughout our discussion, I asked what this term meant to them. When the idea of a 'traditional' Islam came up in some of the interviews – e.g. 'I know that traditional Islam says X, but I think times have changed' – the responses ranged from 'following the five pillars' to 'an Islam tainted with a lot of cultural habits'. For some, 'traditional Islam' means 'the basic principles' of Islam, such as the five pillars. Gahez (77, South Asian origin, married) added that it means 'a person should always act with the confidence that we're accountable to Allah…that we do not intentionally hurt anyone. Just live a peaceful life to have a better society because all the injunctions are there in the Qur'an.' Yet, several others disagreed with this view. Michael (56, married male, white convert), for instance, defined traditional Islam as 'cultural renderings of the religion of God. [It] includes ingredients of the religion and the region [in which it is practised].' Amadou (40, married male, Black), who had identified it as 'tainted with' 'cultural habits', viewed it as 'what's being portrayed by the old *shaikh*s [scholars]'. When I asked Naghma (23, single female, South Asian origin) how she defines the term, she asked, 'You mean like cultural Islam?' I clarified that I wanted to know whatever the term means to her or what comes to her mind when she hears it or what she means by it when she uses it. She replied, 'I guess what comes to mind is Islam in the Middle Ages, in the desert, in the Middle East. Islam makes me question tradition, so traditional Islam is kinda like a contradiction to me. I mean, the Qur'an says not to listen to your forefathers or [to] go against your forefathers.'[122] It is striking that Naghma understands the Qur'an's condemnation of following one's foreparents as a condemnation of following tradition. Through this statement, she recognises the flaws and limitations of those with authority and instead prefers to interpret the Qur'an for herself because she believes the Qur'an promotes critical thinking. 'Tradition', then, has little meaning to most of my participants. While the term is used widely by academic scholars of Islam, it is not as meaningful to my respondents.

Islamic Feminism

Almost all of the discussants believed that the Prophet Muhammad was a feminist – but few of them identified themselves as feminist. In two scaling questions with the statements 'The Prophet Muhammad was a feminist' and 'I am a feminist', the different responses were striking because the informants' definitions for the term differed, they said, based on context: Muhammad was a feminist because he significantly improved the status of women, a status that brought revolutionary changes for not just Arab women but all women worldwide. Today, however, they emphasised, the word 'feminism' and its principles have been misappropriated by the Western feminist movement, which often contradicts Islamic principles, such as female modesty and motherhood. Thus, most comfortably identify the Prophet Muhammad as a feminist while hesitating to identify themselves as feminist, choosing a lower number in their answers for themselves than for Muhammad (e.g. if 5 for Muhammad, 3 or 4 for themselves). Interestingly, some asked, 'What do you mean by "feminist"?' to the second statement about whether they identify as feminist, but hardly anyone asked what I meant by feminist in the statement about Muhammad.

However, most of the participants stated that they did not know anything about 'Islamic feminism' or had never heard of it, but they guessed it was probably a struggle for gender justice. One participant (Scarlet, a 26-year-old white female convert) said she learned about a Facebook group called Feminist Islamic Troublemakers of North America, or FITNA. Whether my respondents self-identified as feminists or not, they admitted that they knew little to nothing about feminism and especially about Islamic feminism. Throughout this book, I use the term Islamic feminism to refer to a movement that works towards gender and sexual justice using Islam as its foundation. This process requires re-engagement with all of Islam's sources, not only the Qur'an and Hadiths but also the historical intellectual tradition of debate, especially concerning issues contemporary Muslim feminists care about, such as female-led prayers, violence against women, same-sex relations, and women's interfaith marriage. Through these ways of engaging with existing interpretations of Islam, often offering critical interventions and contributing meaningful critiques of particular practices, Islamic feminism becomes a part of the Muslim tradition. Islamic feminism, like those who lead the movement, is diverse in its approaches, methods, conclusions, and objectives, but it ultimately assumes that Islam is a fundamental source of equality and justice for people of all genders everywhere.

Table 3: God intended gender equality.

Scale	Single Women	Single Men	Married Women	Married Men	Total
1 (completely disagree)	0	0	1	2	3
2	0	0	1	2	3
3 (I'm not sure)	0	0	1	0	1
4	0	1	1	1	3
5 (completely agree)	10	9	6	5	30

As table 3 shows, it is telling that the single men and women believed that God intended gender equality – even if Islamic law does not always appear to support gender equality, and certainly even if Muslims might not always be just – while the married individuals qualified their answers with certain conditions. When I asked the scaling question about whether God intended gender equality, all single people answered yes (4 or 5), but most of the married participants qualified their answers with 'spiritual equality, but not in the sense that women and men are the same and should have the same roles'. While even the majority of the participants referenced 'Islamic gender roles', such as the husband's financial responsibility over his family, they did not deem it necessary to qualify their responses or their use of 'gender equality'.

However, the married individuals (not necessarily older generation) had different views. Rana (67, married female, South Asian background) stated that she did not like the statement 'God intended gender equality' because 'men and women are different'. Barsala (31, married female, South Asian background) said that if 'gender equality' meant 'to be treated fairly', then yes, God intended gender equality; if it meant 'women and men are the same', then no. Orzala (33, married female, white) vehemently disagreed that God intended gender equality: 'The Qur'an specifically says "God created you differently."'[123] Similarly, Sangin (69, married male, Middle Eastern background) emphasised that while God intended for the fair treatment of women, 'He did not provide the genders equal privileges.' Michael (56, married male, white, convert) paused for several seconds before responding, 'equality as in equalness? There are some differences. Women have some rights that men don't have and vice versa.' Sultan (41, East African married male, convert) also hesitated to respond and offered that 'it depends on what kind of conditions we're talking about. Man was created first, men pray at mosque and women at home, the male is responsible for household, women were created as helpers and caretakers of the house.'

I read these different approaches to gender equality in two ways: first, as reflective of the generational gap in the way language is used to convey meaning, and second as indicative of my respondents' marital experiences. Because 'gender equality' appears to be a part of everyday language for most of the younger generation, for them it is important to acknowledge it and attribute it to Islam; they are less hesitant to use terms such as 'equality' even if they are aware that they carry different meanings in different contexts and communities. Thus, none of the unmarried participants hesitated to offer a 4 or a 5 to the question while fewer of the married ones gave similar answers. Since many of the married respondents were in their early thirties or even late twenties and still qualified their use of 'equality' by saying that equality does not mean sameness, given their closeness in age to many of the younger participants, I do not think generational differences are the only or most useful explanation for this discrepancy. Instead, I suggest that perhaps their marital status informs their opinions on gender roles and gender equality.

Sources of Islam

The majority explicitly listed the Qur'an and the *Sunnah* as the sources of Islam. Some listed their favourite scholars or referenced family members or parents, or even their cultures and communities as their preferred sources of Islam, and one (a white convert single woman) listed the Qur'an alone. However, among those for whom the *Sunnah* is also a source, they explained that there should not be contradictions between the two, and only when the Qur'an is unclear about a matter can or should Muslims turn to the *Sunnah*. While most did not explicitly say 'the scholars' or 'the legal schools', their responses to individual topics, as shown in the following chapters, indicate that they view consensus of the scholars to be a major source of Islam, or at least that consensus shapes their beliefs about many issues in Islam. Malala (37, married female, South Asian origin) insisted in her responses to all of the topics that the Qur'an should be the main source of a Muslim's knowledge on Islam and the main source of consensus, and therefore, one must follow consensus only if it is directly derived from the Qur'an. Others, too, such as Pamir (married, 65, south Asian) stated that the consensus should only be followed when it is supported by the Qur'an.

That the majority of my research participants, primarily the unmarried ones, insisted that consensus is binding only when 'it is clear' is striking because this view does not reflect historical norms according to scholarly practice. My participants suggest that consensus is only valid insofar as it is clearly and unambiguously supported by the Qur'an. This raises questions about the relevance of consensus: if the Qur'an is clear on a matter, what justifies the existence or need of consensus on said matter? In contrast to this view, historically, scholars turned to consensus when an issue was *not clear* in the primary sources and begged debate. Thus, the ideas of my participants on consensus, which guide their attitudes on some issues, differ from historical notions. In fact, the historical doctrine is that consensus is always binding; the sheer idea of consensus being binding only under certain conditions, as my discussants asserted, is itself a break from the traditional doctrine.

The question about what Muslims view to be the sources of Islam is important because it contributes to our understanding of how they conceptualise Islam. That *ijmāʿ*, or the consensus of the scholars, came up in our conversations about the sources of Islam and why they support certain positions, indicates their awareness of some historical thought as well as their (conditional) reliance on scholarly opinions to shape their ideas about the (in)validity of a practice or doctrine.

CONCLUSION

'Traditions' are products of historically contingent communities. Traditions are made collectively, and contemporary intellectuals, past influential individuals, and lay members of society must negotiate and transform those traditions in order to make sense of them in their practice and understanding. As my discussants' views of Islam show, new contexts, issues, and conversations shape tradition; tradition does not shape them. As Kecia Ali proposes, re-interpretation is 'not only an individual project, for application in personal lives; it must also be a collective enterprise of scholars thinking, talking, and writing jointly and in counter-point'.[124] This collective enterprise is not one of the past alone but is a continual process, and lay Muslims are a part of that process. When it comes to issues that my participants either believe are of pressing, urgent concern, or that are no longer officially acceptable, such as child marriage and sexual slavery, then the tradition must be changed to fit a more modern understanding of sexual ethics. Lay Muslims contribute to the tradition by modifying it based on what they believe needs to be re-evaluated and what does not. This re-evaluation is not entirely consistent and predictable, but it is often gendered, such that there appears to be a strong effort to maintain gender hierarchy through a dismissal of largely feminist concerns, such as female-led prayers; other times, however, it is based on lived experience and the impact that a given interpretation or practice of Islam has on one's life. I propose that an effective way to conceptualise this productive inconsistency is by imagining Islam and the Islamic tradition as a rhizome, the complex roots of which allow for it to be morphed (renegotiated) with changing contexts, times, concerns and priorities.

Section 1

The Negotiables: Child Marriage, Sexual Slavery, and Female Inheritance

In this section, I discuss the three issues that my participants consider negotiable and open to change in Islam: child marriage, sexual slavery, and female inheritance. Historically, pre-modern Muslim scholars approved, although frequently with many qualifications, child marriage and slavery as Islamically acceptable while the contemporary global Muslim community reject both. My respondents' attitudes towards these topics illustrate that they understand Islam to be flexible, contextual, and focused on the well-being of particular societies. On the subjects of child marriage and slavery, the Islamic tradition is viewed as one that allows for rejection of past scholarly consensus. However, significantly, this rejection is more than a mere suggestion or belief that the tradition has changed: most of my participants insisted either that Islam never did permit slavery or child marriage, and that the consensus was wrong, or that Islam abolished both. This change is also not necessarily recognised as a change, which suggests a process so thoroughgoing and internalised that it has become naturalised. Their understanding is that it is not *Islam* that changes or can change with time; it is the Islamic *tradition* that changes. That is, 'Islam' in the case of slavery and child marriage refers to an ideal or idealised set of values and ethics that are rooted in the equality and dignity of all humans, including vulnerable groups such as children and enslaved people. Consent lies at the core of human relations, especially sexual relations, and is essential to identifying an act as Islamic. In the case of child marriage in particular, many of my respondents invoked a Hadith attributed to the Prophet (discussed below) that a woman could leave a marriage for which her consent was not sought. In the case of slavery, many claimed that the Prophet never enslaved anyone and that, in fact, he abolished slavery and freed an enslaved person, Zayd ibn Ḥāritha al-Kalbī, whom he adopted as a son.

The topic of female inheritance is addressed in the Qur'an explicitly and in some detail. The prohibitions on female-led prayers and women's marriage to Christians and Jews are not explicitly found in the Qur'an, and neither is the Qur'an's approval of child marriage; the Qur'an acknowledges the existence of slavery, and it appears to permit sexual relations with those whom one (man or woman) enslaves. However, it explicitly states that sons are entitled to receive twice the share of inheritance of daughters. Whether this is a minimum recommendation or the maximum possible allotment for daughters is open to interpretation. Yet, despite the Qur'an's explicit mention of this, most of my respondents believe that this is an unfair allotment for a twenty-first-century Muslim audience, and therefore their own children, male and female, will receive an equal share contrary to what Islamic law designates.

When I initially set out to explore inheritance in Islam and in Muslims' understandings, I had expected my respondents to express hesitance in their disagreement with the established guidelines for female inheritance in Islam. Based on my research and conversations with Muslims on the subject prior to this research, I had assumed that my respondents would largely state that they acknowledge the Qur'anic guidelines and are uncomfortable with them but would be reluctant to defy them. What I found, however, was that most of my respondents supported changing these guidelines – enthusiastically, without any hesitation or reluctance – in favour of an equal share in inheritance for daughters because the historical or existing consensus on inheritance rights is informed by past contexts that do not speak to their current needs and challenges. I also found that inheritance is unlike female-led prayer or women's interfaith marriage because these latter two issues are constantly linked to biology, whereas the question of inheritance is not; past scholars did, however, link higher inheritance privileges for men to their biology. While it was primarily women (both married and unmarried) who supported equal inheritance rights, they did not hesitate to express their disagreement with the Qur'anic text on the matter, or what they understood to be the Qur'anic guidelines. As shown above, many of them explicitly stated that they are aware the Qur'an says otherwise, and they are 'uncomfortable' or 'disagree' with those stipulations. They did not sense a discrepancy between their beliefs and the Qur'anic guidelines on inheritance, because, as many explained, the Qur'anic laws can be practised only if one lives in an ideal world – where men would fulfil their responsibilities – and that is not their reality.

Thus, what makes the subject of female inheritance different from the other topics is that the current dominant lay opinion supports changing the current authoritative opinion on inheritance, which is that daughters receive a share that is half that of their brothers'. Because of the clear shift in attitude towards this issue, female inheritance is a 'negotiable' of Islam, like child marriage and sexual slavery.

This section thus provides an excellent case of Islam as a rhizome because of the way that my respondents (re)negotiate with the Islamic tradition. It is not just Islam and the Islamic tradition that are rhizomatic but also the respondents' relationship with scholarly authority. Specifically, they selectively invoke scholarly authority and Islamic sources (Qur'an, Hadiths, scholars' opinions) to explain their positions. The section reveals how Muslim Americans project their modern ideals of justice, which include consent in sexual relations, onto historical Islam to align contemporary values with Islam and dismiss any claims that Islam may have historically accepted sexual slavery and child marriage as valid by divine decree. I offer an overview of child marriage, (sexual) slavery, and female inheritance, analysing Qur'anic verses and Hadiths on each issue in their respective chapters. I then discuss the pre-nineteenth-century legal tradition's stances on the topics and end with my participants' views on the three.

Chapter 2

Child Marriage

I often think about my own paternal grandmother's situation in conversations on child marriage. She was married at the age of nine to my grandfather, who was twelve at the time, when my grandmother's mother died and her father married another woman. Family legend has it that neither of my grandparents knew that they were getting married, and my grandmother's mother-in-law treated her like a daughter, shared a room together with her (as was/is the norm where I grew up: multiple family members sleeping in the same bedroom) and only after puberty allowed my grandmother to be treated as 'wife' by my grandfather. In this scenario, my grandmother was married off as a child into a trusted family as though she were an orphan to be entrusted to another family for caretaking. This would be viewed as completely acceptable from an Islamic legal standpoint and possibly even as an (at least temporarily) recommended course of action if the child could benefit from such an arrangement and no better alternative existed. Arguably, then, one might posit that in order for child marriage to be treated as impermissible, societies must first eliminate the circumstances that give rise to these choices including poverty, patriarchal views of fathers as inadequate caregivers, and the abuse of children by step-parents.

This chapter investigates the issue of child marriage, or the marriage of prepubescent children, and the discrepancies between historical and contemporary Muslim views on it. As I will discuss in detail, the pre-modern tradition unanimously approved of child marriage as Islamically acceptable, but nearly all of my participants reject it and consider it un-Islamic, *ḥarām* even. Yet, most of them believe that their ideas on child marriage are Islamic, shaped by Islam's views on the subject. They insist that such marriages are fundamentally un-Islamic because Islam requires the consent of the marrying parties for a valid marriage. I suggest that they are projecting onto Islam their ideas of agency and consent by arguing that Islam never supported child marriage – just as historical scholars projected their own ideas onto Islam as well, to be sure. The discrepancy between my discussants' perceptions of Islam's position on child marriage and the legal tradition's dominant viewpoint provides a case that becomes clearer when analysed through the rhizomatic model I proposed in chapter 1. The rhizomatic model describes the selective ways in which my discussants reference 'Islam'. Their sources of Islam change with each new topic discussed. This selectivity is not surprising, since, for them, only the Qur'an and Hadiths are the primary sources of Islam. *Sunnah* is also fluid and rhizomatic – just because Muhammad acted a certain way does not mean Muslims are encouraged to do the same at all times everywhere; they must consciously negotiate with the *Sunnah*, with Islam, to determine when following Muhammad is appropriate and when it is not. This selectivity also speaks to my respondents' ethical priorities.

Below, I offer a historical (pre-twentieth century) view of child marriage in Islam through three of the major sources of Islamic law: the Qur'an, *Sunnah*, and the Islamic legal tradition, focusing on the issue of consent in marriage. I begin with the Qur'an despite the fact that for most pre-modern scholars, the most relevant source of permissibility of child marriage was Muhammad's marriage to Aisha: according to a questionable Hadith report, the two married when Aisha was six and they consummated their marriage when she was nine. I then discuss my respondents' attitudes on the subject, highlighting moments of departure from historical positions and claims. As I move on to analyse my respondents' attitudes toward child marriage, I discuss some of the major themes that emerged in our conversations. These include the following: Aisha's marriage to Muhammad, the reliance on Hadiths specifically in the case of child marriage to support respondents' position that it is un-Islamic, and shifting ideas of what constitutes *Sunnah*, or the way of the Prophet Muhammad.

MARRIAGE AND CONSENT IN THE QUR'AN

Since my respondents argued strongly that Islam does not permit child marriage because 'children cannot consent', and a marriage without consent is invalid, it is worth addressing the Qur'anic verses that implicitly reference consent, which are: 2:221, 2:232, and 65:4. Of these, 65:4 in particular has historically been interpreted to suggest that the marriage of underage girls is acceptable. I will discuss 2:232 and 65:4 here, since 2:221 is discussed in a later chapter:

> 2:232: When you divorce women and they have ended their waiting period, then do not prevent them from remarrying their husbands when they agree among themselves in a lawful manner.
>
> 65:4: And those of your women who do not menstruate, if you have a doubt, their prescribed time shall be three months, and of those too who have not had their courses [*lam yaḥiḍna*]...

Ibn Rushd points out that the scholars believed that 2:232 ('when you divorce women...do not prevent them from marrying...') is addressed to guardians.[1] However, addressing this verse to guardians would mean that the guardian played a role in causing the divorce, per the statement 'when you divorce women'. Thus, it is unlikely that the verse is addressed to guardians and more likely to husbands who have divorced their wives, perhaps referring to threats, intimidations, and other abuse techniques to control women and prevent them from remarrying.

In Q.65:4, a common (but not the only) interpretation of 'and of those too who have not had their courses [menstruation]', in Arabic *wallātī lam yaḥiḍna*, is that it refers to wives who have not yet attained puberty because they have not yet menstruated.[2] Noted Qur'an translators A.J. Arberry and Mohsin Khan are among those who translate the expression to 'those who have not menstruated as yet' (Arberry) and 'those who have no courses [(i.e. they are still immature)]' (Mohsin Khan).[3] According to the influential commentator Abul Ala Maududi (d. 1979), this verse suggests that not only is the marriage (betrothal) of a minor girl valid but so is consummation and that forbidding either is not an option because nothing the Qur'an permits can be made forbidden by humans:

> Making mention of the waiting-period for the girls who have not yet menstruated, clearly proves that it is not only permissible to give away the girl in marriage at this age but it is also permissible for the husband to consummate marriage with her. Now, obviously no Muslim has the right to forbid a thing which the Quran has held as permissible.[4]

Maududi here is permitting child marriage and even consummation despite the Hadith of Aisha in which her marriage is not consummated until three years after her marriage. He does, however, acknowledge that included in the expression are women who have stopped menstruating: 'They may not have menstruated as yet either because of young age, or delayed menstrual discharge as it happens in the case of some women, or because of no discharge at all throughout life which, though rare, may also be the case.'[5] Similarly, interpretations of the verse on popular Islam websites, such as IslamWeb.net, read 'and for those who have no courses [(i.e. they are still immature) their 'Iddah (prescribed period) is three months likewise, except in case of death'].[6] This website explicitly notes, 'So, Allah set rulings of marriage, divorce and waiting period for the women who have not yet had menses, i.e. the young girls.'[7]

While the assessment of child marriage as Qur'anically acceptable abounds in the exegetical tradition, Yasmin Amin's analysis of the Qur'an and its tradition concludes otherwise. She notes that the Qur'an takes into account 'an age at which one is still a child (e.g. verses 24:31; 24:58–9) and an age at which one ceases to be a child (e.g. verses 6:152; 12:22; 17:34; 22:5; 28:14, and 40:67) and reaches maturity'.[8] She highlights that Q. 4:6 'ties the marriageable age to *rushd* [intellectual or economic maturity to handle one's own property[9]], and *rushd* is accepted by the Ḥanafīs, Shāfiʿīs, and Ḥanbalīs to be the age of fifteen, while the Mālikīs set it at eighteen'.[10] She asks, then, 'How then can a prepubescent girl be regarded as having attained marriageable age?'[11]

MARRIAGE AND CONSENT IN THE HADITHS

Four Hadith reports are relevant to our discussion on child marriage and consent in marriage. The first is, 'An orphan virgin girl should be consulted about herself; if she says nothing, that indicates her permission, but if she refuses, the authority of the guardian cannot be exercised against her will.'[12] This Hadith uses the word 'orphan girl' (*yatīma*) in some versions and 'virgin' (*bikr*) in others.[13] The second Hadith is reported as follows: 'The widow [*al-ayyim*] has a greater right over herself than her guardian, and the virgin [*bikr*] is to be asked about herself, and her silence is her consent.'[14] The third, which is the most frequently invoked Hadith in my interviews, involves a woman, Khansa' bint Khidhām, who complains to Muhammad about her forced marriage: 'The Ansari woman, Khansa bint Khidhām, reported that her father contracted her marriage when she was a *thayyib* [divorcee or widow, previously married] and she disliked this, so she went to the Messenger of God and mentioned this to him. He nullified her marriage [*radda nikaḥahā*].'[15]

Other Hadiths on consent in marriage include the following:

> A girl came to the Prophet and said: 'My father married me to his brother's son so that he might raise his status thereby.' The Prophet gave her the choice, and she said: 'I approve of what my father did, but I wanted women to know that their fathers have no right to do that.'[16]

In this report, it is understood that the woman in question was forced to marry against her will, but while she ended up assenting to her father's decision ultimately, she did not think his behaviour should be normalised. The earlier story, Khansa's, is retold in other books, such as *Kitāb al-Ḥujja*, where 'the Prophet separated her from the man to whom she did not wish to be married and "commanded her to marry" the man she wanted to marry'.[17] Scholars from the legal schools of Shāfi'ī and Mālikī cite this case 'as proof that a man loses the power to compel his daughter's marriage once she is a *thayyib* [whereas] Ḥanafī authorities stretch the lesson of Khansa's case further, concluding that any woman who has reached majority escapes her father's power of compulsion'.[18] My discussants who were familiar with Khansa's Hadith did not seem aware that this was a case of a previously married woman, and it seemed irrelevant to them whether the person had been married previously or not. As I discuss below, the legal schools distinguished between women who have previously been married and those who have not: for the founding scholars Mālik and Abu Ḥanīfa, but not al-Shāfi'ī, the prepubescent non-virgin girl could be forced into marriage by her father.[19]

In the fourth Hadith report, perhaps the most significant one that served as the legal basis for the permissibility of child marriage in the pre-modern Islamic tradition, and which continues to be relevant to many Muslims today, Aisha recounts her marriage to Muhammad. According to the report,

Muhammad married her when she was six years old, and he consummated the marriage when she was nine years old, and then she remained with him for nine years.[20] Notably, Aisha was still a minor when consummation occurred according to the Shāfiʿī interpretation.[21] Individual scholars as well as legal schools have historically used this Hadith to allow for the marriage of prepubescent girls against their will. For example, the founding scholar of the school al-Shāfiʿī claims, 'Abu Bakr's marrying Aisha to the Prophet, may God's blessings and peace be upon him, when she was a girl of six, and [the Prophet's] having sex with her when she was a girl of nine indicates that the father has more right over a virgin than she has over herself.'[22] This right of compulsion continues until past puberty in some schools (especially Shāfiʿī, although he 'recommends strongly that daughters who have reached majority be consulted'[23]); Ḥanafī law not only prohibits marriage against the woman's will, but it also does not require a guardian's approval for a woman to contract her marriage.

While the Hadith about Aisha's age was not interrogated in the pre-modern Islamic – or non-Islamic, polemical – tradition, it has been heavily contested in the modern period, and modern and contemporary Muslims have had to explain why it occurred.[24] Discussions about the subject often involve apologetics that specifically respond to criticisms about Islam and Muhammad's marriages. Opinions vary from complete rejection of the Hadiths that mention her age as having been six at the time of marriage and nine during consummation, to explanations that such a marriage was no anomaly for its time and therefore acceptable in the social milieu in which it took place, to revising Aisha's age to during her teenage years or beyond.[25] These opinions indicate the discomfort that Muslims feel about child marriage. Kecia Ali posits that Muhammad's marriage to Aisha provides 'a lens through which to view changed attitudes toward sex and marriage, and unresolved concerns about the appropriateness of applying medieval standards in modern life'.[26]

Many scholars have also critiqued the methods used by those whose support for child marriage is based on the Hadith dealing with Aisha's marriage. Yasmin Amin, for example, shows that the Islamic tradition reached a position of *ijmāʿ* based on faulty and questionable methods and sources. Amin points out that all of the Hadiths cited in support of child marriage in fact 'are ascribed to Aisha herself without being linked to the Prophet', arguing thus that they 'should not be considered *musnad* (supported)'.[27] In the Muslim tradition, the status of Hadiths is distinguished from that of *akhbār* or *athār*. Amin discusses in detail the various reports on child marriage in the

Hadith tradition, the Qur'an (i.e. Qur'anic verses interpreted to permit the marriage of minors), and various other sources such as biographical dictionaries and biographies of the Prophet. Reading these sources collectively, Amin makes a crucial finding: if Aisha and her sister Asma accepted Islam in the first year of Islam, as the biographical dictionaries claim, then 'she could not have been nine at the time of consummating her marriage in the second year after hijra because then she could not have been born yet at the time of her accepting Islam'.[28] She makes the same conclusion by doing similar mathematical calculations using other claims in the tradition as well as conducting a careful, erudite survey of the Qur'an, the interpretive tradition, *fiqh* (Islamic jurisprudence), *maqāṣid* (the divine intents on which Islamic law is based), Islamic legal maxims, and contemporary scientific and medical sources. Others have reached a similar conclusion: Jasser Auda asserts, 'My estimate of Aisha's age when she married the Prophet, peace be upon him, in the first year of the Hijri Calendar, is 19, not 9 as some scholars claimed.'[29] Joshua Little finds that the report about Aisha's marriage was fabricated in the eighth century by a narrator named Hisham ibn Urwa (d. 765), the originator of the report; Little also reads similar Hadiths about Aisha's age during marriage as part of a developing sectarian milieu of eighth-century Iraq and contributing to the canonisation of the Sunni Hadith.[30]

Since contemporary Muslim opinions on the age of marriage as well as on child marriage are at least partly shaped by Muslims' perceptions of Muhammad's marriage to Aisha, as indicated by the Hadith, scholars today are rethinking the issue. That the debate on Aisha's age at the time of marriage is vibrant is a clear sign that Muslims are largely uncomfortable with child marriage. The findings of those who estimate or show either that Aisha appears to have been older or that the Hadiths about her marriage are fabricated have practical implications for Muslim girls and women around the world.

MARRIAGE AND CONSENT IN THE LEGAL SCHOOLS

The legal consensus on the issue of child marriage in pre-nineteenth-century Islam is that a father can contract the marriage of his prepubescent child without the child's consent. Most jurists believed that, while the age for consummation and sexual maturity may coincide, a girl could reach the age of consummation earlier than her first menses.[31] In fact, several *fatwa*s from the pre-modern legal tradition discuss cases in which 'a wife was handed over to the husband and the marriage was consummated prior to the occurrence of her first menstrual period'.[32] Who determined when and whether the child was able to 'bear sexual intercourse' (*tuṭīqu'l-jimā'*)? The point at which a female becomes *muṭīqah lil-wat'* ('able to tolerate the sexual act upon her') is 'undetermined legally'.[33] In the absence of juristic agreement, the decision in classical theory was most likely made by the father, or another male guardian; or if the couple were already living together, then the adult partner would make that choice.[34] Cases of wives (presumably those who had newly attained puberty or were prepubescent) fleeing their husbands' homes to their parental home, where the mother granted them shelter, have also been recorded.[35] Consider the following report, where a minor girl is not to be held back from a husband if she is physically capable of sexual intercourse:

> If she reaches [nine years of age] and does not possess the body and strength [that would allow her to] tolerate a man, her family must keep her away from him… And if she is not yet nine, and she possesses the body and strength that would tolerate a man, they should not keep her away from him. And al-Shāfiʿī said, 'If the bride is husky [*jasīmah*], and others of her type [*mithluhā*] tolerate sexual intercourse, it means they should be allowed to be together. If she cannot tolerate that, then her family should prevent her until she can tolerate sex.'[36]

What is unclear here is, what legal actions, if any, could the bride take against a husband who had sex with her when she was in fact not ready? What regulations were in place to ensure that the girl was protected against her husband's wish to consummate the marriage before she was ready?[37] If no such regulations, or any consequences, existed for the husband's transgression (transgression because the jurists clearly recognised that there was such a thing as a ready and unready bride), is it only one's modern sensibilities that lead us to ask such a question? If so, are our modern sensibilities valid grounds from which to ask these questions? My purpose here is to analyse the structures that enabled and rendered valid such marriages, and to explore how the rules and doctrines established in medieval contexts continue to influence Muslims' opinions about child marriage today. In those cases where Muslims disagree with child marriage, using the logic of changing contexts and shifting norms, we must ask what hinders them from extending this logic to other gender issues, such as female-led prayers or women's right to interfaith marriages.

Carolyn Baugh's study on child marriage shows that while fathers were allowed in earlier *fiqh* to force both minor sons and daughters into marriage, later jurists shifted the ruling to grant the father power over daughters alone.[38] Ibn Ḥazm (d. 1072), for example, posits that the marriage of prepubescent males is invalid because the marriage of prepubescent girls is a result not of *ijmā'* but of *Sunnah*: girls can be married without their consent because of Aisha's marriage to the Prophet.[39] In other words, the minor in this marriage was a girl, not a boy, and therefore boys cannot be married as minors while girls can. Baugh illustrates that the meaning of legal consensus/*ijmā'* is itself inconsistent in the juristic discourse. She shows that Ibn Qudāmah (d. 1223) attributes the following quote to Ibn al-Mundhir (d. 930), who claims that scholarly consensus grants the father the right to marry off his prepubescent virgin daughter so long as the couple is (socio-economically) compatible with each other:

> Ibn al-Mundhir said, *'All of the scholars* from whom we have taken knowledge have reached consensus that a father's contracting of marriage for his prepubescent virgin daughter is permissible, if he marries her to an equal [in terms of social status]' and he is allowed to contract her marriage even if she protests and forbids it.[40]

However, the consensus that Ibn al-Mundhir refers to is not that of all the scholars of religion unanimously, but instead 'that of those scholars with whom he had come in contact, and from whom he had verifiable information'.[41] It appears that 'what are claimed to be areas of agreement are…: 1) the lack of legal capacity of children, and 2) the power of the father. Grounds for justification of both points can be located in the report of 'A'ishah'.[42] Thus, the claim that the scholars by 'consensus' agreed on the marriage of prepubescent girls is questionable because the group of scholars to whom the consensus is attributed is severely limited to a small group that Ibn Mundhir had come in contact with.

Ibn Rushd's *The Distinguished Jurist's Primer* provides extensive details on consent and child marriage, and the many themes related to it (e.g. what constitutes virginity – never married, or someone who's never had sex – and who has the authority to be a guardian) according to the four major Sunni legal schools. He explains that a male's and a non-virgin female's permission takes place through explicit verbal approvals or rejections, whereas the virgin's silence counts as her consent if her guardian is her father.[43] Al-Shāfi'ī, for instance, argued that a father can contract the marriage of his prepubescent children; other jurists similarly believed that 'children are marriageable by fathers seeking their best interests'.[44]

As for the consent of a woman, Ibn Rushd cites a Hadith that states that the consent of a non-virgin woman is to be sought for marriage, which was unanimously accepted by the scholars, though they disagreed on who is included in this category of non-virgin women.[45] They disagreed about a pubescent virgin's and a prepubescent non-virgin's consent in marriage: 'About the *bāligh* [mature] virgin, Mālik, al-Shāfiʿī, and Ibn Abī Laylā said that it is only for the father to force her to marry. Abū Ḥanīfah, al-Thawrī, al-Awzāʿi, Abū Thawr, and a group of jurists said that it is necessary to take her consent into consideration.'[46] Importantly, these legal schools disagreed over the meaning of the virgin or virginity. For Mālik and Abu Ḥanīfa, a virgin woman is one who has never had sexual intercourse, whether legal (e.g. through marriage or as a slave), illegal (*zinā'*/adultery), or under coercion (rape). For Shāfiʿī, each of these types of losses of virginity rendered the female a non-virgin and thus not subject to coercive marriage.[47]

While the guardian has the authority to forcibly marry off both girls and boys, Sarah Eltantawi explains that 'this power ends when the children fulfill the conditions of "emancipation" (*rushd*); a standard that is different for boys and girls': i.e. a male child is believed to attain emancipation upon social and biological maturity, while a female child must obtain juridical decision about her emancipation or satisfy other conditions:

> [Boys are] automatically emancipated upon reaching social and biological maturity…[but] a female child…is not considered emancipated without a judicial decision that she is *rashīda*, or emancipated – the default assumption being that she is not a *rashīda*, and thus her father can compel her to marry. Failing this judicial decree, a girl can be emancipated upon satisfying the following two conditions: she must enter a marital home (i.e., marry), and become the subject of two reliable witnesses testifying to her ability to manage her property.[48]

Baugh argues similarly, showing that women's legal capacity has historically been linked to their virgin or non-virgin status.[49]

Masud's study on child marriage analyses the 'formal sources' (i.e. the Qur'an and Hadiths) and 'material sources' (customs and local social practices) of the practice of child marriage. The main ground for *ijbār* (coercion), Masud explains, 'is restricted capacity' – i.e. the restricted capacity of the ward in question.[50] While insanity is unanimously considered incapacity and is thus grounds for *ijbār*, the jurists disagreed on other criteria. In the Ḥanafī and Ḥanbalī laws, 'minority alone is the ground for *ijbār*', though the guardian's authority is terminated once the child reaches puberty. Shāfi'ī law regards virginity (even of adults) as a justification for *ijbār*. For the Mālikīs, both minority and virginity are grounds for *ijbār*, although the father may revoke his authority over his daughter by declaring her mature enough to take care of her own interests.[51]

Who, though, is permitted to do the coercion, or who counts as legitimate enough authority to force a child into a marriage? The jurists disagreed over who the guardian (*al-walī al-mujbir*) could be – i.e. who could exercise the authority to forcibly marry off a child. All schools agree that the father reserves the right as the *al-walī al-mujbir*. However, while the Ḥanbalīs do not extend this right to anyone else, the Mālikīs do give the authority to the grandfather in the absence of the father, or the executor of the father's will, if available. Otherwise, the power of *ijbār* belongs to the ruler or the judge.[52] The Ḥanafīs 'extend the power to other agnate relatives in the same order of priority as regulated in matters of succession', although the *ijbār* of other relatives is revocable the instant the ward attains puberty.[53] In the other schools, no one else may exercise this authority.[54]

Ibn Rushd explains the rationale for the father's role as a guardian as the father's effort to keep his ward's best interests in mind.[55] But scholars did not, and do not, agree on who can serve as a guardian. Ibn Rushd notes that the reason for the scholars' disagreement over the requirement of a guardian for a woman's marriage is the lack of an explicit Qur'anic verse that stipulates guardianship as a condition of marriage.[56] As far as the marriage of adult parties is concerned, the Ḥanafī school is the only one that considers a marriage valid without the consent of a guardian. In the other schools, including Ẓāhirīs, the consent of the guardian is essential for the validity of a woman's marriage. In the Mālikī school, a guardian's approval is not required in the case of a girl or woman of lower social status, indicating that requiring consent of a guardian was a matter of social class and gender.[57]

It is useful to ask what may have motivated the jurists to allow intercourse with girls who had not reached puberty but whom the husbands could claim were ready. Child marriages were – and still are – often performed for several reasons, though primarily out of poverty and because fathers or guardians could arrange their daughters' marriages in order to transfer responsibility for their daughters to men they found most suitable. Further, in cases where the father deemed his daughter too young for consummation, he could keep his daughter at his house while requiring additional maintenance, such as food, clothing, and education. Masud explores the origins of the practice of *ijbār* (generally compulsion in marriage, whether of minors or adults, but used to mean 'child marriage' in Masud's study) in an effort to explain the inconsistent ways in which *ijbār* is invoked as valid or invalid in different cases across the Muslim world. He explains that child marriage has both sociological and theological motivations, and the practice is supported both by Islamic textual sources (Qur'an and Hadiths) and by extra-textual sources, such as cultural norms (*'urf*).

The fact that the jurists disagreed on the nuances of child marriage (whether a guardian is needed, who the guardian can be, whether consummation is permitted before puberty, etc.) indicates the deeply human processes involved in arriving at conclusions about Islam. There is nothing inherently Islamic about this debate and the scholars' reasoning. Here, I want to address two important questions that should arise from the above discussion. First, why did Muslim scholars permit a child to be married without her consent, forcibly by her guardian, only to grant her permission to end the marriage when she has reached an age of maturity? Her agency was recognised but only after puberty. If she could end the marriage later when she was able to reason and make her own decisions, why allow it in the first place, even in difficult circumstances? And second, what is the significance of the distinction between a virgin and a non-virgin? If a girl is too young to consent, why is she old enough for marriage? Today's Muslims, however, appear to prioritise the consent element such that they seem to be saying that if we have globally decided that children cannot consent, then the spirit of the legal tradition, the Hadiths, and the Qur'an remains alive while the specific, minute details have clearly changed. To the first question, I suggest that their sociohistorical context facilitated child marriage because of several assumptions, realities, and patriarchal family structures. These include, as in the case of my grandmother as mentioned at the beginning of this chapter, the idea that a father is incapable of taking care of his children without the support and involvement of a mother or mother-figure. Discussion of child marriage in Islam needs to account for the structural factors that enable and incentivise this form of child abuse.

CHILD MARRIAGE AND CONTEMPORARY AUTHORITATIVE RESPONSES[58]

In an effort to limit the number of child brides, many Muslim-majority countries have passed laws banning the practice of child marriage, sometimes opposing the religious clergy in those countries.[59] In 2014, for example, Pakistan passed a law called The Child Marriage Restraint Bill.[60] Due to resistance from opponents, including the Council of Islamic Ideology, an adviser to the Pakistani government on Islamic law, the bill was withdrawn in 2016.[61] It is worth exploring how contemporary Muslims are engaging traditional Islamic guidelines and attitudes towards child marriage in this broader discussion of changing norms and new modern attitudes towards marriage generally.

In a *YouTube* video, Yasir Qadhi is asked to shed some light on the issue of the Prophet Muhammad's marriage to Aisha. Qadhi responds that he finds it 'amusing' that women's rights supporters make 'such a big issue' of the marriage 'when Aisha herself didn't make it a big issue'. Not only did Aisha not mind it, but 'she was very proud of it till the day she died that the Prophet was her husband... They had a perfect marriage'. Since even the Prophet's enemies 'did not make an issue about this', it is clear that 'this was something that was culturally the norm'.[62] In another video on Aisha's marriage, he similarly claims that while many Muslims and non-Muslims 'are perturbed' that Aisha was married at a young age, 'frankly, this is a question that people who study anthropology and intelligent researchers that are non-Muslim never bring up'.[63] This is because, he says, those who do question it are taking their 'cultural norms and back-projecting them on to the Arabian society'.[64] This is unacceptable because, he continues, 'the age of marriage has no normative, no standard age'.[65] In other words, the age of marriage is not set by Islam; it differs from time to time and place to place in accordance with a given culture's mores.

Nouman Ali Khan, the second most referenced scholar of Islam in my study, explains in a *YouTube* video on forced marriage and its psychological impact on women that marriages without the consent of either party are forbidden in Islam:

> There is absolutely no room in this religion for the validity of a marriage which was forced in any way. Marriage has to be from the permission of the girl, and not a reluctant permission. They should be completely open and happy about it and want to get married.... A woman comes to

> the Prophet and says, 'My father forced me to get married. So I came under pressure and got married, but I don't like him. He said, 'Your marriage isn't valid; the *nikāḥ* [marriage contract] is *bāṭil* [invalid].'… It's absolutely, outrageously *ḥarām*; you cannot do it.[66]

Influential Muslim teachers and preachers of Islam engage in apologetics to justify Muhammad's marriage to Aisha. They accept the standard view that Muhammad married Aisha when she was six years old and consummated the marriage when she was nine, and they defend the union by assuring their viewers and listeners that this was historically acceptable everywhere, and that one must not judge the practices of the past according to modern standards.

LAY MUSLIMS' PERCEPTIONS OF CHILD MARRIAGE IN ISLAM

I asked all my participants what their own opinions about child marriage were and what they believed Islam's position on the matter was. All except one discussant (Michael, a 56-year-old married male convert) believed that Islam requires the consent of the marrying parties. Many expressed discomfort over the Prophet's marriage to Aisha but maintained that because societal expectations were different at the time, their marriage should not be an issue today.

All except three individuals – a married male and two single females – stated with certainty that Islam prohibits sexual intercourse with wives who have not yet reached puberty because the marriage of underage girls is not permissible in Islam. The three who did not share this position said, 'I don't know.' For those who believed child marriage was always impermissible, the question of consent was essential. They emphasised that the age of the individual did not matter: any marriage without the consent of both parties was invalid in Islam. The marriage of a child is categorically invalid because a child is incapable of giving consent. Pre-modern legal scholars also held that children cannot consent, yet the conclusion they drew was that the father or guardian should consent on their behalf. Contemporary Muslims hold that *since* a child cannot consent, they cannot get married.

My discussants' idea that Islam prohibits child marriages, or marriages without the consent of either party – regardless of whether they have reached puberty or not – coincides with popular contemporary American Muslim ideas about the issue. For instance, Mohammad Ali Syed, in *The Position of Women in Islam*, claims that an Islamic marriage contract can only take place between individuals who have attained puberty. No child marriages took place during the Prophet's time that he endorsed, Syed claims. The Prophet's own marriage to Aisha took place long before the Qur'anic laws on marriage were revealed, and, besides, the marriage was not consummated until Aisha reached puberty, thus indicating that the marriage took place 'when she was either 14 or 16 years old'.[67] Ali continues that while the Qur'an does not mention child marriage, pre-Islamic Arab customs that allowed child marriage shaped the legal rulings on the issue. He recognises that Islamic law permits the marriage of underage children, of any gender.[68] However, he argues, the legal schools' views on child marriage are a form of innovation, and they are not fundamental to Islam, thus allowing Muslims of modern times to change the rules as necessary.[69] Most of my participants, too, believed that the Hadiths override the legal consensus on this matter because, as discussed previously, the scholars' consensus is necessary only in matters on which the Qur'an or Hadiths are silent or unclear. According to my participants, because the Prophet Muhammad clearly issued an opinion on the requirement of consent in marriage, and because Hadiths report that Aisha's marriage to Muhammad was not consummated until three years later – presumably when she had reached puberty – marriages without the consent of the marrying parties are invalid.

AISHA'S AGE AT THE TIME OF HER MARRIAGE TO MUHAMMAD

Since Aisha's marriage is important to the discussion of child marriage in Islam and since it shapes many Muslims' attitudes towards child marriage – e.g. their reluctance to declare it fundamentally immoral or unacceptable – I asked my discussants about their knowledge of Aisha's marriage to Muhammad. The majority believed that Aisha had at least reached puberty by the time she was married to Muhammad, although very few were familiar with the debate about her age.

Table 4: How old was Aisha when Muhammad married her?

	Single Women	Single Men	Married Women	Married Men	Total
I don't know.	1	2	1	1	5
'Puberty' (no specific age)	0	0	1	1	2
6–9 years old	8	3	6	6	23
11+	1	4	2	2	9

* *One married male respondent opted not to answer this question.*

Response 1: She was 6–9 years old.

As the chart illustrates, 23 out of the 40 participants believed that Aisha was between six and nine years old at the time of her marriage to Muhammad. According to Sultan (41, East African male, married, convert):

> He [Muhammad] married her I believe when she was 6. But although he married her when she was 6, the marriage was not consummated until she was 9. Because I think it took maybe three years for her to physically mature and have her period. This is my analysis; I may be wrong. So why does he wait? You see? So I'd say the man has to wait until the woman or girl is ready [to have sexual intercourse]…

He feels no discomfort over Aisha's early marriage or the gap between Aisha's and Muhammad's ages. In fact, he said that given the Prophet's character, he would gladly support the marriage of his hypothetical 6- or 9-year-old daughter to Muhammad:

> I feel great about [their marriage to each other]! See, number one, if it was not right, Aisha's family would not [have allowed] that. And number two, after the Prophet passed away, I never heard of Aisha complaining or regretting him when she was young. So me personally, if I had a daughter, I'd be happy if my daughter married the Prophet at six years old or nine years old. I see nothing wrong with it. Because his quality, his character, he's not a normal person. You can't compare him [to other men]. He's not like a 60-year-old man that we see in this day and age.

For him, it is not just any marriage between an older – 'normal' – man and a prepubescent girl that is acceptable. Since the Prophet did it, it will always be acceptable Islamically, but he himself does not recommend it because other men are not like the Prophet.

Travis (25, married male, white, convert) also believes that Aisha was six at the time of betrothal: 'The strongest opinions that I'm aware of...say that she was 6 when they were betrothed, and that they began cohabiting when she was 9. [Some scholars] point out interesting things like women in certain societies, like Arab societies, would reach puberty earlier.'

Thus, because the marriage was acceptable for its time, it should not be judged as wrong by our current standards.

That the marriage is not an issue because it was not consummated until Aisha reached puberty was a recurrent theme in the discussions. As Barsala (31, married female, South Asian origin) points out:

> At the time of marriage, I understood her to be 9 and for him to be 40-something, I believe? I haven't read much into their marriage relationship... I understand their marriage to be one of him taking care of her, and the marriage wasn't consummated until she reached womanhood. I don't know if there's any truth to this or if this is what I've told myself, but this is what I think.

She acknowledges that what she believes about the marriage between Aisha and Muhammad may not be the truth, but it is her way of coming to terms with what sounds unacceptable for today's standards.

Zala (26, single female, racially mixed background) believes the Prophet was 46 years old at the time of his marriage to Aisha, while Aisha was 9, but 'I have no issue with it because it was a completely cultural thing... It was not an issue at that time, so I have no issues with it.' Zigar (21, single male, South Asian origin) too, guessed that the Prophet was around 50 years old and Aisha around 9 or 10, 'and then the consummation happened around 11 or 12'.

When I asked Michael (56, married male, white, convert) how he felt about Aisha's age as being 6 at the time of marriage, he said, 'How do I feel about that? Ask Louis XIV. [Laughs] Seriously, no orientalist had a complaint about this issue until the nineteenth century. You've heard Jonathan [Brown] on this. It's never been an issue... Islam is what a region understands at the time.' His argument, as some of the others, is that marriages between older men and younger girls should *not* take place anymore because times have changed and other men are not like Muhammad.

Response 2: She was 11+

Several participants believed that Aisha had attained puberty or was an adult at the time of her marriage and therefore the marriage should pose no problems for Muslims today. Malala (37, married female, South Asian background), for instance, said that Aisha could not have been young because she was too knowledgeable to have been 9 years old when she married Muhammad:

> I align with the thought that when it says 8 or 9, they actually mean 18 or 19, because it was just assumed that it's that many years past the first decade of life. I feel that to be more of a realistic answer simply because if you look at the wealth of knowledge that Aisha has contributed to Islamic jurisprudence, that would not be possible for a 9-year-old. Even if you're a really smart kid, you can't understand the nuances of what's being discussed.

Yasin (21, unmarried male, Middle Eastern background), also familiar with the mixed reports about Aisha's age, believes that Aisha was an adult, around 20: 'There's mixed opinions, but I feel like it's 20. I just don't think why someone would marry someone that young. Yes, the Prophet was illiterate, but he had revelations. He had to think about his actions'. Since marrying a child is so obviously unacceptable, Muhammad would not do such a thing.

Others were uncertain, and hesitant to opine, but did not think it was an issue. Scarlet (27, married female, white, convert) said:

> There's so many debates on it. And I saw this article on it recently, which I forwarded to my husband because he says that's one of the only things [in Islam] he has issues with. He's like, man, if she was really that young and they had sex, I feel kinda gross about that. Well, I don't know. There was some stuff that came out recently that she was at least 15. But my deal is that, I'm not gonna pick that apart.... It's not important to me. I don't have the knowledge or the desire to do research on that... It is what it is... There's no way we could really know... Even my father-in-law doesn't know how old he is, so going back to the seventh century?

For her, since it was long ago and we may never know the truth about it, the debate is fruitless, and she has no interest in pursuing it as a topic of interest.

Some respondents were familiar with the argument that Aisha was likely older than 6 and 9, but they were not convinced by the legitimacy of the argument. Turan (24, single male, South Asian origin), for example, suggests that efforts to revisit the sources on Aisha's age in order to conclude she may have been older exist in order to satisfy Western critics who condemn Muhammad's marriage to Aisha:

> There are people who say she was about 12, 13 years old when she got married. There's a huge majority that say she was 9 when she got married. [Others] say she was 9 at the time of the *nikāḥ* [marriage contract] but 12 or 13 when the marriage was consummated. I've also read some narratives that say she was 18, which I think is just trying to appease, in my opinion, these [Western] communities because of the questions these [claims] come with. And it may be true, but in my opinion, from what I've read, she was anywhere between 9 and 12.

Lay Muslims do not agree on Aisha's age at the time of her marriage to Muhammad. Most have heard conflicting references to her age, but their guesses range from 6 years old to 21. They not only disagree over what Aisha's age at the time of marriage was but also over what that marriage meant, and whether contemporary Muslim men of older ages can marry 9-year-old girls today. Significantly, Muhammad as a role model, as a moral exemplar for all Muslims, could never commit a reprehensible action, and therefore, either it did not happen, or we do not know what happened, or it happened but it was not inherently reprehensible because he could do it justly but others cannot.

IS THE PROPHET'S MARRIAGE TO AISHA *SUNNAH* FOR MUSLIMS TODAY?

Response 1: It is *Sunnah*

When I asked the participants in my study about Aisha's age at the time of her marriage to the Prophet, most were aware that Aisha was young while the Prophet was much older. Because the debate on child marriage is intrinsically linked to this marriage, I also asked about whether the Prophet's

Table 5: The Prophet's marriage to Aisha is *Sunnah*.

	Single Women	Single Men	Married Women	Married Men	Total
No	9	6	10	8	33
Yes	1	4	0	2	7

marriage to Aisha can be considered *Sunnah* for Muslims today. I did not define the term *Sunnah* because I wanted to hear their understanding of what it means – and their responses yield a rich, complex picture of diverse potential meanings. However, the *Sunnah* is usually understood as Muhammad's actions that are also recommended for other Muslims to emulate. None of the participants suggested that child marriage similar to the Prophet's marriage to Aisha was recommended for Muslims of all times, but some did note that it was *Sunnah* by virtue of being an action of the Prophet. Their answers fall into two categories: yes, the Prophet's marriage to Aisha (when she was between 6 and 9 years old) is *Sunnah*, but we should not practise it today; no, the Prophet's marriage to Aisha is not *Sunnah*. Notably, all individuals who said that it is *Sunnah* qualified their answers with statements such as it is *Sunnah* because the Prophet did it, but we should not do it because we're not like the Prophet. They also argued that since such marriages are illegal in the US, they would be un-Islamic as well because Muslims must follow the law of the land.[70]

I begin this discussion with my interview with Pamir (65) and Lema (57), who are husband and wife (both of South Asian background). Pamir consistently wanted to know if I was seeking his own opinions or Islam's teachings, implying that his opinions may differ from the Islamic ones. Both he and his wife told me that Islam does not prescribe a minimum age for marriage. When I asked them if parents are allowed to marry a child off without her/his consent, Lema immediately said, 'No, it's *ḥarām* [forbidden] in Islam.' Pamir, however, was hesitant to respond but eventually did say that consent is required in an Islamic marriage. He was not sure if a marriage is *ḥarām* without consent. Lema explained to him, 'It's *ḥarām* because a woman came to the Prophet and said she was married without her consent, and the Prophet said it was not allowed.' Their views on whether Muhammad's marriage to Aisha is *Sunnah* for all Muslims was most fascinating. Both agreed that Aisha was 6 years old at the time of marriage and 9 at the time of consummation – but they disagreed that it was *Sunnah*:

> Lema: It's not obligatory that you follow the *Sunnah*. It was done at the time. The *Sunnah* is that which the Prophet did and you get *sawaab* [good deeds, credit, or merit] for it. That's the definition of *Sunnah*. It's not obligatory, but it's not prohibited. It was the custom of the time. I think if it's allowed, it's fine. If the girl agrees, the father agrees, it's fine.
>
> Pamir: This is not a *Sunnah*? Why? [The Prophet] did it. And anything he did or said is *Sunnah*.
>
> Lema: No, no, no. *Sunnah* is anything he said and did that he told us to follow. He used to like cucumbers, but he didn't say you have to eat cucumbers. It's not *Sunnah*. That was just his way of life. It's what he did.

Pamir was not convinced. I asked him what his definition of '*Sunnah*' is:

> Whatever [Muhammad] did, and whatever he said, is *Sunnah*...For me, this is not *Sunnah*, no, but if someone else [believes it is], they can. I wouldn't encourage [marrying children]. It depends on the situation of the family. But it is *Sunnah*.

Neither Pamir nor Lema believed that the consensus on this issue is binding on Muslims today, because, as Lema explained, 'the law of the land precedes [the consensus]'.

For Lema, the marriage between Aisha and the Prophet is not a *Sunnah* because it is not recommended for everyone else. A *Sunnah*, according to Lema, constitutes only those actions and deeds that Muhammad did that he also encouraged other Muslims to do. Therefore, while marriage between older men and younger girls – with the permission of the girls – is permissible because Muhammad had such a marriage, it is not recommended and it is not obligatory ('it's not obligatory that you follow the *Sunnah*'). For Pamir, however, everything that Muhammad did is *Sunnah* except for this issue.

Response 2: The Prophet Muhammad's marriage to Aisha is *Sunnah* but not for today's Muslims to emulate

Like Pamir in the exchange with his wife, many respondents argued that the Prophet's marriage to Aisha is *Sunnah* by virtue of being an action of the

Prophet, but it is not necessarily recommended for contemporary Muslims. Michael (56, married male, white, convert), for instance, claimed that the Prophet's marriage to Aisha is *Sunnah* today as well because 'the *Sunnah* wouldn't change, but the appropriateness for a ruling – the ruling for any given culture – can be different. The *sharī'a* doesn't change. The *Sunnah* doesn't change. The ruling for cultures are gonna be different.' Sultan, similarly, said, 'Well, who can be like Rasool [the Prophet] in terms of character? That's the problem, see? Will you be able to treat people like Rasool? So I believe that is a unique case… But in terms of the *Sunnah*…it's a little bit different. Today, the stress is different. Expectations are different. Where we live, the cultures, we have to take [them] into account. And also, [Aisha] wasn't his first wife.' Wagma said, 'I think yes [the Prophet's marriage to Aisha is a *Sunnah*] because we don't really know what happened. I don't think the Prophet would do anything that's wrong.' Scarlet also believes that due to the lack of knowledge about the subject of Aisha's age, it is not *Sunnah*: 'He is the Prophet, so I can understand that. But we don't know. If it's *Sunnah*, it has to be in the Hadith, and the Hadith has to be pretty strong and credible, and we don't know enough about this.'

Patang (23, single male, South Asian background) and Turan (24, single male, South Asian background) opined that while the Prophet's marriage to Aisha is *Sunnah*, it's not necessarily recommended for today. Patang explained that not only have times changed and child marriage is no longer acceptable, but Aisha was more mature for a 6-year-old than girls her age today and she was the daughter of Muhammad's closest friend:

> It's a *Sunnah*, yes, but times have changed. There were reasons the Prophet married her. At the age of 6, she was more mature than anyone else at the time. Also, his closest friend was Abu Bakr. To bring their friendship closer, the Prophet married her. You can't practise that in America today. That's not Islam.

Like Patang, Turan argued that it is *Sunnah* because it's the Prophet's action, but since it merely was a part of sixth-century Arab culture, it is not applicable to Muslims universally and eternally:

> It's definitely a *Sunnah*. What is a *Sunnah*? A *Sunnah* is something that the Prophet did, or it could be something he encouraged others to do as well. I think what he did at that time was a tradition that was

> both accepted Islamically just because technically, you're allowed to do so if the person has aged, and secondly, it was a common practice within his particular culture. The Prophet had so many attacks coming his way from all over the place… but this was not something that was even talked about. It was commonly accepted. Also, you need to realise that – and this is again something I've read – over time, the capacity of humans to develop into adults has slightly changed. So a person who at the age of 9 in that day and age might be comparable to someone who's 13 or 14 in our day and age… It's definitely a *Sunnah*, in my opinion, because the Prophet did it. But should we be doing it? Not really, just because of the society that we live in, because of our norms. In the Prophet's time, it did not go against the religion. You can't just isolate a person from his society and say we can do it because he did it when our society doesn't accept it as a norm.

Note that Patang's definition of the *Sunnah* – something that the Prophet did that he also encouraged others to do – is the same as Lema's in the dialogue above with her husband, Pamir. Yet, Patang argues that the Prophet did not recommend it for everyone else – and it is not applicable to all Muslims everywhere because of the specific, unique case of Aisha ('she was more mature than anyone else'); whereas Lema argues that *because* the Prophet did not encourage others to do the same, this does not classify as a *Sunnah*.

Two discussants, Zala (26, single female, racially mixed background) and Michael (56, married male, white, convert), departed from the views of the majority of the other discussants by arguing that while it is 'technically' *Sunnah*, and child marriage is 'technically' allowed in Islam, they do not recommend it. Zala emphasised her position that the Prophet's marriage to Aisha should pose no problems for anyone because that was a different time and place. She said, 'I mean, the Prophet's life is all *Sunnah*. Is it something that we should follow? I don't think it's one of those.' She explained that the reason it is *Sunnah* is that the Prophet did it: 'Whatever the prophet did, we can, too.' This is not to suggest, she clarified, that 'we *should* do it. It's just that we are allowed to because the Prophet did it. Me, personally, I don't recommend it.'

Samandar (29, unmarried male, South Asian background), however, had a different approach to the answer. Like all other participants, he agrees that this is not something Islam requires, and like many others, he defines *Sunnah* as something that the Prophet did that other Muslims are also allowed to do. However, unlike other participants, he said, 'I want to say that everything the Prophet did is *Sunnah*; it's the recommended thing to do. But it's just recommended, not obligatory. But we're not the Prophet. He did it, okay, but it doesn't go with my morality.'

Finally, Travis (25, unmarried male, white, convert) said that defining and following the *Sunnah* entails keeping its spirit of fairness alive:

> Well, we've to define what *Sunnah* means. It exists, and I believe that a sound enough interpretation or conclusion from the fact that they married at that age would be that there can be circumstances in which this may be permissible. That said, Islam is not cut and dry. It's a great ignorance that people try to justify as Islamic things that in all reality practically play out as oppressive and unjust. The fact that it happened means that it's there in and of itself, assuming other conditions are met, and that it is fair. That it is just. That every party's rights are safeguarded. Some apply it coldly and without the prophetic spirit. Or even honestly without any intelligence or understanding of its harms and benefits, or what Islam says on it.

Travis suggests that it is not easily determinable if this is a *Sunnah* or not, that there may be circumstances in which child marriage is beneficial but others in which it is harmful. For him, it is possible to conduct child marriages while keeping with the spirit of Islam and maintaining justice.

Those who said Muhammad's practice of his marriage to Aisha is *Sunnah* all qualified their responses by pointing out that, nevertheless, it is not recommended for Muslims today. They noted that not all of Muhammad's actions are automatically recommended for others because Muslims must remain cognisant of the value of practices in their own contexts.

Response 3: The Prophet's marriage to Aisha is not *Sunnah*

Lejla (24, single, European background) said, 'No. I mean, first of all, there are so many exceptions [about] him [the Prophet]. Like he had way more wives than is permitted for Muslim men. And also, because there's this obvious age discrepancy. And, I don't know, it's been like a thousand years! Maybe, uh, some things don't apply!' Barsala (31, South Asian background, married female), similarly, explained that the Prophet's marriage was 'absolutely not' *Sunnah*: 'There were several things he was permitted to do that the average man should not be allowed to do. He was given special permission as were his wives. But I don't think all women are supposed to be following the Prophet's wives.' For Orzala (33, married, white), the reason it is not *Sunnah* is that 'the *Sunnah* is seen as a preferred way to live our life… I mean, in the Prophet's day and age, it was *Sunnah* for men to wear eyeliner, but if in our time, a man wears eyeliner in 2016, he's perceived as homosexual. That's not encouraged. Similarly, we've evolved to an age where such marriages are not seen as a preferred thing culturally, so I'd say no, it's not *Sunnah*.' Gahez (77, married, South Asian) offered that the marriage is 'not necessarily' *Sunnah* because 'like he had eleven wives, but that does not mean we should. It's clearly mentioned in the Qur'an that he was an exception…' For Amadou (40, married male, Black), too, it is 'absolutely not *Sunnah*'. Finally, Zigar (21, single male, of South Asian origin) explained:

> No [it is not *Sunnah*]. I've talked to multiple scholars on this. Not about child marriage but about having multiple wives. These types of things aren't considered *Sunnah* because the term *Sunnah* is being thrown around too lightly. By this logic, drinking water becomes *Sunnah*, or breathing becomes *Sunnah*. Or not drinking a glass of water is not *Sunnah* because you didn't drink a glass of water; you drank a soda or something. I've heard scholars say that you can't take everything that literally. You need to take general things as *Sunnah*. They give the example of this young Companion [someone who met the Prophet] who'd go and use the restroom in the exact spot that the Prophet had used, and the Prophet said that wasn't *Sunnah*. He himself said that what [the companion was] doing is not *Sunnah*. So in this situation [of child marriage] I wouldn't consider it *Sunnah* because it's circumstantial.

Zigar's response resembles Travis's: whether child marriage is Islamically valid today is determined by the circumstances. Both agree that the Prophet married Aisha under specific circumstances and his actions aren't applicable as a model for Muslims today. However, whereas Travis was unwilling to state whether he would personally classify the marriage as *Sunnah* or not, Zigar is confident that it is not *Sunnah*, and he is critical of using the word *Sunnah* too liberally because such use of the word assumes that everything that Muhammad did was *Sunnah*.

My discussants' responses to the question of whether Muhammad's practice of his marriage to Aisha is *Sunnah* for Muslims today varied drastically. None of them agreed without qualifications; all who agreed explained that the marriage is not still recommended and that the Prophet's marriage is not intrinsically appropriate for everyone else. The majority view, however, clearly is that this specific case is not *Sunnah* because only those of Muhammad's practices that are recommended to others constitute the *Sunnah*.

People's responses demonstrated their uncertainty, conflicting feelings and even disagreement with the precedent of the tradition. Their qualifiers, if they believed Muhammad married Aisha when she was a child, included statements such as Aisha was more mature than other girls of her time; Muhammad was an exemplar and is inherently incapable of committing an immoral act, so this must not have been as bad as we assume; Aisha herself did not complain about the marriage; and it is not for our time even if it were *Sunnah* because it is illegal in the US.

MINIMUM AGE FOR MARRIAGE IN ISLAM

In response to my question about the minimum age for marriage in Islam, for both women and men, most participants said 'puberty', although they qualified that by saying they do not recommend that – puberty is simply the Islamic legal position, they suggested. Others gave a specific age, such as 16 or 18, and one person, a married male, white, convert, said that in Islam, the minimum age for marriage is 6 for girls. Almost all participants had some idea about what the minimum age for marriage in Islam is. Nour (20, single female, Middle Eastern background) and Zala (26, single female, racially mixed background), however, did not know what the age is, and Helen (20, single, white, American convert) said, 'I don't think there's a minimum age in Islam. It wouldn't make sense before modern times because back then the age of consent was fluid.' For most others, the minimum age is either puberty, 6–9, or 18, although some also acknowledged that each culture has a right to set its own standards for the age of marriage.

Response 1: Puberty

The majority of participants stated that the minimum age for marriage in Islam is puberty, whatever age that may be for a given individual. The esti-

Table 6: Is there a minimum age for marriage in Islam? If so, what is it?

	Single Women	Single Men	Married Women	Married Men	Total
No specific age	2	2	2	2	8
I don't know	3	0	0	0	3
Puberty	2	6	7	6	21
6–9	2	0	0	2	4
18+	1	2	1	0	4

mations of this age varied from person to person and gender to gender – from 6 to 18. Sandara (20, single female, South Asian origin) said the minimum age for marriage for both genders is 'after puberty. But if [the girl] gets it [menstruation] really young, like at 9, I think she has to be older than that', suggesting puberty alone doesn't make a marriage licit. Scarlet (26, female, white convert) explained that while puberty is the minimum age of marriage in Islam, 'puberty varies. So I'd say at least 15 or 16. Even though nowadays, I know there are girls getting their period at 7 or 8. I don't consider that true puberty. There's more to puberty than just the period.'

The idea that physical 'maturity' does not suffice came up in other interviews. Sangin (69, married male, Middle Eastern background), who expressed reservation about discussing this topic, briefly mentioning that his sister had been raped as a child, believes that the Islamic position is not to marry until one has reached puberty, but he does not think this is sufficient:

> Let's talk about the woman. A woman not [just] physically but her personality too must become mature enough to get married. If [she is] physically okay but mentally not ready, that's [an] act of rape. That has a psychological impact on her. So it should not [be acceptable]… I don't care if she's even 30, but if she's not emotionally ready for it, no!… In the old days, in my country, if a woman [was] 9 or 11 years old, [it was okay for her to marry], but the reason they changed it is because women stand [sic] up to say, 'Hey, hey, hey! No!' What happens to the girl for the rest of her life? It's not part of *sharīʿa* … You might get upset if I go a little deeper, but *astaghfirullah*,[71] Rasool Allah…over 50 years old? Aisha?'

Sangin's discomfort with Muhammad's marriage to Aisha and with child marriage overall was visible, and he insisted that Islam would never support the marriage of minors because it is *ẓulm*, oppression. He recognised that many Muslims would oppose his position because he was implying that the Prophet may have committed a wrong; he says *astaghfirullah,* revealing a conflict between what he strongly thinks is right in the case of child marriage and the reality of Muhammad's actions according to Islamic tradition. He is certain Aisha was a child when Muhammad married her, and he cannot reconcile the possibility that the Prophet would marry someone who was so young except through the hope that there was some wisdom behind the marriage that he is unaware of. One does not marry someone once they reach an arbitrary minimum age; physical, emotional, sexual, and mental maturity come with older age. Sangin is convinced that the impact of marriage at a young age is harmful for a girl, and should not be permitted.

Several individuals disagreed that puberty should be the minimum, although they predicted that was so in Islam. Gahez (77, married, South Asian) suspected that while this is probably the recommendation in traditional, official Islam, his idea of Islam does not permit it to be so:

> One can marry once he reaches puberty, but [that is not sufficient]. The age should be such that each person or spouse can perform their responsibilities and they understand their responsibilities well. The tradition in the past was for girls, or even for boys, was however young they were, but then they don't understand their responsibility. Like boys can't make their living but they're married, so someone else [has to] take care of them. So that's not the recommendation in Islam. Like the boy, when he becomes old enough and educated enough or skilled enough to take care of his responsibilities, yes, he can [marry]. Same way with girls.

Similarly, Wagma (20, single female, South Asian background), too, believes that the Islamic perspective may be puberty, but she thinks it should be at least 18 for everyone.

> I feel like the girl should be at least 18 or older, and same with the guy… I don't think Islam has any specific age, but I think it's after puberty. But I think from experience, just from, like how the human mind works, I don't think you really mature until you've kind of like experienced a lot of what's out there… I think at least getting a year of college experience is really important, just because you get exposed to so many different things, so many different people, so many different

> cultures, so many different lifestyles, so you get to see, like, a wider perspective and horizon of the world. I also think it's really important because marriage is dynamic. It's not gonna be the same all the time, so I think being accustomed and being familiar with different situations and being able to adapt to different things and being able to cope with them is really important. I'm totally against forcing people to marry, children or not.

For my discussants, then, what they believed to be the Islamic recommendation for the minimum age of marriage – i.e. puberty for both genders – is not practical, at least for contemporary Muslims, and it is certainly not old enough. Holding this opinion, too, did not appear to them as a contradiction of Islamic guidelines because the Islamic guidelines do not require that one *must* be married by or around puberty. Moreover, the recommendation is to be contextualised, they suggested, as puberty was universally acceptable historically as an appropriate age for marriage. This idea of Islam is profoundly significant because Islam here, in this context at least and for nearly all of my participants, is flexible and its guidelines are not set in stone. Even more importantly, the *Sunnah* of the prophet is not a set of agreed-upon practices such that everything the Prophet Muhammad did, Muslims must emulate unthinkingly. Instead, Muslims must constantly re-evaluate and renegotiate Muhammad's actions to determine if those actions are preferable or appropriate in their own contexts.

Response 2: Islam does not specify a minimum age, not even puberty.

Those who were unsure about the minimum age from an Islamic perspective knew that puberty is important in Islam, but they did not agree that puberty constitutes a legitimate marker of maturity, and so did not think it should be used to set the minimum age for marriage. Malala (37, married female, South Asian background) stated that because she sees Islam as able to accommodate evolving social norms, whether child marriage was once acceptable or not is irrelevant to our time period because it is against contemporary social norms:

> When these rules came out, there was no specific age to marry. From my understanding, there's no specific age written in the Qur'an. But it

> does say that puberty is the age you become responsible for your own actions. So from that perspective, yeah, you can say they are marriageable, but only if they're the ones making the decision… Even in the early days of Islam, I don't think it was very common [to marry young] because there are a lot of cases from my understanding of women who were mature and had their own lives and opinions at the time that they were married. So it may have been a large phenomenon, it may have been small, but it's irrelevant because that's what it was at the time. It was general. That's how society was. And I believe that Islam is accommodating to how social norms evolve. So from that perspective…it's probably not okay to marry at puberty today.

Marriage at puberty is therefore perhaps Islamically unacceptable today, according to Malala, because not only have social norms changed but marriage at such a young age was not quite the norm even in the past, as is often assumed. Since Islam accommodates changes in social standards and such marriages are no longer acceptable, they can be safely declared impermissible.

For others, puberty is too complicated to determine the minimum age. Lejla (24, single female, European background) said that the age issue was complicated because puberty cannot easily be marked:

> When you say Islam, you mean like traditional Islam? 'Cause honestly, I have no idea. I've never read anything one way or another. Like I've heard different things. I've heard people say puberty, but then they'll reference Aisha, but she was, like, engaged to the Prophet but didn't move in with the Prophet until puberty. But how do you mark puberty? I guess for women, it's easier because of menstruation, but for men? So I think the age thing is complicated.

Note that Lejla asks what I mean by Islam and whether I am referring to 'traditional' Islam, which implies that there are multiple kinds of Islam, and they all might have different views on the matter. Selma (48, married, African) also questions the meaning of the word 'puberty', pointing out, 'I've never seen it in any *surah* [chapter of the Qur'an] or Hadith about this. It says *bulūgh* [maturity], but it doesn't say exactly what that means, like when the woman starts her cycle, or when she matures? Like emotional maturity or physical?'

With puberty as a prominent focus in the question of marriage, it is important that many respondents are aware that Islamically, one can marry once they reach puberty, but that puberty is not easily recognisable and it is certainly not sufficient for a healthy or good marriage. Many invoked fluctuating and changing social norms and Islam's fluid nature to support their opinions and ground them within an Islamic paradigm.

Response 3: The minimum age is 6–9.

Other participants (strikingly, only single women and married men but no single men or married women) believed that, given Aisha's marriage to Muhammad at the age of 6 and the consummation of the marriage at 9, it is Islamically acceptable to marry in this time range – but they do not recommend it. Athena (21, single, convert, of mixed background), for example, believes that the Islamic position 'may be 9' but she thinks that 'there should be a limit, like you should be fully developed. I like the US idea of 16 or above.' Michael (56, married male, white, convert) unapologetically, and with certainty, stated that the minimum age for marriage in Islam is 6. He was also the only individual to say that 'marrying a prepubescent child without her/his permission is permitted in Islam', though sexual intercourse is not permitted, he clarified, until after puberty.

Nonetheless, most participants overall suggested that puberty was the minimum age for marriage from an Islamic perspective, but almost none agreed with this position personally or believed it was appropriate for today's time. Most of them were clear that puberty is still either too young for marriage, or it is not easily identifiable and therefore should not be the minimum age.

IS THE HISTORICAL POSITION ON CHILD MARRIAGE BINDING ON MUSLIMS TODAY?

I asked my participants if, in their opinion, the historical position of consensus on child marriage is binding on Muslims today. That is, are today's Muslims allowed to revisit or even overturn the position that Muslim scholars historically agreed upon? I did not tell them what the historical position was, so as not to influence their perspective. Almost all assumed that the position would be that child marriage, and any marriage lacking the consent of either or both parties, is invalid in Islam. Some wondered, however, during the discussion, after having noticed a pattern in the conversation – e.g. our discussion on each topic ended with 'Is the historical position binding on today's Muslims?' – and said, 'Wait, the historical position is that it's *ḥarām*, right?' to which I responded, 'According to your knowledge on the matter, is it *ḥarām*?'[72] And some replied, 'I think so. It should be.' My respondents' answers fall into two categories: *yes, it is binding*, and *no, it is not binding.* Significantly, those who said the consensus on child marriage is binding did so because they had previously stated that Islamic law prohibits marrying people without their consent. With few exceptions, the discussants largely simply answered 'yes' or 'no' to the question. The few who offered details are quoted below.

Comparing the results of this table to table 2 from the introduction, one finds an important difference in the responses. A total of 22 participants (6 single women, 8 married men, 4 single men and 4 married women) completely agreed that the scholarly consensus on child marriage is not binding; in contrast, 8 total (3 single women, 2 married men, 2 single men, and 1 married woman) said scholarly consensus is always binding on Muslims. I include table 2 again below for the reader's convenience for comparison. Overall, whereas 8 of the 40 participants completely agreed that following scholarly consensus was obligatory upon Muslims, only 3 believed that it was binding in the context of child marriage.

Table 7: The consensus of the scholars on child marriage is binding.

Scale	Single Women	Single Men	Married Women	Married Men	Total*
1 (completely disagree)	6	4	4	8	22
2	0	1	2	0	3
3 (I don't know)	1	4	0	0	5
3 (it depends/it's circumstantial)	0	0	4	0	4
4	1	1	0	0	2
5 (completely agree)	1	0	0	2	3

* *One married male respondent opted not to answer this question.*

I include here table 2 for reference to compare my respondents' answer to the statement about whether consensus is binding generally to show the ways that their answers changed on this specific issue.

Table 2: The consensus of the scholars is always binding.

Scale	Single Women (10 total)	Single Men (10 total)	Married Women (10 total)	Married Men (10 total)	Total
1 (completely disagree)	3	2	3	3	11
2	1	6	2	3	12
3 (I'm not sure)	2	0	1	2	5
4	1	0	3	0	4
5 (completely agree)	3	2	1	2	8

The consensus is binding

Only three respondents opined that the position is binding on today's Muslims. According to Zala (26, single female, racially mixed background), the historical position is binding because for it to not be binding would mean today's Muslims have to prohibit what has been explicitly allowed. This is not possible, she explained, because it does not make sense to retroactively make something impermissible if it has been established as permissible, especially through an action of the Prophet, because anything made permissible by the Prophet cannot be made prohibited by others:

> I don't think we'd be overturning anything. It's not a commandment… We can't make it *ḥarām* [forbidden], but can we say we shouldn't do it? Yeah!… You can't make something retroactively *ḥarām*. Why would we retroactively make something *ḥarām* when we know the Prophet did it?… Islamic law's position isn't that we have to marry children off. *Ḥalāl* [permissible] is just it's not *ḥarām*… We shouldn't be living along *ḥalāl* and *ḥarām* lines. Not that Islam lacks values or anything, but there's more than just *ḥalāl* or *ḥarām*.

She understands that just because Islamic law permits something does not mean that it is mandatory. This distinction between the permissible and the obligatory is what prompts her to argue that the practice is binding – but binding in the sense that it is simply permissible and cannot be made impermissible. For her, while the position is binding, it carries no implications for today's Muslims because it is not an obligation. Nonetheless, she added, whether it is binding or not 'depends on basic *fiqh* questions and what is *aqīdah* [creed, belief]', explaining that cultural norms would dictate in any given time and place whether a practice for which historical scholars established a consensus is binding on all Muslims everywhere. Notably, some scholars argue against such an approach to Islam and morality: Yasir Qadhi, for examples, condemns such thinking by noting, 'When the anti-slavery movement began to spread in Muslim lands in the 1850s, 1900s, sadly some of our scholars stood in the way of anti-slavery movements. And they said it is *ḥarām* to ban slavery. You cannot ban what Allah has made *ḥalāl.*'[73]

When I asked Zala if, Islamically, a child could be married without her/his consent, she said, 'And live together after marriage? In my contemporary life, not at all.' When I asked her about her position if the couple did not have to live together, she said, 'I think this is a more cultural thing that I can't comment on.' I proceeded to ask her if she knew what the Islamic position on the matter might be, to which she responded, 'As far as I know, I think it would be allowed in Islam… I don't know a hundred percent. But I think especially on child marriage, Islamic law in that sense…didn't negate things that were already on the ground. So it's hard to say. It's not like it's a commandment.' Her answer to the question, 'Is it prohibited to have sex with a wife who has not yet reached puberty?' was 'I don't know.'

The consensus is not binding

Twenty-two individuals opined that the position is not binding – anymore. According to Sandara (20, single, South Asian origin), 'I think it was once allowed, but it is *ḥarām* [impermissible] now. With modern interpretations and scholars, the majority would feel it's *ḥarām*.' Zigar (21, single male, of South Asian origin), too, said:

> I like to take this entire thing into historical context, where it was normal for young people to marry. It wouldn't be okay now because no one does that anymore, children aren't developing at the same rate, people aren't maturing at the same time. Things are completely differ-

> ent now… I would consider it impermissible now, and I'm sure the majority of scholars would, too, because the context has changed. So I consider the past interpretation non-binding.

Travis's (25, married male, white, convert) answer was more complex, noting that whether it is binding or not depends on the impact the practice may have:

> So, my answer to this is going to be in the frame of what a group of many major scholars did perhaps more than once independently. That is that polygyny, despite the fact that it may be legally valid in the majority of cases, it can be harmful… No one has said that polygyny itself is *ḥarām*. But that in most cases, the effects of it render it so. I don't think that addressing stuff like this should necessarily be kind of responding to an *ijmāʿ* [consensus] with a blanket *ijmāʿ* in the opposite direction.

The validity of the practice is determined by its impact, whether it is beneficial or damaging. The scholarly consensus on this issue, then, cannot be applied generally or universally but may be relevant in individual cases. In other words, child marriage generally cannot be considered impermissible or invalid, but if a given case of such a marriage has harmful effects on those involved, then only in that case, it can be rendered impermissible. Further, he suggests, while child marriage is harmful generally, the solution is not to make it impermissible for everyone.

While most respondents willingly and easily stated whether the historical ideas on child marriage were applicable to today's time and whether the historical position of consensus approving child marriage was binding, some hesitated to respond either way. Their reasoning was that permission for or approval of a practice cannot be binding or non-binding. The majority, however, did not hesitate to say that the position was not binding because the consensus on the issue would clearly be rooted in a context that does not fit today's ideals and sense of justice.

ANALYSIS AND DISCUSSION

Several important points emerge here. First, it is worth acknowledging the limited importance that the legal schools, or *madhhabs*, attributed to a

Hadith that is now employed very differently by contemporary Muslims. This is the Hadith about Khansa's complaint to Muhammad about her marriage that took place without her consent, which we have already discussed. While the historical scholars had access to this Hadith, they do not seem to have concluded from it that consent is required for all marriages. Instead, they interpreted this Hadith specifically in terms of women who had previously been married, while Aisha's Hadith about her marriage to Muhammad at the age of 6 is presented as evidence that a virgin girl's permission is not necessary for a marriage. There is no indication in the Hadith about the woman's claim that she was forcibly married or that she had been a non-virgin prior to her marriage. Instead, the scholars seem to have taken these two Hadiths to conclude that a virgin (i.e. previously unmarried), prepubescent girl can be married against her will, but she may later end the marriage per her own volition once she reaches puberty.

In contrast, almost all of my discussants directly or indirectly invoked Khansa's Hadith to argue that consent was unequivocally required in a marriage, without which the marriage is invalid – and that this Hadith proves it – and they were either unaware of Aisha's Hadith about her age at the time of her marriage, or they did not think it applied to Muslims today, at least in the United States. The pre-modern legal schools and Muslim jurists applied different Hadiths with competing viewpoints to arrive at the conclusion that forcibly marrying children was compatible with Islam. Arguably, they chose an interpretation and conclusion of an issue that yields harmful results despite the Qur'anic verse 39:55 directing Muslims 'to follow (from the Qur'an) the best of what has been revealed to you from your Sustainer'. I understand this verse to be encouraging readers of the Qur'an, particularly those with interpretive licence, to choose the best, least harmful, possible interpretation of the many available. However, there remain specific social contexts in which child marriage continues to be practised, and it is likely that the pre-modern legal scholars were not only operating in those contexts but also imagined their interpretations to be especially applicable in those contexts.

Second, my discussants disagree on the meaning of *Sunnah*. For some, *Sunnah* is everything the Prophet Muhammad did, and Muslims should always attempt to emulate his actions – except in the example of his marriage to Aisha. As with his marriages to more than four women while 'only' four are allowed to other Muslim men, his marriage to Aisha is an exception that other Muslims should not follow. For other discussants, the *Sunnah* consists only of those actions that the Prophet Muhammad recommended for others to follow. Marriage without consent and the marriage of children are not acceptable practices, especially not in the United States, where the minimum legal age for marriage is 18 or 16, they incorrectly stated (seemingly unaware that, in the US, a parent or guardian can legally marry off their child without the child's consent in some states).

Third, social norms were commonly advanced as an explanation for Aisha's marriage to Muhammad. While none of my discussants suggested that Muhammad's marriage to Aisha was for political purposes, most who were familiar with Aisha's age at the time of her marriage did maintain that such a marriage was historically and socially appropriate. They explained that child marriage was historically acceptable and is (or was) a 'cultural norm' during Muhammad's time, and that Muhammad's marriage to Aisha is either not *Sunnah* for today's Muslims or is not something for today's Muslims to cast judgement upon. The linear view of cultures and history as progressing towards a better social arrangement, such as one in which child marriages are at least theoretically unacceptable, 'emerge[d] in Muslim thinking in the nineteenth century'.[74] However, as Mohammad Ali Syed recognises, historical context as an explanation largely serves as a response to Western criticisms of Muhammad's multiple marriages and his marriage to Aisha.[75] Carolyn Baugh, too, points out that the medieval legal discourse on child marriage is not one about an issue of culture; it was 'a facet of legal thought on gender'.[76] In other words, the notion of a cultural or historical context's role in shaping opinions was irrelevant to the jurists as they formulated their consensus on child marriage.

Whether or not child marriage was a common practice historically is not, for me, a matter of contention. The issue is instead that historically prevalent ideas on marriage, gender, and sexuality continue to shape contemporary notions of those same topics.[77] We will see later in this book instances in which my participants make this connection in our discussions of other topics, and when they believe that prohibitions are a result of the social, cultural norms of the Prophet Muhammad's Arabia and therefore not relevant or applicable to other time periods and places. For example, while some said that Muhammad's marriage to Aisha was merely *permitted* as opposed to obligatory, that Muhammad's actions were merely *optional* for other Muslims to emulate, are they willing to suggest that the prohibitions on female-led prayer and interfaith marriage may also be equally non-binding?

As with sexual slavery, as we will see, many respondents asked what I meant by 'Islam' or even 'Islamic law' when I asked them what they know or believe Islam's position to be on child marriage. One particularly fascinating response came from Sultan. For him, 'Islamic law' and 'Islam' are different, such that when I asked him if he believes Islamic law permits marriage without an individual's consent, he said, 'I have no knowledge about that, so I don't know.' When I asked him if 'Islam' permits marriage without a woman's or man's consent, he said, 'Absolutely not. Islam prohibits oppression of any kind.' Therefore, Islam – not Islamic law – would not allow any marriage without consent because that is a form of oppression. In this distinction, Islamic law is the realm of experts, while Islam is for everyone.

Finally, none of my participants differentiated between the contracting of the marriage and its consummation, while legal compendia dedicate chapters to this discussion. The *Muṣannaf* (Hadith collection) of 'Abd al-Razzāq (d. 827), for example, includes entire chapters entitled, 'Should a Virgin be Divorced while she is Menstruating?' and 'The Chapter on Divorcing Virgins', indicating that these marriages were not consummated.[78] The annulment of a virgin wife's marriage was a special case referred to as *khiyār* (recession), and legal schools disagreed on its equivalency to *ṭalāq* (divorce).[79] The failure to make this distinction suggests that my discussants also did not differentiate between contracting a marriage and its consummation because, as they almost unanimously argued, a marriage is invalid in Islam if one or both parties are minors. This perception is a significant departure from the historical Islamic legal idea of marriage, and it illustrates what Sarah Eltantawi notes is a moment in which ethical concerns are privileged over jurisprudence. Eltantawi, in her discussion on child marriage in Northern Nigeria, argues that the notion of orthodoxy 'cannot be understood outside human, historical processes', despite perceptions that it is timeless. Her larger questions address the grassroots efforts of Nigerian Muslims, in 1999, to revive the *Ḥudūd*: that is, the punishments derived from the Qur'an, which Nigerian Muslims believe would 'alleviate the poverty and corruption that had reached desperate levels'.[80] (Islamic penal law ended in Nigeria in 1959 and was replaced with an English, colonial code.) She is interested in the apparent incongruence that results from the desire and effort to reinstitute Islamic laws in some instances while resisting them in others, such as child marriage. She shows that this incongruence is best explained through Nigerian society's ethical and social priorities. Eltantawi concludes that 'ethical concerns about *ijbār* were considered so pressing that jurisprudence [where one finds support for child marriage in Islam] was cast aside'.[81] Building on this argument, I propose that my respondents' inconsistent reliance on pre-modern Islam speaks to their social and ethical priorities: Muslims must reject those historical practices that today contradict our sense of ethics, such as child marriage, regardless of what the scholarly position may have been historically.

My respondents' positions can also be identified in the following ways: some have no problem with Muhammad's marriage to Aisha because the time, social norms, and circumstances were different then, but such marriage would not be acceptable today. Others have no problems with the marriage because the Prophet Muhammad would never do something that is immoral, unacceptable, or inappropriate, as a moral exemplar who is incapable of harming others. But a few are bothered by Muhammad's marriage to Aisha and, at least implicitly, believe it was wrong for Muhammad to marry Aisha that young and also believe it is wrong today.

CONCLUSION

Most of my discussants either persistently argued that child marriage is not like the other topics because it is not a *farḍ*, an obligation, or they said this was a good question, and they had never thought about it so had no answer. I am struck by the flexibility afforded to the historical position on the 'urgent' issue of child marriage – urgent because of current notions of human rights violations, sexual agency, and the harmful effects of the practice. Almost all of my participants assume that the historical schools and scholars would prohibit the practice of child marriage or marriage without the consent of either party. It is not simply that ordinary, observant Muslims' practice and understanding of Islam are complex and varied, but it is also that they attribute their attitudes to 'Islam', even where Islam's textual sources can be said to contradict them. While my participants' sources for their assumptions about Islam change depending on the topic, their position is clear: Islam prohibits child marriage and sexual slavery. Participants would go to great lengths in order to defend this position.

The discrepancies between Muslims' perceptions of Islam's position on child marriage, or even consent in marriage, and the textual legal attitudes towards consent and marriage in Islam testify to the fact that contemporary Muslims project their own ideas onto 'Islam'; that is, their construction of Islam involves a reflective engagement with contemporary and past engagements of ethics and justice. More importantly, 'Islam' is not simply a tradition derived from texts alone, but lived realities contribute to its conceptualisation as well. Because my discussants perceive child marriage as illegal and unethical universally, they read it as prohibited in Islam. While all my participants agreed that consent is essential for a valid marriage in Islam, a few did say that children were capable of giving consent while others said that was inherently impossible.

I suggest that contemporary projections of consent in marriage onto Islam can occur and make sense particularly because Islam is a rhizome. This explains why these contemporary ideas are not seen as contradictory to the pre-modern textual ideas on marriage and consent. This is made possible by the multiple sources of Islam. That is, my participants wavered between choosing the legal schools or Qur'an and *Sunnah* as the authoritative source of Islam on a given issue. On the issue of child marriage, or consent in marriage, they prioritised Hadiths and either rejected the legal schools' consensus or scholars' opinions that child marriage is acceptable (if they were aware of this position), or assumed that the legal schools would forbid child marriage. That they assumed that the legal schools, and Islam generally, would prohibit the practice of child marriage is significant because such an approach to Islam indicates the flexibility of both Islam and its sources to accommodate shifting moral structures and compasses.

Chapter 3

Sexual Slavery in Islam

INTRODUCTION

Slavery, and sexual slavery in particular, has been a common topic of discussion since the attempt by ISIS to revive it in 2014. ISIS argued that since God never prohibited slavery, or sexual relations with slaves, Muslims today are entitled to practise both. While most Muslim legal scholars declare slavery illegal in today's context, the issue of slavery is relevant in conversations on the meanings and boundaries of tradition and tradition-making because it raises the question of how and when the notion of sociohistorical context is invoked to defend or oppose a practice. Indeed, slavery is (officially) illegal in today's world, but how do Muslims think about this illegality, particularly those who know that Islamic law historically approved the practice? Does a practice have to be explicitly, textually prohibited for it to be un-Islamic? Given that slavery was historically accepted by Muslims, what rationales do Muslims offer for its prohibition today? If the idea is that Muslims approved of slavery in the past merely because it was universally acceptable already, what does that mean about the role of cultural, historical contexts in prohibiting or permitting other unjust, immoral, or otherwise exploitative and hierarchical practices? If slavery can be declared impermissible today, after its historical acceptance has been contextualised, can the same level of contextualisation be extended to the more explicitly gendered practices such as female-led prayer and women's interfaith marriage?

In this chapter, I discuss historical views on men's right to sexual relations with enslaved females, and contemporary Muslims' understandings of slavery in Islam. I analyse Qur'anic verses that arguably support sexual relations with enslaved people, while also briefly addressing the argument that the Qur'anic verses about 'those whom your right hands possess' do not necessarily permit sexual contact with enslaved people. We will then look at attitudes towards slavery within the historical legal tradition. I highlight the case of Māriya the Copt, a woman who the earlier Islamic sources acknowledge as a concubine of the Prophet, but whose status as a wife or concubine is ambiguous. The implications of Māriya being a wife or a concubine are significant: if Māriya was Muhammad's concubine, then enslaving women and having sexual relations with them are sanctioned in the *Sunnah* (prophetic practice) and not just in the legal tradition. Like in the case of child marriage in the previous chapter, Muhammad's practice – in this case, his relationship with Māriya the Copt – and the permissibility of slavery in the historical Islamic tradition are instances where a clash occurs between prophetic *Sunnah*, classical jurisprudence and modern notions of sexuality, justice and sexual ethics.[1] I move on to my discussants' views towards slavery and their understandings of Islam's position on slavery. I conclude with the argument that contemporary Muslims' views on slavery and its contemporary impermissibility in Islam require distinguishing between 'Islam' and 'Islamic law'. I argue that switching between different terms for 'Islam', in order to explain the relationship between religious practice, religious ideals, and lived reality, demonstrates a rhizomatic conceptualisation, even if it is not consciously conceived in those terms. While several of my discussants had initially told me that 'Islamic law' and 'Islam' are the same, they, too, eventually acknowledged the distinction between the two, arguing that Islamic law would not permit something that Islam prohibits or vice versa. My respondents believe that Islam is a system of principles guided fundamentally by equality and compassion, for everyone at all times. Although a few of my respondents believed slavery is still technically acceptable in Islam because it was never scripturally prohibited, they qualified their positions with statements such as 'but only if the slaves are treated with respect and dignity'. Those who believed slavery was permissible in the past but not today also explained that slavery was permissible on the grounds that those enslaved would be treated with dignity and equality, clearly believing that it is possible to enslave someone while also respecting them and seemingly rejecting the view that enslavement is inherently degrading and undignified. Others believed it was always and still is impermissible because it goes against the core of Islam, which is to treat others respectfully and equally, which to them, intrinsically precludes enslavement.

MĀ MALAKAT AYMĀNUKUM ('WHAT YOUR RIGHT HANDS POSSESS'): THE QUR'AN AND SEXUAL RELATIONS WITH ENSLAVED PEOPLE

The pre-modern Islamic tradition unanimously permitted slavery, including male ownership of and sexual intercourse with enslaved women. Islamic law put in place specific rulings about how to deal with enslaved people (slaves) and what the rights of the enslaved and enslavers (slave owners/masters) were. The Qur'an, too, appears to sanction sexual contact, including sexual intercourse, with one's slaves. I do not engage the exegetical tradition here because all pre-modern exegetes unanimously took for granted the existence of slavery and the permission for men to have sexual access to the women they enslaved. Only in the modern period has slavery been viewed as detestable and abolished by the Qur'an. However, I discuss below some of the Islamic legal ideas on sexual slavery. Relevant verses include the following:

> 4:3: If you fear that you cannot act equitably towards orphans, then marry such women as seem good to you, two or three or four. But if you fear that you will not be just, then only one or what your right hands possess.

> 4:23-25: Forbidden to you [presumably for marriage] are your mothers and your daughters and your sisters... And *muḥṣanāt* [married women] except those whom your right hands possess[2]... And whoever among you does not have the means to marry free believing women, then marry of those whom your right hands possess of believing slave girls...

> 23:6: [Successful indeed are those who believe... [23:1]]...and those who guard their private parts [23:5]...except before their spouses or those whom their right hands possess...

> 70:30: …except before their spouses or those whom their right hands possess.

> 33:50: O Prophet! We have made lawful to you your wives whom you have given their dowers, and those whom your right hand possesses out of those whom God has given to you as prisoners of war…exclusively for you, not for the (rest of the) believers. We know what We have ordained for them concerning their wives and those whom their right hands possess in order that no blame may attach to you.

> 33:52: It is not allowed to you to take [additional] wives afterwards, nor that you should exchange them for other wives, though their beauty be pleasing to you, except what your right hand possesses.

It is difficult to conclude absolutely whether the Qur'an permits sexual contact with those whom one has enslaved. Collectively, the above verses distinguish between spouses and 'those whom your right hands possess', and although the phrase *mā malakat aymānukum* is not gendered, it is believed to grant permission only to male enslavers to have sexual contact with the women they enslave. Kecia Ali recounts an incident recorded in the tradition in which a woman reveals to the Caliph Umar that she engages in sexual relations with her male slaves, a male concubine in particular: Umar tells her she is prohibited from doing so, and the woman replies, 'I thought… that ownership by the right hand made lawful to me what it makes lawful to men.' Umar disagrees but consults the other (male) companions about the matter, and they unanimously tell him, 'She has [given] the book of Exalted God an interpretation that is not its interpretation.' Although Umar does not punish her for having illicit sex, he forbids her from 'ever marrying any free man' and he 'put an end to the liaison by 'order[ing] the slave not to approach her'.[3]

Assuming *mā malakat aymānukum* refers to enslaved women, most of these verses do not explicitly permit sexual intercourse with enslaved women. In fact, by stating that men can marry *mā malakat aymānuhum* if they do not have sufficient means to marry free women, Q. 4:3 suggests that in order to have sexual access to enslaved women, one must first marry them. In the verses where 'spouses' and *mā malakat aymānuhum* appear (e.g. 23:6 and 70:30), they do so with the Arabic *aw* – 'or' rather than 'and'. However, verses 23:6 and 70:30 complicate this point because they refer to chastity or guarding one's private parts 'except from spouses *or* those whom their right hands possess', which may mean that not all men have wives in addition to slaves, hence the word 'or'.

Verses 4:23–25 also pose a dilemma: men are told that they cannot marry women who are already married *except* (*illā*) those whom their right hands possess. The *tafsīr* tradition explains that these verses were revealed in response to Muslims' capture of new communities, and while they gained the right to sexual access to the women captured, some of the men were concerned about the marital status of the women. Q. 4:25 was revealed to permit them to have sexual intercourse with the married women who had been captured because their marriages were automatically annulled upon capture. Jurists disagreed, however, about what to do in a case where both husbands and wives were captured together.

Some contemporary scholars entirely reject the classical doctrine that the Qur'an/scripture supports a man's sexual access to his female slaves.[4] Asifa Quraishi-Landes, for example, states, 'I, personally, am not convinced that sex with one's female slave is approved by the Quran in the first place.'[5] She suggests that 'it is plausible to read the critical Quranic phrase "what your right hands possess" as referring not to slaves but to some form of preliminary marital arrangement, such as we might today say someone has "pledged their hand in marriage"'.[6] Thus, the idea of sexual contact with enslaved females is at best Qur'anically ambiguous. Jonathan Brockopp seems to support this position: he observes a pattern in the Qur'an where the two clear references to sexual relations with slaves are in Meccan verses while the Medinan verses 'refer to sex with slaves in terms of a strict hierarchy: marriage to a free woman (Q. 4:25); marriage to a believing slave (Q. 2:221 and 24:32); and finally abstinence (Q. 4:25 and 24:30), suggesting that a new ethic was promulgated in Medina, where sexual intercourse was to be entirely within marriage bonds'.[7] What appears to be the Qur'an's ambiguous stance on sexual relations with slaves, then, can be explained through Brockopp's suggestion of the differences in the Meccan and Medinan verses. Nonetheless, historical scholars – and the major schools of law – unanimously agreed that the Qur'an grants a man sexual access to the women he enslaves.

SEXUAL RELATIONS WITH ENSLAVED WOMEN IN THE LEGAL TRADITION

The enslaved woman who bore her enslaver (master) a child was called *umm al-walad*, literally 'mother of [her enslaver's] child'. The children born to enslaved women are recognised legally and are therefore entitled to inheritance and other rights that the enslaver's children with his free wives are owed. While it is popularly believed that the slave woman who bears her master a child could not be sold on to another owner and that she became free upon her enslaver's death, Ibn Rushd offers differing views on the status of the *umm walad.* According to the caliphs Umar and Uthman as well as the majority of the scholars after them, the *umm walad* is not to be sold, and she becomes a free woman upon the death of her enslaver. However, according to Abu Bakr, Ali, Ibn ʻAbbās, and several others, the sale of the *umm walad* is permitted, and she does not necessarily gain freedom upon the death of her master. Those who held the latter position 'argued on the basis of what is related from Jabir, who said, "We used to sell the *ummahāt al-walad* [plural of *umm walad*] in the period of the Prophet, in that of Abu Bakr, and in the early days of the caliphate of Umar. It was then that Umar prohibited us from selling them."'[8] The side supporting the mother's freedom and the prohibition on her being sold cites a Hadith attributed to Muhammad 'who said about Māriya his slave-girl when she gave birth to Ibrahim, "Her child has set her free."'[9]

Umar's rationale for forbidding the selling of a female slave who had given birth to her enslaver's child was the Qur'anic principle of maintaining family bonds. Hearing that the mother of a slave girl had been sold, Umar gathered his community, 'read from the Qur'an, reciting a verse that supported the bonds of family, then declared, "What greater breaking of kindred could there be than the sale of a mother of one of your children…?"' The crowd suggested that he do whatever he believed necessary to settle the issue, 'so he decreed that, throughout the realm, it was forbidden to sell the female slave who gives birth to her master's child'.[10] Younus Mirza writes that 'during the early period, Umar was identified as the advocate for the freedom of the *umm al-walad* and, thereafter, Sunnis, who believed his rule and religious judgment to be correct, continued to ascribe to his opinion'.[11] Before Umar's ruling, 'the master designated…whether his female slave could bear the title of *umm al-walad* and thus if she was free after his death'.[12] After his ruling, however, 'a female slave who bore the child of her master was given the title of the *umm al-walad* automatically and the master was bound by law not to sell her'.[13] While the consensus on not selling the *umm al-walad* once she gave birth to her master's child and her freedom upon her master's death was established, it was contested at times as well.[14] These shifting positions show that the status of the *umm al-walad* was not consistent in Islamic history, even in the earlier period, and that Umar is believed to have played a vital role in ensuring the relatively secured status of the *umm al-walad*.

We will not examine the broader role of slavery in Islam, the intricacies around buying or selling slaves, or debates around the legal status of the *umm al-walad*, as they are not relevant here. However, I will analyse some of the relevant views surrounding slavery in Islam and in particular sexual slavery, the ways in which contemporary lay Muslims perceive these debates today, and what their understanding reveals about how change is negotiated in Islam. For instance, most of my participants had little knowledge about Muhammad's relationship with Māriya Qibṭiyya, or Māriya the Copt.

MUHAMMAD AND MĀRIYA THE COPT

According to the Muslim tradition, Māriya the Copt was an Egyptian woman whom the Coptic king Muqawqis gave to Muhammad as a gift and concubine, along with another concubine – Māriya's sister Sirin – together with a eunuch, some gold, and other gifts. Muhammad 'liked Maria and was satisfied with her, while he offered her sister Sirin to his poet Hassan ibn Thabit'.[15] The tradition is replete with conflicting portrayals of Māriya, including her status as a wife or a concubine of Muhammad, a confusion that persists until today when Muslims write about Muhammad's life and his wives.

In the English translation of Aisha Abd al-Rahman Bint al-Shāṭi's (d. 1988) book, *Biographies of the Ladies of the House of the Prophet* (1987), Matti Moosa translates the word *surriyya* (concubine, bondswoman) as 'wife' when referring to Māriya. In his introduction to her section, Moosa says that 'in a special home lived one of [Muhammad's] wives'.[16] By contrast, Abd al-Rahman's original words are that 'in a special home lived the Prophet's *surriyya*'.[17] While Bint al-Shāṭi acknowledges and reports that Māriya was one of Muhammad's bondswomen but nonetheless chooses to portray her as his wife because she gave birth to Muhammad's son Ibrahim, Moosa goes farther and presents her as having married the Prophet. Where Bint al-Shāṭi writes in the Arabic, 'Throughout the second year of her life with the Prophet' (*istaqbalat Māriya 'āmiha al-thāni fī ḥayāt al-nabī*), Moosa translates, 'throughout the second year of her marriage'.[18] However, Moosa cannot completely avoid acknowledging Māriya's slave status in his translation. Moosa presents Māriya's status as a slave ('bonds-woman') mainly when referring to the Prophet's wives' jealousy of Māriya ('a bonds-woman, sent as a gift').[19] He also uses the term 'bondswomen' when discussing the parallels between Māriya and Hagar: 'Whenever she was alone, Maria was accustomed to think of Hagar, her Egyptian ancestry…and dwelt on the similarities of her own and Hagar's position. For both were Egyptian bondswomen…both of them aroused the jealousy of the Mistresses of the households', and both were 'gifts' to prophets.[20] Māriya is also depicted as longing to give Muhammad a male child just as Hagar had given Abraham one; Māriya eventually becomes Muhammad's only living 'wife' to have a male child. The differences in emphasis in Bint al-Shāṭi's portrayal of Māriya and her depiction in Moosa's rendering demonstrate that her relationship with/to Muhammad can be interpreted in multiple ways, and such interpretations are informed by the prevailing moral assumptions in a given historical context. Contemporary writers and translators like Moosa are much more uncomfortable with the idea that Muhammad had concubines and hence downplay this aspect of the relationship. This makes it unsurprising that my respondents were unaware of her status, or that Muhammad had concubines at all.

Aysha Hidayatullah, in her study on the status of Māriya in relation to the Prophet in Muslim sources, writes that the sources 'are exceedingly indecisive, at times likening her to a wife (*zawja*) of the Prophet Muhammad and at other times, referring to her only as his female slave (*mawlā*)'.[21] The earlier texts (from the ninth to the fifteenth century) 'are generally clear in referring to Māriya as the Prophet's slave by using the terms *milk al-yamīn*, *surriyya*, *jāriya*, *ama*, *umm al-walad*, and *mawlā*'.[22] Yet, in the twentieth century, as with Bint al-Shāṭi's text, Muslim authors inconsistently employ 'the terms *milk al-yamīn*, *surriyya*, *jāriya*, and *mawlā* to refer to Māriya at the same time as using contradictory terms that imply that she was married to the Prophet'.[23] Later sources either omit references to Muhammad's sexual interactions with Māriya in translations, or they deny that such incidents ever took place.[24] A striking example is found in the English translations of modern Arabic sources on the Prophet's life and his wives.[25] For example, in his 1933 biography of the Prophet, Muhammad Husayn Haykal writes that the Prophet used to visit Māriya at the chamber allotted for her 'frequently as would a man his female slaves'.[26] Yet, in its 1973 English translation by Ismail al-Fāruqi, 'the equivalent of this line is nowhere to be found, and [al-Fāruqi] provides no explanation for this omission. This exclusion appears to be deliberate, given that the translator remains faithful to all surrounding portions of Haykal's Arabic text.'[27] The omission can be attributed to how the unexpurgated passage would be received by the audience: 'For Haykal's

Egyptian audience in the 1930s, the practice of concubinage among the elite was a recent memory; Al-Fāruqi adapts the text for a 1970 American audience, for whom Muhammad's having a sexual relationship with a female he owned would have been deeply troubling.'[28]

The Qur'an arguably legitimates Muhammad's relationship with Māriya. The first five verses of the chapter *al-Taḥrīm* (*The Prohibition*) were reportedly revealed in order to free Muhammad of having prohibited sexual relations with Māriya after Ḥafṣa, one of his wives, caught him with Māriya in her house on a day allotted to Ḥafṣa.[29] According to Ibn Sa'd:

> The Messenger of God was alone with his female slave [*jāriya*] Māriyya in the home of Ḥafṣa. The Prophet came out, and Ḥafṣa was sitting at the door. She exclaimed, 'Oh Messenger of God! In my house? On my day?' The Prophet declared, 'She is forbidden to me. Keep yourself away from me!' She said, 'I will not accept [that] unless you swear that to me.' So he said, 'By God, I will never touch her.'[30]

In response to Muhammad's prohibiting Māriya for himself, God sends the following verses to assure him that his oath is void and invalid: 'O Prophet! Why do you forbid yourself that which God has made lawful for you; you seek to please your wives… God indeed has sanctioned for you the expiation of your oaths and God is your Protector… Maybe his Sustainer [*rabb*], if he divorces you, will give him in your place wives better than you, submissive, faithful, obedient, penitent, adorers, fasters, widows and virgins.' (Q. 66:1-5) The Qur'an validates his desire for Māriya, encourages Muhammad to revoke his oath, and reminds Muhammad's wives that God can replace them with better ones – and a variety – if they are dissatisfied with him. The Prophet had asked Ḥafṣa to keep his affair with Māriya a secret, but Ḥafṣa

> could keep no secret from Aisha and the incident kindled her [Aisha's] jealousy [of the Prophet's interest in Māriya]. She, in turn, also incited the other wives who, forgetting their jealousy of her [Aisha], joined ranks. They exclaimed: 'We have been patient all this while over the Prophet's favoritism to the daughter of Abu Bakr and now we see him favouring this Coptic slave. What a humiliation!'[31]

In this report, Ḥafṣa reports what she saw to Aisha, who then immediately informs the other wives, stirring disharmony in the family, almost conspiratorially. The wives are 'humiliated' that their husband would choose a 'slave' over them, the free ones.

While my discussants either did not know about Māriya or rejected any notion of Muhammad having sexual relations with someone he was not married to, contemporary Muslim preachers and teachers continue to tell the story without modifying its message for a contemporary audience. In his telling of the story of Ḥafṣa/Māriya, for example, Yasir Qadhi explains that the image of the Prophet as portrayed in this story challenges people's superhuman image of Muhammad when there is nothing wrong with what he did because Māriya was *ḥalāl* (permissible) to him.[32] In other words, while Muslims might view Muhammad as a 'superhuman', by which Qadhi perhaps means someone with more sexual restraint and a lack of desire for women, Muhammad in fact did nothing wrong by sleeping with Māriya because the two were sexually permissible to each other, even if not married.

Since contemporary Muslims portray Muhammad as a champion of women's rights and of justice more broadly, they tend to find it unthinkable that Muhammad would have a slave and/or have sexual relations with a woman to whom he was not married – especially when he could have more than four wives and therefore had the option to marry her. Most of my respondents either had no knowledge of the existence of Māriya al-Qibṭiyya or they believed Muhammad freed her and then married her. Some mentioned a 'woman' who had been 'given to Muhammad as a concubine' but insisted that Muhammad had freed and married before he slept with her to highlight their point that Muhammad himself had no slaves and thus did not support slavery. The sheer possibility that Muhammad may have had a slave likely offends 'many Muslims who hold the Prophet in the highest esteem and who might adamantly defend his character against any suggestion that he might have treated Māriya in a manner that does not neatly accord with contemporary criteria for just interpersonal relations'.[33] In fact, a part of Hidayatullah's argument is precisely that the different ways that Māriya's life story is told serves 'to uphold the moral purity of the Prophet and the members of his household'.[34] Thus, Māriya's existence in the historical tradition poses a dilemma for today's Muslims, challenging the dominant view of Muhammad today, as slavery is now seen as immoral.

Besides Māriya, the Prophet had other concubines as well. An example is Rayhāna bint Zayd, a Jewish woman who was captured during an attack on her tribe, Banu Qurayza. (Bint al-Shāṭi, in *Wives of the Prophet*, writes in her introduction that she chooses not to write about Rayhāna because she offered herself to the Prophet but did not have a major influence on his life that is recorded.) Other concubines included Jamīla, Nafīsa, and Rubayha, also known as Zulaykha al-Qaraziya.[35] Finally, Zaynab bint Jahsh is said to have provided Muhammad with a concubine 'to appease him after he had deserted her for three months'.[36] But none of my respondents mentioned these women.

The significant discrepancies between Muslims' perceptions of Muhammad's life (whether he had slaves or not) on the one hand, and his life according to textual sources on the other, reveal much about what matters to Muslims. These are not contradictions so much as representations of the rhizomatic multiplicity of ways that Islam and its sources are constructed and conceptualised. That is, while Muhammad's image in the contemporary Muslim American imagination may contradict the reality of Muhammad's life and practices, competing perceptions of Muhammad are at play here. Muhammad's relations with women whom he did not marry are re-imagined by contemporary Muslim Americans as having actually been marital relations and therefore Islamically licit according to modern Muslim understandings of sexual ethics. As Islam and the ways it is conceptualised change, so too do the images of the historical Muhammad and the conceptualisation of his sexual relations.

CONTEMPORARY AUTHORITATIVE VIEWS OF SEXUAL SLAVERY

The topic of sexual intercourse with slaves is popular among Muslim preachers. Some, like Nouman Ali Khan, are more apologetic and polemical in their discussions of it, while others, such as Yasir Qadhi, find nothing to be ashamed of in acknowledging that Islam accepted slavery in the past and even that Muhammad had sexual relations with enslaved females.

Yasir Qadhi states that 'I don't like using the term "slavery" because the English term "slavery" comes with a connotation in Western history that the Arabic term and Islamic terms never had... When we use the term, we get images of...American slavery, which was one of the worst manifestations of this institution in human history.'[37] He suggests that Muslims look at Islamic notions of slavery 'within the context of their times. We need to understand that slavery, or *'ubudiyya*, was a universal practice...Islam was the first and only to institute laws for *'ubudiyya*.'[38] Here, he makes a false claim about how other Abrahamic religions approached slavery in order to convince his audience that Islam's way of dealing with slavery was more ethical.[39] By comparing the reality of American slavery to the ideals of Islamic slavery, he avoids examining how slavery functioned in Islamic societies in practice, making it appear more humane. Islam, he states, began to institute laws for slavery by restricting who could be enslaved: only prisoners of war who were not ransomed.[40] He also stresses the virtue of freeing enslaved people and treating them well, again using this emphasis to suggest that Islamic practices were more ethical than those prevalent in other societies. As for slavery in contemporary times, Qadhi explains that no legislation exists in Islam 'that requires the existence of slavery, and therefore, in our times, when there is no such institution as slavery, Islamic law is full and valid and it doesn't need their existence'.[41] The fact that slavery no longer exists 'clearly demonstrates that God intended for this institution to be something that is not necessary and required'.[42] When it was present, there were laws that covered it. Specifically in relation to sexual relations with slaves, Qadhi claims: 'Previous civilisations and cultures did not have any rules, and in many cultures including pre-Islamic Arabian culture, your *ama* [female slave] didn't just have to be yours; you could lend her to other people, and of course what would happen was you'd hire her to other people… And the Qur'an references this fact; you cannot do this.'[43] 'Islam' thus intervened in such treatment of enslaved females by declaring them legitimate only to their owners/enslavers, and by granting the status of *umm al-walad* to slaves who gave birth to children of their masters. Enslavers could then no longer sell such slaves to others, and these slaves became free upon the death of their masters.[44] Qadhi tells his listeners that 'the fact of the matter is that we don't have to deal with this in the modern world',[45] since slavery no longer exists. God put in place rules and regulations that would lead to the elimination of slavery, and now that 'it is eliminated, *alhamdulillah*, we don't have to call for it to be brought back'.[46] Finally, Muhammad had no slaves as servants; he freed them all, Qadhi states.[47]

Nouman Ali Khan's explanations of female sexual slavery are more apologetic. Khan insists that enslaved females enjoyed a status equal to wives, and, in fact, they were practically the enslavers' wives. The only difference was that a *nikāḥ* (marriage contract) was not necessary for sexual relations with slaves, he specifies. The *nikāḥ* was unnecessary because the purpose of the *nikāḥ* is to transfer responsibility over a woman from one *walī* (guardian) to another, which would be redundant because the slave was already under the man's guardianship:

> The *nikāḥ* is a transfer of responsibility…from the previous *walī* to the new *walī*. The previous *walī* is … the man of the house. And now who's the new *walī*? The husband. In situations where the woman was already inside your house… who are they transferring the responsibility from? Themselves? It doesn't make sense…[48]

Khan continues to explain that Islam's approach to slavery and sexual slavery is practical because Islam merely acknowledges the existence of slaves as sexual partners and offers guidelines for treating them well:

> Historically speaking, in any civilisation, when are women taken as prisoners? Either under prostitution or under war… The practical reality is that this situation will occur… So what do you do with them? Allah put them under the authority of the believers…They [enslaved people] have rights. Their children have a shared inheritance. Practically, they enjoy everything a wife enjoys.[49]

Nouman Ali Khan sees slavery as an inevitability in certain historical conditions, such as in times of war. Hence Islam doesn't explicitly forbid slavery because for him, it's easy to imagine situations in which slavery might be revived, and Islamic guidelines will become relevant once more.

Khan's explanation contradicts the historical legal views on *nikāḥ* and sexual relations with enslaved people. It is a dramatic departure from the historical legal scholars' conception of marriage and *nikāḥ* and why a man was permitted to have sexual intercourse with either his wives or the women he enslaved. A man's wife and the same man's concubine were not equal in theory or in practice. The legal tradition permits a male slave owner to marry his slave himself, though she must be freed before she can marry him. An enslaved woman is not automatically married to her enslaver on the virtue of being his slave, as Khan claims. After all, it is the 'valid contract of sexual ownership, or *milk al-bud'a*', that entitles the male enslaver to have sexual access to the enslaved woman.[50] This is precisely one of the major points of scholarship on slavery and the connection between marriage and slavery: the historical legal tradition treats marriage as a form of slavery (*riqq*) and ownership (*milk*). Further, as already discussed, the tradition debates whether a male enslaver can have sexual intercourse with an already married woman he is enslaving, and many scholars forbade it. Kecia Ali shows that enslaved people, men and women, 'could validly marry either other slaves or free persons, though never their own masters or mistresses'.[51] The legal schools grant the master sexual access to the women he enslaved, but once the woman was married, right to sexual access passed to her husband instead.[52] In his discussion, however, Khan is assuming that the woman in question being enslaved in the examples he provides is necessarily single and that she automatically becomes the master's wife through enslavement.

While my respondents did not explicitly reference Nouman Ali Khan or Yasir Qadhi in our discussion on slavery, they share similar views, which might suggest a causal relationship between these preachers' teachings and their audiences' views. Like these scholars, my respondents reference a socio-historical context in which slavery was acceptable, they contest the use of the word 'slave' in the context of Islam, they invoke the idea that Islam commanded kind treatment of slaves, and they have a vastly different idea of sexual relations between the enslaver and the enslaved from what the legal tradition provides. However, the majority of my participants do not believe Islam or Islamic law ever granted men sexual access to the women they enslaved, whereas Yasir Qadhi and Nouman Ali Khan acknowledge it as a man's right. As I show below, Muslims absorb and internalise the discrepancies between the textual sources and contemporary revisions of narratives of (sexual) slavery, and these discrepancies reinforce the idea of a rhizomatic Islam.

While my respondents do not seem to be intimately familiar with the discourse on slavery in either historical or contemporary Islam, their ideas on slavery make sense. As Bernard Freamon argues, while Islamic jurisprudence makes it 'abundantly clear' that there is an Islamic basis for maintaining slavery, Islamic law also can and should abolish slavery.[53] These two points are not necessarily in contradiction with one another. Freamon notes that the unequivocal abolition of slavery is possible Islamically not only because of Islam's notions of justice, freedom, and the equality of all humans, but also because of foundational Islamic legal concepts such as scholarly consensus and public interest.[54] He also points out that 'the Prophet Muhammad actually condemned the capture and sale of free persons. After his death, however, the demands of empire caused jurists to look the other way, ignoring the immorality of what was essentially an illegal trade, and permitting their patrons to get rich on the traffic in human beings.'[55] He provides not only the examples of Muhammad in freeing enslaved people but also those of Muhammad's Companions to support his argument that slavery entered Islam through sources outside of the Qur'an and prophetic examples.

But is slavery truly abolished? Freamon argues that much remains to be done in practically abolishing slavery and its legacies in Muslim contexts, such as in the treatment of migrant workers in the Arabian Gulf. He shows that slavery and slave trading never completely went away, and continue to flourish in the forms of 'human trafficking' and 'modern-day slavery', a bigger problem in the Middle East, per capita, than anywhere else in the world.[56] The Middle East continues to traffick women and girls from East Africa, for example. He also discusses the abuse and violence that families in countries like Jordan, Saudi Arabia, and Oman inflict on their domestic migrant workers, such as through the system of *kafala* (sponsorship) that regulates employment of foreigners.[57] Similarly, Khaled Abou El Fadl writes about a high-ranking Saudi jurist, Shaykh Saleh al-Fawzan, who claims that slavery is still lawful in Islam and should be legalised in Saudi Arabia. Abou El Fadl points out, though, that this jurist's *fatwa* 'seemed to be a part of a theological and moral apparatus designed to legitimate the sexual exploitation of domestic workers in Saudi Arabia'.[58] To insist that the Islamic legal rulings on slavery no longer apply because slavery does not exist anymore is therefore an injustice to those who do endure forms of slavery.

SEXUAL SLAVERY IN LAY MUSLIM PERSPECTIVES

As the chart below shows, only 5 of my 40 respondents 'completely agree' that Islam permits slavery, while 20 believe that it does not. None, however, believe that Islam supports slavery *today*, since all those who believed Islam supports slavery qualified their opinions with 'in the past'.

Table 8: Islamic law permits slavery.

Scale	Single Women	Single Men	Married Women	Married Men	Total*
1 (completely disagree)	3	7	5	5	20
2	1	1	0	0	2
3 (It's complicated)	3	1	3	1	8
4	1	1	1	1	4
5 (completely agree)	2	0	1	2	5

* *One of the married male participants declined to answer almost all questions on slavery, citing his lack of knowledge on the subject.*

Let's start at my discussion with the married couple Pamir (65) and Lema (57) of South Asian background, who held similar views on slavery. They agreed that 'those whom your right hands possess' is a Qur'anic phrase that refers to enslaved females – with qualifications. Lema explained, 'But the definition of slave in this age and the Prophet's age is very different. As long as they abide by the rules of slavery in Islam, it's okay.' Pamir agreed. I asked them what Islam says about slavery. Lema: 'Modern times? These days, slavery is for profit. It's a business.' Pamir: 'She's not talking about that, though. She's talking about in general, what is Islam's position on sexual slavery.' Lema clarified:

> Slaves in those times were the women who came after the battles and they were divided among the men, but they were not divided according to their looks [race] or anything. And it was more of protection for the women because they didn't have men to take care of them or to protect them. And keeping in mind, the natural desires of any human beings – women, men – the men were given these women and they could have sexual relations with them. But then those women had their own rights. They were supposed to be treated in an equal manner.

Pamir concurred with this, 'So instead of throwing the women on the street once you conquer them, you take them as your slaves and protect them and take care of them.' Lema continued, 'Yeah. It wasn't like the African slaves brought into America. It's not prohibited, so as long as we abide by those rules, I think it's okay. If not, then it's *ḥarām*.' Pamir added, 'Yeah, there are rules and regulations in Islam, and if the people don't follow them, it's the people's fault, not the religion's.' They both agreed that slavery can be moral or immoral 'depending on the conditions' and that slavery today is permissible 'as long as you follow the rules'. Both assumed that only women could be enslaved and neither considered the possibility of enslaving men.

I now proceed to the rest of my respondents' attitudes towards slavery. As the above and following charts show, Muslims' understandings of Islam's stance on slavery are not only complicated, but their definitions of 'slaves' as well as their idea of 'Islamic' slavery vary widely. The majority of those who believed that Islam did not outlaw slavery argued that it is still impermissible because the context in which slavery would be legitimate today no longer exists.

Table 9: Islam outlawed slavery.

	Single Women	Single Men	Married Women	Married Men	Total*
Yes	5	4	4	6	19
No	4	4	3	2	13
I don't know	1	2	3	1	7

* *Recall that one married male participant opted not to answer most questions about slavery.*

Table 10: Slavery in any form is morally wrong.

	Single Women	Single Men	Married Women	Married Men	Total
Yes	9	7	7	9	32
No	1	2	1	0	4
I don't know	0	1	2	1	4

Few of my respondents were willing to say whether Islam outlawed or permits slavery. Notably, as can be seen in Tables 9 and 10, they largely consider slavery to be immoral but do not all believe that Islam outlawed it. All those who said Islam permits slavery also added qualifiers such as 'but in the past', 'but only if the slaves are treated well', or 'but not the American kind'. Yet 32 of the 40 agreed with the statement 'Slavery of any sort is morally wrong.' They did not view these statements as contradictory because all those who believe Islam 'permits' slavery emphasised that Islam also recognised slavery as an evil and sought to end it, such as by deeming the freeing of slaves a virtuous deed. The contradiction would exist only if Islam considered slavery an evil, while promoting it as a practice, rather than merely allowing it.

The majority view among my respondents was that Islamic law does not permit slavery today. For example, Gahez (77, South Asian male, married) said, 'Slavery is not permitted in these days. So all the questions about slavery are moot today.' Zigar (21, South Asian male, single) and Turan (24, South Asian male, single), explained that because Islam encouraged the freeing of slaves, rather than enslaving people, slavery is impermissible now that it has ended. Turan explained, though, that technically, since slavery is not explicitly impermissible in Islam, Muslims have no right to make it impermissible today, but since it was discouraged, Muslims are not allowed to practise it, either. This made sense to Turan because his point is that were slavery *mandatory* or even *encouraged*, then there would be no possibility to say that 'we should not do it'.

Zigar (21, South Asian male, single), however, insisted that it is absolutely impermissible today, and added that he knew of no scholar of Islam who claims that slavery is permissible:

> The Qur'an didn't say keep slaves; it says free slaves, re-integrate slaves. Slavery is a holding system because we don't have prisons in a giant complex, so while the system exists, use it to the benefit of people. Don't keep it as a means of oppression because oppression is not good. You have the Hadith *qudsi* [a category of Hadith that directly reports God's speech to Muhammad] that 'Oh my servants, I have forbidden oppression for myself, and so I've made it forbidden upon you.' You can't take these contradictory ideas and say that they're compatible. I've never met a scholar of the religion…that believes that this is permissible.

In other words, slavery is inherently oppressive, and Islam encourages freeing slaves, not maintaining them. Once slavery has ended, Muslims have no divine permission to revive it because God has forbidden all forms of oppression.

Others believed that the form of slavery that Islam approves of is actually servitude, not ownership or enslavement of other humans. Sultan (41, married male, East African) explained that since only God is the owner of all humans, humans are not allowed to own each other, but one can have servants:

> Islam allows slavery as in serving other humans where your rights are respected… When I was in Africa, we had a maid. She works, and she gets paid, and she's considered almost like a slave. She eats. Some families, they beat her, but I don't believe she should be touched. I don't support that. She's not valued less because of her skin colour… To me, slavery is what Africans went through in the US. I don't believe that should exist right now. To me, working for someone and I have my God-given rights, I'm okay with that. But you can't own people, because in Islam, the owner is only Allah. Allah owns all of us.

He implies that as a servant, a person's rights are protected and respected, which is what Islam expects of those who have servants, or 'maids', or anyone simply working for someone else. He defines slavery as the ownership of individuals because of their skin colour, as with American slavery, and argues that only God can 'own' people. He also believes that Islam outlawed slavery, that before Islam, people did not have any problems with the idea of 'owning' people until Islam came:

> The Prophet said in his last sermon that a black man is not better than a white man, and an Arab is not better than a [non-Arab] man… You're only better than someone based on your work. So the slavery concept that someone's superior than someone else and therefore they can own them, that's not in Islam.

Again, because Sultan conceives of slavery as related necessarily to racial superiority in the way that America subjected Africans historically, it does not exist in Islam. Islam outlawed it, and it is un-Islamic to continue it.

Patang (23, South Asian male, single) agrees with Sultan, stating that when Islam speaks about slaves, it is actually referring to 'servants' or 'secretaries':

> [We have to keep in mind] that the Prophet and the Companions had a different [idea of] slavery than America did… Slaves in those times were more like servants. But when we translate servants in modern-day English, it comes out as slave. Because a slave, according to the Prophet, is a servant that you hire, and he gets to live with you. He [the slave] is free and can do whatever he wants. He's free to leave you if he wants. There's a Hadith of the Prophet that if a slave comes up to you and hands you food and you can tell by the expression of the slave and by the sweat that it took him a lot of effort to make the food for you, then it is obligatory upon you to have the slave sit right next to you and eat with you.[59] That's basically treating the slave equally. It's like a secretary… When past scholars supported slavery, that was mentioned at that time according to the Qur'an and Hadiths, not the slavery we consider it today according to American history… Even today, in Saudi Arabia, every major family has a servant. They're not slaves. They're given equal rights, they're allowed to go wherever they want whenever they want, they're given paid leave, they're given vacation, they're given housing. They're employees of the families, just like you're

> an employee with a company. Would your CEO call you a slave? No, that has a negative connotation to it.

Like Sultan, Patang insists that the kind of slavery that was once permitted in Islam is actually servitude. Patang denies the existence of slaves, invoking his experiences in Saudi Arabia, where the human rights violations of migrant servants are in fact a major problem. Because he cannot imagine an Islam that would allow one to purchase and own another person, he reasons that when past scholars permitted slavery, they were actually speaking about servants, maids, secretaries, and other employees who work for someone in a position of power over them. His reference to a Hadith in which the Prophet Muhammad demands that slaves be fed properly supports his belief that Islamic slavery is merely servitude. For him, certainly, as for nearly all the other respondents, the American form of slavery, in which people were enslaved because of their skin colour and were bought and sold and forcibly removed from their homes, does not exist in Islam; however, also for him, neither does any other form of slavery that involves the ownership of other humans. It is quite apt that Patang invokes the problem of slavery or abuse of domestic servants in the context of slavery, since, as discussed earlier, some Gulf countries are notorious for their exploitation of migrant workers.

A few respondents believed Islam never permitted slavery, in any form. Those who held this position were primarily in the single/unmarried category, although some married respondents also believed this. Wagma (20, South Asian female, single), for example, said:

> I don't think slavery's allowed in Islam. You can have maids and stuff but not enslave them. There was slavery in the pagan times, but Muslims aren't allowed to have them. I think Muslims did have them, though, right? I think if we had them, we treated them well, but from the knowledge I have of Islam, it was never allowed because Islam requires equal treatment of all people.

Yasin (21, unmarried male, Middle Eastern) also explained that 'Islam prohibits slavery. It says no one should have slaves. We should free a slave if we see one.' Khalil (51, married male, Middle Eastern) not only believed that slavery of any form is not permissible today, but he also recited a Qur'anic verse that explicitly declares all humans to be free: 'My interpretation of Islam is that slavery is not allowed, period, ever. The Qur'an says, "*wa khalaqnā insāna ahrāran*" [literally, "And We created the human to be free"].[60] It says, "If we created them free, how can you enslave them?"' This is striking particularly because this verse is not in the Qur'an. However, the saying does appear in *Nahj al-Balāgha* (*Peak of Eloquence*, also *Path of Eloquence*), a collection of sayings of Ali, the Prophet Muhammad's cousin and son-in-law, the first Shi'i imam, that were compiled by Al-Sharīf al-Rāḍī, a Shi'i Muslim scholar from the tenth century. Al-Rāḍī attributes the quote to Ali, who reportedly wrote a will to one of his sons in which he advised, 'Do not make yourself a slave of anything. God has created you a free man.'[61] When I later contacted Khalil to ask if he can find a reference of the verse, he sent me verses 49:13 and 4:1, neither of which explicitly speaks to the freedom granted to humans by divine decree but which Khalil argued should be interpreted to prohibit slavery because they point to the equal dignity and status of all humans in God's view.[62]

While some denied that slavery was ever, even in the past, permitted in Islam, others were uncomfortable with Islam's past acceptance of slavery. Malala (37, South Asian female, married) expressed her personal conflict with what she believed was Islam's position, because Islam never prohibited or outlawed slavery, although it did encourage freeing slaves:

> I'm conflicted, quite honestly. It wasn't prohibited, but Islam encouraged freeing slaves. Slaves were to be treated like your own family; they just didn't inherit from you… I'm on defence quite honestly because it's not prohibited, so, yes, it's [permissible]. But there are very firm guidelines as to what's okay and not. Treatment of slaves, for example. I read a research paper…about why slavery was so prevalent and why West Africans allowed for ships of slaves to be brought to the New World was because slaves there were treated like family. The masters there had no idea what the slaves in the Americas would have to face.

Here, Malala admits being conflicted, indicating she does not share the Islamic position on slavery, but seems to appreciate the rules in place to ensure better treatment. In other words, Islam did not prohibit slavery – although it would have been preferrable to – but it did issue clear guidelines to prevent harm.

Diwa (67, South Asian female, married) also expressed her personal discomfort with the existence of slavery in the Qur'an, although she refers specifically to sexual contact with slaves: 'That is a very problematic thing in the Qur'an - it says it in the Qur'an clearly: whoever your right hands possess, the girl who's working in your house. It is a problem for me. I don't know how to interpret it, and I don't believe in other people's interpretations.' It is a 'problem' for her because of the possibility of sexual exploitation.

Other participants explained that since slavery is not an essential element of Islam, 'the tradition' is opposed to it. Travis (25, single male, white, convert) said:

> Slavery is not an essential of Islam. It was an institution that was regulated in accordance with divine will, but it is not intrinsically something that God loves necessarily. The tradition may argue the opposite, actually. There are scholars from West Africa who took beautiful stances on slavery. There's a scholar who was gifted a slave by the ruler, and he asks the ruler, 'You own this man? He's your slave?' The ruler's like, 'Yeah.' The scholar's like, 'That means I'm your slave, too, because this man and I have the same Lord.'... So slavery is not something that you have to do; it's not something that you even should do.

In other words, since slavery is not an essential, fundamental teaching of Islam, not something required of Muslims to participate in but rather discouraged, it need not be maintained as a social practice. He invokes a story that he attributes to the tradition to argue against it and to conclude from it that at least those who have 'the same Lord' are one people, one group, who are secure in their worship of the same God and cannot be subjected to slavery.[63] If one of them is enslaved, then so are all the others.

Turan's (24, South Asian male, single) attitude towards slavery also rests on the idea that slavery is not integral to Islam and therefore abolishing it would not be contradictory to Islam:

> When society evolves or changes, you can reach an opinion that does not contradict Islam but that is relevant to the day and age you're living in... Islam doesn't promote slavery, and it doesn't say it's an integral part of Islam. Islam actually discourages slavery. So if we reach a point where slavery is no longer acceptable, Islam is completely comfortable with that.

The idea that in order for a practice to be maintained, it must be essential to Islam helps answer the question of how these individuals perceive change in Islam. They imagine a clear set of essential and non-essential values or fundamentals of Islam, and the essential ones cannot change while the non-essential ones can. Altering or rejecting the essential elements of Islam may pose a threat to the foundations of Islam.

It is clear that Muslims not only disagree on what Islam's position on slavery is today but also whether the religion ever accepted it in the past. The dominant opinion, however, appears to be that Islam historically accepted slavery because it was a common practice universally, but it also recognised it as an evil that needed to be eradicated and put in place clear guidelines to minimise its harm. The form of slavery that Islam approved of in the past was not the slavery of the American past but one in which those enslaved were treated with fairness. Now that slavery has been abolished, Islam's goal of eradicating it is met, and it does not need to be revived. It is therefore no longer permissible.

WHAT DOES 'THOSE WHOM YOUR RIGHT HANDS POSSESS' MEAN?

The phrase 'those whom your right hands possess' appears fifteen times in the Qur'an and 'in almost all instances, it legislates rules of behavior in relationships between free male owners and their lawfully owned concubines'.[64] It is typically understood to be a euphemism for the enslaved. However, my respondents offered a wide range of meaning for this term. One of the first questions on sexual slavery that I asked them was if they had ever heard about the Qur'anic phrase 'those whom your right hands possess', or *mā malakat aymānukum,* and if so, what they think it means. Many had heard of it and believed it was probably a reference to slavery, while a few said it had nothing to do with slavery and just meant 'those in your care'. Their understanding of the phrase is not outlandish, however: as Freamon argues, the Qur'anic phrase does not simply refer to an enslaved person but also connotes a specific kind of treatment of the enslaved – the *milk al yamīn* must be treated with honour, kindness, mutuality. He argues that the way the Qur'an uses the phrase as well as the examples of the Prophet and his Companions all 'sought reforms lessening the injustices associated with concubinage'.[65] Thus, even if my respondents are not aware of the discourse on slavery in the Islamic past, their understanding of it is not discordant with Islamic history.

Table 11: Men can have sexual relations with women they enslave.

	Single Women	Single Men	Married Women	Married Men	Total
Yes	4	1	1	1	7
No	5	8	6	5	24
I don't know	1	1	3	4	9

As we've seen in the issue of child marriage, married men and single women had more similar opinions while married women and single men had more in common with each other. For example, 5 married men and 5 single women said that Islam prohibits sexual relations between men and their enslaved females. The greatest number of people who agreed that Islam permits men to have sexual intercourse with their slaves fell in the single category: 4 women. A total of 7 out of 40 individuals said that men were never permitted to engage sexually with their slaves. The category with the most participants who said Islam does not allow such contact between a man and the women whom he enslaves were single men: 8 of the 10 single men believed Islam prohibits it. Of the remaining 2, 1 said he does not know, and the other said, 'Yes, but under a specific framework with specific guidelines', i.e. the rules put in place by historical Islamic law.

Gahez (77, South Asian male, married) was among those who interpreted the Qur'anic phrase 'those whom your right hands possess', or *mā malakat aymānukum*, as a reference to slave ownership of females. 'It was in that context when slavery was common and acceptable by the society. So that doesn't apply today because there is no slavery and there should not be any slavery', he explained. Michael (56, white male, married, convert), who otherwise refused to speak on slavery because he said he had no knowledge about it, said he is not sure if 'it means the same thing in all places, but sometimes it can mean a slave, sometimes a prisoner of war. It may mean both of those.' He added that 'the answer to the idea of intimacy without permission [raping one's slaves], is no, no, no, no. They have to have permission', regardless of status. This is important because he is emphasising that, for him, sexual relations with one's slaves are prohibited without consent. Malala (37, South Asian female, married) responded that the idea of a man's sexual relations with a slave 'is completely against everything Islam stands for. People can justify it however they want, but a) consent is required, and b) Islam says that women and men are supposed to be chaste. How can you be chaste and have sex with someone you're not married to?' Scarlet (27, white female, married, convert) also said, 'if the woman consented, I'd say it was okay, and not because she was scared because she was the slave. Not some weird power dynamics.' Adam (21, South Asian male, single) similarly said, 'Yes [men could have sex with their slaves], but with [the slave's] consent.' These ideas, relevant to modern sensibilities, are contrary to the legal schools' positions, given that none of them consider consent essential for sexual contact between a man and his female slave, or the enslaver and the enslaved.

Some respondents believed the phrase refers to the women of newly conquered communities who must be protected. Selma (48, African, married), for example, said:

> Back then, women were losing their husbands as Islam was spreading, so a lot of the companions and the Prophet, they got all the women to be married to the men to protect them. If you marry them, that's okay. But I've never seen a strong Hadith that says you can sleep with your slaves. Especially without the slave's permission. *Mā malakat* could be talking about your extra wives, not the slaves.

For Selma, the phrase does not refer to enslaved people but to all wives after the first one.

Others had different and differing ideas. Sultan (41, African male, married, convert), suggested the Qur'anic phrase meant 'booty…including women'. Khalil (51, Middle Eastern male, married) replied, 'I don't know. Whatever you think the righteous thing to do is you can do it' – that is, the Qur'anic phrase refers to good deeds. Sandara (20, South Asian female, single) shared Khalil's opinion: 'I always thought it was talking about your good deeds.' For Zalaan (42, South Asian male, married), it means 'anyone under your guardianship', like children. These respondents have heard the term, believe they know its meaning, which makes sense to them, but they have not thought about it more closely because the term is not relevant today.

Clearly, *mā malakat aymānukum* evokes various ideas in Muslims' minds. Whereas some believed it referred to slaves, enslaved females in particular, others believed it had no connection to slavery. Their understanding is not distant from what some contemporary scholars, such as Asifa Quraishi-Landes, argue – i.e. that the Qur'anic phrase *mā malakat aymānukum* does not refer to one's enslaved females and/or that the Qur'an does not support men's sexual relations with their female slaves – but the views expressed by my participants certainly diverge from the textual historical tradition's ideas of slavery and sexual relations with enslaved females. For example, whereas some of my participants believed that sexual relations with slaves could never have been acceptable in Islam because Islam requires marriage for such relations, the legal tradition unanimously allowed men such access, arguably supported by the Qur'an. The dominant idea among my participants' views of sexual slavery is a part of the way that the historical practices and theories of slavery in Islamic contexts undergo revisions as Muslims reflect on past historical issues to make sense of them in contemporary contexts. They continue to project onto and attribute to Islam their vision of a just society, where slavery and other forms of exploitation either are prohibited or practised with compassion and justice. The creative explanations they offer for their opinions and understanding are meaningful: these narratives help them maintain their idea of Islam as a religion of God that continues to guide their sense of ethics and justice.

IS SCHOLARLY CONSENSUS ON SLAVERY BINDING ON TODAY'S MUSLIMS?[66]

Table 12: Islamic law's position on slavery is binding on Muslims today.

	Single Women	Single Men	Married Women	Married Men	Total
Yes	2	3	2	2	9
No	7	4	6	7	24
It's complicated	1	3	2	1	7

As with the issue of child marriage, I include table 2 (on the next page) about whether consensus is always binding.

As table 12 shows, the majority of my respondents (24 out of 40) believed that the *ijmāʿ* position on slavery is not binding. Those who said it is binding did so on the understanding that Islamic law never actually permitted slavery. Those whose views fall under 'It's complicated' explained that the idea of an opinion being binding does not apply in the case of slavery because slavery is not a necessary part of Islam.

Table 2: The consensus of the scholars is always binding.

Scale	Single Women (10 total)	Single Men (10 total)	Married Women (10 total)	Married Men (10 total)	Total
1 (completely disagree)	3	2	3	3	11
2	1	6	2	3	12
3 (I'm not sure)	2		1	2	5
4	1		3		4
5 (completely agree)	3	2	1	2	8

While the majority of the respondents either said simply yes or no, two individuals' views are particularly worth addressing because they point to the complexity of a position's status as binding or non-binding. Zala (26, racially mixed, single female) said that Islamic law's position on slavery, like its position on child marriage, was not a command and therefore it is irrelevant whether the position is binding or not. Only commands are binding, such as if Islamic law had required that all people own slaves and/or have sexual relations with their slaves. Therefore, 'We can't make it *ḥarām*. It's not *ḥarām* in Islamic law. [But that's because] it was normal back then.' Travis (25, single male, white, convert) held a similar position: because it is not something that Muslims 'have to do, or even *should* do', what does it even mean for it to be binding or non-binding? Both Zala and Travis said they are personally opposed to slavery.

Most of the respondents believe that the historical position on slavery or sexual relations with slaves is not binding on Muslims today. What are their criteria for determining whether a posion is binding? Travis and Zala, as well as many of the others who pointed out that slavery is not essential to Islam, offer one possible criterion: in order for a position to be binding, 'it must maintain its value throughout history', Travis said. The position is not binding if any of the following apply: a historical position of consensus does not offer any value to today's Muslims; Islam can survive with a change to that position; or Muslims today collectively disagree with the position.

ANALYSIS AND DISCUSSION

What does it mean that my participants did not all agree on the meaning of 'those whom your right hands possess'? This important disagreement suggests that the Qur'anic phrase can have multiple meanings and that it need not be limited to the meanings attached to it in historical legal and exegetical texts. The disagreement also points to something more striking: the Qur'an uses a euphemism for slaves ('those whom your/their right hand possesses') but no generic, consistent term for 'slave' itself. It uses the term *ama* for 'female slave' (Q. 2:221); *'abd* for 'male slave' (Q. 2:221), although '*abd* is also used in other verses to mean simply a servant of God or a worshipper, as in Q. 17:1, which is specifically referring to Muhammad; *ghilmān* for, arguably, 'slave boys' (Q. 52:24); *rajul* for 'slave man' (Q. 39:29), although *rajul* otherwise means 'man'. This may be what has led some scholars to point out that the permission for sexual relations with slaves is not scripturally supported.

Contemporary scholars have discussed in great detail the ways in which the historical scholars' assumptions that men could have sexual relations with their slaves were incorporated into the legal system and explained through Qur'anic verses, such as those referring to 'those whom your right hands possess'. Kecia Ali's scholarship, for example, has highlighted the ways in which the relationship between slavery and sexuality influenced the legal school's approaches to marriage and sex. Quraishi-Landes writes, 'Because of their presumption that a man may legally have sex with his female slave, classical Muslim jurists draw an analogy between a marriage contract and a contract for sale of a concubine'.[67] Critical of the historical model, Quraishi-Landes states, 'Established Islamic marriage contract law uses the contract of sale as its basic conceptual framework – a model which leads to some uncomfortable conclusions about what is being sold and the role of women's agency in that sale.'[68] She offers a new model for approaching gender, sexuality, and marriage that retains parts of historical jurisprudence while rejecting those parts that are troubling from a contemporary ethical standpoint. She argues, for example, that Muslims today can apply the tool of *ijtihād* (legal reasoning) 'on Islamic marriage law that does not presume an analogy to slavery' to 'create different doctrinal rules than those' established in the historical legal system.[69] She proposes that Islamic business partnership contracts, a precedented field in Islamic legal practice, 'may be a fruitful area for new ijtihad on marriage contract law' because of its emphasis on mutuality, consent, and partnership.[70] I will return to this idea of the relationship between marriage, sex, and slavery in chapter 5 on interfaith marriage.

While most of my participants believe slavery is impermissible today because Islam aimed to eradicate it gradually and succeeded, a few believe that since Islam never prohibited it, it is permissible under certain conditions. As Nouman Ali Khan points out, there may come a time when Islamic rulings on the treatment of slaves are relevant, and he claims that they already are in the case of prisoners of war today. Those of my respondents who believed that slavery may be acceptable in Islam similarly explained that hypothetically a future society could practise slavery again. Since Islam is an eternal and universal religion, there must be a reason it did not explicitly prohibit it. This notion is echoed in the views of some of the scholars whom Karen Bauer interviewed for her study on gender hierarchy in the Qur'an. She conducted an interview with the Iranian scholar Muhammad Ghazizadeh, who believes that once a law has been established, it is fixed and eternal, not open to change, because 'a law is a law'.[71] Bauer asked him about slavery and whether the Qur'anic rulings on slavery are still fixed even though 'we don't have slaves' any more. Ghazizadeh replied, 'This example actually confirms that this is a rule for all time. In one period of time we may use the rule, and in another period, we don't use it, but the rule is fixed.' Similarly, my respondents who were hesitant to say that slavery is impermissible did so because they believe Islam to be a universal religion with wisdom behind each of its guidelines, including the lack of prohibition on something that almost all my respondents believe is immoral.

The meaning of 'Islamic law' changed for my respondents in our discussions on child marriage and sexual slavery, especially the latter. They repeatedly asked if I was talking about 'current Islamic law' when I asked them what they believed 'Islamic law's position' is. The few who were aware that Islamic law and/or Islam had once permitted slavery made sure I understood that was the Islamic law of the past. For the topics on which contemporary mainstream Muslim viewpoints remain aligned with classical *fiqh*, the term 'Islamic law' did not provoke qualification. In those instances, 'Islamic law' and 'Islam' were often interchangeable in our conversations. In contrast, for topics on which mainstream Muslim perspectives diverge from the historical tradition, such as the validity and acceptance of slavery, the respondents described Islamic law as fluid. When participants expressed disagreement with Islamic legal positions they either suspected or were certain were not in line with contemporary notions of human rights, they preferred drawing a distinction between 'Islam' and 'Islamic law'. Rokhan (39, South Asian male, single) said 'Islam' does not allow slavery, but 'Islamic law' does, and therefore, his position is that it is wrong. While discussing slavery, Orzala (33, white female, married) explained that

'Islamic law does not exist on its own, or in a bubble', that today's Islamic law is not the same as that of the past. It was Sangin (69, Middle Eastern male, married) who most explicitly distinguished between Islamic law and Islam, asking me if we could skip the slavery topic because 'it is too difficult for me'. He did not elaborate, and I did not ask for more information. Islam, he said, is a simple religion, clear and reasonable, that does not support or allow oppressing anyone else, but Islamic law and the scholars of Islam allowed for oppressing others by permitting child marriage and slavery. While Islamic law allows slavery and sexual relations with slaves, he argued, Islam prohibits it and outlawed it on the principle that all humans are equal and oppressing others is prohibited.

The participants' views on men's sexual encounters with their slaves were more similar than they were different. All participants who believed that Islam permits men to engage sexually with their enslaved females clarified that the consent of the slaves was still required. Others, both married and unmarried, insisted that since Islam prohibits sexual contact between people who are not married, it would certainly not allow a man to have sexual intercourse with his slaves. Among those who held this position were the individuals who said that 'those whom your right hands possess' refers to slaves – but never in the context of sexual engagement with them. Others found it unfathomable that the Qur'anic phrase would refer to slaves and said, 'it means those under your care'. The assumption that sexual relations with slaves are permissible only with the consent of the slaves also figures in scholarly academic works. Intisar Rabb, for example, claims that not only does the Qur'an generally 'forbid non-consensual relationships between owners and their female slaves', but also that 'the master–slave relationship creates a status through which sexual relations may become licit, provided both parties consent'.[72] In her discussion of consent in sexual relations with slaves, Ali notes that the jurists do not mention the need for consent in relations with slaves. However, since they unanimously allowed for a slave to be married against her will, 'It strains logic to suggest that an enslaved woman is subject to being married off without her consent or against her will to whomever her owner chooses but that he cannot have sex with her himself without her consent.'[73] The female slave's permission was also not necessary for a man to practise withdrawal (*'azl*) as a method of contraception – while the wife's permission was essential.[74] It is therefore safe to assume that the enslaved woman's permission or consent was unnecessary for sexual contact with her.

Finally, my respondents' belief that Islamic slavery was designed to be just is what Bernard Freamon calls emancipatory piety, an attitude that 'provided the building blocks for an emancipatory ethic that colored and sometimes even dominated Islam's theoretical appraoch to slavery since that time'.[75] Freamon offers many examples of this ethical imperative toward social change, including the example of Muhammad himself and his Companions like Abu Bakr.[76]

CONCLUSION

There is a striking generational gap in the perspectives shared by my respondents. While the married and older ones largely believe that Islam does or did permit slavery under certain circumstances and with specific guidelines, the younger and unmarried ones largely believe that the slavery that Islam permits/permitted is, in fact, merely servitude, not the ownership of other humans. This difference can be attributed to the influence of teachers and scholars of Islam who propagate a revised idea of slavery in Islam. The younger generation seems to have absorbed this influence in such a way that it is unimaginable for them that Islam, a religion rooted in the equality of all humans in their view, would ever allow enslaving others. These differences also reveal something important about the way that change occurs: in this case, the older generation's rather positive assumptions about Islam's guidelines on slavery do not really sound like slavery, or at least not the kinds of slavery practised in the Americas. Islam certainly prohibits that kind of slavery, all participants agreed, but the younger generation cannot fathom a different kind of slavery. They make sense of what Islam did permit by giving the institution a different name: servitude.

What does this discussion reveal about the ways that change occurs in Islam? Since most of my participants either implicitly or explicitly distinguish between Islam and Islamic law, the idea seems to be that Islam as a religion of goodness, justice, and equality condemns enslaving other human beings on principle. Islamic law, however, permitted it in the past, but only because it was the reality of the time. Islam never encouraged it or endorsed the institution; it merely acknowledged that it was a practice, and it issued guidelines *through Islamic law* that would enable as good a treatment of slaves as possible. A few did believe that slavery could still be allowed within Islam – but only if those enslaved are treated with dignity and respect, per

Islam's requirements. The majority, however, believed that since slavery no longer (officially) exists, to revive it would be against Islam because Islam strove to abolish it, and it succeeded. Moreover, slavery is not an essential component of Islam. Because it is unnecessary for Islam's survival, it is no longer permissible, and it should not be revived. However, permitting it in the past was not necessarily a problem because there were still guidelines to ensure fairness and past Islamic slavery was not like the slavery of the American past.

For my respondents, Islam and Islamic law are very different from each other in that Islam is more flexible and just, while Islamic law is more inflexible. Even if Islam had once in the past permitted slavery, that permission does not hold today because permissions are not 'binding' – but, as we learn in the coming chapters, prohibitions are. There appears to be a very clear idea of what is 'essential' and 'necessary' for Islam's survival, which determines whether it is binding or negotiable. Since Islam does not need slavery in order to survive or flourish, it cannot be an essential. Importantly, their knowledge of American chattel slavery informs their opinions on Islamic notions of slavery: Islam does not permit the kind of slavery practised in the Americas. This is related to the lack of agreement among my respondents over what constitutes slavery, what slavery means, or what the Qur'an means by 'those whom your right hands possess'. When they invoke Islamic sources to justify their positions on slavery, it is clear that they are aware of Islamic sources, to some extent, and that they are selective about the evidence they use to support their positions, reinforcing the idea of Islam as a rhizome.

Chapter 4

Female Inheritance in Islam

INTRODUCTION

Inheritance laws appear to be one of the areas in Islamic law where there is greatest clarity, supported to an extent by the Qur'an, although the Qur'anic prescriptions are not always sufficient in practice. While the Qur'an tends to be ambiguous in most of its guidelines, particularly gender-centered ones, its laws on inheritance are detailed. The guidelines are complex, and Muslim jurists did not, and do not, agree on the details. One historical point of agreement, however, has been that daughters receive half the share of the sons, or as the Qur'an states, 'to the male [child], a portion equal to that of two females' (Q. 4:11). This point is the most relevant for this study. This ruling is widely known among Muslims, even if they do not know the remaining laws on inheritance, such as who receives what percentage of the wealth after the siblings, or even how much sisters may receive if they have no brothers.

The three authorities who my respondents referenced the most in our discussions – Yasir Qadhi, Nouman Ali Khan, and Yasmin Mogahed – have no publicly available lectures on female inheritance laws in Islam, and so I do not engage those thinkers' viewpoints here. Instead, I cite other popular Muslim preachers, some of whom my discussants referenced, where relevant. I also engage those authorities who propose equal inheritance rights for women.

The current authoritative ruling that daughters receive half the inheritance share of sons is not popularly perceived as unequal or an infringement on Muslim women's rights. In fact, women's right to inheritance in the Qur'an is a commonly invoked explanation for Muslims to argue that Islam supports women's rights and that it in fact revolutionised women's rights in the seventh century, when such a right was not common in much of the world and when women were themselves viewed as property to be inherited upon their husbands' death.[1] Additionally, that women receive half when they have no responsibility towards their families is considered a privilege, as some of my respondents in support of this ruling pointed out.[2]

I provide an analysis of Qur'anic and extra-Qur'anic Islamic laws on inheritance, alternative interpretations of these rulings, and the ways in which contemporary Muslims approach this subject. This chapter pays special attention to how contemporary Muslims are negotiating the traditional guidelines as they attempt to apply them to their lives in circumstances that are different from those in which the laws emerged.

THE QUR'AN AND *TAFSĪR* ON FEMALE INHERITANCE

Three verses in the Qur'an speak of the relative shares of women and men in inheritance. These are 4:11–12 and 4:176. According to parts of Qur'anic verses 4:11-12: 'God directs you [*yūṣīkum*] as regards your children: to the male, a portion equal to that of two females: if only daughters [*nisā'*], two or more, their share is two-thirds of the inheritance; if only one, her share is a half.'[3] Similarly, 4:176 addresses the question of women's shares versus men's as follows: 'If one dies, leaving no child but [only] a sister, she will have half of what he left. And he inherits from her if she has no child. But if there are two [or more] sisters, they will have two-thirds of what he left. If there are both brothers and sisters, the male will have the share of two females.'

The Qur'an does not always afford *all* females a lesser portion than males. As 4:11 stipulates, if the deceased leaves behind parents, both parents receive an equal portion (a sixth of the share). This distribution is subject to qualifications, as the verse continues with exceptions and other details. Verse 4:12 states that grandparents also receive an equal share regardless of their gender, as do the deceased's sisters and brothers. However, daughters receive half of what the sons receive: 'to the male, a portion equal to that of two females'. It is this part of the verse that this study concentrates on, not on women's inheritance laws or inheritance laws more generally.

Muslim scholars, both contemporary and historical, explain the unequal distribution of inheritance by pointing to male responsibility to provide for the women in their family, arguing that half a share is a privilege in the context in which the Qur'an was revealed. According to pre-Islamic customs, they state, women received no inheritance whatsoever and were in fact a part of a deceased man's inheritance.[4] As Ziba Mir-Hosseini points out, the logic was that 'since men provide for their wives, justice requires that they be entitled to a greater share in inheritance'.[5] However, she adds, men's higher portion of inheritance was also 'rationalized and justified by other arguments, based on assumptions about innate, natural differences between the sexes: women are by nature weaker and more emotional, qualities inappropriate in a leader; they are created for childbearing, a function that confines them to the home, which means that men must protect and provide for them.'[6] Because women are presumed to lack the biological capacity to be leaders and providers, men must work and take care of women, on account of their vulnerability. Men's responsibility to provide for women in turn entitles men to a higher share of inheritance to help them fulfill their responsibility. Similarly, amina wadud proposes that when the Qur'anic verse 4:34 speaks of the preference for 'some' (men) 'over others', it is a reference to the higher inheritance portion that males receive, since 'they spend of their property (for the support of women)'.[7]

Medieval scholars, such as Fakhr al-Dīn al-Rāzī (d. 1209), also link male responsibility (and authority) over women to their higher inheritance share.[8] One could argue, therefore – as does al-Rāzī – that inheritance rules are not inherently unjust or unequal but are justified because of the male's responsibility over his female household members. Nor are the verses seen as unjust in their context; they are seen as equitable.

Yet, when these verses on inheritance were revealed, the male members of the early Muslim community were unhappy, felt deprived of their privilege as the only gender to inherit, and challenged the rulings. The pre-modern scholar al-Ṭabarī discusses the conflict between the Prophet Muhammad and his companions. His companions asked him why it was that anyone who had not fought in a battle, or one who had not acquired any booty, should receive any inheritance at all (*wa-laysa min hā'ulā'i aḥadun yuqātilū al-qawma wa-lā yaḥizu al-ghanīma*).[9] They hoped God would retract the ruling, and said among themselves: 'Be silent over this statement in the hopes that the Prophet, peace be upon him, forgets or we ask him to change it.'[10] In other words, Muhammad's male companions struggled to accept this change and questioned the new regulations' legitimacy given that, for them, one's inheritance could be due only to one's participation in battle. These arguments were invoked during a prominent case in the Muslim tradition involving the widow Umm Kajja. When her husband died, his brothers attempted to deny her inheritance by claiming that '"women don't mount horses and don't go into battle" and therefore could not inherit since inheritance is a compensation for the danger of engaging in war'.[11] His brothers' argument was clearly in line with what Muhammad's own companions also believed.

Fatima Mernissi attributes the revelation of the verses on inheritance to the demands and concerns of the women of Muhammad's time about their rights:

> They were so successful that a *sura* [chapter of the Qur'an] bears their name, *sura* 4, An-Nisa ('Women'), containing the new laws on inheritance, which deprived men of their privileges. Not only would a woman no longer be 'inherited' like camels and palm trees, but she would herself inherit... This little verse had the effect of a bombshell among the male population of Medina, who found themselves for the first time in direct, personal conflict with the Muslim God. Before this verse, only men were assured the right of inheritance in Arabia, and women were usually part of the inherited goods.[12]

Mernissi frames the revelation on inheritance as an impediment to male privilege, leading the men in Muhammad's community to protest. The men challenged these rulings because they believed that inheritance, like their relations with women, was a matter 'in which Islam should not intervene'.[13] These new rules affected the men doubly: 'Their inherited goods were reduced, since women, who constituted a good part of it, were no longer included; in addition, they had to share with women the little that remained to be inherited.'[14] Mernissi writes that Muhammad's male companions opposed women's right to inheritance by first rejecting the decree altogether; they then complained to the Prophet and attempted to pressure him to change the laws.[15] Women, however, reported to the Prophet when they were denied inheritance due to them in line with the new verses.

Pre-modern Sunni legal scholars unanimously read the inheritance verses to mean that daughters can receive only half the share that sons receive. As Ibn Rushd recounts, 'Muslims agreed' that daughters receive half that of the sons: the son receives the entire wealth if he is the only inheritor; and in the case of daughters, one alone gets half, but three or more daughters receive two-thirds of the wealth; that is, even where daughters were the only direct heirs, they still had to divide their inheritance with the wider family.[16] The scholars disagreed about the inheritance of two daughters: 'the majority maintained that they get two-thirds, and it is related from Ibn 'Abbās that two daughters get half'.[17] While the scholars clearly disagreed on the nuances of the inheritance, they did agree, by consensus, that daughters receive half the share of their brothers.

The injunctions in the verses, however, are not unanimously accepted as immutable. As the next section discusses, many scholars today reject the idea that the Qur'anic verses on female inheritance are universal and eternal. They instead argue that because of changes in gender roles, with women earning an income and sharing household responsibilities with their husbands, equal inheritance is necessary today.

MODERN AND CONTEMPORARY MUSLIM SCHOLARS ON EQUAL INHERITANCE

Many modern and contemporary Muslim scholars, reformists and liberal as well as more traditionally conservative ones, propose that the historical rulings about female inheritance no longer apply in today's context. Those who support equal inheritance rights for daughters include Ṭāhir al-Ḥaddād (d. 1935), Nasr Hamid Abu Zayd (d. 2010) – and Olfa Youssef, a contemporary Tunisian Muslim feminist scholar who specialises in Arabic linguistics and is the author of *Ḥayratu Muslimah* (translated into English as *The Perplexity of a Muslim Woman*).[18] Besides these individuals, some Muslim-majority countries (as well as Muslim feminist groups) have offered alternative readings of the inheritance verses.[19] These countries include Tunisia, which extended equal inheritance rights to women in August 2017, much to the disgust of many Muslims, including women.[20] In this section, I discuss the above-mentioned scholars' interpretations of the inheritance rulings and their rationales for departing from the previous consensus position, rationales that many of my respondents offered as well.

Ṭāhir al-Ḥaddād, a Tunisian scholar, was critical of the historical *fiqh* positions on various issues, including female inheritance, and urged the re-evaluation of these rulings to suit modern realities. He explains that the reason the Qur'an did not prescribe daughters and sons an equal share in inheritance is that 'it was difficult for Arabs and people from other nations who converted to Islam to accept the new laws of inheritance since the man assumed on his own the responsibilities for providing for his family and defending them as well as his tribe and his people [in warfare]'.[21] However, these conditions are no longer met, and women are 'fully engaged in all areas of life as a consequence of the changes in attitudes that have occurred over time'.[22] Women have now attained their independence and look after their own affairs, their achievements proving that 'their previous condition had nothing to do with gender, but was merely one of many chapters in social evolution'.[23] Therefore, he explains, 'Islam in essence does not contest such equality in all aspects since the causes of man's superiority over woman have vanished.'[24] Islam merely prescribed the rulings as they are in the Qur'an in response to the social order of the time.

Nasr Hamid Abu Zayd, an Egyptian scholar, interprets the Qur'anic verses on inheritance to mean that daughters must receive a minimum of half what their brothers receive, and the brothers can receive a maximum of double their sisters' portion. This is because, as he writes, 'prescribing a half share for the female was a great forward step in a context when inheritance was for males who were able to fight; male children and females were excluded'.[25] His holistic reading of the Qur'an allows him to believe that 'the world of the Qur'an, on the cosmological level as well as on the ethical-spiritual level, sustains absolute human equality'.[26] He argues that gender discrimination on the societal level, however, is extra-Qur'anic, rooted in the *fiqh* literature (jurisprudence) 'due to a certain cultural and socio-historical context', rather than in the Qur'an itself.[27] He agrees with other scholars, whom he cites, among them Munawir Sjadzali (d. 2004), that the Qur'anic text must be re-interpreted according to the Muslim community's social circumstances. Abu Zayd views the Qur'anic laws on inheritance as contextually based and inapplicable to Muslims' current realities where the idea of female inheritance is no longer revolutionary but instead a basic human right.

Olfa Youssef, a Tunisian feminist scholar, challenges the historical ruling and its application to contemporary Muslim life. In *The Perplexity of a Muslim Woman*, her discussion on inheritance focuses on Q. 4:176, which reads, 'if one dies, leaving no child but a sister, she will have half of what he left... But if there are two sisters [or more], they will have two-thirds of what he left. If there are both brothers and sisters, the male will have the share of two females.' Youssef disagrees with Ṭabarī's position that 'based on precedence', the *Sunnah* (in this case meaning the inherited tradition) 'cannot be doubted' – that is, by virtue of being results of scholarly consensus, these interpretations are correct and not subject to doubt.[28] She recounts the Hadith report in which the widow of Sa'd Ibn Rabi' expressed her complaint to the Prophet that her husband had died and left behind two daughters and a brother, and the brother had usurped the entire inheritance. The Prophet summoned the brother and ordered him to 'pay two thirds to [the deceased's] daughters, one eighth to his wife, and to you the rest'.[29] While this report supports the traditional interpretation of the verses that daughters are to receive half the inheritance of their brothers, Youssef takes from this that the Prophet intervened in a man's effort to deny women their inheritance, however much it was. In another Hadith, with different individuals involved, a man died and left behind his three daughters and a wife. Two men from his paternal side claimed his wealth. His wife approached the Prophet to demand her share of the inheritance, and Qur'anic verse 4:7 was revealed: 'For men [it] is a share of what the parents and close relatives leave, and for women [it] is a share of what the parents and close relatives leave, be it little or much – an obligatory share'. The Tunisian scholar Muhammad al-Ṭāhir Ibn 'Āshūr (d. 1973) dismisses the Hadith involving Sa'd's wife because 'it is not appropriate to determine the share of two females because in his account, there is disagreement whether the daughters left behind were two or three'.[30] He rejects the Hadith because of what Youssef views as a minor discrepancy in the number of daughters involved, a point that is irrelevant to the Hadith's message. Youssef views this rejection as commentators and scholars allowing 'themselves to distort the explicit meaning of the text in violation of that which is linguistic and historical'.[31] She questions Ibn 'Āshūr's claim that God's intention in verse 4:137 is to emphasise the double portion that men are entitled to. Youssef asks, 'Why isn't it possible that God's silence over the share of two females is at the same time a silence over the share of the male, implicitly opening up the door for *ijtihad* (independent judicial reasoning) in the question of inheritance which like all legislations and laws is closely tied to its historical context?'[32] The historical context that made women entitled to an inheritance is essential, for Youssef, to proposing re-interpretations of inheritance rules in Islam.

The dominant scholarly view that unequal inheritance rights for sons and daughters remain unaltered is an example of preserving historical rulings through new justifications. While contemporary Muslim scholars justify the unequal distribution of inheritance by referencing male responsibility over female family members, pre-modern scholars had other rationales. As Youssef points out, classical and pre-modern scholars did not hesitate to explain the rulings as proof that God favours men over women, which is no longer used as a justification to support the ruling.[33] It is interesting that while the justifications have clearly changed, as have the realities – since women are contributing financially to their households in larger number than likely they did in the seventh century – the ruling remains the same.

The individuals discussed above are departing from the more traditional, historical viewpoint on inheritance, but the dominant opinion of Muslim authorities remains that the Qur'an requires that daughters receive only half (maximum allotment). This literal approach to the Qur'an 'results in the interpretation that Muslims should literally adhere to the above verses at all times and in any situation, without looking at the changing roles and responsibilities of men and women'.[34]

CONTEMPORARY LAY MUSLIM RESPONSES

Almost all of my participants were aware that the existing laws of inheritance grant daughters half the share of the sons. Those who were familiar with the ruling offered the explanations discussed above – that is, that sons receive a larger portion because they are financially responsible for the women in their families, including their sisters and their wives. Women in both single and married categories were more likely to disagree with this majority ruling, arguing that this does not apply in a context where men cannot be relied upon to take care of the women in their lives, while the married men were more likely to support the ruling. I organise the discussion below into four of the main questions I asked my respondents: whether daughters' share of inheritance in Islam is half that of sons', whether a daughter's inheritance *should* be half that of a son's, whether the respondent's daughters and sons would receive an equal share of inheritance, and whether the existing consensus on this matter is binding.

As the chart below shows, most of the respondents are familiar with the idea that daughters receive half the inheritance that sons are entitled to. Only three individuals disagreed, and one was uncertain. This means that 36 out of the 40 individuals (90%) of my participants are aware of the majority ruling.

Table 13: In Islamic law, a daughter's inheritance is half that of a son's.

	Single Women	**Single Men**	**Married Women**	**Married Men**	**Total**
Yes	9	8	9	10	36
No	1	2	0	0	3
I'm not sure	0	0	1	0	1

However, as table 14 shows, only 12 out of 40 (or 30%) of the respondents personally agree that daughters' inheritance should be lower than sons', and 22 out of 40 (55%) do not personally agree with the idea that daughters' inheritance should be half that of sons'. This distinction is important because it shows that there is an openness to disagreeing with Islamic legal rulings even if they are believed to be clearly articulated in the Qur'an. Most of my respondents are aware that inheritance rulings are outlined in the Qur'an, or at least that the Islamic legal rulings stem from the Qur'an directly. When they disagree with the current ruling, then, they are disagreeing with the predominant traditional interpretation of the Qur'anic verses on inheritance. These individuals' critical engagement with the Qur'anic text reflects their own realities and contexts. Given that the ruling does not appeal to participants' sense of justice in a contemporary setting, or even according to their sense of justice as concluded from their overall understanding of the Qur'an, they believe it is acceptable to hold the opinion that the rulings are unjust for their times.

Table 14: I think a daughter's inheritance should be half that of a son's.

	Single Women	**Single Men**	**Married Women**	**Married Men**	**Total**
I agree	3	2	2	5	12
I disagree	6	6	6	4	22
I'm not sure	1	2	2	1	6

When I asked them what they knew the inheritance guidelines to be in Islam for sons and daughters, almost all said, 'half for girls'. Most did not explain further until I asked them if they knew why this was the case. Others first explained why the distribution was unequal and then said what the ruling was. In the latter case, they wanted to clarify their position and Islam's position so as not to be misunderstood, carefully stating that while the Qur'an ordains half a share for daughters, they themselves support an equal share.

That the wisdom behind the ruling is male responsibility over females is widely known. Sultan (41, African male, married), for example, explained that daughters receive half because 'when a man gets married, he's expected to provide, not the woman. I'm not gonna have my daughter get married and do her husband's job.' Since it is exclusively a man's responsibility to provide for his family, Sultan understands, when a woman works with the intention of providing for her family, she is assuming men's responsibilities. In fact, Sultan made it very clear that all men should be working to take care of their families, and if they cannot find a well-paying job, they need to switch careers so they can fulfill their God-ordained responsibilities. He believes women pursuing jobs and careers creates more obligations for them, on top of the duties they already have, which are demanding enough. His wife, he said, does not work; she has no need.

While many others did not share Sultan's opinion that it is always a man's job to provide for his family, they did explain the traditional ruling in terms of male responsibility. According to Barsala (31, South Asian female, married), for example, the Qur'anic laws of inheritance are not relevant anymore because they reflect the context in which they were revealed, where women's source of income was their husband or other male family members. To accommodate that expectation, the Qur'an stipulated that the man receive a larger share so he has a sufficient amount to spend on his family. This is no longer the case, however, she said, since women now have more access to financial independence. Orzala (33, married female, white), also stated that the ruling is 'rooted in the assumption that the men will take care of the women'. Athena (21, single female, convert, of mixed background), said that men receive a higher portion because 'traditionally, men are the breadwinners. At least women get something, so at the time, maybe that was progressive.' None of the women, married or unmarried, believed that women do not need to or should not work. However, several did say that it is the husband's job to provide for his family whether the wife works or not. A few of my married female participants (e.g. Orzala and Malala) earn their own income, but they do not spend it on their families because, they said, that is their husband's responsibility. Some mentioned that they do buy gifts and other items for their family with their money, but that essential household expenses, such as bills, were their husband's Islamic obligations.

Not all participants were certain about the rationales behind the distribution. Selma (48, married female, African background) assumed it was because of male responsibility over females, but she disagrees with both the reason and the ruling strongly:

> I really don't know [why it's half for daughters]. I'm so confused. I think because the women, they get support from the husbands, and the man has to support the family? I strongly disagree with this. I don't get it… But I know that in Islam, there are ways to get around this. Like you can give a *hadiya* [gift], like leaving a will where you can be fair to both sons and daughters. So in the will, it can be different.

Strongly opposed to the ruling, Selma believes that there are ways to subvert the stipulations in order to give equal shares to sons and daughters while remaining faithful to the traditional ruling. Not only does she explicitly disagree with the Qur'anic text, but she is also informed about ways to work around the text to allow a more equal distribution.

Amadou (40, married male, Black) also stated that 'in Islamic law, daughters get half what the sons get. But that doesn't sit well with me.' He recognises that the rulings are grounded in past realities: 'The reality back then was that the man has to get out and work to provide for the family. But that's not the case today.' Similarly, Diwa (67, married female, South Asian background) said, 'I don't think women should get half. The *sharīʿa* says that, but I disagree with it.' Rokhan (39, South Asian male, single) expressed profound discomfort with the ruling, saying that it makes him question Islam:

> I know that there is a greater percentage that goes to sons than to daughters. This is an area where I'm confused because this is very specifically mentioned in the Qur'an, to my knowledge… Normally, when something doesn't make sense, it comes from the Hadiths and whatnot; but this is explicitly in the Qur'an, and it makes no sense to me…it really bugs me. Quite honestly, it sometimes makes me question Islam.

His attempts to rationalise it, he said, still don't explain why the guidelines are in the Qur'an. If they are rooted in a specific context that differs dramatically from the context in which he lives today, it makes no sense that the Qur'an would be so explicit on them:

> To me, [the existing ruling] makes more sense in a historical context when men were the main earners of [income for] the household, but in this day and age, particularly in this society, where women earn just as much as men, and you've got stay-at-home husbands as well, I don't think it makes sense.

For others, the existing rulings have always been generous for women. Malala (37, married female, South Asian origin), for example, said:

> Men have twice as much as women. In a perfect world, where everybody was distributing what they were supposed to, then women would still end up with a very comfortable life. I would inherit from my father, my husband, my brother, and any children that I may have, sons or daughters [if they die before me]… And any money I make as a woman is mine alone; I'm not obligated to spend it on my husband or family or anyone else, but if I do so, I am doing it as a charity and I get rewarded for it. So this is very generous in a perfect world. I think Islam is very ahead of its time with this concept.

Like several other participants, she reiterates that the ruling works comfortably 'in a perfect world', where everyone follows the rules, and men fulfill their responsibilities towards their families. In such a case, a woman ends up with more because she is not required to spend her inheritance on anyone. Malala recognised that the ruling assumes that all men will be responsible enough to take care of the women in their lives, but that this is a flaw in the way that society functions, not in the Islamic rulings themselves. The ruling must remain in place as it is, for Malala, because it cannot be changed simply because people do not fulfil their roles.

Clearly, all participants who were familiar with the idea that sons are entitled to a higher portion of inheritance believed that the ruling stems from the notion of male responsibility to women. Most support changing this ruling in order to fit the reality in which they operate today, while others believe in maintaining the guidelines as they are because they can be beneficial to women if followed properly – in an ideal world.

Their responses varied on the question of whether they would grant their children an equal share in inheritance regardless of their gender. According to table 15, more single women – than the rest of the categories – said they would. Only 1 single woman said she would not give an equal share, and another 1 was unsure. The least likely category to agree with this statement was married men, although an equal number of them agreed and disagreed with the statement (4 agreed, 4 disagreed). Those respondents who expressed that their children would receive an equal share regardless of their gender did not believe their statements contradicted Islam's guidelines, although they had previously stated otherwise. Many invoked the idea that these laws do not work in a context like today's where men do not uphold their responsibilities as fathers, brothers, husbands or sons.

Table 15: My children, sons and daughters, will receive an equal share in inheritance.

	Single Women	Single Men	Married Women	Married Men	Total
I agree	7	5	5	4	21
I disagree	1	2	2	4	9
I'm not sure	2	3	3	2	10

Those who stated that they are uncomfortable with the existing ruling and will not apply it in their lives included Barsala (31, South Asian female, married), who said, 'I know Islam does say daughters should have half, but I don't personally like that, and I don't plan to leave my daughter half. So I personally won't follow that.' Orzala (33, married) also supports the idea of equal shares, saying that her own children would all receive an equal share 'independent of who's working more and all'. Selma (48, married) was not sure about how she feels but believes that giving daughters an equal share is allowed and she will definitely do that.

There is much resistance to the existing laws among single participants. Sarbaz (28, South Asian male, single), for example, 'fundamentally disagree[s] with the reason behind why daughters receive half the share of sons' and does not believe Muslims are obligated to follow the consensus. It gets complicated, however: he believes that Muslims who recognise and accept the ruling that daughters are to receive half the share but still work around the law using bequests to equalise the children's inheritance 'are cheating God'. For him, the more honest and appropriate way to deal with the current consensus is to reject and challenge it without finding 'loopholes'.

Another respondent, Rokhan (39, South Asian male, single), finds the inheritance rulings to be very confusing, he says. He is confident that God's true intent is justice and fairness, and given the historical context in which the Qur'anic verses of inheritance are revealed in – male leadership, men as financially responsible for the family, etc. – the rules may have been fair at the time. However, today, they 'go against any understanding of Islam's greater moral guidelines. So even if I have to go against the law, I'd give my children equal shares in inheritance because I believe that's what God would want for us today. So the scholars' consensus is not binding on us today.' Similarly, Yasin (21, Middle Eastern male, single) does not believe the rules of inheritance should have anything to do with gender: they should 'depend on who is smarter' and should be determined on a case-by-case basis, not generalised. He admitted to not knowing what the Islamic ideals were but maintained that they should not be based on gender.

Several respondents suggested that the existing rulings would work well only in a world where men followed the rulings in the Qur'an – but unlike Malala (37, married female, South Asian origin), who believes the rulings should remain as they are, these individuals support modifying them. Naghma (23, unmarried, female, of South Asian origin), for instance, said that her own children would receive an equal share because the social structures necessary for the Qur'anic rules on inheritance to prosper do not exist today:

> I feel like these things can be applied only when everything else can be applied as well. In an ideal world, a woman would be provided for by her husband…so she wouldn't even need any of that inheritance. But these days, that sort of structure doesn't exist everywhere, and men don't fulfill that obligation. So I feel like we can't just take one law and think that's it without context.

For her, this stance is not contradictory to the Qur'an because 'I feel like whatever you think is morally right in today's world, Islam probably does not ban it.'

Similarly, Wadaan (21, unmarried male, South Asian origin) believes that the law as it exists currently has 'economic reasons' (i.e. man as the breadwinner gets a higher portion of inheritance), but he disagrees with this thinking in today's time, and his own children will get an equal share regardless of gender. This is because 'I feel like no one really lives in a Muslim society today, so that it'd be fair to do that [follow the Islamic legal ruling]' – that is, it might *not* be fair to follow the traditional legal rulings.

One respondent, Zala (26, single female, racially mixed background), was not uncomfortable with the existing rulings but believes in equal inheritance portions for sons and daughters. For her, the Qur'an is 'pretty clear' on inheritance rules, 'but in Islamic law, it's pretty complicated'. She plans for her own children to receive an equal share. When I asked her if she believes there is a discrepancy between her belief that equal inheritance is allowed and the Qur'anic ruling, she said, 'No, because I have a third [of my inheritance] that I can mark out [and do whatever I want with it]. So I'd make it work out that way.' Since according to the rules, once she has distributed two-thirds of the inheritance in accordance with what she believes the law requires, the remaining one-third can be distributed among the daughters so as to equalise their share.

While Scarlet (26, married female, white, convert) was not uncomfortable with the rulings as they are and believes that Muslims should try to work with the existing guidelines, she does support equal inheritance rights:

> I'm probably not gonna be passing on much because I'm a stay-at-home mom. I'm like in today's financial times, you can really take advantage of a woman the way that things are...because the sons are supposed to take care of their sisters...I can see in a system where all of the men in a woman's life are obligated to take care of her. But if the men don't practise Islam but want Islamic inheritance, then no, especially if a woman marries a non-Muslim man who won't honour this obligation and her brothers don't protect her, this is a problem. I think in today's world and system, it's okay if brothers and sisters receive an equal share.

For her, then, as with a few others, men's higher inheritance portion is contingent upon their recognition of the greater responsibility that accompanies their inheritance share. It is also contingent upon whether they practise Islam properly. There is a direct correlation between a man's proper practice of Islam and his fulfilment of his responsibilities because any good practicing Muslim man would be aware of his responsibilities and fulfil them.

Some respondents stated that whether their children will receive equal shares will depend on various factors. For Michael (56, married male, white, convert), a major factor is the sons' *taqwa* (God-consciousness). He said:

> No [my children will not receive equal shares]. Because the boys have the obligation to provide for the girls. There's an exception, though. If I recognise that my boys don't have any *taqwa*, then there has to be a process to deal with that. But the ruling is clear.

Abigail (39, married female, white), too, said, 'I would allow [equal shares], but I would also allow the traditional way of giving the son more as long as he's of sound mind, moral, and responsible. I'm not opposed to either one. But if my son turns out to be immoral, I would not give him more.' For them, then, the rulings are not absolute, and not all sons are entitled to a higher share in inheritance.

Others believed that the current guidelines must be maintained because, since they are Qur'anically grounded, there must be wisdom behind them that human beings may not comprehend. Malala (37, married female, South Asian origin), for instance, said, 'I'd probably align with the Islamic distribution, but it'd be my responsibility to make sure that my sons understand that it's their responsibility to take care of their sisters.' Sandara (20, female, unmarried, South Asian) believes that the consensus on inheritance is not binding for all Muslims everywhere but that Muslims should still try to follow the guidelines as they are because 'there's a reasoning for it even if we don't completely understand it'. The idea that humans do not always comprehend God's wisdom came up in my conversations with Sangin (69, married male, Middle Eastern background) as well, who said 'I don't have any reasons for it, but it's the law of Allah, and I accept that.'

Patang's response is particularly useful here. While he has never thought about the issue before, he says that when it becomes relevant to him, he'll go with whatever Islamic law says – 'if I even have any inheritance to leave!' However, he believes that the law applies only if there is no will; if there is a will, the person is not required to follow the Islamic legal guidelines. This is not the understanding that most of my other respondents hold. Table 16 below captures their response to the question of whether the existing scholarly consensus is binding and must be maintained.

Table 16: The consensus on female inheritance is binding today.

	Single Women	Single Men	Married Women	Married Men	Total
I agree	4	5	4	7	20
I disagree	6	3	5	3	17
I'm not sure	0	2	1	0	3

Should the share be equal if women are contributing to their households?

Since my respondents all explained that the ruling exists because of the assumption that males are providing for their female family members, I asked them if they believe that the shares should be equal if women are contributing to their households, especially if they are the primary breadwinners. While most agreed that this should be the case, a few suggested that the point was not whether women are working or contributing to their households or not; it is that they are not obligated to do so and men are. Essentially, then, women's contributions to their household income are always a choice, even if they work out of necessity.

Some acknowledged that the rules are perhaps flexible. According to Orzala (33, married female, white):

> I think the laws are probably flexible for every family… I don't think men in this society take care of their sisters or anybody else… I don't contribute to our household at all. I work, and my husband works, but his money is our money, and mine is mine alone. I can do whatever with it that I want… If my husband dies, I would assume I'd get all the money and pass it on to my daughter. If I die, I wouldn't leave any to my husband or daughter; I'd give it to my parents and my sister who would need it more.

Since her husband works and provides for her and her daughter, she expects that her daughter will not need her (Orzala's) inheritance. Instead of leaving her inheritance to her daughter or husband, she will distribute it between her sister and mother because they need it more. In other words, whether someone is entitled to inheritance or not is a matter of need and not of gender.

Others explained that whether women work or not is not relevant to the discussion. Zala (26, single female, racially mixed background) explained that 'the idea is more about responsibility. The woman can work or not, but the man is still responsible… I don't think you've to change the law to allow the woman to get equal. You just take that one-third you can do whatever with.' Michael (56, married male, white, convert) agrees: 'I don't think that would change anything. The responsibility is still on the man to provide for his family. I could see other criteria that would change this ruling, like his *taqwa* [God-consciousness]. Making or not making money is not part of the equation.' For Abigail (39, married female, white), not only do women not need an equal share, but they also should not work because working to provide for their family would add more pressure on them:

> I don't think a woman should receive an equal share just because she works and earns an income of her own. I think that's just more pressure on women to work and be out in the workforce and I just feel like unless that's absolutely necessary, that's not the ideal way to be. I think it's acceptable for women to work if there's need, but I just see so many cases where it's not a need. If it's a choice, that's fine, but I don't think that's preferable… I don't work.

Sultan (41, married male, East African) shared this perspective, suggesting that there should never be a reason for a woman to work – she should only ever work out of genuine desire:

> I'm sure Allah knows best, but we can't make exceptions to Allah's rulings. We should be changing our environment, not Allah's rulings or making our wives work. If I'm not making enough, maybe I need to get a new job, maybe I need to move somewhere else, maybe I need to gain new knowledge for promotion… Islam doesn't forbid a woman to work, but the husband is expected to shoulder the expenses. What a woman does by choice is fine, but she cannot be forced.

Among those reluctant to support modifying the existing inheritance guidelines if the wife contributes equally to the household was Sandara (20, unmarried, female, South Asian), who said, 'I think the scholars should interpret it and figure this out. Because what if the sister is really old and the brother is really young, and he gets the inheritance but she's the one taking care of him? Shouldn't she get more?'

As with their views on the other questions above, the respondents' approaches to the question of whether a female breadwinner should receive an equal share of inheritance varied. While some absolutely supported modifying the rulings in such circumstances, others believed that perhaps the ruling does not need to change but the circumstances should (e.g. the men in her family need to fulfill their responsibilities, or find better jobs); yet others suggested that the rulings should be equal regardless of who earns an income or a higher income.

ANALYSIS AND DISCUSSION

Here, I address some of the important points from my discussions with participants on inheritance. These points involve: explanations of the complicated relationship that Muslims clearly have with the Qur'anic text or with Islamic legal rulings and what they (plan to) do in practice; an acknowledgment of my respondents' own circumstances and lived reality, which shape their opinions; and a gap in the rationales provided, not just by respondents but also by historical and contemporary scholars, for the unequal distribution of inheritance between sons and daughters.

First, a striking result in this discussion is that while almost all (36 total) respondents agreed that Islamic law designates for sons twice the share of daughters, a little more than half (21 total) said that their own children will (or would hypothetically, if they currently have no children) receive an equal share. They reasoned that the Qur'anic guidelines are not relevant in an American context or generally in today's global context, where women work often out of need. These individuals justified their position by linking existing inheritance laws with income-earning, whereas those in support of the historical position of consensus argued that these rules have no relation with income-earning; they represent a male's responsibility towards his female family members and the females' entitlement to being taken care of. Thus, the Qur'anic verses on inheritance must be contextualised, they explained, in order to make sense of them in accordance with current social norms.

Second, the opinions expressed in these interviews appear to be rooted in the individual respondents' current financial situation. For the men, if they are currently employed and make enough money to provide for their families and do not need additional income for support, they believe that all men are responsible financially for their families, whether or not their wives work. While all the women believe that men are financially responsible for their families, the single women were likely to admit that that is not always the reality, and so men should not be entitled to a higher portion of inheritance. Among the individuals who support the existing rulings were married women who work but said they do not contribute to their household expenses and that their husbands financially take care of them, as well as married men who work and recognise their responsibilities over their families. Few of these men's wives worked at the time the interview took place. The single women, however, fear that the distribution allotted to them, which they perceive as unequal, denies them access to wealth in a way that jeopardises their rights because they do or will likely work out of necessity.

Sa'diyya Shaikh would identify what my respondents are doing here as a '*tafsir* through praxis', as discussed earlier in the book.[35] That a majority of my respondents, men and women, speak about the changes in social norms and in their personal realities as grounds to interpret the Qur'anic verses on inheritance to allow for equal inheritance means that they do not view the Qur'an as an unchanging, fixed set of rules.

Third, those who support the existing rulings on inheritance explained that the reality of whether a woman works or not plays no role in why her share is half. They explained that the issue at hand was not one's circumstances but the fact that Islam has placed on the man the responsibility of providing for his family. Thus, whether a woman works or not does not affect the ruling. All participants, regardless of their opinions, assumed that the rulings are rooted in male financial responsibility when asked why they believe daughters receive a half share. Yet, as Olfa Youssef asks, if the double share of men is because of their financial obligations towards their families, then why do women receive any portion of inheritance at all 'since all of [their] expenses are covered by the man'?[36] As several of my respondents pointed out, it is irrelevant whether a woman works or not; the husband is obligated to provide for her and the rest of his family.

Fourth, I want to reiterate here that none of my respondents who support equal inheritance rights believed that they were contradicting the Qur'anic message. For them, because the Qur'an's overall message is one of justice, it would in fact be an injustice to today's Muslim families if daughters did not receive an equal share. They also emphasised the historical roots of the ruling as based on the assumption that all men take care of the women in their families and/or that women are not financially responsible for their families. Since female-run households are common today, the change in family dynamics then legitimates the opinion supporting equal inheritance ruling.

Finally, my respondents' complex views on inheritance resemble the views espoused by Muslims universally on the question of female inheritance rights, including the gendered support for equal inheritance rights. According to a study conducted by the Pew Research Center in 2013, 'in 12 of the 23 countries where the question was asked, at least half of Muslims say that sons and daughters should have equal inheritance rights'.[37] The distribution varies, however, by region, such that 76% of the Indonesians surveyed support equal inheritance rights, 15% support them in Morocco and Tunisia each, 88% in Turkey, and 30% in Afghanistan.[38] The views also vary based on the nation's legal attitudes towards inheritance – i.e. 'levels of support for equal inheritance by sons and daughters is often more widespread in countries where laws do not specify that sons should receive greater shares'.[39]

The opinions of many Muslims today contradict those of the historical Muslim legal tradition. That a son is entitled to a higher share of inheritance makes sense to Muslims even if they are aware that the ruling rests on assumptions that the men in women's lives do indeed fulfill their responsibilities. Since this is not always the case, according to my respondents, men and women should in today's time be entitled to an equal share. For many of them, to not provide equal shares in a context like today's would be a violation of the Qur'anic ideal of justice and fairness and the spirit of inheritance guidelines.

CONCLUSION

Many scholars, and many lay Muslims, including some of my respondents, contextualise the Qur'anic verses on inheritance to argue that in the context in which the inheritance rules were revealed, it was a great justice to women to receive a share in inheritance. Given this context, the verses indicate Islam's attempt to improve women's rights. Moreover, since males are required to take care of their female counterparts, the inheritance portions assigned to women suggest that they are in fact receiving a privilege, since their inheritance (theoretically) belongs solely to them, whereas men are required to spend theirs on their families. In the seventh century when women's inheritance rights were revealed, the Qur'an was doing something revolutionary, as contemporary scholars of Islam and some of my respondents have pointed out. If, as Fatima Mernissi suggests, the message of the Qur'anic verses is understood to be to speak up in favour of the marginalised and to be a force of revolutionary rights for them, and to always pursue and implement justice, then the verses should not be implemented literally.

Since the context in which the verses were revealed originally does not reflect my discussants' context, as the above discussion shows, most of them support equal inheritance for daughters and sons. It is striking that the majority of those who supported existing laws on inheritance for daughters were married men, who appear to be supporting their wives or families. They explained that the current laws are not unequal but are actually fair because women are not financially responsible for their families; only men are. Even women who work and provide for their families, whether out of necessity or of personal choice, are not financially responsible for their families. Women's choice to work and earn an income is irrelevant to the discussion of inheritance, these (married male) respondents argued. By contrast, most female participants, single and married, as well as half of the single men, disagreed with this line of thinking and suggested instead that these laws are in fact unfair for today's context because women do in reality work, many out of necessity, and that this should change the conversation on inheritance laws.

An important conclusion from this discussion, then, is that female inheritance laws *are* being renegotiated, and those individuals who have been or are negatively affected by the current laws oppose them. Besides the relevance of gender in these conversations, however – because those who opposed these laws are primarily women – the respondents' generation bears relevance as well: that single (i.e. younger) men supported equal inheritance laws for sons and daughters is significant because their support for equal distribution shows that current broader discourses on gender equality are creating an awareness of women's rights in the minds of younger generations of Muslims. Their own lived reality is an important motivator for change. Inheritance laws are based on assumptions that the younger generation does not believe reflect current realities in their American context. There is a general sense or expectation that these (currently unmarried) men's wives may have to work, or may work, and thus be entitled to an equal share of inheritance. Thus, while the older generation of my respondents do not perceive a relationship between earning an income and existing inheritance laws, the younger generation does, because they can rationalise the existing laws solely on the basis of men's working to support their families. None of the participants, however, believe that women should or are required to work. All participants acknowledged a man's responsibility over his female family members.

Finally, the shift in attitude regarding existing inheritance laws among my respondents, most of whom acknowledge that their views depart from the position of consensus on the subject, reaffirms my overall conclusion in this book: the negotiables and non-negotiables of Islam are determined based on their perceived relevance, or lack thereof, to the lives of individuals and groups. When an existing ruling has a negative impact on a group's or individual's life, they support amending the ruling in order to better reflect their reality. Because the existing rulings on female inheritance adversely affect most women – of all generations – they are the largest group in my study to support women's equal inheritance rights.

The direct impact that existing laws have on women's lives explains women's support for equal inheritance rights, but why do single men support equality in inheritance while married men do not? The answer to this question is connected to a part of my overall argument in this book: lived reality. All men are affected by the unequal distribution of inheritance for girls because of the assumption and expectation that they must provide for their female family members. They are therefore personally adversely affected by the existing inheritance rules, and since changing them will alleviate the burden for them to provide, they prefer the law be equal. They also imagine their own female family members (mothers, sisters, daughters) in situations where their husbands do not fulfil their financial responsibilities over them, or they recognise that the women they marry will most likely work and have their own income, and in their eyes this entitles them to an equal share in inheritance. This is because the younger generation approaches the existing laws of inheritance as being related to one's earning of an income, such that those who earn an income are entitled to a higher share in inheritance since they take on the role of providers, while those who do not earn an income may expect to be taken care of by family members who do. In both cases, then, they support modifying rulings to fit their social contexts. Another possible explanation points to a generational gap in the ways gender equality is understood. The younger generation, as gauged through their marital status for this study, is more comfortable using language that includes 'gender equality' and expresses its support for equality in a way that the older generation, both women and men, were reluctant to show. Young men's support for equal inheritance rights, then, is connected to the broader discourse on gender equality. However, gender equality appears to be conditional, since it does not apply for all gendered issues, as we will see in the remaining chapters.

Conclusion to Section 1

In this section, I discussed sexual slavery, child marriage, and female inheritance. The issue of whether the *ijmā*ʿ on child marriage and sexual slavery is binding on today's Muslims raises complex questions about the meaning of the term *ijmā*ʿ itself. Only when discussing slavery and child marriage did some of my respondents wonder about my question of a position's being binding. Travis (25, single male, white, convert), Zala (26, single female, racially mixed background), Michael (56, married male, white, convert), and Orzala (33, married, white), for example, all seemed perplexed that I was even asking the question. These individuals' views are probably best summarised and expressed by Zala, who said, 'You can't make something retroactively *ḥarām*.' In other words, if Islamic law permitted child marriage and slavery, Muslims have no right to make them impermissible. These issues are unlike interfaith marriage and female-led prayer because the latter are prohibitions, as we will see. Such views suggest that only positions of consensus *on prohibitions* are binding. Were slavery or child marriage a requirement for all Muslims, rather than merely being permissible, the discussion would have taken a different course. Thus, the *ijmā*ʿ on these issues is not binding because they are not essential parts of Islam, an argument put forth by traditional scholars of Islam as well. This seems to be the opinion of many contemporary scholars when they point out that Islamic law 'merely permits' practices such as child marriage or slavery (e.g. Yasir Qadhi, Nouman Ali Khan). Zaid Shakir, too, claims, 'The first and highest objective of Islamic law is the preservation of religion itself. When an action, such as sexual slavery, which in no way, shape, or form could be described as an essential of the religion, is undermining the religion, that action is to be rejected.'[1] Not only is slavery, maintaining it or encouraging it, not essential to Islam, but it in fact also undermines the religion. As we will see, while this statement explains my respondents' rejection of slavery and child marriage, it does not explain why they support the consensus on the prohibition against women's interfaith marriage and female-led mixed-gender prayer. Are female-led prayer and women's interfaith marriage a threat to Islam? Do they undermine the religion?

Moreover, my respondents' approach to the *Sunnah* specifically on the topics of child marriage and sexual slavery evinces a rhizomatic strategy. They clearly see the *Sunnah* as complex and multivalent, rather than being a set of unambiguous guidelines on how to follow the practice of Prophet Muhammad absolutely. In his discussion of the nuances of the *Sunnah*, Khaled Abou El Fadl suggests:

> the Sunna contains a large number of traditions that could be very empowering to women, but it also contains a large number of traditions that are demeaning and deprecating toward women. To engage the Sunna on this subject, analyse it systematically, interpret it consistently with the Qur'an, and read it in such a fashion that would promote, and not undermine, the ethical objectives of Islam calls for a well-informed and sagaciously balanced intellectual and moral outlook.[2]

However, my respondents are only able to take a critical approach to the *Sunnah* selectively – and what they include in their definition of the *Sunnah* can change according to the issue discussed, as we will see.

The conceptualisation of the Islamic tradition as a rhizome is most visible, I believe, through my respondents' views on female inheritance. Most of them not only support changing the consensus to allow equal inheritance to sons and daughters even while recognising that their opinion does not align with a literal reading of the Qur'anic verses, but they do not wait for a new consensus to emerge: they hold their opinions in disagreement with the consensus. Their approach to scholarly authority in this issue is significantly different than on the other issues. In this case, it is not just the Islamic tradition that is rhizomatic, but so is the respondents' relationship to the Qur'an and its interpretations: once they have confidently concluded that the Qur'anic verses on inheritance do not reflect their lived realities, they refer to alternative sources, such as experiential knowledge, to justify their positions.

Section 2

The Non-Negotiables: Women's Interfaith Marriage and Female-Led Prayers

This section analyses the two issues in the study that are perceived as non-negotiable because of the historical tradition's position of (imagined) consensus on them: women's interfaith marriage and female-led communal prayers. The former is more complex, because the Qur'an does address interfaith marriage and explicitly permits men's marriage to People of the Book (*kitābīs*), i.e. women of other Abrahamic faiths, without prohibiting women from marrying men who are Jews or Christians. However, the commonly perceived prohibition on female-led prayers has no textual foundation in either the Qur'an or *Sunnah*. On both issues, the Qur'an is silent, and the text's silence was taken to be a source of prohibition, despite the legal maxim that nothing is prohibited unless expressly written (*lā taḥrīm illā bi naṣṣ*).[1]

Both prohibitions are results of *ijmā'*, the collective consensus of (male) scholars and the four Sunni legal schools – a seeming majority of scholars today continue to hold this view. This is why I categorise them as 'non-negotiables' in this study. Both are also rooted in gendered and hierarchical assumptions that do not account for today's family dynamics and constructions of gender and of Islam. Although the Islamic tradition, Islam, Islamic law, and the Islamic legal schools are widely acknowledged to be diverse and nuanced, conversations on Muslim women's marriage to non-Muslims (specifically to *kitābīs*) often present Islam as a monolith on the matter.

My respondents' opinions on these two prohibitions demonstrate further that they view Islam and the Islamic tradition (the Islamic past) as rhizomatic. With child marriage and slavery, most of them confidently concluded that Islam does not permit them, and they therefore appealed to different sources to justify their positions; yet, with female-led prayer and women's marriage to non-Muslims, many have decided that Islam prohibits these two, whether explicitly through the Qur'an or through scholarly consensus, and therefore, these are not negotiable even though some of them personally support change. Again, it is their selective reliance on different sources to justify a claim and arrive at a conclusion that suggests they conceptualise the Islamic tradition as a rhizome. The 'picking and choosing' from multiple sources, rather than the same consistent sources, means that they recognise the flexibility afforded to them through the Islamic tradition – but that flexibility is not limitless: certain explicitly gendered issues remain unalterable except through scholarly disruption and the emergence of a new scholarly consensus to legitimate new opinions.

The first chapter in this section deals with women's interfaith marriage and the second chapter with female-led mixed-gender prayers. Both chapters include historical interpretations of the topics while highlighting contemporary approaches to these issues, primarily through the ethnographic data I collected for the study. The conclusion to this section discusses the parallels between the two topics, particularly as they arose in conversations with my research participants, and reiterates what I consider to be the weakness of the arguments against both prohibitions in the contemporary Muslim American context. In this conclusion, I highlight the commonalities between the topics, such as similarities in the explanations given for why these issues are not open to renegotiations in contemporary contexts. I argue that the reluctance to approach these topics as negotiable reflects a larger sense of gender hierarchy and, particularly, of a gendered notion of authority. I show that these 'non-negotiable' prohibitions are maintained for two main reasons: they are not perceived as urgent, necessary, or relevant enough to warrant departure from the historical consensus, and they serve an inegalitarian gender framework on which Islam is believed to be founded.

Chapter 5

Muslim Women's Interfaith Marriage

INTRODUCTION

The Sunni Islamic tradition prohibits marriage between Muslim women and all non-Muslim men.[1] It permits, however, Muslim men to marry women from among the People of the Book, or *kitābī*s, historically understood as Christians and Jews. As previously mentioned, the Qur'an's silence on women's marriage to *kitābī*s in this instance has served as a source of prohibition, despite the legal maxim that nothing is prohibited unless expressly written. To reiterate, this book defines 'the (Sunni) Islamic tradition' broadly as the collection of legal and exegetical scholarship on Sunni Islam, the sources of which range from the Qur'an and *Sunnah* to scholars' personal opinions and customary practices.

This chapter deals with Muslim women's marriage to People of the Book, as opposed to other groups of non-Muslims, because scholarly consensus dictates that neither women nor men may marry the *mushrikīn*: literally, 'polytheists'. Thus, the prohibition on marriage to disbelievers is not gendered and applies to all Muslims. Since the Qur'an does not explicitly prohibit women's marriage to *kitābī*s, I am interested in the justifications for this traditional prohibition put forward by contemporary Muslims, despite their willingness to discard other traditional doctrines given new contexts, such as the popular mainstream rejection of the idea of male superiority over females (with qualifications). Emphasising the Qur'an's silence on women's marriage to *kitābī* men in verse 5:5, which allows men's marriage with *kitābī* women, I explore the following question posed by Kecia Ali: 'If the Qur'an does not directly address the marriage of Muslim women to *kitābī* men, and if the presumptions about male supremacy and dominance in the home [that justified the prohibition] no longer hold [then]...what rationale exists for continuing to prohibit marriage between Muslim women and *kitābī* men?'[2] If Muslims expect or assume the Qur'an to be the frame of reference for all things prohibited and permitted, then what leads to the popular assumption that the Qur'an explicitly and inarguably prohibits Muslim women's marriage to the People of the Book? How do lay Muslims renegotiate the changing realities of Muslim women and family dynamics when considering classical justifications against the prohibition?

The question of women's marriage to *ahl al-kitāb* (the Qur'anic term for 'People of the Book', understood by Muslim scholars to refer to Christians and Jews) appears frequently in online Muslim discussions, forums, blogs, and other Islam-related websites. In these spaces, Muslim women often ask for Qur'anic evidence that they are indeed not allowed to marry Christians and Jews, while men are. Although the responses to their questions vary, indicating there are more cracks in the contemporary consensus than assumed, the predominant view remains that the Qur'an prohibits such marriages; this is presented as the correct 'Islamic' position and often goes unchallenged by academic scholars of Islam, traditionally trained Muslim scholars and preachers, and lay Muslims.[3] The explanations provided for the prohibition by contemporary scholars and preachers are profoundly influenced by the historical assumptions about marriage on which the prohibition is grounded, such as male superiority and the husband's authority over the wife.[4]

LITERATURE ON THE PHENOMENON OF MUSLIM WOMEN'S INTERFAITH MARRIAGE

The legal prohibition on Muslim women's marriage to non-Muslims is not always reflected in current practice. For example, marriage among Muslim women and Hindu men is not uncommon in India, where Muslims are approximately 14% of the total population. As Akbar Ahmed writes, 'While Muslim men married Hindu women when they were dominant [in India], today the picture is reversed, with large numbers of Muslim women marrying non-Muslim men in India'.[5] Moreover, roughly 40% of Muslim women in Canada are married to non-Muslim men, half of whom never convert to Islam (i.e. approximately 20% of Muslim Canadian women are married to non-Muslims).[6] According to a Pew study published in July 2017, 13% of married American Muslims have non-Muslim spouses: 'most married U.S. Muslims have a spouse who is also Muslim (87%). Just 9% have a Christian spouse, 1% are married to someone who has no religious affiliation and 3% are married to someone of another faith' (their gender is not specified).[7] Finally, in research I am conducting currently on Muslim women's marriage to non-Muslims, within the first three months of my call for participants, I interviewed more than 30 Muslim American women who are married to or are in romantic relationships with non-Muslim men.[8] In practice, many Muslim women marry non-Muslim men, whether People of the Book or not, despite the popular idea that such unions are prohibited.

Much of the conversation on women's interfaith marriage is currently taking place online in op-eds, social media discussions, news articles, blog articles, and other non-academic platforms. However, there has been a surge in interest in the topic in the last few years. One of the most detailed studies of the pre-modern secondary sources on interreligious marriage (not exclusive to People of the Book) is Yohanan Friedmann's chapter on interfaith marriage in *Tolerance and Coercion in Islam*.[9] Kecia Ali also discusses the issue briefly in *Sexual Ethics and Islam* and notes the non-existence of the prohibition in the Qur'an and questions its relevance in contemporary contexts.[10] One of the most recent discussions on this topic is Mohammed Gamal Abdelnour's 'The Islamic Theology of Interfaith Marriages', which surveys various Muslim scholarly positions on interreligious marriage for women and men.[11] Most such studies focus on the opinions of male scholarly authorities. Friedman, for example, provides the authoritative legal opinions of male scholars before the nineteenth century, all of whom rejected the idea of women's interfaith marriage.[12] Alex Leeman examines only male Islamic scholars' attitudes towards the subject, past and contemporary, some of whom support such marriages.[13] Abdelnour also highlights exclusively the opinions of male Muslim scholars, both pre-modern and modern, on marriage to non-Muslims – again, some of these writers support the practice.[14] Other scholars who have critiqued the prohibition as not stemming from the Qur'an but from scholarly patriarchal assumptions and biases include Johanna Buisson and Leena Azzam. Buisson discusses both Shi'i and Sunni interpretations of the interfaith marriage verses in the Qur'an, noting also the debate in the Shi'i tradition about Muslim men's *mut'a* marriages (marriages of pleasure, temporary marriages) to non-Muslim women. Buisson discusses several layers of the prohibition, such as the control of female bodies and sexuality and the scholars' patriarchal biases and assumptions. She offers an alternative interpretation of the relevant verses to argue in support of women's marriage to non-Muslims.[15] Azzam explicitly argues that the prohibition is rooted in a contextual understanding of the concept of *qiwāmah* (male authority, leadership), discussed later in this chapter.[16]

Scholarship on the reality of women's interreligious marriage practices, however, is more limited. Among those who have investigated interfaith marriages are the various scholars included in the edited volume by Abdullahi Ahmed An-Na'im, *Inter-religious Marriages among Muslims*, Haifaa Jawad and Ayse Elmali-Karakaya, 'Interfaith Marriages in Islam', and Heather al-Yousuf's 'Negotiating Faith and Identity in Christian–Muslim Marriages in Britain'.[17] In addition, Jawad and Elmali-Karakaya's ethnographic study surveys Turkish-British Muslim women married to non-Muslims in the United Kingdom.[18] Significantly, the underlying assumption in much ethnographic research remains that 'Islam' does not allow women to marry non-Muslims. Jawad and Elmali-Karakaya, for instance, claim that it is incorrect to suggest that the Qur'an does not prohibit such marriages because 'all classical scholars of Islam' have explicitly interpreted the Qur'anic verses as a prohibition. This itself needs to be analysed.[19]

Naomi Riley's discussion on interfaith marriage among Muslims in America attempts to shed light on the lives and experiences of Muslim men in interfaith marriages, whom she interviewed for her book.[20] She finds that in interfaith Muslim marriages, while 'there was an initial objection on the part of one family or the other to either the couple dating or to their wedding…over the long term, there [was] general acceptance and even a kind of embrace'.[21] Citing a Pew Religious Landscape Survey from 2007, she also notes that the rate of interfaith marriage among Muslims is 'roughly the same as for other Americans, about one in five American Muslims have married outside their religion'.[22] A 2015 version of the Pew study shows, however, that 79% of Muslims are married to or living with a partner of the same religion and that roughly 21% of American Muslims have non-

Muslim spouses or partners.[23] Neither the Pew studies nor Riley accounts for gender in the statistics – i.e. what the gender of the Muslim partner in these marriages or relationships is. In fact, all those whom Riley interviewed for her study who are married to non-Muslims are men, and she does not qualify her use of 'Muslim' in the book. That is, instead of speaking about 'Muslim men' marrying non-Muslim women, she speaks about Muslims marrying non-Muslims. Citing Muslim community leaders who are in positions to respond to the challenges that come with interfaith marriages, Riley notes that counsellors, such as Munira Ezzeldine, a marriage counselor in Irvine, California, points out that 'the number of men marrying out has actually created a severe gender imbalance, leaving many Muslim women without partners. In other words, the religiously sanctioned intermarriages are forcing more religiously forbidden interfaith marriages.'[24] A part of the problem resulting from the religious double standard is that the non-Muslim (wife or husband) often converts only nominally for marriage, which, Ezzeldine is quoted as saying, 'is kind of funny because it's almost a charade' where they claim they are Muslim but are actually not.[25] Riley points out that 'Muslim and Catholic theologians apparently both believe that the rights of "their" women will not be protected in a marriage with the other. Both Catholic and Muslim leaders, though, suggest that they are under their own religious obligation to protect the rights of women of other faiths.'[26] Here, Riley includes a deeply problematic statement that reinforces Islamophobic myths about Muslim women's realities, or ignores equally patriarchal violence in other religious traditions, by claiming, '[g]iven the treatment of women in much of the modern Islamic world, the Pope probably has more cause for concern, but the parallel theological statements are noteworthy'.[27] In other words, since Muslim women are demonstrably treated unfairly 'in much of the modern Islamic world', the Pope's concern for Catholic women at the hands of Muslim men is legitimate, as is his disapproval of Catholic women's marriage to Muslim men.[28] This lack of awareness of the complicated realities of Muslim women's lives and their relationship with their faith and traditions may explain why Riley does not interview Muslim women who have married non-Muslims: Riley repeatedly states that Muslim women are prohibited from marrying non-Muslims, and she implies that Muslim women observe this prohibition in the main, failing to do due diligence as to the reality of Muslim women's interfaith marriage.

Others, too, claim that the reason Muslim women cannot marry non-Muslims is that a non-Muslim husband would not honour her rights. Mashood

Baderin, for example, claims that Muslim women are unanimously prohibited from marrying non-Muslims because:

> under Islamic law, a Muslim man who marries a Christian or Jewish woman has a religious obligation to honour and respect both Christianity and Judaism. Thus the woman's religious beliefs and rights are not in jeopardy through the marriage, because she would be free to maintain and practice her religion… Conversely, a Christian or Jewish man who marries a Muslim woman is not under such obligation within his own faith, so allowing a Muslim woman to marry a Christian or Jewish man may expose her religious beliefs and rights to jeopardy.[29]

In this view, the prohibition exists in the interest of women.

In the context of Muslims in North America or the West more broadly, the conversation is also one about the availability of (compatible) Muslim husbands for Muslim women in the West. As Jane I. Smith notes, because Islamic law permits men to marry Christians and Jews but denies women this right, Muslim men 'naturally take advantage of this alternative more often in the United States and Canada than in societies where Islam is the dominant culture, putting an additional burden on young Muslim women who may find that the pool of available partners is very small'.[30] Thus, 'to the alarm of many families, the incidence of interfaith marriage is on the rise, with Muslim women marrying Christians, Jews, Buddhists, Hindus, and others', an option more tempting to 'some young American converts [who] are expressing their frustration that potential marriage partners are inaccessible to them because of the insistence of families that their children, especially their daughters, marry "one of their own"'.[31] Because of the problem of unavailable Muslim husbands for Muslim women, a phenomenon that many Muslims consider 'a crisis',[32] Lori Peek notes that 'compromises have been offered…including restricting Muslim men from marrying outside the faith, or allowing Muslim women to marry non-Muslims'.[33] For Peek, 'these changes are problematic' because 'neither corresponds with Islamic law'.[34]

Besides an uncritical acceptance of the idea that Muslim women cannot or do not marry non-Muslims, another issue with much of the current research is the passive acceptance of patriarchal justifications of the limits placed on women's choices. According to the study conducted by Hassan Hamdani, referenced above:

> Roughly 77 per cent of Canadian children raised by a Muslim mother and non-Muslim father do not count themselves Muslim (the Muslim drop-out rate is 60 per cent of children raised by a Muslim father and non-Muslim mother). By contrast, when both Canadian parents are Muslims, Hamdani's study suggests 99 per cent of their children maintain a commitment to the religion.[35]

Cila and Lalonde, in their study on Muslims' interfaith marriage in Canada, find that Muslim men in Canada are almost twice as likely as Muslim women to marry someone outside the faith.[36] They suggest that 'these gendered norms [i.e. the permissibility of men's dating and marrying non-Muslims] can be explained in part by the women's role within the household. Since women traditionally have been the ones responsible for the upbringing of children, women are often considered as the primary carriers of cultural and religious continuity for future generations'.[37] However, this statement does not explain but contradicts the prohibition. Since it assumes that women have the responsibility of raising the children, one would expect that it is the mother's religious identity that would have more influence on the children and therefore be the ones permitted to marry non-Muslims.

Other scholars are more careful, however. In his research on interfaith marriage between Muslims and Christians among Zongo communities in Accra, Stephen Owoahene-Acheampong briefly discusses Muslim women's interfaith marriages and the broader reaction to them. He notes that while only men are typically permitted to marry non-Muslims – though still discouraged – Muslim men who marry Christian women do not face any social ostracisation. Interestingly, however, contrary to what is popularly assumed, many such men 'allow their children to attend church services and other religious and social activities in the churches of their wives'.[38] Yet, 'although some Muslim men who marry Christian women had to present them with copies of the Bible, they do not allow their wives to read them'.[39] He also interviews Muslim women who have dated Christian men, although he concludes that many would only marry a Muslim man even after such interfaith dating experiences.

More research is needed, particularly on Muslims' marriage to Jews because of the rabbinic Jewish principle that religion is passed from the mother to the children. This principle exists because, Dvora Weisberg notes, 'rabbinic law refuses to recognise the rights of the non-Jewish father', although not all forms of Judaism permit interfaith marriages for any gender.[40] That religious identity is passed down by the mother raises the question of whether either Jewish or Islamic laws are based on principles or ideals, or the reality that children necessarily take the religion of one parent or the other. That is, since these two religious traditions hold such contrasting views towards whose religion/identity the children adopt, neither of these ideas are grounded in reality; they cannot actually be lived in reality as they are mutually incompatible. The principle also points to the inconsistent and subjective ways in which ideas about the validity and invalidity of marriage are fostered. How might Muslim legal scholars consider addressing the conflict of the Jewish principle that children take on the mother's religious identity and the popular Muslim understanding that they take the father's?

WOMEN'S INTERFAITH MARRIAGE IN THE QUR'AN AND THE EXEGETICAL TRADITION[41]

Three verses address the question of marriage between Muslims and non-Muslims, revealed in the following order: Q. 2:221, which generally prohibits marriage between Muslims[42] and polytheists; Q. 60:10, which says that after converting to Islam, neither Muslim women nor Muslim men can stay married to their polytheist spouses; and Q. 5:5, which says that marriage between Muslim men and People of the Book is permissible.[43] These three verses are referenced as Qur'anic evidence for the prohibition on women's intermarriage. In this section, I show that a reading of the three verses together complicates the claim that women's marriage to *ahl al-kitāb* is prohibited because two of the three verses (Q. 2:221 and Q. 60:10) apply to men too, and the third (Q. 5:5) does not prohibit such marriages.

The first verse involving interfaith marriage is 2:221.

> Q. 2:221: Do not marry polytheist women [*lā tankiḥū'l-mushrikāti*] until they believe [in one God]: A believing enslaved woman is better than a polytheist, even though she may please you. And do not marry women to polytheists [*lā tunkiḥū'l-mushrikīna*] until they believe: A believing, enslaved male is better than a polytheist, even though he may please you. They [the polytheists] invite you to hellfire, while God invites you to the Garden of bliss and forgiveness.[44]

This verse is identical in its prohibition for women and men: neither can marry a *mushrik*.[45] It prioritises belief in one God and appears to be addressed to a

Muslim male audience. The only difference between the prohibition for women and men lies in the diacritical marking: *lā tankiḥū* as a command to men, and *lā tunkiḥū* as a command to (or about) women. The phrase becomes gendered as a result of the gender of the object, the *mushrik*: *mushrikāt* (feminine plural) for men and *mushrikūn* (masculine plural) for women. Moreover, when given the choice between a free *mushrik* person and an enslaved *mu'min* (a believer), the believer should choose the enslaved *mu'min* because their belief in God makes them preferable to the *mushrik*. That is, a person's faith is more important when it comes to marriage than their social or economic status. The rationale in the verse for the prohibition is that *mushrik*s 'invite you to hellfire', implying that they are likely to influence the *mu'min* towards *shirk*, 'polytheism', a major sin in the Qur'an (e.g. Q. 4:48). This prohibition applies to both women and men – i.e. it is not women alone who are advised not to marry *mushrik*s. Strikingly, while the verse states that the *mushrik* calls one to hellfire, it does not state that the *mu'min* calls one to heaven; only God calls one to heaven; in other words, the alternative to the *mushrik* is not a *mu'min* but God.

The second verse relevant to interfaith marriage in the Qur'an reads:

> Q. 60:10: O you who believe! When there come to you believing women refugees [*al-mu'mināt u muhājirātin*], examine them [*imtaḥinūhunna*]...if you conclude that they are believing women [*mu'minātin*], then do not send them back to the deniers [*kuffār*]. They [i.e. the women] are not lawful [in marriage] for them [i.e. the male deniers], nor are the men lawful [in marriage] for them [i.e. the women]... There is no sin upon you if you marry them... Do not maintain marriage bonds with the women deniers [*wa-lā tumsikū bi-ʿiṣami'l-kawāfiri*]...[46]

Like Q. 2:221, this verse is explicitly directed towards both women and men: women who leave their communities of *kufr* (those who deny God's oneness) are allowed in marriage to believing men, and their marriages to their previous 'denier' (*kāfir*) husbands are dissolved; believing men, too, may not maintain their marriages with *kāfir*s, or women who commit *kufr*. That is, the prohibition is not gendered – marriage between believers and *kāfir*s is prohibited regardless of the gender of the believer. While the first half of the verse indirectly addresses believing women, the latter half directly addresses believing men, as the verse reads, 'Do not maintain marriage bonds [*ʿiṣam*] with the women deniers'. The root *ʿ-ṣ-m* connotes 'to adhere to' and 'to preserve', among other similar meanings. As in Q. 2:221, too, the direct audience of this verse is believing men, although women are addressed indirectly. As I show below, this verse is invoked in contemporary conversations about intermarriage for Muslim women in order to oppose women's right to marry non-Muslims, without any mention of the same textual prohibition for men.

Significantly, the category of non-believers is not *mushrik* but *kāfir* (pl. *kuffār*); the two terms are not inherently or always interchangeable. *Kufr* entails the denial of truth, specifically the truth of monotheism from an Islamic viewpoint, while *shirk* denotes the association of multiple or other deities with the one God and is the root word for *mushrik*; thus, *kufr* is more general than *shirk*. However, in this verse, the Qur'an is referring to Meccan *mushrik*s exclusively, not the People of the Book: the first verse speaks of the *kuffār* evicting Muhammad and his followers out of Mecca, a point repeated in verses 8–9, and the fact that the believing women are identified as 'emigrants' in verse 10 indicates that the *kuffār* in question are the *mushrik*s from whom flight to Medina was necessary.

The final verse on interfaith marriage in the Qur'an is 5:5, which reads:

> This day, all things good and pure [*ṭayyibāt*] are made lawful for you. The food of the People of the Book is lawful for you and yours is lawful for them. And [lawful for you] are *muḥṣanāt* [chaste or free women] who are believers and *muḥṣanāt* among the people who received a scripture before you if you give them their due compensation [*ujūrahunna*]…

This is the most relevant verse to the question of interreligious marriage in the Qur'an, as this is where permission is granted explicitly to men. It is also the verse that has the potential to permit Muslim women's marriage to people of the same religious communities that Muslim men are permitted to marry. The verse allows men explicitly to marry women from the *ahl al-kitāb* but does not prohibit the same for women. Arguably, the permission in Q. 5:5 does not extend to women because it allows intermarriage only to *muḥṣanāt*, a feminine plural that means either 'chaste' or 'free'.[47] (Pre-modern scholars' interpretations of this verse will be discussed below.) The Qur'an had the option to use a masculine plural that can apply to mixed-gender groups, such as *muḥṣinīn,* to refer to chaste or free people. However, the verse begins with the phrase *al-yawma uḥilla lakum al-ṭayyibātu* ('all good things are permissible for you all'), *-kum* being gender-inclusive in this context. It thus implies that marriage to the People of the Book is among the 'good things' that have been made lawful. But who is the *-kum* here? One might expect that just as the food of the People of the Book is permissible for Muslims (of all genders), so are marriages with them. That is, if the audience of this verse is a gender-inclusive 'you all', then both women and men are allowed to marry *ahl al-kitāb*. Another observation to be made about this verse, in conjunction with the other two verses discussed, is that it can be read as limiting *only* men's options while permitting women to marry everyone except *mushrik*s (Q. 2:221 and Q. 60:10). That is, scholars of the Qur'an have the interpretive authority to assume that all Muslims are allowed to marry all non-Muslims except *mushrik*s, and Q. 5:5 limits men further to only People of the Book and Muslims.

In order to consider the possibility that this verse applies to women also, we must understand an important linguistic device in Arabic, *iktifā'* (sufficiency, or truncation), a rhetorical strategy in Arabic. 'Abd Allāh al-'Alāylī (d. 1990), a Lebanese linguist and scholar of Islam who argues in support of women's marriage to non-Muslims (People of the Book and others), has pointed out that the rhetorical tool of *iktifā'* allows an interpreter to argue that because the verse has already addressed its audience once, it does not need to do so again.[48] Al-'Alāylī proposes that since the verse begins by permitting the food of the People of the Book to Muslims and vice versa, 'there is no need for it to repeat the same linguistic emphasis when it moves to intermarriage'.[49] It is sufficient for the verse to say, 'So are chaste women from the people who were given the scripture before you', without needing to explicitly add, *and your women are lawful to them*, because 'it is clear from the context that the same rule applying for food applies also to marriage and hence the Qur'an is putting both together'.[50] Al-'Alāylī further supports his reading by noting that the Qur'an uses the conjunction *wa-* (and) to connect food and marriage, indicating the similar permissible status of the two.[51] In other words, it is implausible that this verse is speaking to men alone because that would mean that the part of the verse about food is also directed to men alone, leading to the conclusion that Muslim men are permitted to eat more food than Muslim women.

Contrary to the above argument, the dominant interpretation of the verse is that only the beginning part of the verse, which concerns food, is applicable for all Muslims regardless of gender. It is not obvious, however, that the first part of the verse applies to all Muslims if the latter part is addressed to men specifically; *-kum*, after all, can be either masculine or gender-neutral, and an interpretive decision has to be made for either reading. Some interpreters of the Qur'an insist that it is only 'chaste' women of the People of the Book who are permitted to Muslim men; for them, the chasteness of the men is irrelevant, and the woman's chasteness is relevant only if she is non-Muslim, explicitly overlooking the Qur'anic phrase *al-muḥṣanātu min al-mu'mināti* (see, for example, al-Ṭabarī's commentary below). According to the text itself, chaste women from the believers as well as chaste women from the People of the Book are permitted in marriage. Therefore, if unchaste women are excluded from the category of marriageable women among the People of the Book, then they are also excluded from those women who are marriageable among Muslims. That is, if Muslim men are allowed to marry 'only chaste' women of the People of the Book, then they are also allowed to marry 'only chaste' believing/Muslim women. Finally, even if the permission to marry the *muḥṣanāt* must be read to mean that only men can marry women from the People of the Book, the prohibition against Muslim women marrying the men of the People of the Book is non-existent in this verse. As Kecia Ali points out, 'although Surah 5, verse 5 does not explicitly grant permission for such marriages [women's marriage to *kitābī* men], there are numerous other instances in the Qur'an where commands addressed to men regarding women are taken to apply, *mutatis mutandis*, to women'.[52] One such example is found in Q. 5:6, which explicitly refers to intimacy with one's wives or women (*nisā'*) with regards to attaining ritual purity but is interpreted as applying to women's intimacy with their husbands as well.[53] Another example can be seen in the presumed prohibition on homosexuality for all humans based on one reading of the story of the people of Lot, which is addressed to men specifically and never addresses women's attraction to other women.[54] This latter example suggests that in some instances exegetes took Qur'anic prohibitions exclusively addressed to men as applying to all genders, but Qur'anic privileges afforded to men were read as exclusively for men. In other words, the exegetes' starting point is subjective, not neutral.

I have argued in a separate article that interpreters of the Qur'an have the option to interpret Q. 5:5 as being applicable to women, as other such verses often are, and any choice against doing so is a result of the scholar's interpretive agenda and priorities.[55] Yet, while the historical commentators of the Qur'an all differ in the specific points they emphasise, as I will show, they remain united in their conclusion that Muslim women's marriage to all non-Muslim men is prohibited. Contemporary scholars recycle those same arguments with different rationales and explanations.

In my article on this topic, I analyse the interpretations of five specific exegetes, but here I will merely provide a quick summary of some of their main conclusions. The works I have looked closely at are the *Asbāb al-Nuzūl* (*Occasions of Revelation*) of ʿAlī b. Aḥmad al-Wāḥidī (d. 1075), within which I focus on the interpretations attributed to ʿAbd Allāh b. ʿAbbās (d. 687); *Jāmiʿ al-bayān ʿan taʾwīl āy al-Qurʾān* (*A Collection of Statements on the Interpretation of the Verses of the Qurʾan*) by Abū Jaʿfar Muḥammad b. Jarīr al-Ṭabarī (d. 923); *al-Jāmiʿ li-aḥkām al-Qurʾān* (*The Comprehensive Legal Rulings of the Qurʾan*), also known as *Tafsīr al-Qurṭubī* (i.e. al-Qurṭubī's *tafsīr*) by Abū ʿAbd Allāh Muḥammad b. Aḥmad al-Qurṭubī (d. 1273); *Tafsīr Ibn Kathīr* by Ismāʿīl b. Kathīr (d. 1373) and *Tafsīr fī ẓilāl al-Qurʾān* (*In the Shade of the Qurʾan*) by Sayyed Quṭb (d. 1966). These exegetical engagements offer a variety of interpretive possibilities on account of the different issues that each exegete highlights, and because of the different interpretive choices they make and the methods they employ to arrive at their respective interpretations.[56]

Before I discuss the commentaries on the three verses, however, I want to briefly discuss the case of Zaynab, Muhammad's daughter, who was married to a *mushrik* for twenty years. Of the commentators I look at in this article, only Ibn Kathīr and al-Qurṭubī address the issue of Zaynab's marriage to a *mushrik*. Zaynab was Muhammad's daughter, but he never explicitly condemned the marriage or declared them divorced. While a more detailed discussion is not essential in this study, which focuses on Christians and Jews, it is worth mentioning Zaynab's story briefly because her marriage challenges a literal reading of any of the verses discussed in this study. Zaynab and her husband, Abū al-ʿĀṣ b. al-Rabīʿ, who was also her maternal cousin, married before the Qur'an was revealed, and while Zaynab accepted Islam immediately, Abū al-ʿĀṣ refused and even fought against the Muslims in the Battle of Badr (624 CE/2 AH).[57] When captured by the Muslims, Zaynab granted him refuge and protection on at least one occasion. In fact, when Zaynab publicly declared to her father that she was granting her husband protection, Muhammad responded with an announcement that he was now authorising Muslims to grant protection to anyone who requested it, even hostile non-Muslims.[58]

Although the details of Zaynab's story differ in the various available sources, including whether Muhammad ever asked her to deny her husband sexual access unless he converted, none of them provide any evidence referencing Muhammad's order that the two divorce.[59] Some note that after Abū al-ʿĀṣ's conversion, the couple reunited with a new *mahr* (dower, bridal gift from the groom to the bride) and a new marriage, and others (e.g. Ibn Kathīr, al-Qurṭubī) claim that the couple did not need a new marriage contract or *mahr*. This disagreement is significant because it suggests a lack of unanimity on the interpretation that their marriage was invalidated by Zaynab's conversion, as well as challenging a literal reading of Q. 2:221 and Q. 60:10; it means that the Qur'anic verses were not interpreted literally by Muhammad when they applied to his own daughter. Muhammad's two other daughters, Ruqayya and Umm Kulthūm, were married to the sons of Muhammad's other prominent enemy, Abū Lahab, whom the Qur'an condemns in Q. 111, the *sūra* (chapter) which is named after him. In their cases, however, Abū Lahab, not Muhammad or his daughters, annulled the marriages.

I suggest that we take the literature addressing Zaynab's marriage seriously because it offers an important glimpse into commentators' struggles to reconcile a literal reading of the Qur'an with reality.[60] Zaynab's marriage even throws into question whether the issue of marriage between Muslims and polytheists is indeed a matter of politics and alliances, given that Abū al-ʿĀṣ was no friend of the Muslims and actively fought Muhammad and his community. Yet, Zaynab's case is not seen as setting precedent for marriage between Muslim women and non-Muslim men. My point here is to problematise the claim that the Qur'an is very clear that all Muslims' marriages to non-Muslims other than People of the Book are prohibited, especially since Zaynab's case complicates a literal reading of the prohibition of marriage to *mushrik*s. Still, while the explicit prohibition on intermarriage with *mushrik*s makes sense in Muhammad's context, since it was the *mushrik*s of Mecca with whom Muhammad was constantly in conflict, the Qur'an complicates the story of Zaynab. The story suggests that either the marriage did not happen, that she divorced her husband, or that she remained married to him and that this verse is not intended to be applied universally and categorically.

Q. 2:221

In the exegetical tradition, there is disagreement about the context of the revelation of this verse. For some, it was revealed in response to a Muslim man's desire to marry his polytheist concubine, a relationship that pre-dated his conversion to Islam. The verse was reportedly revealed to discourage him from marrying her. Others claim the verse was revealed to criticise the early Muslims who ridiculed each other for freeing enslaved women in order to marry them. The verse thus encourages marrying enslaved people who are

Muslims, and who should be preferred over unbelieving free people.[61] The focus of the discussion in the *Asbāb al-Nuzūl* on this issue is the concept that the ideal spouse for a Muslim person is another believing person, whether enslaved or free, and not a polytheist, and that monotheism should be prioritised over lineage and social status when seeking a spouse.

Many exegetes' interpretations of this verse highlight the scholarly disagreement over the meaning of *mushrik*. Al-Ṭabarī notes that not all scholars limited the term's meaning to 'one who associates partners (with God)' or 'polytheist'. For some, it is about only a select group of *mushrik*s, such as those at war with Muslims; for others, all of them.[62] Some included monotheists such as Jews, Christians, and Zoroastrians in their definition but argued that this ruling was abrogated by Q. 5:5 to allow Muslim men to marry some non-Muslim women.[63] For others, Q. 2:221 did not apply to the People of the Book, and *mushrikāt* refers exclusively to 'Arab polytheist women who do not have a holy scripture to recite'.[64] Al-Ṭabarī's position appears to be that the verse does not apply to women from the People of the Book, who do not count as *mushrik*. Still, he discusses reports attributed to the caliph Umar (d. 644) in which Umar, after the Prophet's death, ordered Ḥudhayfa and Ṭalha, two of Muhammad's Companions, to divorce their, respectively, Christian and Jewish wives. Ḥudhayfa asked, 'Are you alleging that this is impermissible?' Umar responded that no, he was simply concerned that Muslim men might marry 'whores' (*al-mūmisāt*) from these religious communities.[65] In other versions of the report, Umar discourages marriage between Muslim men and non-Muslim women to prevent Muslim men from favouring non-Muslim women over Muslim women. Al-Ṭabarī includes another report, also attributed to Umar, stating, 'A Muslim man can marry a Christian woman, but a Christian man cannot marry a Muslim woman',[66] but al-Ṭabarī himself doubts the authenticity of the report and emphasises that it is not a statement of the Prophet himself, therefore not reliable. A report similar to that detailing Umar's claim that Christian men cannot marry Muslim women is also attributed to the Prophet Muhammad: 'We can marry women from the People of the Book, but they cannot marry our women.'[67] Al-Ṭabarī notes clearly that this Hadith is unreliable because of a weak chain of transmitters (*isnād*) but opts to accept the prohibition on the grounds of *ijmāʿ*. He uses the phrase *hādhā al-khabr wa in kāna fī isnādihī mā fīhi* ('this report has a chain that has what it has') to mean a weak chain, whether because of missing links or unreliable narrators – an equivalent phrase in English would be, 'it is what it is'. As a result, he states, *f-al-qawlu bihī li-ijmāʿ al-jamīʿ ʿala ṣiḥḥat al-qawl* ('but there is consensus that its content is correct').[68] Al-Ṭabarī's discussion is an excellent demonstration of the ambiguity of select words of the Qur'an that different commentators found debatable, which points to the subjectivity of the conclusions drawn from the text.

Al-Qurṭubī disagrees that *mushrikāt* in this verse include women from the People of the Book because, he explains, Surah 5 cannot have been abrogated by Surah 2, since 2 came before. Moreover, he notes, several Companions and *tābiʿūn* (the first two generations of Muslims) married women of the People of the Book, identifying some of them as 'Uthmān, Ṭalḥa, Ibn 'Abbās, Jābir, and Ḥudhayfa.[69] He is clear that People of the Book are permitted in marriage to Muslims as long as they are not at war with Muslims, referencing Q. 9:29.[70] In his commentary on Q. 2:221, al-Qurṭubī also discusses whether the Qur'an permits marriage between Muslims and enslaved Christians and Jews (his position is that it is permissible, although some disagree) and marriage between Muslims and Zoroastrians. For the latter case, his own position is not explicitly stated, but he seems to lean toward the view that sexual relations and marriage with free and chaste Zoroastrian (Magian) women are acceptable, per Q. 5:5, because they have a scripture; he cites others, such as Mālik, al-Shāfiʿī, Abū Ḥanīfa, and al-Awzāʿī, who forbid it.[71] Note that he is finding gaps in the verse and filling them – e.g. while the Qur'an speaks only of 'women', he and others wonder if that means enslaved or free women. Much of his commentary also focuses on whether women can contract their own marriages. His conclusion is that they may not, and there is 'no sense in opposing' this position.[72] Somehow, he concludes from Q 2:221 that the verse stipulates that a Muslim woman's marriage is valid only when contracted in the presence of a *walī* (male guardian). If God was granting women the right to contract their own marriages, he argues, God would have addressed women directly in the same way men are addressed in this verse: 'if women had that right, [God] would have mentioned them', he states.[73] But not all women are equal for him: he provides extensive details about which women may be allowed to contract their marriage without a guardian's permission, the social status of a woman, and even the skin colour. For example, a noble woman of high status cannot contract her own marriage, but a 'lowly woman' (*danīʿa*), such as a freed woman or a black woman (*al-sawdāʾ*), or a 'prostitute', or someone with 'no status', the *walī* plays no role and she can contract her own marriage.[74]

For Ibn Kathīr, too, while Q. 2:221 establishes the prohibition for all Muslims against marrying all *mushrik*s (here 'polytheists') as well as *kitābīs*, an exception is later made for believing men to marry *kitābī* women in Q. 5:5.[75] He argues for the prohibition of intermarriage for all Muslim women by invoking just part of Q. 60:10, which he uses to argue that Muslim women are not lawful wives for *mushrik* men.

Sayyid Quṭb explains in his commentary on Q. 2:221 that the reason marriages between Muslims and *mushriks* are prohibited is that the two do not share a common belief in God or a common worldview.[76] He acknowledges that God does not forbid Muslim men's marriage to Christians and Jews but points out that scholarly opinions differ on whether Christians and Jews are *mushrik* and himself discourages them. He argues that such interfaith marriage is permissible as long as the Christian and Jewish women believe in the unconditional oneness of God.[77] Quṭb claims that Muslim women's marriage to non-Muslims, including People of the Book, is forbidden (*maḥẓūr*). This is because, he explains, children take their father's religious identity, which he claims is a requirement in the *sharī'a*, and because in many societies, the woman moves into her husband's family upon marriage. To him, this means that a Muslim woman would become part of a non-Muslim community and household if she married a non-Muslim, and would therefore raise her children in a non-Muslim environment.[78] He devotes a considerable amount of space to criticising the West for its ill treatment of women, because in Western societies the pressure on women to work deprives their children of a mother's love, leading to psychological illness.[79] Yet, this discussion on the importance of mothers' care for their children stands in tension with his statements about the need for a woman to marry a Muslim man. For example, if children are so attached to their mothers, rather than to their fathers, then why are Muslim women not permitted to marry non-Muslims, since the Muslim father supposedly does not play as important a role in nurturing his children as the mother does?

Contrary to these scholars' views, contemporary Muslim feminist Asma Lamrabet argues that Q 2:221 'stipulates that Muslim men and women are allowed to contract marriage with believers (*mu'minīn*) and prohibited to marry polytheists (*mushrikīn*). It is worth mentioning that the Qur'anic verse clearly stresses the totally egalitarian approach in favour of both men and women and which is not confusing at all.'[80] Even though the verse applies to women and men equally, none of the classical exegetes acknowledge that. In fact, 'all of the classical interpretations' of verse Q 2:221 'focused on the first part of the verse which is addressed to Muslim men'.[81] Contemporary discourse on women's interfaith marriage and Q 2:221 also focuses on the first part and gives little to no attention to the latter part addressing women. For Lamrabet, the verse is not intended to place a prohibition on believing women, but to protect them from the hostility they faced in their communities.[82] She also reads the context of Q. 60:10 as ensuring the safety of Meccan women who converted to Islam after they escaped the hostile environment of the *mushrik* community.[83]

Q. 60:10

While past and present commentators invoke Q. 60:10 to point out that women's marriage to all non-Muslims is prohibited, any prohibition here is applicable to both genders. According to a report attributed to Ibn ʿAbbās, Q. 60:10 was revealed about Subayʿa bint al-Ḥārith al-Aslamiyya, who approached Muhammad and declared her conversion to Islam in the year of al-Ḥudaybiyya, but her husband Musāfir came after her to take her back.[84] The Treaty of Ḥudaybiyya (628 CE), a peace accord between Mecca and Medina, allowed for Meccan polytheists who had converted to Islam or left Mecca for another reason to be returned to their Meccan leaders, but it did not allow Muslims who left Medina to be returned to Muhammad. Reportedly, according to Ibn ʿAbbās, Subayʿa's husband demanded that she be returned to him in accord with this agreement, and the verse was revealed to allow Subayʿa to stay with the Muslims.[85] Significantly, one way to interpret Muhammad's decision here is that he willingly broke the terms of a treaty in order to protect a woman, an issue that leads al-Qurṭubī to wonder whether the treaty originally applied to women in the first place. In al-Wāḥidī's commentary on this verse, the portion of the verse reading 'hold not to marriage bonds with *kuffār* women' is ignored; instead, we see a detailed discussion claiming that once the marriage bond is broken by a Muslim woman's conversion, she is not required to observe a waiting period and can marry (Muslim men) immediately.[86] How he arrives at this conclusion is unclear, as the verse does not address the question of waiting periods at all, but his conclusion speaks to the interpretive possibilities available.

Al-Ṭabarī includes in his commentary a Hadith attributed to Ibn Zayd, a Companion, who reported that when the *mushrikāt* fought with their husbands, they would threaten to go to the Muslims, seemingly as a way to get back at their husbands rather than due to a genuine desire to become Muslim. This explains God's command that these women's faith be tested for sincerity. If their faith was sincere, they were not to be returned to their non-Muslim husbands.[87] Unlike Ibn ʿAbbās, al-Ṭabarī does acknowledge the latter half of the verse and provides a detailed commentary on the meaning of the phrase *wa-lā tumsikū bi-ʿiṣami'l-kawāfiri* ('do not maintain marriage bonds with the women deniers') which, he argues, referencing others who agree, means that Muslim men should not remain married to polytheist women. However, he believes this is not a universal prohibition and is only applicable in the context of this specific treaty between the Muslims and the Meccans.

What is unique in Ibn Kathīr's commentary on this verse is that he discusses Zaynab's marriage to her *mushrik* husband, Abū al-ʿĀṣ b. al-Rabīʿ: while Muslims were previously allowed to marry *mushrik*s, this verse invalidated all such marriages, including that of Zaynab. As a result, in exchange for her husband's freedom after he was captured by the Muslims, Ibn Kathīr claims, Zaynab was to be returned to her father's home and stay there until her husband converted to Islam. When the two were reunited, according to Ibn Kathīr, their *nikāḥ* was not renewed. It is significant that Ibn Kathīr states that they did not need a new marriage contract because this would mean that their marriage was never invalidated in the first place. Clearly, he is struggling to justify Zaynab's marriage to her husband after it had been, in his opinion, invalidated by Q. 2:221, causing her to return to her father's home. It is likely that for him, Zaynab's return to her father's home until her husband converted is sufficient grounds for her not to renew the *nikāḥ*.

According to al-Qurṭubī, this verse abrogates the conditions of Ḥudaybiyya by prohibiting the Muslims from returning any Meccan women seeking refuge in Medina, a position Ibn Kathīr also shares. He asks whether women were even included in the original stipulation – i.e. were both *mushrik* men and women to be returned to the Meccans? – and spends a great deal of time discussing scholarly disagreements on the answer. Ultimately, he suggests, the Prophet performed *ijtihād* (independent reasoning), and concluded that the women should stay, and God approved.[88] In case one wonders why the men are to be returned and the women kept by the Muslims, al-Qurṭubī has an explanation: women have vaginas and softer hearts, and they are indecisive.[89] For him, no marriage between a believer and a *kāfir*, regardless of gender, is valid in Islam after the revelation of this verse.

Al-Qurṭubī discusses Zaynab's interreligious marriage, claiming that her husband converted either two or six years after her conversion, the time depending on the source. Like Ibn Kathīr, he mentions some sources note that when she returned to her husband, the two did not renew their marriage. However, al-Qurṭubī clearly struggles with this lack of renewal of the marriage contract because he tries to justify it. First, he highlights that Zaynab's case is a special one because her marriage had taken place before Islam, treating it as a unique case despite the fact that many other Muslims had likewise married their non-Muslim spouses before Islam. He writes that if the story as told is true, then, according to some of his sources, the entire issue is abrogated due to Q. 2:228, which states that husbands are entitled to reinstate the marriage after an initial divorce; he adds that Q. 2:228 is only applicable while the wives are on their waiting period.[90] He does not comment on the fact that a waiting period cannot be two or six years, which is how long Zaynab was reportedly separated from her husband, according to different sources. Moreover, what he does not seem to admit here is that this would mean that Q. 2:228 applies to non-Muslim husbands and not just Muslim ones.

Sayyid Quṭb interprets the verse to mean that the terms of the treaty were not applicable to women, only to men, and that the reason the women were not to be returned was the fear that they would be persecuted by their polytheist community for accepting Islam.[91] He highlights the importance of marriage, which 'cannot be properly established when the primary bond of faith is absent'.[92] Since faith must be present in a Muslim marriage – regardless of gender – Muslim men's marriages to unbelieving women are invalidated by this verse, he concludes.

Note that only Ibn Kathīr and al-Qurṭubī take up the case of Zaynab, Muhammad's daughter, who was married to a *mushrik* before the advent of Islam but appears to have remained married to him even after her conversion and his refusal to convert. These commentators instead address other issues that appear less relevant for our topic, such as whether women must perform the *ʿidda*, or waiting period, before being able to marry men from the Muslim community and, if so, how long their *ʿidda* should be, or whether a woman's marriage is valid without the approval of a guardian. Some also discuss whether the prohibition on interfaith marriage extends to sexual relations with enslaved women of the prohibited group. That each selected different issues to highlight and prioritise indicates that readers of the Qur'an insert their own assumptions and expectations into the text's meaning.

Q. 5:5

According to the interpretation attributed to Ibn ʿAbbās in al-Wāḥidī, this verse was one of the last verses to be revealed, and it makes lawful to Muslim men marriage to free, chaste, believing women in addition to virtuous women who have received scripture before them - i.e. who follow a religion with a sacred text.[93] However, while the exegesis attributed to Ibn ʿAbbās makes clear that this guideline applies only to chaste women of the People of the Book, he is cited in other reports as having claimed that it applies only to People of the Book under Muslim rule – not to women of the People of the Book living in the regions that were at war with Muslims or were living in a territory controlled by non-Muslims.[94] There seems to have been little agreement on whether it referred only to Christians and Jews, or included Sabians (a religious group the Qur'an mentions a few times) as well, given that the Sabians are considered believers in the Qur'an (e.g. Q. 2:62). Abū Ḥanīfa, for instance, permitted the marriage of Muslim men to Christians, Jews, and Sabians, while his disciples did not permit it to Sabians.[95]

Although the Qur'an is not clear about the religion of the *muḥṣanāt* mentioned in Q. 4:24, the legal and exegetical traditions go to great lengths to arrive at their preferred conclusions on this point, supporting my larger point that these interpretations reflect the interpreters' biases, preferences, and priorities.

Al-Qurṭubī, too, discusses extensively who is included in the category of the People of the Book in this verse. According to some, he writes, it refers only to the People of the Book with whom Muslims have a treaty, while others insist that it applies to all – both the *dhimmī* (non-Muslims granted legal protections) and the *ḥarbī* (non-Muslims at war with Muslims, and thus without such legal protections) – because the verse is general. As for his understanding of *muḥṣan*, he defines it to mean a woman who has not engaged in any illicit sexual activity, or, according to others he references, one who guards her vagina and performs *ghusl* (a ritual purification) after sexual activity.[96] Significantly, he summarises the debate around where the vowel on the word *muḥṣan* should be: some opine that it should be a *kasra* (i.e. a case ending below an Arabic letter, pronounced as a short *i*), while others argue it is a *fatḥa* (i.e. a case ending above an Arabic letter, pronounced as a short *a*). This is important because these case endings can determine whether the word is passive or active: if it is *muḥṣan*, the woman herself decides to guard herself, while *muḥṣin* denotes that someone else is in charge of her, hence the enslaved/free distinction. When scholars debate the meaning of the term *muḥṣan*, they generally proceed to decide whether, first, the verse applies to only free, or also enslaved, People of the Book; and second, are these slaves owned by People of the Book or slaves who are themselves People of the Book? Also significantly, al-Qurṭubī does not address the question of women's marriage to the People of the Book in his commentary on Q. 5:5.

Ibn Kathīr interprets Q. 2:221 as applying to all Muslims' marriage with all non-Muslims, not just *mushriks*, and reads Q. 5:5 as an exception to Q. 2:221 – but for men only. In other words, for him, all Muslims are prohibited from marrying all non-Muslims (as opposed to only *mushriks*, as Q. 2:221 states); however, God, conveniently, made an exception for Muslim men to marry some non-Muslims, namely chaste Christian and Jewish women.[97]

Quṭb's discussion focuses on the dowers Muslim men are required to give to the Christian and Jewish women they marry. The dower, he insists, must be paid for a legitimate Islamic marriage (*al-nikāḥ al-shar'ī*), which serves the purpose of protecting the wife, but not for a marriageless relationship that treats the woman as a mistress.[98] He insists that women's marriage to *ahl al-kitāb* is forbidden. He first argues that the permission for marriage with *ahl al-kitāb* only applies to non-Muslims living under Muslim rule and then classifies the permission as part of a social set-up based on mutual friendship and hospitality.[99] Despite forbidding the *ahl al-kitāb* men of these communities to marry Muslim women, Quṭb claims that only Muslims are tolerant and friendly towards people of other faiths.[100] Notably, Quṭb is the only exegete among the five studied here who attempts to rationalise the prohibition; the others appear to assume that their readers accept the prohibition and agree that it needs no defence or justification other than a reminder that the Qur'an prohibits it.

ANALYSIS AND CRITIQUE OF THE INTERPRETATIONS OF Q 2:221, Q 60:10, AND Q 5:5

While none of the verses above (or other Qur'anic verses on marriage) explicitly prohibit marriage between Muslim women and *kitābīs*, the exegetes read the above verses collectively to prohibit such unions. Few scholars acknowledge that the prohibition stems not from the Qur'an but from a scholarly consensus, but among them are Muhammad al-Ṭāhir ibn ʿĀshūr (d. 1973) and Ḥasan al-Turābi (d. 2015).[101] In fact, this claim of 'consensus' was accepted so widely that, as Kecia Ali observes, Ibn Rushd (d. 1198.) does not address it in his *Bidāyat al-Mujtahid* (*The Distinguished Jurist's Primer*), a legal manual that discusses the diverse opinions of five Sunni legal schools on reportedly every issue there was disagreement on by Ibn Rushd's time.[102] That he does not address women's marriage to People of the Book demonstrates that the later scholars had no question about whether such marriages were lawful; it was understood as a prohibition and made sense as such. The earlier generation, however, appear to have considered it important to assert that there was an explicit prohibition.

The above scholars' interpretations of Q. 2:221 and Q. 5:5 combined suggest that, with regards to marriage, the status of the *kāfir* (denier) depends on their gender.[103] That is, for Muslim women, all non-Muslims are treated as disbelievers or deniers, even though they are not classified as such in other contexts; for Muslim men, only polytheists are treated as deniers. Asma Lamrabet and Johanna Buisson corroborate my analysis on this point.[104] As the exegetes keep claiming, seemingly unanimously, marriage to *mushrik*s is not permitted, where *mushrik* somehow means all non-Muslims, but God conveniently makes an exception for Muslim men to marry People of the Book. This suggests that Christians and Jews were treated as *mushrik*s by some commentators except in the context of marriage to Muslim men. The lengths to which these exegetes go to defend their argument that the category of *mushrik* includes all non-Muslims suggests that the scholars began with the premise that women absolutely could not intermarry (and men could) and then read the Qur'an in a way that supported that conclusion, which is not an unusual strategy.[105] Yet, while Q. 2:221 is commonly invoked as the source of this prohibition, the verse exclusively applies to *mushrik*s. One can speculate whether scholars would have interpreted the word *mushrik* to include Christians and Jews in Q. 2:221 if there were no Q. 5:5, since that would mean that men, too, would not be allowed to marry Christians and Jews. Scholars had the option to read Q. 2:221 as inapplicable to Christians and Jews – and as al-Ṭabarī acknowledges, many actually did – and Q. 5:5 as applicable to both men and women, relying on the general language of the verse seen in its reference to food – but the majority of the pre-modern scholars took a path that reinforces a gender and religious hierarchy, and which maintains the male privilege of being able to choose between a variety of marital options. Similarly, the fact that the exegetes debated whether the word *muḥṣanāt* in Q. 5:5 meant 'pure, free, chaste' women, not to mention whether the Christian/Jewish women permitted to men in marriage were required to be chaste, speaks to the interpretive choices available to readers of the Qur'an. In a clear demonstration of power, these exegetes decided which Qur'anic terms and guidelines were indisputable mandates and which ones were debatable.

As we shall see, contemporary Muslims have no qualms over the meaning of either term: *muḥṣanāt* simply means 'chaste' or 'virtuous', and *mushrik* simply means 'polytheist'. The specific conclusions interpreters of the Qur'an arrive at, then, speak to the different assumptions and priorities of each interpreter's time.

In his commentary on Q. 2:221, al-Qurṭubī, like others, takes a Qur'anic verse and makes it about something that it is not obviously about (e.g. guardianship).[106] He distinguishes between free and enslaved, Black and non-Black, 'noble' and lower-class, chaste and unchaste women. This shows how norms of freedom, social status, and prejudice against people based on social hierarchies, professions, and skin colour are read into the Qur'an in commentaries. The fact that Q. 2:221 does not actually speak of social status, for example, or guardianship, but the phrase *tunkiḥu'l-mushrikīna* elicits such a detailed discussion on these subjects speaks to the ways that personal and societal biases affect the meanings and applications of the Qur'an. Even if we assume that the Qur'anic text in Q. 2:221 is *suggesting* – not requiring – that a woman's marriage must always be contracted by a male person, the verse certainly does not provide any details of who that person must be and does not distinguish between women of different statuses. Notably, when al-Qurṭubī disagrees with others, he states that the other side's opinion is to be ignored. For example, when discussing whether a son can be his mother's *walī*, referencing Umm Salama's marriage to Muhammad by her son, he writes, 'Our scholars often cite this as proof, but it counts for nothing.'[107] Such assertions of exegetical power also leave other readers of the Qur'an free to make choices about the meaning and applicability of the text. It also means that these commentators' opinions should not be taken at face value and that contemporary Muslims can generate their own interpretations, making interpretive choices about which terms, phrases, and verses warrant detailed commentaries and which ones are 'clear'.

There are many other gaps and inconsistencies in these commentaries. I'll analyse Quṭb's here because he offers the most extensive explanations for the prohibition of women's interfaith marriage, which are repeated by other opponents of the practice. Given the significant theological differences between Muslims and Christians, one might argue that marriages between these two groups would also be prohibited if one were to accept Quṭb's reasoning for the prohibition of marriage between Muslims and polytheists. However, he argues that because of the fundamental belief in the Oneness of God that Muslims share with *kitābī*s, marriage between *kitābī* women and

Muslim men is acceptable. He finds it noteworthy to add that Muslim men can marry Christian women, despite their belief in the Trinity, because at least they share a belief in God.[108] Here, he fails to explain why this does not apply to Muslim women too. Similarly, his rationale of the theological differences is also flawed: it does not explain why Muslim men are allowed to marry only *some* monotheists, and not all – e.g. Zoroastrians are excluded. His third rationale, about the religious identity of children that are born into such relationships, does not explain why Muslim men are not allowed to marry polytheists. He rationalises the prohibition on women by arguing for the supremacy of the husband's religious identity. According to this patriarchal and patrilineal logic, since identity is passed down through the father, the religion of the mother, whether she is Muslim, Jewish, Christian, or a polytheist, has no practical significance. But according to this logic, Muslim men should therefore be allowed to marry polytheists too. Of course, the prohibition between polytheists and all Muslims is Qur'anic, and he does not have to rationalise it; not doing so, however, weakens his reliance on claims of patrilineality.

Further, Quṭb's argument supporting the prohibition on grounds of childrearing fails to account for several issues. Namely, it assumes that religious identity is passed down through the father alone. This view is not shared by other religions and cultures. Judaism, for example, is traditionally passed down through the mother, raising the question of a child's presumed identity in a marriage involving a Muslim father and a Jewish mother. Moreover, this assumption also ignores the modern ideal that both parents (should) play an equal role in childrearing, and not all couples wish to or can have children. Curiously, although childrearing today has been designated the mother's responsibility, her role in passing on her religion to her children is unacknowledged. Yet, contrary to contemporary Muslim perceptions, classical jurists agreed that children take on the religious identity of any Muslim parent, whether that is the mother or the father.[109] Nor did they consider it a woman's responsibility to raise her children; in fact, according to the jurists, a child can legally be raised by a woman other than his or her mother, as in the Prophet Muhammad's own example. Perhaps, in an ironic and unintended twist, the patriarchal rationale that women are responsible for childrearing can be applied to argue that it is Muslim women, not men, who should be allowed to marry non-Muslims, since, according to the logic posited here, mothers are the ones best equipped with the task of childrearing and thus pass on their beliefs and identity to their children.

Finally, while Quṭb founds his argument against marriage between Muslim women and non-Muslim men on the sanctity of Muslim identity, he notes, 'our societies today [mid-1900s] are only nominally Muslim'.[110] This comment challenges his assumption that marriage to non-Muslim men is a threat to the proper practice of Islam and Muslim identity: if Muslims are only nominally Muslims, why is it necessary that the children be raised in the father's community? Moreover, while Qutb places great emphasis on the role of mothers in raising Muslim children, it is unclear why he does not acknowledge the possible role that a non-Muslim mother would play in raising her children in an interfaith marriage, shaping the child's identity and faith. Ultimately, then, Quṭb's discussion, like those of the other exegetes, speaks to the arbitrary theological boundaries that scholars draw because they are convenient, not necessarily because they are logical or scripturally founded.

I have shown here that there are inconsistencies in the logic and assumptions of the male exegetes who argue that the Qur'an prohibits women's marriage to People of the Book. I have interrogated their interpretations by highlighting the ways in which the scholars attempt to fill apparent ambiguities or silences in the Qur'an through their own lenses, and I have concluded that their choice to focus on specific elements of each individual verse while reading all three collectively to conclude something that is not obvious speaks to their interpretive choices and power and the arbitrariness of what is deemed debatable.

CONTEMPORARY PERSPECTIVES AND JUSTIFICATIONS FOR THE PROHIBITION

Contemporary opinions on interfaith marriage at first seem to reflect the scholarly consensus, but a closer examination reveals points of conflict. All but 2 participants (1 single male, 1 married female) believed that Muslim men are allowed to marry Christians and Jews, but almost all of them also qualified this permission by pointing out that it applies to only 'chaste' women of the People of the Book, and, some also added, those who reject the doctrine of the Trinity.[111] 35 out of 40 participants, when asked if Islam prohibits women from marrying People of the Book, replied along the lines of: 'Yes, the Qur'an is pretty clear that men can marry People of the Book and women can't' – although they disagreed whether this ruling is binding on Muslims today or not. This response is striking because of its popularity and the certainty of those who hold that it is indeed explicitly in the Qur'an. When asked what they understand the reasons of the prohibition to be, most explained, 'Because in Islam, religion is taught to a child by the mother.' A few participants – 2 single men and 1 single woman – paused as they explained this to comment, in variation, 'Wait, that doesn't make any sense. It should be the other way around. But Islam does forbid it, right? I don't know actually.' Some of those who said that the reason was because of men's dominance in the family as well as because religious identity is passed down by the father noted that they disagreed this was true for most families today but they did not think they had the authority to challenge the prohibition. A common response was that the prohibition may be reconsidered if scholars collectively re-evaluated it and offered a new position on it, but that they trust historical scholars to have made the correct decision.

Table 17: Islamic law's position on women's interfaith marriage is binding today.

Scale	Single Women	Single Men	Married Women	Married Men	Total
1 (completely disagree)	4	3	3	3	13
2	1	1	0	3	5
3 (I'm not sure)	4	0	3	0	7
4	0	2	0	0	2
5 (completely agree)	1	4	4	4	13

I asked the question about whether the consensus on this issue is binding at the beginning of the interview, but I also asked a similar question toward the end of our discussion. Table 18 shows the responses to the statement about whether women's interfaith marriages are un-Islamic:

Table 18: Women's marriage to People of the Book is not allowed in Islam, and Muslims today must maintain the consensus.

Single Women	Single Men	Married Women	Married Men	Total
2	6	5	4	17

Table 18 includes only those who agreed with the statement. Since the figures for agreement are lower here than those who considered it to be prohibited, it can be concluded that either they began to change their minds, or were not completely certain about how to deal with this issue when it came to the reality of women's marriages today. At this point in the interview, some were also beginning to see the pattern of the questions for each issue, recognising that all topics came with a question about consensus, the 'Islamic' position, and their own. Among the participants who were aware of the prohibition and were willing either to guess the wisdom behind it or had looked into the issue before, the most commonly invoked justification was that the husband has a natural tendency to be dominant, or so he believes, and thus a non-Muslim husband would not allow his wife or children to be Muslim. Most participants referred to this idea even if they did not agree with it, commenting at least that they had heard this. The most common answer, however, involved the idea that only a father's religion is passed down to the children. The notion that a non-Muslim man would not recognise his Muslim wife's rights and thus deprive her of the rights Islam has granted her hardly came up in my interviews as the opinion of the respondents themselves, although a couple of participants mentioned that they have heard this explanation.[112] Another reason given was that a woman would follow her husband's tradition and by doing so, she would subject herself and her children to a non-Muslim tradition.[113]

In what follows, I discuss my respondents' opinions and rationales about the practice and the prohibition. I organise their responses into the following categories: 1) women are not, and should not be, allowed to marry non-Muslims because Islam is a patrilineal religion and/or because of male dominance in marriage; 2) the prohibition is 'Islamic', but it does not reflect current realities and should therefore be open to change; 3) the prohibition is not fair and is rooted in false assumptions of male superiority, but it should not be changed because it is in the Qur'an; and 4) the prohibition is not Islamic and Muslims are not bound by it – i.e. Muslim women can marry People of the Book.

To demonstrate the complexity of the conversations that took place on this topic with all my participants, I begin, as in the previous chapters, with an interview that took place with a married couple of South Asian background, who had different positions on the issue. The 57-year-old wife, Lema, and 65-year-old husband, Pamir, frequently disagreed on what Islam's positions were and what they believed those positions should be. They disagreed about whether the prohibition should be maintained as well as about its historical and contemporary rationales. According to Lema, women cannot marry People of the Book because:

> we have the example of the Prophet. His two daughters were married to non-Muslims, and they waited for them to convert but they didn't, so he made them get divorced from their husbands. So we have an example and we follow that example… They were *mushrik*s, I think, but then again, we have examples in our Islamic history… I don't have much knowledge of this, but whatever the scholars said.

Lema's rationale here appears to be the Prophet's example: the Prophet's daughters, she believes, were married to non-Muslims, and when these non-Muslim husbands refused to convert to Islam, the Prophet compelled them to divorce their husbands.[114] She acknowledges that while I am asking about women's marriage to Christians and Jews (given the explicit textual permission to men to marry Christians and Jews), her example of the Prophet's daughters may not be useful here; in that case, she adds, 'whatever the scholars said'. And the scholars concluded that a woman may not marry a non-Muslim man regardless of his faith.

Pamir, Lema's husband, asked her if the prohibition was found in the Qur'an, because he remembered that the Qur'an allows such marriages to men, but he did not think the Qur'an prohibits women such marriages. Lema replied, 'But after the Qur'an, we have the *Sunnah* and Hadiths and scholars. And all the great scholars, the four scholars, interpreted it that it is prohibited. That's what we follow right now because that's our guiding light.' For Lema here, the conclusion ('women cannot marry non-Muslims') is the premise, and if one source does not support this conclusion, then there must be another, more authoritative source that does. Women's marriage to non-Muslims is by default prohibited, and if the prohibition is not in the Qur'an, then Muslims must approach the second most authoritative source to find justification for this claim; if it is not there either, then the third most authoritative source, and so on.

Pamir believed that the reasons of the prohibition concern the husband's authority over his wife: 'At that time, men could influence the women to get them to convert, whereas the other way around, a woman would have difficulty to convert the husband. So it makes sense to me that would be the reason.' Lema was reluctant to speculate: 'I think it's the law. We don't know the wisdom behind it, and we should accept it. Because later on, we might find that there was wisdom behind it.' Pamir responded, 'But she's asking about your opinion. We can have opinions. It doesn't mean it's true or it will make a difference. She's just asking why do you think it was like that.' Lema, still reluctant, offered, 'I think also the kids. They follow the religion of the father. Maybe that's why.' However, Pamir disagreed: 'I think it's the other way around right now. Because the husband stays away from home, and the woman is at home with the kids, so the kids follow whatever the mother follows. And back then, too. Which is the opposite of what I said earlier… On one side of the coin, you have the husband's authority over the woman, but on the other side, the woman could influence the kids.' The couple believed that the consensus is binding on Muslims today; Lema did not think any changes needed to be made to it, and Pamir suggested that it be changed because times and family dynamics have changed. This is an example of Muslims simultaneously believing that consensus *is* binding but that it should or can be changed in their opinion. This couple's differing views on the issue point to the wide-ranging views across the Muslim American community. The exchange provided here reflects my discussions with my other respondents as well.

Below, I discuss some of the most common responses I received as explanations for the prohibition against women's marriage to non-Muslims. Even if the individual did not personally hold the opinion, I include their explanation in its respective category or theme because the prevalence of these opinions reveals the ways the discourse on women's interfaith marriage is constructed.

Position 1: Women's interfaith marriages are un-Islamic because of male dominance and Islam's patrilineal nature

The two most common positions were that a woman cannot marry a non-Muslim man due to the husband's natural dominance over his wife and the patrilineal nature of Islam. Michael (56, married male, white, convert), who divorced his non-Muslim wife after his conversion to Islam, believes neither men nor women should marry non-Muslims:

> In places like the US, I think Muslims shouldn't marry non-Muslims, regardless of the sex. I know the classical definitions make a difference for Muslim-majority situations allowing Muslim men to do it. But to

> be honest, I haven't really seen an opinion from a scholar that clearly permits that to women. And also, is the woman really a Christian? Is she somebody who is really sincere religiously? Do you really want your household to be raising your kids with somebody that doesn't really care about God's opinion on something?... I hear that opinion a lot [that men are allowed to marry non-Muslims] and I think it's the correct opinion. But only if we're in a society where there aren't enough Muslim women for someone to marry. The permissibility of it may relate only to the necessity of it.

He explained that one of the purposes of marriage is to bring the couple closer to God and Islam and to raise 'sincerely religious' children. This is why he divorced his non-Muslim wife after his conversion. Although Muslim men are allowed to marry Christian and Jewish women, he does not encourage it and certainly chose not to apply this permission to himself; besides, he explains, the only context in which a Muslim man may marry a non-Muslim woman is if there are no Muslim women available to him for marriage.

For Michael, the scholarly consensus on this issue is crucial: whatever the rationales might be, the most important thing to him is that the scholars prohibited it, and there must thus be some wisdom behind it. He believes the reason the prohibition on women's interfaith marriage exists is that 'men are prone to being domineering and to be too prone to violence and pushing their opinions on others. Plus preservation of religion. The likelihood decreases of a child being Muslim if the father is not Muslim.' When I asked him if he believes that is true according to his observations or experiences, he did not give a clear answer but noted that exceptions are possible and insinuated that there is no reason for the prohibition except that that it is the scholarly position.

Sultan (41, African male, married, convert) invoked the idea of male dominance to rationalise the prohibition:

> I believe when a woman marries a man, he's in charge. He's the leader of the house. So he's not gonna be good for her *dīn* [faith]. Yeah, he might not force her to leave her *dīn*, but on top of that, children! If I'm to marry People of the Book, the rule is the children have to be raised as Muslims. But with a woman, the children would follow the footsteps of the father. It's the natural way. Men are dominant. I mean

> whether you talk about physically, whether the emotional balances because we don't go through our periodic cycles, our hormones don't fluctuate. So we're kind of like stable for the most part. Women tend to be emotional. I mean, women cry when they're happy! Men don't cry even when they're supposed to cry for the most part! So a woman marrying a non-Muslim man, eventually is going to lead her towards *jahannam* [hell]. And I've seen women married to non-Muslims and their children are gone [i.e. astray].

Sultan is explicitly stating that as the head of the household, the husband is responsible for raising Muslim children, and therefore his religion must be Islam. To rationalise male dominance, he appeals to women's presumed physical and emotional weakness ('women cry when they're happy', menstruation) and concludes that since men are 'stable for the most part', they have the right to marry non-Muslims because only they have the power to raise Muslim children. He also appeals to his personal experiences with Muslim women who have married non-Muslim men and whose children 'are gone' to explain his position.

When I asked if he knows of cases where Muslim men are married to non-Muslims and, if so, how their children might have turned out, he said, 'Hmm…lemme think…yes, I do, actually. That's a good point. I have a Muslim friend married to a non-Muslim. Their children goes [sic] to church with their mom.' He added, after a pause, that 'you know, he's not even in the *dīn* [Islam]. I don't see him praying. I don't think he eats pork, but he's not in the *dīn*. But for me, if the *dīn* is not there… I don't know why you'd marry someone. For me as a Muslim, I can't imagine marrying a non-Muslim.' He clearly admits that interfaith marriage in general, regardless of the Muslim spouse's gender, may create challenges for the couple in raising Muslim children. However, after pausing while narrating his Muslim male friend's experience in an interfaith marriage, he asserts that his friend is not even a Muslim anyway, since he (Sultan) does not see this friend praying. He concludes that because he himself cannot imagine marrying a non-Muslim person, other men should not either, but women are absolutely prohibited from doing so. Examples he knows contradict his claim that men are always naturally in charge of the children's religious upbringing and that only the father's religion determines that of the children's.

When I asked Zalaan (42, married male, South Asian background) why he believes women cannot marry non-Muslims, he said, 'I don't know one hundred percent, but I went to this lecture ten years ago, and it mentioned because of the kids and the household dynamics. What they say is that it derails the fabric of the family or something.' I asked him if he believed that, or if according to his observations, that statement might hold some truth. He responded, 'In Undergrad, I knew about 6 families – or 10 total. They're all messed up.' Seeking clarification, I asked him if these were cases where women married Christians or Jews or the men did. He responded:

> Both ways, but more so with the Muslim woman marrying a non-Muslim. So I know about 10, actually 11 – I just ran into [another one]. And they're all messed up. The couple doesn't practise Islam, so forget the kids. It takes the Islam out of the person. It took religion out of both people, forget Islam. Even the other one who's Christian is no longer Christian…the marriage just completely dissolves religion.

He remained unclear about whether there were any differences in the way the children of the Muslim women turned out compared to the Muslim men, except that the issue was 'more so with the Muslim woman' who had married a non-Muslim. While he initially estimated the number of interfaith couples he knew with a Muslim spouse as 6, he ended by claiming it was 11. Despite the similar problems he believes an interfaith couple may face raising their children as Muslims, he believes men are allowed to and can marry non-Muslims but that women cannot, stating that 'the Qur'an makes it clear that men can marry People of the Book, but women can't. But a specific kind of Christian and Jew. And she has to be chaste and can't believe in the Trinity, and a lot of other stuff.' When I asked, 'Just to clarify, your understanding is that the Qur'an makes it clear that it's prohibited for women, right?' he said, 'The Qur'an didn't specify it, but it makes it clear, and the Hadiths explain why.' He thus does not believe that it is Islamic for women to marry non-Muslims but understands that:

> it happens all over. In London, it's like twenty-five percent. It doesn't bother me. It's just not relevant to me… But you have lesbian and gay Muslims claiming they can be gay and Muslim at the same time, and they say it's because the Qur'an isn't clear about it. And Canada has the highest population of gay and lesbian Muslims in the world. They even have mosques for lesbian and gay Muslims. So you have people

> finding all kinds of excuses to do what they want to do. But that's why I said Hadiths explain things that are left out in the Qur'an.

He views such marriages as Muslim women 'finding all kinds of excuses to do what they want to do' and justifying it through the Qur'an. He connects the existence of LGBTQ+ Muslims and mosques accommodating them to Muslim women seeking the right to marry non-Muslims: both, for him, are unacceptable and serve to show that just because these are realities does not mean that they are Islamically acceptable.

While almost all participants knew that it is lawful for Muslim men to marry *kitābī* women, Patang (23, single male, South Asian background) said the Qur'an does not allow either women or men to marry non-Muslims because 'the Qur'an says not to trust Christians and Jews because they're not friends [to Muslims]. You can have relations with them up to a certain point, like be friends with them, sure, but marriage or romance?' When I asked him why he thinks that scholars prohibited such marriages for women, he responded, 'Maybe because women are the ones who bear the kids, so if they marry Christians or Jews, sometimes when they bear the kids, the mother is the one who takes care of the kids and she makes decisions for them. So if the scholars said women are allowed but men aren't, I'd think that's why.' He expressed shock when I clarified that the ruling had been that women were *not* allowed: 'They're not? Oh! That's just – I've never heard of that, but I don't know what to think of that. I always thought the Qur'an and *Sunnah* treated and mentioned women [and men] together, or equal rather.'

The notion of male leadership in the family was a recurrent theme in this discussion. The respondents quoted above viewed Islam to be a patrilineal religion, passed down from father to child, and argued that this is why the Qur'an prohibits women's marriage to all non-Muslims. Men are entitled to marry non-Muslim women because they are the ones whose religion and identity are passed down to their children, and they are the ones with the influence to raise a Muslim family. Since women innately lack the same power and influence, it is in Islam's interest, it appears, not to permit women to marry non-Muslims.

Other respondents had also heard that the reasons might have to do with male superiority but realised the argument did not make sense as they were speaking. Sarbaz (28, unmarried male, South Asian background), for example, proposed that the reason the prohibition persists must have to do with 'childrearing' but paused and said, 'Wait, that doesn't make sense. Maybe a balance of power?' He believes that the prohibition is only Islamic and legitimate if it is explicit in the Qur'an.

Position 2: The prohibition is Islamic but should or can change.

Table 19: It is not allowed in Islam but should be.

Single Women	Single Men	Married Women	Married Men	Total
7	3	3	6	19

Table 19 includes only those who agreed with the statement that Muslim women are not allowed to marry non-Muslims but that they should be. Those who fall into this category believe that the prohibition is Islamically grounded – whether in the Qur'an or the consensus of the legal schools – but that it is negotiable, although the majority said that the current consensus is binding until it changes.

Scarlet (27, white, convert to Islam) has heard that it is prohibited for women to marry non-Muslims, but she is personally conflicted about the issue: 'There's a verse that says that men can marry People of the Book and women should marry Muslim men. So it's mentioned in the Qur'an.' However, the prohibition should be 'at least reconsidered' if not totally lifted, and 'scholars should talk about it' because the context in which the prohibition emerged is not relevant for Muslims today. The reason for the prohibition, she has heard, 'is that the husband is the responsible caretaker of the family, and I can sort of see that, but it does not affect me' – because she is married to a Muslim man. She adds that she is happy for any Muslim woman who is happily married to a non-Muslim because 'it is hard to find a good husband'.

Zigar (21, single male, of South Asian origin) agrees that the prohibition is connected to the father's religion – but believes it needs to be contextualised and revoked because that is no longer the reality today: the prohibition emerged because of 'the fact that people seem to follow the religion of the father. But then again, this is why I'm really big on interpretations. Societies have changed. If it's not an explicitly stated rule, then I think we can read it in a modern context.' He was not sure if the prohibition is Qur'anic or not but believes that contemporary scholars need to review it: 'I'm really big on a group of *'ulama* [scholars] going through it and re-interpreting it. Because family dynamics have changed. The whole social fabric of family has changed. I feel like if there's a purpose behind it, and you're not achieving that purpose, then relook at it.' For him, then, since the reason the prohibition emerged is premised on patriarchal notions of identity and male supremacy, which are no longer recognised as valid justifications for any rulings, the prohibition on women's marriage to non-Muslims needs to be revisited to reflect the more contemporary family dynamics of Muslim life. The prohibition especially deserves to be recontextualised, he states, if it is not explicitly found in the Qur'an. However, the prohibition remains valid until a new scholarly consensus emerges, an opinion that points to the importance of scholarly authority in Zigar's understanding of Islam. New interpretations of Islam, particularly those that contradict historical consensus, must be validated by scholars in order to carry legitimacy and authenticity for Zigar.

Naghma (23, single female, South Asian background) had also heard the reason women cannot marry non-Muslims is because of the role of the father in raising Muslim children: 'Religion is passed by the father, or the father is the one who takes the kids to the *masjid* [mosque] or teaches them about Islam. So it's a very patriarchal thing… And if you marry a man who's not Muslim, then he'll want to impose his religion on you and the kids.' She does not accept these explanations as rational and valid but points to their pervasiveness. Careful not to speak on behalf of Islam, Naghma does not classify women's choice to marry non-Muslims as 'un-Islamic' and thinks that there are reasons why Muslim women might marry non-Muslim men: 'I've been thinking about it a lot recently because I've met a few older women who've been marrying non-Muslim men because they can't find anyone to marry because Muslim men just don't want to marry an older woman.' That older Muslim women are marrying non-Muslim men speaks to a common trend in North America. As I discussed earlier, many Muslims, including in the scholarly community, consider it to be a crisis that single Muslim women are facing difficulty finding Muslim husbands. Naghma shared her own experience as well of going to matrimonial events organised by Muslim communities across Texas to find a Muslim husband. As she stated, older Muslim women marry non-Muslim men because Muslim men 'don't want to marry' older women. Muslim men have a larger pool of available spouses to choose from, including non-Muslims; however, Muslim women's options are more restricted for multiple reasons, among which are patriarchal standards – such as many eligible men's and their families' preference for younger and less educated women, and also for lighter-skinned women. Being older, more educated or darker-skinned may therefore decrease a woman's desirability. For such women, considering non-Muslim men as potential spouses increases their chances of getting married.

Other single female discussants expressed similar sentiments regarding their failed searches for Muslim husbands. Fatima (29, East African female, single) shared her struggle to find a Muslim husband and her current consideration of a non-Muslim man for marriage, despite believing that she is prohibited from marrying him. She stated that according to her research on the matter, which she pursued because of her personal situation, Muslim women are explicitly prohibited from marrying non-Muslims, even though she sees nothing wrong with such marriages. 'I mean, this guy I am interested in is amazing. He's everything I want in a partner, we're so compatible, he gets me...but I can't even bring it up with my family because they'll say it's *ḥarām*', she said. Her current decision is that she will marry this non-Muslim man only if he converts to Islam, and she is hopeful because he has been expressing an interest in Islam and asking questions that suggest he might convert soon. However, since the concept of family has changed, Fatima suggests, and since Muslim American women are widely struggling to find suitable Muslim husbands, it is the responsibility of today's scholars to revisit the ruling and make sure that it is something more applicable to women today. Until the scholars form a new consensus, the current consensus is only somewhat binding on Muslims (for Fatima, 3.5 on a scale of 1 to 5, 1 being 'completely disagree', and 5 'completely agree'). She understands Muslim women who defy the consensus on this issue because of her own experiences of not being able to find a compatible Muslim husband. However, she does not recommend Muslims' marriage to non-Muslims regardless of gender because of the challenges that interfaith marital relations can create, especially when children are involved. Like Naghma above, Fatima believes that the prohibition needs to be revisited in light of the struggles that single Muslim women are facing.

Aisyah (20, unmarried female, Southeast Asian background) was taught that 'men could marry *ahl al-kitāb* [People of the Book] just because we didn't have all this Muslim meet-up apps and matchmaking apps. But now we do... In terms of women, I'm guessing it has to do with how culture or religion, you get it from the father or something? Actually, that's not true. Because some religions are matriarchal'. Over the course of the discussion, however, she suggested that perhaps the prohibition exists 'to keep the integrity of the religion. Because I'm thinking of all these friends I have who have Christian moms or dads and they take faith into like their own beliefs [they mix Islam with their personal beliefs].' I asked her if, at least in her experience, the faith can be jeopardised when men marry non-Muslims too, to which she said, 'Honestly, I've seen it jeopardised in interfaith marriages in general. Because I know plenty of non-Muslim women and it's like, these kids know that their dad is Muslim but they don't follow [him]. Because most kids grow up spending time with their moms anyway.'

While none of the single women believed that marriages between Muslim women and non-Muslim men were permissible in Islam, a majority of them (70%) said that they believe it should be allowed. It is significant that the single females are the only category to unanimously state that women's marriage to non-Muslims is prohibited – this reveals the impact of the popular teachings of Islam through online videos and social media. Muslim preachers are vocal about this issue, and they have successfully convinced many among their primary target audience that they are not permitted to marry non-Muslims. For many of them, the conclusion that it is prohibited for women to marry a non-Muslim man is based on research they did because of their personal circumstances (interest in a non-Muslim man, friends in similar situation, and so on). However, even as they believe – have been taught – that such marriages are invalid and impermissible, a majority of them support these marriages and believe that the prohibition does not reflect lived reality and should therefore be changed to accommodate new concerns. Nour (20, single female, Middle Eastern background), for example, said:

> I've heard it's not allowed, but I think it should be. Isn't the assumption that the woman will convert to the man's religion if she marries a non-Muslim?... I just don't think anyone should do it because faith is important so it shouldn't be separate or different in your marriage. I think that you shouldn't co-exist believing in different things... Also, something I just thought of – doesn't it make more sense for the woman to be able to marry a non-Muslim since she spends more time with the kids?

Again, the idea of male superiority through the man's presumed power to influence his wife's faith and his role in childrearing comes up. However, in this case, Nour catches the contradiction almost mid-sentence to point out that the justification she had been given makes no sense because mothers are typically the ones to spend more time with children.

When I asked her what she thinks about women's marriage to People of the Book generally, she said, 'I don't think it's a negative thing because, again, I feel like women do most of the raising. Not that men don't have an influence – they definitely, definitely do, but… I mean, I think it makes more sense to marry someone who's on the same page about God as you.'

Similarly, Zala (26, of mixed background, single), has heard that such marriages are not permissible, but she is not sure whether it should be acceptable or not:

> I was interested in that question, too. I don't really have an opinion on whether this is okay or not. I'm just interested in the Qur'anic *ayah* [verse] and why it's interpreted that way. Because all the verses for marriage are for women and men - men can't marry XYZ, therefore women can't marry XYZ; men can marry this, therefore…you'd expect women can, too! I'd like to have someone I respect explain this to me… I don't know what their reasons were. I've heard ideas about kids – like religion is passed on to the kids through the man, but I'm not convinced. I'd like to hear something better. I mean, if it is, it is – but I want a better reason… I mean, I wouldn't say let's advocate for Muslim women to marry non-Muslims, but let's stop Muslim men from doing it.

She indicates that if the prohibition is Qur'anic, she has no problem with it, but it does not look to her like it is, and she is more interested in finding some convincing rationales for it. Also, like the other single women, she does not believe that men should marry non-Muslim women, hinting at the wider pool of potential spouses available for Muslim men but not for Muslim women. If Muslim men's marital options were restricted, she suggests, then Muslim women would not be struggling so much to find a Muslim spouse.

The single women are relying on their own experiences as well as those of their peers to express their opposition to the prohibition on women's interfaith marriage. Even if they themselves would not marry non-Muslim men because that is not their ideal or preference, they do support a re-interpretation of the interfaith-marriage-related verses to allow women to intermarry today. More importantly, however, they are not convinced by the reasons they have been given to justify the prohibition. Foremost among their reasons seems to be that there is a contradiction at play: on the one hand, women as mothers are expected to – and often do – spend more time with their children and generally contribute to childrearing more than men as husbands tend to; on the other hand, fathers are assumed to be the teachers and guardians of their children's faith, and their religious identity is privileged over the mother's. Even if this contradiction did not exist and pre-modern justifications made sense in the historical context, they do not generally apply to my discussants' familial situations.

Position 3: The prohibition does not reflect reality, but it cannot be changed

Some respondents disagreed with the reason behind the prohibition (as they understood it: a husband's dominance over his wife or patrilineal family structures) but believed it to be Qur'anically grounded and thus not open to change. Among these was Turan (24, single male, South Asian background), who said that the historical justifications included the husband's authority and power over his family, including his family's faith – and that these reasons, even if not convincing to anyone today, must still be accepted because those are Islam's reasons:

> Primarily the reason was that – and has sort of died in our day and age – technically when a woman marries, she moves into another family and the lineage that follows is that of the father's, not the mother's; as well as historically men have been in a stronger position of authority. And those are the primary reasons why Islam does not allow for such marriages. Because if a woman is married to a Jew or Christian, high probability of the children not being raised as Muslims, lineage-wise definitely, as well as perhaps religiously, just because a father has historically had a greater authority in the family structure. And one of those things being that you have to respect the Islamic understanding of things even if you don't believe in it. The *ayah* [verse] goes that the person must believe in what has been revealed before to her and what has been revealed to you… And the definition given was *muḥṣanāt* [chaste or free women], and that definition can't really apply to Christian and Jewish men.

That he acknowledges that these reasons have 'sort of died' today yet accepts their validity because they are the 'Islamic understanding' on the issue is significant because his position reveals an unconditional commitment and loyalty to what he understands Islam – or rather historical Islam – to be. Even as time and context change, and the rationales offered for a specific position no longer make sense in a different time period, the position must be maintained because of its 'Islamic' status. Further, for him, even if the reasons *did* make sense, the important thing is that the prohibition is textually, Qur'anically, grounded – because the Qur'anic verse that allows marriage to the People of the Book explicitly speaks of *muḥṣanāt*, an inherently gendered word ('chaste women'). That is, since the word *muḥṣanāt* explicitly applies only to chaste women, the permission is also only for men and the use of this term removes the possibility for women to marry 'chaste men'.[115]

Another discussant who believed the prohibition is textual is Adam (21, single male, South Asian origin). For him, the historical reasons still apply because Islam is very clear about gender roles; even if gender roles change with time and place, they do not change in Islam:

> In Islam, the roles for women and men are different. [Women] have complete gender equality, but what's prescribed to them is different. Islam gives men a responsibility, and so if the man is Muslim, then the children will be Muslim, but if it's the other way, then the chances are lower [for the children to be Muslim]… When I say the woman's primary role is to raise the kids, I don't mean the husband can't. It's not that she has to; it's her choice. But I just feel like because the woman gives birth and all, she nurses the kids or whatever.

Again, while women are the ones with the responsiblity to raise children – because that is their prescribed Islamic role, he suggests – one might expect that women should have the freedom to marry non-Muslims. When I asked him if he would say that since the mother spends more time with her children, she is more likely to influence her children's faith, he said, 'Ahh, that's a hard question. Honestly, my opinion is that no one should marry non-Muslims. But I guess, yeah, I don't know.' This lack of clarity on the relationship between these two ideas was common in conversations with many other participants as well. Many changed their answers during the interview to 'I don't know, actually' (primarily single women, such as Aisyah, Nour, and Sandara), but many others said as Adam did, 'I guess women can do whatever they want, but we can't change this ruling since it's clearly in the Qur'an. The Qur'an is very clear it's *ḥarām* – I've read it.'

Several other respondents gradually noticed that their explanations in support of the prohibition were not making sense and ended with, 'I don't know.' Sandara (20, single female, South Asian origin) initially said that the prohibition 'has to do with the religion of the children. The mother's like the foundation of the family, and I think it'd be difficult for her to marry a non-Muslim and then try to teach her kids about Islam when their father is not Muslim.' When I sought her clarification about why, if the mother's role is foundational in the family, Muslim men are allowed to marry non-Muslims and women are not, she said, 'Oh, that's a good question. I don't know. I've never thought about this.' That she, like many other discussants, had never thought about the explanations given to them suggests an uncritical acceptance of conventional justifications even if they make little or no sense. Many of my respondents became silent for a moment after realising themselves or through my clarification that the justifications they were giving me in fact supported women's interfaith marriage and opposed men's.

Malala (37, married female, South Asian origin), who believes that the prohibition is Qur'anically grounded, does not accept the traditional justification for the prohibition but believes that there must be some wisdom behind it:

> People will say that the reasoning behind it is that religion is enforced by the father and blah, blah, blah. But in reality, it's the women who're teaching their kids. If that wasn't the case, then men who married non-Muslim women, their kids would be practising Islam. But that doesn't happen.

Her opinions on women who marry non-Muslim men, and men who marry non-Muslim women are starkly different. Regarding men's marriage to non-Muslims, she states:

> I mean, if it's permitted, it's permitted. Who'm I to disagree with it?… I know men who've married Christian and Jewish women who're doing great, you know. Sometimes they [the wives] convert, sometimes they don't. They are good people. I feel like for a lot of people, if they're marrying outside the faith, they're really not thinking about

> how it's going to affect the next generation… Realistically, there is an effect on the next generation. Your legs are in two different directions. Your children are gonna end up neither in most cases, because you're not affiliated with either religion.

She does not recommend it, and it affects children's faith negatively. But as far as women's marriage to non-Muslims is concerned, she said, after stating that it is prohibited according to the 'classical texts':

> I do feel that if you're marrying outside the faith as a woman, you are clearly doing something that is not permitted, but then we all do things that are clearly not permitted all the time. So why focus on the one or the other? Personally, I wouldn't endorse it, but I've had people in my own family who've married non-Muslims. I've gone to their weddings, I've sent them wedding gifts. I do feel guilty sending them gifts and going to their weddings, because they're doing something that's clearly not allowed. If these people were close family, I'd probably feel different about it, but the fact that they are distant family, it's like, whatever, you know?… Obviously, I believe you're not attached to your faith if you're doing something like that. If you're attached enough to your faith to say you're not gonna drink, then really you should be attached to all aspects of the faith, versus saying, 'Oh, I'm not gonna do this, this, this, but it's okay for me to do this.' So it is a personal association with how you do your faith. It's not for others to judge, though.

Her different attitude towards men who marry non-Muslims and women who do is, of course, driven by the acceptance of the traditional prohibition. Since it is impermissible for a Muslim woman to marry a non-Muslim man, then when she does it, she is sinning. But since everyone sins and everyone is responsible before God for their own actions, it should not be anyone else's concern that a Muslim woman has married a non-Muslim man. Still, for her, women who marry non-Muslims are 'obviously okay with the religion ending with them. The practising of the faith ending with them. Because realistically, that's what happens. Your kids won't be associating with the faith, either.' When I asked her if she knew whether this prohibition stems from the Qur'an, she said, 'I don't know if it's in the Qur'an; I've only read translations. But I know that the general consensus prohibits it.' She believes that when Muslim women do marry non-Muslims, they 'should not ask for people to think it's okay that they're doing that. I don't think it's right to ostracise, but endorsing is a different story. I support the consensus because I don't know enough about the subject.'

Another discussant who was certain that the prohibition is Qur'anically grounded is Selma (48, married woman, African background), whose husband converted to Islam to facilitate the marriage. When explaining the Qur'anic roots of the prohibition, she used an Arabic phrase that she said was from the Qur'an. When asked if she knows whether Islam permits women's marriage to People of the Book, Selma, who personally does not believe it should be forbidden but merely discouraged, responded, 'it's very clear that Islam does not allow women to marry non-Muslims. It is in the Qur'an. It is in *Surat al-Baqarah* [chapter 2 of the Qur'an]… I don't know exactly the verse but it says, "We allow you to marry the People of the Book", but for women, it says, "*harramnā 'alaikum* [we have prohibited for you]"… it's like that. It's *taḥrīm* [a case of prohibition]; it says "forbid".' When she offered to show me the verse, I declined, saying that the important point was what she knows about this topic and what her opinion is. She nonetheless looked up the verse, was not able to find it, and concluded, 'I can't find it now, but I know it's in the Qur'an.' There are two important points to analyse here. First, she is deeply certain that the prohibition is Qur'anic and recited a verse that does not exist in the Qur'an to insist that the prohibition is Qur'anic. As an Arabic speaker, she assumes or expects that, since she has been taught that the Qur'an explicitly forbids it, it must appear in the Qur'an as a *taḥrīm*. Second, and importantly, even though she is convinced the prohibition stems explicitly from the Qur'an, she does not accept it and believes that interfaith marriage for women should not be prohibited, only discouraged. Her position differs from several other respondents, whether those who confidently asserted that the Qur'an explicitly prohibits women's marriage to Christians and Jews and should therefore be maintained in all times, or those who were not sure if the prohibition is Qur'anic but should still be preserved because it was a result of scholarly consensus. In other words, Selma does not consider the Qur'anic text to be binding at all times, let alone its interpretations.

Wadaan, a 21-year-old single male of South Asian origins, believes that because the prohibition is strictly in the Qur'an, it cannot and should not be changed even when the context changes. He is not entirely sure what the reasons for the prohibition are but suggests that there is context: 'They [the early Muslims] were trying to spread Islam. The woman has a closer relationship to the child.' He does not support men's interfaith marriage either: 'I mean, I honestly don't understand [why it's allowed for men] because my best friend, her dad is Muslim and her mom is Christian... And I would say she's more Christian than anything. I think people end up following whatever their mom does. Maybe it was a different time back then? I don't know.' Here, he realises that if it is the mother who is supposed to be 'closer' to her child, then her religious influence matters more. He repeatedly noted that he would not marry a non-Muslim and does not think Muslim men should marry non-Muslims:

> I can't speak for anyone else, but I know I would marry a Muslim, just because it's easier. I know that men are allowed to marry Christians and Jews, but I don't understand why. I've friends married to Christians, and I've seen it's, like, really contradicting on their lifestyles and kind of led them away from religion. I think if you really believe in religion, why would you want to marry anyone else?

Since interfaith marriage leads to problems in raising Muslim children as well as in allowing one to maintain their faith in their own religion, the correct choice, according to Wadaan, is to marry someone of the same faith. This is because, as with several other respondents, anecdotally speaking, they do not believe interfaith marriages work very well.

Finally, Orzala (33, married, white) has heard that women are not permitted to marry non-Muslims and has never questioned or thought about it and does not 'feel strongly about it'. However, even if it becomes religiously permissible for a Muslim woman to marry a non-Muslim – that is, if Muslim scholars today collectively came to an agreement to permit it – she would not allow her daughter, or her son, to marry a non-Muslim. The existing scholarly consensus is binding, according to her.

Position 4: Muslim women are allowed to marry non-Muslims

Table 20: Women are allowed to marry People of the Book.

Single Women	Single Men	Married Women	Married Men	Total
0	1	3	2	6

Table 20 accounts for those respondents who agreed with the statement that Muslim women *are* allowed to marry non-Muslims. Some respondents believed that women *are* – not just should be – allowed to marry non-Muslims because the context in which the prohibition emerged does not reflect contemporary Muslim American women's realities. For example, Amadou (40, married male, Black) stated that the prohibition for Muslim women to marry Christians and Jews was imposed 'because maybe the reality was to grow the community, and in that type of society, man had a lot more influence in the family. The likelihood of men converting to join the ranks of Islam was stronger than women converting. Men had more authority and were more dominant. But that's not the reality today.' He supports women's right to interfaith marriages, explaining, 'We live in a non-Muslim society, and there are more non-Muslim men. It's supply and demand. It's what's there. So I think it's completely fine.' He is hinting at what the single female discussants said above about having difficulty finding Muslim husbands in America. Yet, significantly, while none of the single women were willing to say that interfaith marriages are permissible – they argued that such marriages *should* be permissible but that they currently are not – some married participants said that they are permissible. The single women's reluctance to declare it permissible perhaps speaks to their belief that they do not have the authority to disagree with scholarly consensus, while the married participants, perhaps because of their age and their experience with both marriage and religion, felt more comfortable making such a statement. It also speaks to single women's reluctance to make an argument that sounds self-interested.

One participant who openly stated that he does not trust scholars unconditionally because some of their conclusions and rulings may not be correct is Sangin (69, married male, Middle Eastern background). In fact, he said, because scholars have historically been predominantly male, they 'did not care about women'. Men have historically ruled in favour of themselves but to the detriment of women:

> Scholars are prone to making a lot of mistakes, and perhaps more of their rulings are incorrect than they are correct. So I'm very careful about how much I trust scholars. They have a very strong belief that 'the road is this way'. So they don't realise that they must open their eyes to find out exactly what is correct. So I've come to this understanding that during the 1,400 years [of Islamic history] and before

> that, the opinion of the man was against woman. So any time they come to any law, it was to benefit man and they didn't care about women... In my opinion, we must teach women to defend themselves against the opinions of men.

Therefore, Sangin concluded, the prohibition on women's marriage to non-Muslims is not accurate and not 'Islamic'. Given that the prohibition limits women's options and rights, it is rooted in patriarchy and not in 'Islam' for Sangin – and women should protect themselves against rulings like these because they do not serve them but instead control them; these rules are not well-intentioned.

Five married women stated that women *are* permitted to marry non-Muslim men. Osai (41, South Asian background) believed that the prohibition is not Islamic but 'scholarly' and not 'what God intended'. Abigail (39, married female, white) believes that it is not prohibited for women to marry non-Muslims but 'if you're a practising Muslim, you'd want a Muslim spouse'. She was surprised to learn that many scholars consider it prohibited. She does not support the consensus because the Qur'an and the *Sunnah* should hold priority over scholarly opinions. Mina (36, Middle Eastern background) believes that women should be and are allowed to marry 'true People of the Book' and that the prohibition is not Islamic. Diwa (67, married female, South Asian background), began by explaining that she does not support the position that men can marry non-Muslims because 'I can name at least fifteen families where the men married non-Muslims, and none of their children are Muslim. Not a single child.' She recognises that the permission is granted to men explicitly, and notes that since the prohibition is not explicit in the Qur'an, women are permitted to marry non-Muslims as well:

> In the Qur'an there's a verse that is addressed only to men and it says... that a man can marry the women of [the] People of the Book. Now that does not mean that He [God] is asking the women not to marry the People of the Book. There's a difference. People say only men can and women cannot, but it's not clearly saying in the *ayah* [verse] that women cannot! It says, 'You can marry women who are believers.' This is my problem with the scholars. They can choose whatever they want to, and I don't agree with them... It's the man who finds excuses in the Qur'an to marry whoever he wants.

Diwa understands the verse to be permission only for men to marry People of the Book – but not as prohibition for women. Significantly, she believes that the unanimous reading of the verse as a prohibition is because of the gender of the scholars: as males, not only did they fail to consider the implications of their rulings and interpretations, but they also sought to read the Qur'an in ways that benefited them personally.

Like Diwa, Barsalai (31, married female, South Asian background) said that she has read 'a verse in the Qur'an that says men can marry Christians and Jews, but it doesn't explicitly say if women can't'. She added that 'there should be flexibility. Like if kids don't follow the father's religion, then [women's marriage to Christians and Jews] should be allowed. It shouldn't be considered sinful.' She added that 'only God can decide what's sinful or not'. She is suggesting that since God has not declared such marriages sinful through the Qur'an – via an explicit prohibition – Muslims should not declare them sinful either.

While some respondents stated that the prohibition is only Islamically valid if it is Qur'anically grounded, others disagree so strongly with it that even if it is in the Qur'an, they believe it no longer applies. Athena (21, single female, mixed) held such a view. Lejla (20, single female, European background) believes that because Muslim gender dynamics have shifted so significantly in our times, the prohibition should only remain valid if it is explicitly in the Qur'an.

CONTEMPORARY AUTHORITATIVE RESPONSES TO WOMEN'S INTERFAITH MARRIAGE[116]

This section deals with contemporary authoritative responses to the historical prohibition on women's marriage to non-Muslims, both supporting and opposing it. The popular opinion on the practice of Muslim women's interfaith marriage remains that it is prohibited. *Fatwa*s (legal opinions) issued by contemporary Muslim scholars adamantly state that the Qur'anic position is that 'it is forbidden for a Muslim woman to be married to a non-Muslim', where the 'non-Muslim' is assumed to include People of the Book as well.[117] Scholars both historically and currently disagree over the question of the validity of a marriage between two non-Muslims in which the wife converts to Islam: should she leave the marriage – or does her choice to stay married to her non-Muslim husband invalidate her marriage or her conversion? In contemporary conversations on the issue, scholars reference minority opinions from the past legal tradition to validate their preferences, sometimes contravening and departing from the historical consensus, such as allowing a woman who converts to Islam to stay in a marriage with a non-Muslim husband because of the family's circumstances.[118]

The question of women's marriage to the People of the Book appears frequently in online Muslim discussions, forums, blogs, and other Islam-related websites. The Egyptian website *Dār al-Iftā' al-Miṣriyyah*, for example, features a question titled 'Why a Muslim woman can't marry a non Muslim?' [sic] in which a Muslim woman asks: 'I know the rule but where in the Qur'an that allows ONLY men [sic] to marry from '*Ketabia* i.e. Christian or Jew. Please quote from Al Quran what has been practiced by giving the right to men and prohibit women when the result is one family of different beliefs and their impact on children.'[119] In response, the *fatwa* website states:

> This is mentioned in the words of God Almighty, [in verse 5:5]… In this noble verse, God Almighty only allowed Muslims to feed the non-Muslims from their foods. This way God draws Muslims' attention to the fact that the matter of eating slaughtered animals differs from marriage, since it is allowed for Muslims to eat the meat slaughtered by the People of the Book and vice-versa. On the contrary, it is only permissible for Muslim men to marry women from the people of the Book and not the other way round. Hence, it is impermissible for a non-Muslim man to marry a Muslim woman.[120]

Here, the woman is told that Qur'anic verse 5:5 prohibits such marriages, but no clear explanation and certainly no evidence is offered for how the verse accomplishes that. The *fatwa* goes on to explain the reason: 'If non-Muslim men were allowed to marry Muslim women, they will have a legal authority over them and God never allows non-Muslims to have authority over Muslims. Unlike food, it is allowed to exchange food with non-Muslims since there are no legal restrictions on it in Islamic law.'[121] The idea that a husband has legal authority over his wife and that the legal authority must come only from a Muslim man is read into the Qur'an to conclude that a woman's marriage to non-Muslims is impermissible.

Claims of the 'clarity' of the Qur'anic prohibition abound in the research. Zahidul Islam, writing in the Malaysian context, insists that the prohibition is 'very clear' and that it exists because such marriages would 'definitely' jeopardise a Muslim woman's faith and identity:

> This category of marriage [between a Muslim woman and any non-Muslim man] is haram in its totality regardless of whether the man is from the people of the Scripture or other types of unbelievers. The prohibition is very clear. Allah has stated in the Holy Quran [2:221]: 'Nor give (your women) in marriage to idolater men until they believe; and certainly a believing servant is preferable to an idolater (free man), though he may please you...'... The reason or wisdom behind the prohibition is also evident and unambiguous. As we know, the paramount objective of Shari'ah is to protect religion. If Islam allows such marriage, it will definitely jeopardise the Muslim woman's faith. Not only would the Muslim woman be influenced by her non-Muslim husband's faith and lifestyle, it is also not beyond expectation that the latter will prevent the former from performing religious obligations or duties. This is simply because the husband is the head of family and he is generally more dominant as compared to the wife.[122]

Islam goes on to explain that the focus of his research is Muslim men's marriage to *kitābī* women because of the 'very clear and unequivocal' proof of the prohibition on Muslim women's interfaith marriage. He respects the views of Muslim jurists and scholars (he identifies Rashid Rida among them) who have extended the word *kitābī* to apply to 'Zoroastrians as well as idolaters in India' – because their religion 'promotes the oneness of God'.[123] Still, he recommends prohibiting all interfaith marriages between Muslims and non-Muslims in Malaysia, men or women, because one cannot really be sure if a woman 'genuinely' believes in the oneness of God, even if in principle the Qur'an permits interfaith marriage for a man.[124] He rejects 'without hesitation' any claims by a Muslim scholar challenging the prohibition on women's interfaith marriage.[125]

While the majority opinion remains that women's interfaith marriages are prohibited, many Muslims have challenged this notion and offered alternative viewpoints. On National Women's Day in August 2017, the Tunisian president Mohamed Beji Caid Essebsi spoke up in support of 'comprehensive equal treatment for Tunisian women' and argued that they should be allowed to marry non-Muslims and receive equal shares in inheritance.[126] While some news reports claim that 'Tunisia's authority on Islamic fatwas' supported his position,[127] others claimed that religious leaders opposed his position because 'the religious texts [are] clear about them'.[128]

In April 2017, Junaid Jahangir, a Canadian gender-justice activist, published an article on the *Huffington Post* in support of Muslim women's interfaith marriage.[129] Jahangir presented a list of ten contemporary scholars – nine men and one woman, Asma Lamrabet – who either support women's interfaith marriages or argue against the prohibition, including Khaled Abou El-Fadl and Hasan al-Turābi (d. 2015). The article underlines the significance of the subject by recounting the struggle of an interfaith couple, a Muslim woman and Jewish man, who were unable to find an imam to officiate their marriage. The response to Jahangir's article included negative reactions where readers attempted to correct his claims. Among those who responded critically to Jahangir publicly was Abdullah Ali, an instructor at Zaytuna College and at Lamppost Education Initiative, a website committed to 'providing access to high level and relevant Islamic scholarship' that affects Muslims in the West.[130] Lamppost announced days in advance that Imam Abdullah Ali would be giving a live lecture on Facebook explaining why Muslim women are not allowed to marry non-Muslims. Referring to Jahangir's article, the Lamppost announcement promoting Ali's talk provides details about the talk:

> A recent article suggests that restrictions on Muslim women preventing marriage to non-Muslims are unfair and unreasonable. In response to this and questions that Muslims have had about the issue, Shaykh Abdullah Ali will be on our Lamppost Education Initiative Facebook page on 'Facebook Live' from 6:30 to 7:30 pm Eastern Standard Time on Friday, March 24th to briefly address the issue and answer your questions about it.[131]

The talk is now published on Lamppost and available to the public.[132] Abdullah Ali begins by assuring his viewers that he will focus on the Qur'an, rather than on tradition, and show that the Qur'an does prohibit women's interfaith marriages, highlighting the three Qur'anic verses that reference the issue. However, he repeatedly returns to his point that the view permitting such marriages 'is against the historical tradition, which says that a Muslim woman cannot marry a non-Muslim man'. In his discussion of Q. 2:221, he references the scholarly disagreement over the meaning of the word 'polytheist' (*mushrik*). Ali suggests that one interpretation of the verse is to prohibit both women and men from marrying all non-Muslims, be they Christian, Jewish, or others.[133] The second verse he addresses is Q. 5:5, which, as discussed above, explicitly permits men's marriage to the People of the Book. Discussing Q. 2:221, Ali states:

> Some will say this verse excludes women from marrying Christians and Jews. So God starts by saying neither women nor men can marry polytheists, but this verse says men can marry Christians/Jews and Shiites will say Zoroastrians, too… Others will say this verse…is introducing a new injunction…that the Jews and Christians are not under the category of polytheists… So Islam not only limits the different types of men that a woman can marry but it also limits the different types of women a man can marry…[134]

Curiously, he reads Q. 5:5 and 2:221 together as limiting men's right to marriage – to only three groups of women: Muslims, Jews, and Christians – and conveniently does not seem to recognise that women are even more limited, to Muslim men only. It is also striking that he views this as a limitation upon men, as though to suggest that Muslim men should really be at liberty to marry women of any faith, including polytheists.[135] Finally, for verse Q. 60:10, he states: 'This verse is more explicit, which would outlaw the intermarriage of Muslim women and non-Muslim men. Allah refers to the unbelieving men as *kuffār*, which *includes* Christian and Jewish men. So that's an important thing to reflect on.' However, he fails to reflect on the portion of the verse that also orders men to end their marital ties with disbelieving women.

Ali challenges the idea that the Qur'an does not explicitly prohibit women's interfaith marriages and therefore it cannot be forbidden. He asks that if silence is read as permission, then how does one deal with the fact that the Qur'an gives men explicit permission to marry multiple wives but is silent on polyandry?[136] Here, he is clearly admitting that the Qur'an is silent on the matter but interprets the silence as upholding the existing prohibition. He concludes:

> Fundamentally, the Qur'an, or the understanding that scholars have had, not only the scholars of the four schools, but scholars among the Companions, all the way down to the present day, and…for all of Islamic history, both Shias and Sunnis have held the view that it is

> unlawful for Muslim women to marry a non-Muslim man… Now if you want to practise historical Islam, this has meaning to you. If you're not interested in practising historical Islam, and you're interested in something that is a bit more 'progressive' or evolutionary…where you believe only in God but not in religion, or you're spiritual but not religious, then follow your fancy, and I'm not here trying to impose on anyone; I'm just here to try to articulate what historical Islam has said about this issue. And people are free to do whatever they want to… Allah says, whoever wants to, let him reject faith. But Allah says there are consequences that come with that.[137]

Thus, while he began his talk with the claim that he will focus on Qur'anic verses that prohibit such marriages, he does not mention those in his concluding statement and instead emphasises the historical view. He also speaks unkindly of those who disagree with his views, dismissing them as those who 'reject faith' and who 'follow [their] fancy'. In the Question and Answer part of the talk, he states that this topic is not one of *ijtihād*, not open to re-interpretations, because it falls under the 'non-negotiables' of Islam, like the prohibition on *ribā* (usury).

Ali is not alone in using Q. 60:10 to prohibit only women's marriage to non-Muslims, despite the fact that the verse is not about People of the Book and that it applies to both women and men. Historical commentators have unanimously agreed that this verse was about Meccan *mushrik*s and that it was revealed to address the specific case of women who were leaving their polytheist communities for the Muslim community. According to the Muslim tradition, Muhammad himself had Christian and Jewish wives (or concubines, depending on the source).[138] This is further evidence that contemporary references to Q. 60:10 are not accurate, as they disregard its context and fail to account for its original audience and instead claim that it applies to Christians and Jews today, not just Meccan *mushrik*s in Muhammad's time.[139]

Other scholars, such as Feisal Abdul Rauf, an American imam at Park51, have proposed extending the permission of marriage with *kitābī*s to Muslim women. Abdul Rauf recognises that Muslim women's opportunities to find and marry Muslim men are reduced when Muslim men marry non-Muslim women.[140] He writes that religious scholars, both in the West and in traditional Muslim societies, are being forced to address this issue, which speaks to the depth of the problem and the lack of available Muslim men for Muslim women. Abdul Rauf supports the marriage of Muslim women to non-Muslim (Christian and Jewish) men, stating that not supporting interfaith couples where the wife is a Muslim sends them the message that 'the Muslim community can do nothing for them religiously', which would cause them to 'flee, religiously, psychologically, and even physically, seeking out a justice of the peace for a civil ceremony'.[141] He adds, 'The choice I have made, and now promote, is to accept these couples, help them, and hope that they will help sustain and build our community.'[142] He also suggests that this is because the Qur'an does not explicitly forbid such a marriage. Narrating the story of the Prophet's daughter Zaynab, who was married to a cousin before the Prophet received revelation, and who herself converted to Islam while her husband did not, Abdul Rauf reminds his Muslim readers that the Prophet never compelled her to leave her husband and never declared their marriage invalid.[143] Yet, even though the case of the Prophet's daughter is one involving a polytheist – not a Christian or a Jew – it is not viewed as setting precedent even for marriage between Muslim women and People of the Book.

Similarly, Imam Khaleel Mohammed, Professor of Religion at San Diego State University, supports a re-evaluation of the prohibition and opposes relying on the Qur'an for explicit permission rather than for prohibitions.[144] Challenging the historical and patriarchal idea of the husband's dominance over his wife, Mohammed concludes that, given contemporary ideas on gender equality, 'an inter-faith marriage can take place on [the] condition that neither spouse will be forcibly converted to the other's religion'.[145]

Others express reluctance to either allow or prohibit women's interfaith marriages. Khaled Abou El Fadl, for example, does not consider it a prohibition but does believe it to be *makrūh*, or reprehensible, because, he observes, 'the children of these Muslim/non-Muslim marriages in most cases do not grow up with a strong sense of their Islamic identity. It seems to me that in countries like the U.S. it is best for the children if they grow up with a Muslim father and mother.'[146] Despite his opinion, he writes:

> Surprising to me, all schools of thought prohibited a Muslim woman from marrying a man who is a *kitābī* (among the people of the book). I am not aware of a single dissenting opinion on this, which is rather unusual for Islamic jurisprudence because Muslim jurists often disagreed on many issues, but this is not one of them.[147]

Struck by the unanimous agreement of historical scholars on the issue of women's marriage to Christians and Jews, Abou El Fadl is reluctant to support such a marriage from a theological standpoint because he assumes there must be some wisdom behind the scholarly position. Despite having the religious authority to issue an opinion on the matter even if it contradicts the consensus, Abou El Fadl is concerned about the potential theological implications of permitting women to marry non-Muslims when (presumably) all scholars before him have forbidden it.

The contemporary conversation on this topic, as can be seen in the many responses to this commonly asked question, relies on the pre-modern ideas discussed above, inasmuch as they support the prohibition. These rationales include assumptions about the husband's leadership, authority, and supremacy, the importance of male lineage and irrelevance of female lineage, and a fear of the possibility that a non-Muslim husband might convert his wife to his religion, if he has one.[148] All of these reasons can be questioned, as can be the claims about spousal compatibility discussed above. For instance, if women cannot marry non-Muslims because of issues of children's identity and religious upbringing, what of cases in which a couple do not want to have any children, or cannot have children, or have mutually agreed on how to raise their children? If it is because the two are not compatible, contemporary notions of compatibility are different from those of pre-modern Muslim scholars. For them, marital compatibility was determined by social standing, which involved a heavy emphasis on one's lineage in a way that many contemporary Muslims do not take so seriously. The concept of compatibility is currently being redefined to extend beyond lineage and a shared culture, language, or background. Pre-modern Muslim jurists assumed that all Muslim women were incompatible with all non-Muslim men, while all Muslim men could be compatible with all 'chaste' Christians and Jews. Indeed, while the notion of compatibility remains important, it is not governed by the legal rules of Muslim jurists, but instead by contemporary social rules and considerations. Still, the argument of compatibility can be used to contemporary Muslim women's advantage: expanding the definition of compatibility to include intellectual compatibility rather than limiting it to the same social status, for example, would validate many potential interreligious marriages. I have shown elsewhere that the same methods of interpretation that classical exegetes used, e.g. *qiyās* (analogical reasoning), *ijmāʿ* (scholarly consensus), and *takhṣīṣ* (particularising a general statement) to prohibit women's interfaith marriage can be used by contemporary Muslims to argue in support of women's interfaith marriages.[149]

Contemporary scholarly views on intermarriage offer different and new possibilities for Muslims seeking such unions. While the premodern stance remains powerful and convincing for many Muslims, alternative scholarly views not only exist but indicate that there is a lack of consensus on the matter. The difference between the historical and contemporary discussion highlights interpretive possibilities afforded to scholars and other readers of the Qur'an in order to arrive at novel conclusions.

Essential to this discussion is the historical context in which the scholars concluded that women's marriage to all non-Muslims is prohibited, as we will see. The historical and social contexts in which the scholars were reading the Qur'an are integral to the conclusions they derived from the three verses, because these contexts provided the premises.

SLAVERY AND MARRIAGE[150]

> The dominion of marriage is a kind of enslavement, and the dominion over right hand possessions is absolute enslavement. God allowed Muslim men to marry the People of the Book, but He did not allow the People of the Book to marry their (Muslim) women. This is because marriage is a kind of slavery, as Umar said: 'Marriage is enslavement, so let each of you think carefully about who will enslave his daughter.'[151]

Why were the scholars so confident in declaring prohibited something that, at least to a contemporary reader of the Qur'an, does not appear Qur'anically founded? Presumably, they did not hesitate to question their own and their predecessors' assumptions about the prohibition because the idea sounded natural to them. Perhaps, as Ayesha Chaudhry argues in the context of Qur'anic verse 4:34, which has historically been read unanimously to allow a husband to physically discipline his wife, the scholars did not question their interpretation because such an understanding of the verse fit their shared cosmology, or 'visions of the universe as it would exist if all humans submitted entirely to God's laws' that relied necessarily on gender hierarchy, with men above women.[152] This makes sense for the unanimous prohibition of women's marriage to non-Muslims: it made sense that women would not, or should not, be allowed to marry outside the faith because such marriages would disrupt the gender hierarchy on which patriarchies have functioned historically. Although this proposal does not account for the contemporary tendency to maintain the consensus on the issue, I will return to this point later, in my conclusion when emphasising the relevance of the primary argument of my study. I suggest that issues that predominantly affect women are not considered, by scholars and those to whom they are not relevant, as urgent enough to warrant a re-examination, despite their impact on women's lives today. This requires an in-depth discussion of which issues are deemed 'urgent' and 'relevant' as well as a discussion of the connection between patriarchal constructions of Islam and authority.

I will show here that the prohibition on intermarriage by female Muslims is rooted in assumptions of male superiority over women and Muslim superiority over non-Muslims. It is a product of the assumptions about women and women's (in)abilities upheld by scholars of patriarchal, male-dominated societies. Marriage between a Muslim man and a non-Muslim woman is potentially the utmost form of male superiority over women: the Muslim man may display his superiority over his wife on the grounds of both her gender and her religion. Since few of my participants support the arguments on which the prohibition stands, I ask why the prohibition remains compelling enough to be maintained as a predominant position.

The idea that a woman cannot marry (or cannot be married to) a Person of the Book is not only an extra-Qur'anic notion but is more importantly a product of a conception of marriage that views the husband as the owner of his wife's sexuality – i.e. as having usufructuary rights over his wife's sexuality/sexual body – since female sexuality was historically viewed as a type of commodity.[153] As Hina Azam explains:

> For early jurists, sexual relations were only lawful in those contexts where the man possessed a usufructory right over the sexuality of the woman in question. Such ownership (*milk*) could only be acquired through purchasing those rights from the proprietor of her sexuality through payment of an exchange value (later called *'iwaḍ* or *badal*)… Ownership of the exclusive right to enjoy her sexuality (*buḍ'*), however, was transferred to her husband, as a usufructory right secured through paying a dower (*mahr*, *ṣadāq*, or *'uqr*).[154]

Thus, the female sexuality (although, importantly, not the woman herself) was viewed as a commodity to be purchased through marriage or enslavement. The notion of marriage as ownership occurs in pre-modern (pre-nineteenth century) Muslim legal literature. In these texts, the institutions of marriage and slavery are so similar that the guidelines of slavery are applicable, to some extent, to marriage as well.

Kecia Ali has demonstrated that classical legal analogies between wife and slave as well as marriage and purchase significantly shaped Muslim jurisprudence on marriage.[155] As she points out, the prohibition of women's marriage to non-Muslims 'presupposed two kinds of hierarchies: Muslims were to be dominant over non-Muslims and husbands over wives. As wives were to be subordinate to their husbands, the marriage of a non-Muslim man to a Muslim woman would challenge this authority structure'.[156]

As a first premise, legal scholars considered marriage a form of slavery (*al-nikāḥ naw'u riqqin*) and a wife was required to obey her husband the way a slave would his master.[157] As a second premise, Muslims could enslave non-Muslims but not vice versa. The conclusion thus followed that a Muslim man could marry (or enslave) a non-Muslim woman, but a non-Muslim could not marry (or enslave) a Muslim woman.

Yohanan Friedmann similarly discusses in detail the views of legal scholars, such as Ibn Ḥanbal and Ibn Ḥazm, on marriages between Muslim women and non-Muslims.[158] Ibn Ḥanbal stated, in the question of the marriage between two *kitābī*s once the wife converts to Islam, 'We can possess them, but they cannot possess us' (*namlikuhum wa-lā yamlikūnanā*). These marriages were such a violation of the law that not only was the offender – the non-Muslim (specifically a *dhimmī*, a non-Muslim of protected status living under Muslim rule) who married a Muslim woman – corporally punished, but so was the individual who facilitated the marriage.[159] In the case that a non-Muslim married a female Muslim slave, his entire community was to be punished along with him.[160]

Similarly, Friedmann analyses Ibn Ḥanbal's justification against Muslim women's marriage to non-Muslims on the basis that such marriages are akin to non-Muslims' ownership of Muslims. As Friedmann explains:

> A marriage of a Muslim woman to a non-Muslim man would result in an unacceptable incongruity between the superiority which the woman should enjoy by virtue of being Muslim, and her unavoidable wifely subservience to her infidel husband. In terms of Islamic law, such

> a marriage would involve an extreme lack of *kafā'a*, that is, of the compatibility between husband and wife, which requires that a woman not marry a man lower in status than herself.[161]

The gender hierarchy that pre-modern jurists conceptualised favoured men above women and privileged Muslims above non-Muslms. A Muslim man marrying a non-Muslim woman was superior to his wife on both counts – the hierarchy was stable. But a Muslim woman marrying a non-Muslim man had a claim of superiority over her husband in her religion. This disruption of the hierarchy couldn't be tolerated.

The idea of ownership was also attributed to Umar, who reportedly said, in the context of inheritance, that a Muslim can inherit from a disbeliever, but a disbeliever cannot inherit from a Muslim because Islam is superior – 'in the same way that we [Muslim men] can marry their women, but they cannot marry our women'.[162] (For Umar, the category of *kāfir* reportedy included the People of the Book, and, as mentioned earlier, he discouraged marriage between Muslim men and People of the Book, although some exegetes are not convinced Umar would have issued such a claim.) The statement that Muslims can inherit from non-Muslims but not vice versa, just as Muslims can marry their women but not vice versa, also appears in Zarqāni's (d. 1710) commentary on Mālik's *al-Muwaṭṭa'*. Ibn Qudāmah (d. 1212), too, invokes a Hadith attributed to the Prophet Muhammad to support his interpretation that Islam is superior to other religions because 'we can marry their women, but they cannot marry ours', and 'therefore, we can inherit from them (the non-Muslims) but they cannot inherit from us'.[163] Similarly, Ibn Taymiyya (d. 1328) states:

> *milk al-nikāḥ* [the classical Islamic legal term for marriage, literally dominion of marriage] is a type of enslavement [*naw'u riqqin*] and dominion over right hand possession [slavery] is absolute enslavement [*wa milk al-yamīn riqqu tām*]. God allowed Muslim men [*lil-muslimīn*] to marry the People of the Book, but He did not allow the People of the Book to marry their [Muslims'] women. This is because marriage is a kind of slavery, as 'Umar said: 'Marriage is enslavement, so be careful, each of you, with regard to who will enslave his daughter [*al-nikāḥu riqqin; faliyandhur aḥadukum 'inda man yaraq karimatahu*].' Zaid Ibn Thabit said, 'The husband is master in God's Book,' and recited the verse of God 'and they found her master [*sayyidihā*] at the door'

> (Q. 12:25). And the Prophet said, 'Fear God regarding women, for they are prisoners with you [*'awān 'indakum*].' So it is permissible for a Muslim to enslave [*yastariqq*] a *kāfirah*, but a *kāfir* is not allowed to enslave a Muslim woman [*Muslimah*] because Islam is superior and nothing can be above it, just as a Muslim can own [*yamlik*] a *kāfir*, while a *kāfir* can never own a Muslim.[164]

As shown in Ibn Ḥanbal's position above, other reasons for the prohibition included claims regarding marital incompatibility between a Muslim woman and all non-Muslim men – but not between Muslim men and *kitābī* women. If the reason for the prohibition is indeed concern over compatibility between the husband and the wife, what explains the permission for men to enter such marriages? I am reluctant to accept the prohibition as rooted in a genuine concern for the well-being of the Muslim woman. The logic is that while a wife's status – but not necessarily her well-being – was inferior to that of her husband's by virtue of being a woman, it was superior to that of a non-Muslim's by virtue of being a Muslim. However, this rationale is suspect because of the severity of the punishment ordained for the man who failed to heed it. The case of a Muslim man of low social standing who marries a Muslim woman of a higher status is not discussed in the same way as the non-Muslim (of any class) who marries a Muslim woman (of any class). That the community thought it worth asking if a *dhimmī* who marries a Muslim woman was to be put to death, along with the woman's guardian who consented to the marriage, points to the possibility that this was not a question of marital compatibility but an infringement of Muslim male privilege. In fact, 'Severe punishment is ordained for a *dhimmī* who weds a Muslim woman and consummates the marriage; according to a view attributed to Mālik b. Anas, the culprit is even liable to be executed since he broke the conditions of his *dhimma* treaty.'[165] There is disagreement on the severity of the penalty for the offending *dhimmī*, some scholars even going so far as to say that a collective punishment should be inflicted on all *dhimmī*s in a given community if a *dhimmī* has sexual relations with an enslaved Muslim woman.[166] Even if the *dhimmī* converted to Islam after marriage, the marriage was still invalid because it was invalid originally and conversion does not validate an invalid marriage.[167]

The parallel that jurists drew between marriage and slavery is not merely a thing of the past, however; it continues to affect Muslim family law today.[168] Ali notes that this analogy:

> is key to understanding Muslim marriage law. The strict gender differentiation of marital rights, the importance of women's sexual exclusivity, and above all the strict imposition of rules about unilateral divorce, however contested in practice, all facilitate and flow from the key idea that marriage and licit sex require male control or dominion. Analogy makes this possible.[169]

Licit sex is only possible, for pre-modern jurists, 'when a man wielded exclusive control over a particular woman's sexual capacity'.[170] In her dissertation on Muslim women's interfaith marriage, Leena Azzam argues that the prohibition on women's interfaith marriage is rooted in a contextual understanding of the concept of *qiwāmah* (male authority/leadership) and, like Ali, connects it to the idea of ownership and slavery; she discusses the views of several scholars who saw marriage as a form of slavery and humiliation, among them al-Ghazālī (d. 1111), al-Marghinānī (d. 1197), and al-Sarakhsī (d. 1090).[171] Azzam argues that this 'perception of marital life as a form of enslavement (*riqq*) continues to exist today as a result of the concept of male authority (*qiwāmah*)'. As she explains, 'this does not mean that in Islamic legal discourse, a wife is a slave, but rather that slavery allows for understanding one of the central notions that has shaped the jurists' views of marriage which is that licit sexual relations are hierarchical'.[172] My research corroborates Azzam's claims, as I have shown in the discussion of my interviews above that the concepts of gender hierarchy and male authority and supremacy continue to shape contemporary Muslim opinions on women's interfaith marriage.

Muslims have the option to reject this hierarchical view of marriage, one that is founded on a parallel with slavery. Muslim scholars and activists have already provided excellent suggestions for the practical ways in which the Islamic idea of marriage *can* be shifted from an inegalitarian, hierarchical one that requires wifely obedience in exchange for maintenance from her husband.[173] Neither the Islamic tradition, nor its texts, nor the framework within which marriage is understood in pre-modern *fiqh* is frozen in time; each is subject to change.[174] Mir-Hosseini *et al.* have insightfully observed that while the Qur'anic idea of marriage rests on *mawaddah* (love), *raḥmah* (mercy), and *ma'rūf* (common good) in multiple verses and only once does the idea of men as *qawwām* (maintainers, leaders) appear, the Islamic legal tradition's approach to marriage is founded on the framework of *qiwāmah* (male leadership, authority) rather than on love, beauty, and justice, as the Qur'an mandates.[175] They ask, 'Why did the classical jurists not choose to translate these two terms [love and mercy] into legal rulings?' Asking similar questions on many gender-related issues, they argue 'for an egalitarian construction of family laws from within Muslim legal tradition'.[176]

Rooted, therefore, in supremacist, hierarchical assumptions that have largely been debunked, the claims of the scholars discussed above rely on circular logic to reinforce or legitimate their own assumptions and expectations of women and non-Muslims. That is, the scholars imagine the husband as his wife's master, require wifely obedience to the husband and believe Muslims are superior to non-Muslims. Their legal rulings for marriage follow from these premises. The twin ideas that Muslims are superior to non-Muslims and that a wife owes her husband obedience create a contradiction in the case of female interfaith marriage: since this is the case, a Muslim woman cannot be married to a non-Muslim man. The prohibition is a product of the assumptions about women and women's (in)abilities, upheld by members of patriarchal, male-dominated societies. Hence, it perpetuates the subjugation of women.

DISCUSSION AND ANALYSIS

The charts in this chapter illustrate the opinions of my participants on statements I read to them about interfaith marriage. Note that in each chart, single women – for whom the question of interfaith marriage is most relevant – are the group that supports the practice the most. Single women unanimously said Islam prohibits such marriages, and they proposed that contemporary scholars of Islam re-evaluate the prohibition in favour of women's marital options. Married men came the second closest in support of women's choice to intermarry. For some of them, like Gahez (77), Sangin (69), Pamir (65), their own daughters or other single women's experiences and struggles were a strong motivator to support this choice. Sangin said, 'If I had a daughter, I'd have no right to tell her what to do. Even the majority of Muslim men are worse than non-Muslim men. But I'd tell her to marry a man who believes in God, who respects her, and has a wonderful personality. If he comes and says his *shahādah* [statement of faith upon conversion to Islam] but he's a corrupted, wrong person, no, no, no!' Similarly, Gahez (77, married male, South Asian background) explained that Muslim women today are marrying non-Muslims 'maybe because women don't find as compatible Muslim husbands! Women are expected to be subjugated [in Muslim communities], and women in America don't like that. Islam emphasises compatibility between the partners for marriage.' However, while he does not believe it is prohibited, he believes 'it's less preferable because they [the women] have to raise the children right', suggesting not only that the husband does not have such a role but also that an interfaith marriage would complicate raising children in accordance with Islamic principles. None of my participants recommended marriages between Muslims and non-Muslims as a first choice.

Most of the married women and most of the single men did not approve of women's interfaith marriage. Both groups acknowledged that Muslim women are involved in such marriages but that the option is 'clearly' prohibited in the Qur'an, and therefore they are committing a sin by marrying outside of the faith. Recall that one married woman recited a verse she insisted was from the Qur'an that explicitly says, 'We have made marriage to *kitābīs* impermissible for you (women).'

If they could find Muslim husbands, some of them pointed out, then so can other Muslim women; and if they cannot, their struggle to find a Muslim husband is a test from God, and they must remain patient. They did, however, acknowledge that some of their single Muslim female friends were struggling to find Muslim husbands. None of the single men, however, were aware that Muslim women face difficulties finding Muslim husbands. For them, the choice was 'clearly' not afforded by the Qur'an. Those who did support such marriages did so based on gender equality and a lack of faith in the idea that scholars would take women's rights seriously.

Why is the idea that the Qur'an prohibits Muslim women's marriage to non-Muslims so widely shared, when the verse does not explicitly prohibit women's marriage to Christians and Jews but merely permits it to men? It is tempting to suggest that the idea exists due to a lack of direct reading of the Qur'an, but two of my female participants, one married and one single, had done their research for their situations: the first decided that marrying a non-Muslim man she is interested in would be disobedience to God, and she still does not plan to marry him until he converts. The second participant married a man who, in her words, converted to Islam but is 'only nominally Muslim', because she was not going to break God's law to marry a man she loved. Only two discussants, a married couple (wife in her sixties, husband in his seventies), stated that they have done their research and concluded that such marriages are not *ḥarām*. While the husband did not tell me this himself, his wife revealed that he officiates the marriage of couples with a Muslim bride and a non-Muslim groom, because no imam they know is willing to do it.

A justifaction for the prohibition based on the necessity of raising children Islamically does not account for the possibility that a couple in an interfaith marriage may be unable to have children or may not wish to have any. If the primary reason that women cannot marry non-Muslims is linked to the issue of children's identity and religious upbringing, how does one judge the cases where a couple plan not to have any children, they cannot have any children, or they have agreed mutually on how to raise their children?[177]

In what ways, then, does the prohibition or the popular understanding around it reflect the reality of interfaith marriages? Some studies have also shown that interreligious couples 'consciously regulate the influence of religion in their families with the goal of maintaining interfaith harmony'.[178] But we still lack sufficient empirical data to confirm or deny some of the claims made about the consequences of Muslim women's marriage to non-Muslims, especially the effects on the children and on the woman. In how many, and which, cases does the wife leave Islam for her husband, and/or in which and how many cases do the children adopt the father's religion? Did the jurists propose these ideas according to their assumptions and fears, and to what extent – if at all – are these ideas rooted in some reality, particularly for contemporary Muslims? In his study on interreligious marriage in Indonesia, Noryamin Aini notes that it 'is widely believed that [interreligious marriage] may jeopardize a woman's faith, because it is assumed that women, being inferior to men, will end up converting to their husband's religion'.[179] Challenging this claim, he writes that 'A study based on Yogyakarta province census data from 1980, 1990, and 2000 found that, on average, 70% of children born to inter-religious married couples became Muslim if their mother was Muslim, whereas only about 50% of the children became Muslim if their father was Muslim.'[180] Another study conducted on Indonesian interreligious marriages concludes that such couples may decide to allow one partner to take over the religious upbringing of the children (not necessarily gendered), raise one/some children with one religion and others with another, or agree to raise the children in both religious environments and traditions. All, however, want their children to be raised with universal values of kindness, justice, and love.[181]

This is not to deny the importance of the challenges that can arise in an interfaith marriage; however, this applies regardless of whether a Muslim woman is marrying a non-Muslim man or a Muslim man is marrying a non-Muslim woman, and is a universal concern in interfaith marriages with some religious traditions opting for paternal supremacy.[182] The difference here is that with Muslim men, the assumption is that the Muslim husband will be rightfully in charge of his wife and children, but non-Muslim men are not trusted to ensure that the wife maintains her religious identity or that of her children. In both cases, the expectation is that the children should be Muslim.

Research is now growing on the phenomenon of Muslim women's marriage to non-Muslims. In their research on British-Turkish Muslim women married to non-Muslims, Jawad and Elmali-Karakaya find that the couple (Muslim woman, non-Muslim husband) do not argue or fight over religious issues or decisions if at least one of them does not care about religion; if they both care about religion, then they argue. In their study, 6 out of 20 women identified as religious, the remaining 14 as cultural and non-practising. The study also finds that Muslim women largely (11 out of 20 in their study) regret marrying non-Muslims because they begin to have issues primarily after having children, even if the Muslim woman is not practising but is a cultural Muslim only; the spouses cannot agree on how to raise their children: 'Although initially interfaith couples had an agreement on some issues before their marriage and found a way to deal with the potential difficulties stemming from religious differences in their family, having children had a major impact on their relationship for all women, whether devout or cultural-Muslims.'[183] Yet, several of their respondents question the idea that Muslim women should not marry non-Muslims because of concerns about their children's identity: they insist that as the primary caretakers of their children, they would have more influence on their children than their husbands would.[184] Finally, 2 of the 20 women in their study said that their husbands changed their minds and went back on their word regarding how they would raise their children.[185] Heather al-Yousuf, too, finds that Muslims (men and women) in mixed marriages face similar issues raising their children, and similar factors determine how the children will be raised. For example, the parents' own faith history influences how a child identifies with and relates to the parents' religion(s). Al-Yousuf also finds that children in Muslim–Christian interfaith marriages tend to identify with Islam when one parent is Muslim, as the Christian partner is more likely to treat religious identification as autonomous and personally negotiable;[186] or that raising the children as Muslims is 'a default assumption' in such unions.[187] Significantly, Al-Yousuf notes that none of the Muslim partners in the 230 couples involving a Muslim and a Christian considered converting to Christianity; conversely, 'formal conversion' by the non-Muslim partner was 'relatively frequent'.[188] There also seems to be a competition for supremacy between Catholicism and Islam, as both religions expect that any children in mixed marriages involving a Catholic or a Muslim be raised within their own faith, even as the reality might be different. In a separate study, Elmali-Karamaya finds that, contrary to popular anxieties around non-Muslim husbands' negative influence on Muslim wives, interreligiously married women in fact report that the marriage has either positively affected their religious practice or had no impact at all – but none reported a negative impact.[189] This finding parallels findings in my own research on Muslim American women's marriage to non-Muslims, conducted separately from the research in this book. In this new research group, nearly all of my respondents (37 as of July 2023) state that their spouses, or partners if unmarried, had agreed to raise any children as either Muslim only, part Muslim and part non-Muslim, or with no specific faith but exposed to the religions of both parents; that is, none of them agreed to raise their children outside of Islam. Moreover, those with adult children speak positively of their decision about how their children were raised, whether exclusively Muslim or with interfaith teachings. Essential to this decision is clear communication between the partners, and the negotiation process is mutual.[190]

Although the claim that a non-Muslim husband will not honour his Muslim wife's rights did not come up much in my interviews, I believe it is worth addressing because of its prominence in other contemporary discussions on the issue. This claim is founded on the assumption that a Muslim man necessarily honours his wife's rights, by virtue of being Muslim. As with the other justifications, it infantilises the Muslim wife, portraying her as the object of men's potential exploitation and domination, a common view in conservative discourse broadly. While more empirical data has yet to test these assumptions, a study of interreligious marriages in Senegal has found that 'wives in inter-religious marriages deal with the same issues as wives in same-religion marriages, such as polygamy, bride price, male headship of the family, submission to husband, attempts from in-laws to control their life and freedom of faith whether the husband is Muslim or Christian'.[191] The claim, therefore, that a Muslim husband will necessarily treat his wife better than a non-Muslim husband is not grounded in reality and seems to be an attempt to compare which patriarchy is better for women.

CONCLUSION

The traditional prohibition on women's marriage to People of the Book, not explicitly stated in the Qur'an but widely perceived to be so, rests on gendered and social hierarchical assumptions that Muslims have largely departed from or do not adhere to in the same ways as classical jurists expected. The sociological contexts in which this ruling emerged do not speak to the realities and experiences of Muslims today, particularly in non-Muslim majority countries and communities where Muslims are a minority. Importantly also, while the legal tradition that is invoked in honouring this restriction has historically not been static, components of the *sharīʿa* that speak to gender issues have witnessed the least change. It is clear, I suggest, that the existing legal tradition, in its selective application and interpretation, must be reconciled with and re-interpreted in light of contemporary standards relating to gender and sexual justice.

Importantly, while both my married and unmarried participants largely believe that the Qur'an 'clearly' prohibits women's marriage to non-Muslims (Christians and Jews), single women are most supportive of the prohibition being modified. This is significant because it speaks to their relationship with their faith based on their experiences and struggles. Most of my single participants are of marriageable age, and most of the women have been looking for partners for a few years (e.g. Zala, Fatima, Lejla) but are reluctant to marry non-Muslims because they fear compromising their faith in their efforts to marry.

The issue of women's interfaith marriage is clearly not irrelevant, as some have claimed. It is a reality that many practising Muslim women have to grapple with. As scholarship on change in religious traditions shows, religions adapt to new times according to what works and what does not work for the community in question. The Islamic tradition, as I've established, has been a rhizomatic one in its methods of selecting and preserving particular doctrines and practice. But this process has rarely taken into account gender issues in terms of determining issues that may be re-evaluated nor does it see practices or doctrines pertaining to women as negotiable to the same extent as others. The issue of Muslim women struggling to find a Muslim husband, or marrying outside of their faith, shows that it is time for a re-examination. What can be said of the consequences of a prohibition that is not only extra-Qur'anic but affects a significant part of the Muslim population today? As most of the single women in my study assert, while they take the current prohibition seriously, they believe it is necessary for contemporary Muslim scholars to reconsider the prohibition and arrive at a conclusion that reflects current real, lived struggles of Muslims, including and especially single Muslim women.

Clearly, the tradition is changing, has changed, or is open to change according to what Muslims consider necessary and urgent. Those whom the prohibition affects most negatively, single Muslim women, support a re-evaluation of the practice, but do not see themselves as qualified to change the Islamic position themselves. Meanwhile, many male scholars and married Muslims continue to see the issue as irrelevant, and hence continue to refer to an old consensus, even as the facts on the ground are shifting.

Chapter 6

Female-Led Mixed-Gender Prayer

Female sexuality has always been conceptualised
on the basis of masculine parameters.

Luce Irigaray[1]

INTRODUCTION

In this chapter, I address current opinions regarding mixed-gender female-led prayers – i.e. women leading people of all genders in prayer, not just other women – highlighting scholarly debates and my participants' perceptions of the subject. I begin with an analysis of the pre-modern tradition's views on female-led prayers and the ways they shape or depart from contemporary scholarly and authoritative ideas on the issue. I then present and analyse the responses of my research participants to questions related to female-led prayers. Looking for patterns in their responses that help answer my larger question of which positions of consensus are negotiable and which are non-negotiable, and how this is determined, I discuss the three most common responses my respondents offered as explanations for the prohibition on female-led prayer: female modesty and male sexuality (i.e. it is immodest for women to lead men in prayer because men naturally lack the capacity to control their sexual urges and will therefore be distracted by a woman leading them), a lack of precedent (the assumption that no Muslim woman has ever led a mixed prayer in history before), and the notion that it is an unnecessary, irrelevant goal (i.e. Muslim women have more urgent concerns to address than prayer leadership). I argue that the prohibition on female-led mixed-gender prayer remains and is supported by most of my respondents because it is perceived as an irrelevant issue and a lack of support for it is rooted in popular misconceptions and anxieties around sexuality. As with the issue on women's interfaith marriage, many of my respondents support a re-evaluation of the prohibition on female-led prayer but feel bound by the prevailing scholarly opinion – although admittedly there was less support for female-led prayer. Still, what makes the issue non-negotiable is not my discussants' views towards it but the current dominant scholarly consensus. Female-led prayer leads to a fascinating discussion where scholars and lay Muslims clash because the latter are slightly more accepting of change than the former appear to be. Many of my respondents note that they are open to changing their view *if* Muslim scholars change the consensus.

I will show that the sources of Islam (i.e. the Qur'an, Hadiths, scholars' opinions, etc.) are different from those relating to previous discussions. In this case, a lack of precedent, weak and inauthentic Hadith reports, and the majority scholarly view (assumed to be unanimous) are invoked to justify the prohibition against female-led mixed-gender prayer when scripture (the Qur'an or Hadith) fails as evidence. This is even the case when the same individuals had earlier argued that all prohibitions must come from the Qur'an ideally but at least the *Sunnah*. In this case, however, many of my respondents wanted explicit scriptural evidence in support before they were willing to consider female-led prayer as permissible. As other scholars have pointed out already, on the matter of female-led prayer, the conclusion is prioritised and the sources selectively used to find support for that conclusion, rather than asking a question and then using the sources to find an answer. Calderini argues, for example, that 'laws and customs themselves are the starting point, and that legal arguments are developed to reconcile the laws with the textual sources'.[2] I propose that the reason for such an approach to this topic (and not the others) is that female-led prayer is perceived as an irrelevant issue, as many of my respondents explicitly stated. My overall argument in this book is that lived experience and the impact of a given Islamic position on a community or group prompts an issue being re-evaluated in the tradition. Because only one of my forty respondents had any personal interest in leading prayer, the issue is clearly not of personal relevance to them.

I structure this chapter differently than some of the others, beginning with the contemporary scholarly authoritative views on female-led prayers. This is because the Qur'an is famously silent on prayer leadership (men's or women's), there is only one questionable and unreliable Hadith about women not being allowed to lead prayer, and the legal tradition offers a variety of opinions on the matter. Discussion of the relevant Hadiths and pre-modern legal perspectives is dispersed throughout this chapter in the religious scholars' and my respondents' explanations as well as in my analysis. Once I discuss some of the points of departure between historical and contemporary, scholarly and lay opinions on the issue, I discuss in detail one of the most frequent claims supporting the prohibition on female-led prayer: women's leadership of prayer as a distraction for men, which I argue treats women as sexual objects in a sacred space rather than as full humans equally entitled to freedom of worship.

CONTEMPORARY SCHOLARLY VIEWS ON FEMALE-LED PRAYERS

The notion of female-led prayers is one of the most contested subjects in contemporary Muslim discourse.[3] The spectrum of opinions on this issue is emblematic of a broader set of issues regarding female authority and the acceptability of women in public view. Much of the contemporary scholarship on female-led prayers was a response to amina wadud's highly publicised leadership of a mixed-gender prayer on 18 March 2005. Discussed more commonly on the Internet than in academic publications, wadud's action received mixed reactions from Muslims and continues to be a source of controversy in Muslim American communities. Below I engage many of the relevant articles, published in both academic and mainstream spaces. Among the essential academic books on the topic are Juliane Hammer's *American Muslim Women, Religious Authority, and Activism: More Than a Prayer* (2012), Behnam Sadeghi's *The Logic of Law Making in Islam* (2013), Simonetta Calderini's *Women as Imams* (2020), Sa'diyya Shaikh's *Sufi Narratives of Intimacy* (2014), and Sa'diyya Shaikh and Fatima Seedat's *The Women's Khutbah Book* (2022).[4] Hammer highlights women's contributions to the debate on female-led prayer, explores the ways that authority has been negotiated through interpretations of religious texts and traditions, and frames amina wadud's leadership of a mixed congregation as connected to tradition, community, leadership, and representation. She argues that female-led prayers are not simply about prayer but also about larger questions of recognition, authority, and women's spaces more broadly.[5] Sadeghi's argument broadly extends to the question of change in Islamic law and the legal schools' consensus on a matter without textual evidence for that consensus.[6] Calderini explores the wide range of opinions on female-led prayers in the Sunni and Shi'i traditions of women leading mixed and women-only congregations, surveying especially Hadiths, *fiqh* (Islamic jurisprudence), and biographical dictionaries of women who led prayers. She argues that the contemporary debate on female-led prayer reveals not only a lot about Muslim understandings of Islam but also larger conceptions of religious authority, tradition, and the past. For Calderini, the debate especially brings to light the role that a 'normative past' is imagined to play in contemporary Muslim views about Islam, even when textual and scriptural evidence is contrary to the dominant attitude.[7] Shaikh offers an innovative and liberating reading of the thirteenth century Sufi scholar Ibn 'Arabi's understanding of gender, sexuality, and spirituality – to be applied, conditionally and carefully, to contemporary Islamic practice for those seeking a fulfilling and egalitarian practice of Islam. Shaikh rethinks the patriarchal, traditional approach to sexuality, maleness, and femaleness by asking what it means to be human to shape a new discourse in the study of religion and gender. These re-readings invite readers to question existing assumptions of masculinity and femininity, and human interpersonal relationships, that continue to hinder humans' full spiritual potential.[8] Shaikh's work is particularly relevant to my discussion in this chapter because of her close attention to the idea of female imamate, or leadership of prayer. Like her, I interrogate the idea of the male and masculine as the default, which assumes the feminine exists only for male interest. Her book also raises questions about what it means to focus so much on male and female sexuality in ways that prevent worshippers from developing a full spiritual connection with the divine as humans.

Finally, Sa'diyya Shaikh and Fatima Seedat's *The Women's Khutbah Book* is crucial to this conversation as well. The authors treat the *minbar* (the pulpit) as 'a space for religious authority', thus symbolically significant if denied to women.[9] The authors frame this first-ever collection of *khutbah*s (sermons) by Muslim women around the world as part of, as representing, a global shift toward gender-inclusive and ethical forms of religious authority and practice. The book reveals 'an innovative body of religious knowledge and literature', which serves as a 'source of feminist Muslim theology'.[10] This theology is drawn from the *khatibahs*' (the women giving these *khutbahs*) 'own experiences and understandings of the Qur'an and tradition'.[11] Significantly, the authors highlight the incongruence between women's inclusion in mosques and the sacred in the early Muslim tradition, including Muhammad's practice of Islam, and later, dominant patriarchal Islam's treatment of women, which they argue does not coincide with an ethical and just Islam. Thus, they argue, these *khatibahs* are operating within an Islamic paradigm, 'following in the powerful lineage of our Qur'anic ancestors', like Hajar, Khawla, and Maryam.[12] The mere existence of the book speaks to the fact that women's presence and authority in sacred contexts remain controversial.

In mainstream, non-academic Muslim spaces, however, the responses to wadud's prayer leadership included both supporters and detractors. I want to discuss here some of the reasons given on both sides. While opponents of female-led prayers are many, I limit this discussion to Imam Zaid Shakir, the Assembly of Muslim Jurists of America (AMJA), and two scholars mentioned by my respondents, that is, Yasmin Mogahed and Yasir Qadhi. Those who have challenged the prohibition or have offered alternative opinions from the historical tradition include Juliane Hammer, Ahmed Elawa, Laury Silvers, and Nevin Reda.[13] I discuss these individuals' views as a dialogue with each other because their arguments are often responses to each other's claims.

Zaid Shakir, critical of female-led prayers, frames wadud's prayer as a form of *fitna* (disruption, temptation), not necessarily an evil but that which creates division in the community, 'that which clarifies the state of a person, be that good or evil' or a 'strife breaking out among various peoples'.[14] He does not explain his presumptuous claim about 'the state of a person'. He elaborates that 'in both of these meanings the controversy surrounding the "historic" female-led *jum'a* [Friday] prayer is a *fitna* for many Muslims in this country. This is undeniable when we see the divisions, bitter contestation, and outright enmity it is creating in the ranks of the believers.'[15] Here, he is not condemning the injustice that leads to women's demand for respect and inclusion but the response itself; in other words, for him, the bigger problem is not that women are denied access to sacred spaces and religious authority but that they are speaking up. Apparently, the treatment of women in mosques and the rejection of their authority is not what is or creates *fitna* but their response is. He informs his readers that his position is based on the Sunni legal and linguistic tradition as historically understood, 'the tradition of the Islamic orthodoxy'. Like other opponents of the practice, Shakir neglects to acknowledge the historical debate on the subject, including its proponents such as Ibn 'Arabi (scholar and mystic, 1165–1240), Ṭabarī (scholar and exegete, 838–923), and Abu Thawr (jurist, d. 860), all of whom Ibn Rushd explicitly identifies as permitting mixed female-led prayers. Besides them, other scholars who found female-led prayers of mixed congregation permissible include Muzanī (Shāfi'ī scholar, 791-876), and Dāwūd al-Zāhirī (founder of the Zāhirī legal school, 815–83). In fact, Ibn 'Arabi even went so far in his support for female-led prayers for a mixed congregation that he stated, 'women's *imamate* is sound. The basic principle is allowing women's *imamate*. Thus, whoever asserts that it is forbidden without proof, he should be ignored. The one who forbids this has no explicit text [*naṣṣ*]. His only proof in forbidding this is a shared [negative] opinion of her.'[16] However, Shakir rejects the opinions in support of such prayers because he claims these scholars used an inauthentic Hadith to support their position, a point I address below.

Shakir's article is primarily a critical response to Nevin Reda, Associate Professor of Muslim Studies at University of Toronto, who offered a response in support for female-led prayers on the same website. Reda set out to show 'the Islamic basis' for female-led prayers and argued that 'research from the Qur'an and the customs of Prophet Muhammad demonstrate that there is no prohibition precluding women from leading mixed-gender prayer and, further, that Prophet Muhammad approved the practice of women leading mixed-gender prayer'.[17] She argues that there was no explicit prohibition on women leading men in prayers in early Islam, and that the prohibition emerged in the ninth to tenth centuries. She shows that the practice is in fact Islamically valid and permissible for three reasons. First, the Prophet allowed Umm Waraqa to lead her *dār* (community or household) in prayer, and this serves as precedent. The theme of precedent is significant here: it is an important source of Islamic law and Islam, and many of my respondents invoke it in their opinions on female-led prayer. Second, support for female-led prayers has legal precedence in Islamic history from several scholars, such as those identified above (e.g. al-Ṭabarī, Abu Thawr, Muzanī). Third, the Qur'an affirms the suitability of female leadership through the example of the Queen of Sheba, and the Qur'an commands justice of its followers. Shakir writes that 'only one' of Reda's pieces of evidence 'is substantive' – namely, that the Prophet Muhammad commanded Umm Waraqa to lead the people of her *dār* in prayer.[18] Nevin Reda posits that the Umm Waraqa Hadith supports mixed prayers because the word *dār* includes neighbourhood and community. This is evident because the Prophet ordered her to lead her *dār* in prayer specifically because the mosque of the Prophet was too far from her community, the logic being that the community needed another, closer place to pray in. Moreover, Reda argues that the Prophet would not have assigned her a *mu'adhdhin*, someone who performs the call to prayer, if she led only her household in prayer.[19]

Shakir, explicitly responding to Reda, disagrees and questions the legitimacy of this Hadith because two of its narrators are deemed unreliable by some scholars. As such, for him, the Hadith does not stand as a reasonable basis for female-led prayers. He insists that Umm Waraqa must have led only her own household in prayer and likely in the privacy of her home because, he notes, the Prophet had ordered her to stay at home. Shakir disregards Reda's point about the individuals whom Umm Waraqa likely led in prayer. Regarding the scholars such as Muzani, Ṭabarī, Abu Thawr, and Zāhirī, Shakir claims that these scholars supported female-led prayer only because of the Hadith of Umm Waraqa. Shakir accepts the narration in which Umm Waraqa was ordered specifically to lead 'her women' (*nisā'ihā*), and not necessarily the rest of the community.[20] Calderini's findings in 2013, however, show that earlier versions of the Hadith use the word 'household' (*dār*) while later ones replace it with 'her women'.[21] She argues that this shift reflects the change in the development of ritual identity in the community:

> From the 10th century onwards, scholars cite the same narratives centered about Umm Waraqa's prayer leadership but with different wording than those of earlier versions. By doing so, these scholars might be seen to reflect widespread changes in perceptions about the status and ritual role of women, thus echoing the socio-cultural and legal concerns of their times.[22]

Later additions to the Hadith even add that the *mu'adhdhin* she was designated was 'an old man', which Calderini reads as 'a form of crafting serving as a response to possible concerns of female modesty and propriety due to the presence in Umm Waraqa's house of an unrelated man!'[23] The older version of this Hadith uses the gender-neutral term *dār* (household or community), whereas the later version has only one transmitter using the term 'her women'. Calderini discusses in detail the Umm Waraqa Hadith and its reception, development, and role in Islamic history in chapter 3 of her book *Women as Imams*.[24]

Note that Shakir dismisses the Hadith about Umm Waraqa on grounds of weak narration, despite, as others have shown, its wide acceptance by many early scholars. One would expect, then, that since he admits to finding no authentic textual evidence against female-led prayers, it must not be divinely impermissible. However, that is not the case: finding only weak Hadiths, he then resorts to scholarly opinions that resemble his, and dismisses the ones that disagree because, he incorrectly states, they use the Hadith of Umm Waraqa as the basis for their argument. This claim is incorrect because the scholars who supported female-led mixed-gender prayers did not do so on the basis of the Umm Waraqa Hadith but on the basis that there is no textual evidence to prohibit it. Shakir is not alone in this approach to female-led prayer, as I show below, and his approach is aligned with Sadeghi's analysis of other scholars who deal with female-led prayer.

In response to Reda's article supporting wadud's prayer, the Assembly of Muslim Jurists of America (AMJA) – which issues Islamic legal opinions – compiled a collection of *fatwa*s to express opposition to women's prayer leadership. Their arguments include the following five reasons: 1) The consensus of the scholars is decisive proof, 'for Allah made it impossible that the body of the Muslims to be united upon misguidance, and whoever strays away from the consensus of the Muslims over the generations open[s] a door of misguidance'; 2) 'the whole Muslim Ummah in the East and West has collectively agreed that there is no leeway for women to deliver the Friday Khutbah or to lead the Friday prayer'; 3) women must pray behind men 'to protect them from tribulation and blocking the steps leading to fitnah [disruption, temptation, chaos] from all aspects', a claim I return to in my analysis towards the conclusion of this chapter; 4) women are not obligated to attend the Friday prayer; and 5) 'it has never been established that even one woman in all of Islamic history has went [sic] forth to do this act or even asked to do it, throughout the consecutive ages, from the birth of Islam'.[25] Note that in none of these reasons is it shown that female-led prayers, whether Friday or otherwise, are prohibited in the Qur'an or the Hadiths. Instead, AMJA appeals to popular Muslim anxieties regarding female modesty, a theme we will return to, to render such prayers null and void. In her discussion of AMJA's *fatwa* compilation, Calderini writes:

> Their evidence is gathered from selected, yet widely circulated and well known hadiths and Sunni legal sources. Their arguments are only partially constructed according to classical legal and exegetical frameworks and are pervasively enriched by current political and social concerns. Most contributors not only show limited critical approach to the hadiths but also little awareness of contextualization of the legal

sources as they refrain from any explanation of the rationale for the rulings beyond the literal meaning of their selected texts.[26]

AMJA's claims beg to be interrogated. First, AMJA fails to define 'consensus', but implicitly the term refers to the opinion of those scholars with whom AMJA agrees, since not all scholars hold this view. Moreover, one must ask which group of scholars' consensus matters; are contemporary Muslim views considered? The idea that God made it impossible that Muslims would unite upon a misguidance is deeply flawed and troubling: indeed, as I showed in the previous chapters, Muslim scholars historically unanimously agreed with slavery and child marriage as morally acceptable. Finally, the idea of 'the whole Muslim ummah in the East and West', while clearly intended to lay a claim to a collective voice rejecting the notion of female-led prayer, is a false generalisation, unless the *ummah* excludes those voices calling for the legitimacy of female-led prayer.

Yasmin Mogahed appeals to women's role as mothers to argue for female uniqueness. She argues that wadud's prayer is 'a huge step towards being more like men', rather than toward progress.[27] She offers female-led prayers as an example of the Western feminist paradigm of using men as the standard: 'What we so often forget is that God has honored the woman by giving her value in relation to God – not in relation to men. But as Western feminism erases God from the scene, there is no standard left – except men. As a result, the Western feminist is forced to find her value in relation to a man.'[28] While her critique of Western feminist ideas of the male as the standard is legitimate and one many contemporary feminists of all backgrounds share, her article does not in fact explain what the problem with female-led prayers is, and instead dismisses it as the result of women wanting to be like men. She claims that leading prayer is not an honour for women: 'A Muslim woman does not need to degrade herself in this way. She has God as a standard. She has God to give her value; she doesn't need a man. In fact, in our crusade to follow men, we as women never even stopped to examine the possibility that what we have is better for us. In some cases we even gave up what was higher only to be like men.'[29] She does not elaborate what 'higher' thing women sacrifice to lead prayer. For her, the prohibition on women's leadership in prayer is grounded in the idea that 'God dignifies both men and women in their distinctiveness – not their sameness'. She draws a parallel between prayer leadership and motherhood to insist that since women have the privilege of being mothers, they don't need to strive towards anything men have or do:

> For 1,400 years there has been a consensus of the scholars that men are to lead prayer. As a Muslim woman, why does this matter? The one who leads prayer is not spiritually superior in any way. Something is not better just because a man does it… On the other hand, only a woman can be a mother. And God has given special privilege to a mother. The Prophet taught us that heaven lies at the feet of mothers. But no matter what a man does he can never be a mother. So why is that not unfair?[30]

She does not explain why the parallel between motherhood and prayer leadership makes sense (but a parallel between, say, fatherhood and prayer does not), but instead repeatedly insists that women need to stop mimicking men and appreciate the value God has already given them. Let's examine her argument about why we don't ask why Allah has deprived men the privilege of motherhood. First, she is addressing the claim that it is 'unfair' that women are denied the right to lead prayer. Women arguing for the right to lead prayers do not ground their arguments on 'unfairness', but on the basis that there is neither a Qur'anic prohibition nor an explicit prohibition in the *Sunnah*. Second, while (cis) men cannot be mothers, they can be fathers. The issue is not about who is better and more valuable, or whose labour is more important, but about entitlement to religious spaces and leadership. Finally, the Hadith about heaven lying at the feet of mothers is commonly used to silence women and teach them to accept subordinate treatment in society on the promise of a better afterlife. Motherhood does not have to exclude leadership: one can be a mother and a leader simultaneously, just as men can be leaders and fathers at the same time. Significantly, her argument about women wanting to be like men simply for seeking religious authority could be extended to other areas, such as women speaking in public and seeking education and employment; in fact, she seems to do precisely this when she treats women not having to work as a privilege given to them by God. The arguments that Mogahed makes, however, show up in my conversations with my respondents. I will return later to the idea of women's status as mothers meaning that women should not want or need anything else, as well as the notion of women competing with men.

Yusuf al-Qaraḍāwi, who is opposed to female-led prayers of mixed congregations, accepts the above-mentioned Hadith of Umm Waraqa as weak and 'not well-authenticated' because the 'eminent scholars of Hadith say that the chain of reporters of this hadith is extremely weak, and hence, it is not to be taken as evidence in the question in hand'.[31] He rejects the Hadith but claims at the same time that 'Rulings pertaining to leadership in prayer are established by evidence of authentic hadiths as well as the scholarly unanimity of Muslims. They are based on religious teachings, not on social customs as it is has been claimed.'[32] While claiming that these rulings result from authentic Hadiths in addition to scholarly consensus, he does not in fact cite any Hadiths in support of the prohibition. He argues against female-led prayer because of the scholarly consensus, because of a lack of precedent, and because:

> [prayer in Islam] requires concentration of the mind, humility, and complete submission of the heart to Almighty Allah. Hence, it does not befit a woman, whose structure of physique naturally arouses instincts in men, to lead men in Prayer and stand in front of them, for this may divert the men's attention from concentrating in the prayer and the spiritual atmosphere required.[33]

Like the other authorities, he attributes these reasons to Islam, stating, 'Islam...does not treat people as super angels; it admits that they are humans with instincts and desires. So it is wise of Islam to lay down for them the rulings that avert them from succumbing to their desires, especially during acts of worship where spiritual uplifting is required.'[34] While he speaks about 'people', he implies that only men are 'humans with instincts and desires': when men lead prayers with women behind them, the idea that women, too, might be sexually attracted to the men does not cross his or other scholars' minds. In fact, when women express that sexual thoughts occur to them during prayer, they are advised to perform more *dhikr* (remembrance of God), 'to ignore it', 'try hard to pay attention' to continue the prayer until the sexual desire 'goes away', and they are assured not to worry about whether they will be held accountable because they will not be.[35] We must ask why men are not taught to try harder to focus on their prayers as well; instead, their desires are taken so seriously that women are prohibited from leading prayers as a result. I return to this idea of the gendering of patience and endurance (*ṣabr*) later in this chapter in my analysis of the prevailing misconceptions around female and male sexualities.

In his lecture on the negotiables and non-negotiables in Islam, Yasir Qadhi offers the example of female-led prayers as a non-negotiable, a fixed principle that cannot be changed under any circumstances.[36] The easiest way to determine what can be changed and what cannot be changed, he explains, is 'when the scholarly body of the entire *ummah* [universal Muslim community] agrees that something is *ḥarām* [forbidden]'.[37] He claims (incorrectly) that no scholar in Islamic history has ever disagreed or challenged the prohibition on female-led mixed-gender prayers. He even adds that this prohibition, and accepting it, is among the 'basic principles' of Islam.[38] As an example of his methodology, he cites the fifteenth-century prohibition of the printing press as an incorrect prohibition, on the basis that *some* scholars disagreed with it at the time, meaning there was no consensus. Yet, he does not apply this definition of consensus to the issue of female-led prayer, arguing that this is impermissible according to the unanimous consensus of the scholars. Qadhi seems unaware that some scholars in Islamic history did in fact support mixed-gender female-led prayer, certainly by the time that Ibn Rushd was writing *The Distinguished Jurist's Primer*, but Qadhi does not address this in any of his lectures or writing. Moreover, his notion of the *ummah* appears to be limited to historical Muslim male scholars who supported this prohibition, and certainly excludes the Muslim women and men, including figures of authority, who challenge the prohibition. According to Ibn Rushd, the majority of the scholars maintained that a woman cannot lead men in prayer, but they disagreed about her leading other women in prayer (*ikhtalafū fī imāmati-l-mar'ah*):

> The majority maintained that she is not allowed to lead men in prayer, but they disagreed about her being an imam for [other] women. Shāfi'ī allowed it, but Mālik opposed it [*fa-l-jumhūr 'alā 'annahū lā yajūz 'an ta'umm al-rijāl, wa ikhtalafū fī 'imāmat al-nisā', fa-ajāza dhālik al-Shāfi'ī, wa māna'a dhālik Mālik*]. Abū Thawr [d. 854] and Ṭabarī [d. 923] departed [from the others' view] and allowed a woman to be an imam with no restrictions at all [*wa shadhdha Abū Thawr, wa al-Ṭabarī, fa-'ajāzā 'imāmatihā 'alā al-'iṭlāq*].[39]

In addition to the scholars mentioned in the above quote, Yaḥya al-Nawawī (Shāfi'ī jurist and Hadith scholar, d. 1277) also includes Ismā'il bin Yaḥyā al-Muzanī (d. 878) as among those who argued for the validity of men's prayer if behind a woman: 'Abū Thawr, al-Muzanī, and Ibn Jarīr [al-Ṭabarī] said that man's prayer is valid when behind a woman' (*qāla Abū Thawr wa al-Muzanī wa Ibn Jarīr taṣiḥḥ ṣalāh al-rijāl warā'ahā*).[40] Thus, while the prohibition on female-led prayer is valid, according to Qadhi, because it is a result of the consensus of the scholars, Qadhi's argument is inconsistent even with his own definition of the term consensus because all historical scholars did not agree with it and many today do not.

Besides the historical disagreement among scholars, some contemporary scholars also support female-led prayers, at least conditionally. Khaled Abou El-Fadl, for example, believes that women can lead communal prayers if their community finds it acceptable and if the men are not directly positioned behind the woman imam – e.g. the genders pray side by side.[41] He acknowledges that the exclusion of women from prayer leadership is 'an issue of customary practice and male consensus rather than direct textual evidence'.[42]

amina wadud's primary argument, too, is that no textual evidence existed against the prohibition of female-led prayers in communal settings:

> There is very, very little precedent for it [female-led mixed-gender prayers] but there is no textual restriction. That is, women are not prohibited by the sacred text, the Qur'an, or even by the Prophet's statements, nor are men specified by the Qur'an or by the Prophet that it must be a man. Yet, the way the law was encoded 300 years after the Prophet restricted women from this position by a majority rule....[43]

In her book *Inside the Gender Jihad*, wadud elaborates on the absence of textual support for the prohibition of female-led prayers, arguing that both gender segregation during prayer and the prohibition of female-led prayers reflect

> social and historical customs as they developed after the advent of Islam in seventh-century Arabia. There is no single Qur'anic passage to support these arguments... Since such practices of gender disparity reflect social praxis, not theological rationale, then all legal codification of such rationales were built upon the status quo and can be reformed by the collective and conscientious alterations in the status quo.[44]

wadud's point that there is no prohibition on female-led prayers in the Qur'an and the Sunnah and that it is therefore permissible was later rediscovered by male scholars.[45] Not only is there no textual evidence against mixed female-led prayers, but the only Hadith that exists to oppose the practice has always been classified as weak. This Hadith reads: 'A woman will not lead a man in prayer, nor a Bedouin a townsman, nor an iniquitous [impious] man a believer.'[46] Muslim scholars have never accepted this Hadith as authentic because of a weak chain of transmitters.[47]

In addition to arguing that there is no scriptural prohibition on female-led prayers, wadud writes that:

> the cultural and historical precedent of exclusive male leadership in the role of religious ritual is not a requirement. Although it has served as a convenience which later became legally inscribed, it was merely customary and should not be prescribed as a religious mandate. Women's tawhidic humanity allows them to function in all roles for which they develop the prerequisite qualifications.[48]

The tawhidic paradigm is wadud's coinage, a theoretical term based on the essential Islamic doctrine of *tawḥīd*, God's unity and incomparability. According to the tawhidic paradigm, there is a triangular relationship among humans and God, in which God stands above in a vertical relationship with humans, and humans are in a horizontal relationship with each other. Women and men are equal to each other 'because the divine function establishes their reciprocal relationship. If human beings really are horizontally equal, independent, and mutually co-dependent, each has the same potential for performing any social, religious, political, or economic task.'[49] For wadud, the concept of *tawḥīd*, 'or the unicity of Allah', entails that 'all of nature is interconnected' and everything in nature, including humans, is 'under a single divine reality', held together by the tension of God.[50]

Pre-modern Islamic law didn't account for the tawhidic paradigm – instead, it constructed hierarchies between human beings. In these systems, enslaved women were treated as men with regards to modesty: unlike free women, slave women were allowed theoretically to pray while showing their hair and even their breasts, and it was considered 'reprehensible' for enslaved women to cover because doing so was an imitation of free women.[51] Since an enslaved woman could show her bare breasts during prayer, while a free woman could neither pray alongside men nor lead them, the social construction of womanhood or femininity dictated whether a woman posed to men the threat of distraction from prayer. In either scenario, the social status of the woman defined the confinement of her liberty in the male gaze. To be sure, the legal tradition did not allow any women, enslaved or free, to lead mixed-gender prayers, even as modesty rules were different for both. But here I am questioning the inconsistent treatment of enslaved women *as* men. That is, the jurists decided that (free) women could not lead mixed prayers because of modesty concerns; yet, these same modesty concerns simply did not apply to enslaved women, who were still women, as they were permitted to show their hair and even breasts during prayer. Interestingly and perhaps in an ironic twist, according to this logic and the distinction that the scholars drew between enslaved and free women, then enslaved women could be allowed to lead prayer.[52]

Attributing the restriction on female-led prayer to 'Islam' is thus suspect and relies on inconstant and illogical framing of womanhood and the male gaze. Moreover, it was not just (free) women alone who were presumed to pose a distraction for men: beardless young men were also not to pray next to men, as some scholars ruled that a man's prayer was invalidated if he prayed next to a beardless male youth 'because it induces sexual thoughts'.[53] Similarly, a woman's age was relevant in determining whether she should even pray at the mosque or not. In her discussion of the Mālikī view on women's presence in mosques, Marion Katz shows that by the eleventh century, for whatever reasons, 'the division between mature and young women with respect to mosque attendance was so well established among jurists of all regions and schools' that Ibn 'Abd al-Barr (d. 1070) 'was able to declare, "The scholars consider it unobjectionable for mature women… to attend congregational and Friday prayers, and they consider it objectionable for young women to do so."'[54] Older women were understood to be unattractive to (presumably all) men, although some might still be alluring to men despite old age. The unattractive older woman 'is like a man' in that she can pray wherever men can pray.[55] This was not only a Mālikī position, however: al-Shāfi'ī, too, believed that while women and enslaved people were not obligated to attend Friday prayers, he preferred that 'aged women and those who do not have [attractive] appearances attend [congregational] prayers and festivals; I prefer more strongly that they attend the festival [prayers] than that they attend other obligatory prayers'. Moreover, Shāfi'ī wrote that 'I do not consider it objectionable for a woman who does not have splendid appearance or for an old woman or a young girl to attend [prayers performed on the occasion of an eclipse]; I consider it desirable for them. I prefer that those women who have [attractive] appearances to perform it in their homes.'[56] In her discussion on women's prayer leadership in the legal tradition, Calderini also finds that 'because of more extensive application of the concept of 'awrah [something to be concealed, private parts], women are further subdivided according to age (young, childbearing age, old) and level of attractiveness (in men's eyes)'.[57] Gradually, however, 'the association of fitna [disruption, chaos] to young attractive women gives way to a more general association with all women, irrespective of looks and age'.[58] It is significant that references to enslaved women's and older women's prayer and their sexual attractiveness are not part of today's debate on female-led prayer. The debate has experienced an important shift from pre-modern times. We are working out the position from different premises from earlier generations of scholars.

That women are still widely believed not to have access to religious authority and prayer leadership in the mosque is a remnant of the early Muslim debates on women's presence in the mosque and women praying with men. Seedat and Shaikh highlight two important layers of this early debate:

> namely, the 'contaminating' effects of women's presence among men and the idea that women's presence induces men to lustful thoughts. Importantly, these discussions begin in prescriptions on the transmission of ritual impurity through water used for ritual purification (*wudu*) but conclude in the prohibition of men and women praying side by side or in proximity to one another.[59]

I discuss below the language categorising women as sources of distraction and as objects of male fantasy and desire. These ideas merit being problematised in the context of prayer and worship.

PRECEDENT AS A SOURCE OF ISLAM

The expectation that every interpretation must have precedent in the past in order to be legitimate is commonly shared among Muslims in discussions of female-led prayers. According to 95.5% of my respondents, the reason women's prayer leadership is not acceptable and is un-Islamic is that it 'has never taken place in history before'. Calderini addresses this notion in her 2014 guest lecture at George Mason University, titled 'Citing the Past to Address the Present: Authorities and Unexpected Interlocutors on Female Leadership of Salat [prayer]'.[60] She states that: 'Precedence or alleged precedence in past history, meta-history, or sacred history provide legitimacy to interpretations, which, far from being presented as new, are shown as a continuity, a reaffirmation, a revival of the past.'[61] Addressing the collection of *fatwa*s issued in April 2005 against women's leadership of obligatory prayers, Calderini quotes the anonymous editor of the collection who cautions that while the *fatwa*s are not a complete collection of Islamic legal opinion on the issue, 'it does...represent a consensus amongst contemporary Islamic and Muslim legal scholars on this specific issue'.[62] She comments that 'such a consensus is hardly surprising given that all the contributors are Sunni and are arguing, on slightly different grounds, against the female leadership of mixed congregation in *salat*'.[63] The *fatwa*s included are by nine scholars from different parts of the world – eight of whom are males, one female – as well as by AMJA. While the discourse following the event included opinions both supporting and opposing the prayer, this collection selected only the opinions opposed to the prayer, and it presents them as the 'consensus amongst contemporary Islamic and Muslim legal scholars' on the issue. Clearly, then, the issue is not one of consensus, not even of majority necessarily, since that is difficult to determine, given that only one perspective is presented as the Islamic one. The rejection of the alternative perspective begs an important question: when disagreement arises, why is the inegalitarian perspective considered more Islamic? It appears that consensus is of interest primarily when it benefits male dominance.

Besides Umm Waraqa and Aisha, other female Companions of Muhammad known to have led women in prayer include Umm Salama (the Prophet's wife), who was 'personally entrusted by the Prophet Muhammad with ritual leadership'.[64] Calderini finds several more instances of women leading female-only congregations: while Sa'da bint Qumama is explicitly named in the tradition, others are referenced in other ways, such as Ibn Hazm's mention that Abdullah Ibn Umar 'appointed an unnamed woman to lead in prayer a female congregation during Ramadan'.[65] A *jāriya* (slavegirl, an enslaved child) of 'Ali ibn al-Husayn led prayer; 'Amra, a well-known Hadith transmitter, instructed a woman to lead women in prayer. Further, Ibn Ḥanbal permitted women to lead men in *tarāwīḥ*, voluntary night prayers performed in Ramadhan,[66] and Imam al-Shāfi'ī's teacher Nafīsa bint al-Hassan led his funeral prayer.[67]

Significantly, there is also precedent for women leading men in the historical Islamic tradition. Ghazala al-Haruriyya (d. 695–6) was an Iraqi Kharijī woman who 'actively participated in battles, was referred to as an imam, and...very publicly performed prayer in front of men in the mosque of Kufa'.[68] Her 'presence in the mosque and her ascending the pulpit (minbar) and praying there are mentioned in a number of sources'.[69] The sources that Calderini finds on Ghazala, however, are polemical anti-Kharijī sources that tell us more about attitudes towards Kharijīs than Ghazala herself or female-led prayers.

In chapter 3 of her book *Women as Imams*, Calderini discusses in detail the different attitudes towards Umm Waraqa and Ghazala:

> The relation between these women and their ritual performances was sidelined, partially censored and almost forgotten. When it was reported, I argue that it was done in a way so as to serve as a warning to other women not to overstep male bounds. It might be no coincidence that Umm Waraqa and Ghazala were both reported to have met a violent death.[70]

For Calderini, it is also significant that both the Umm Salama and the Umm Waraqa Hadiths meet the criteria to qualify as precedents in legal terms but 'the destiny of their uses as precedents' developed in different directions, 'with Umm Salama's being uncontroversially used across Islamic legal schools, while Umm Waraqa's were, as a whole, sidelined or obscured'.[71]

Further, Calderini finds that the reasons against the prohibition are as follows, in order of frequency based on the legal sources she consulted:

> firstly, historical precedence, whereby they claim…there's no recorded instance of a woman imam during the formative and normative early centuries of Islam, [so] no innovation should be introduced nor accepted. Secondly, on textual evidence from hadiths like the one by Abu Hurayrah, ritual and social practices are introduced; as women pray behind men in mosques, they cannot lead them in prayer. Thirdly…the legal consensus, *ijmā'*… Fourthly, textual evidence from the Qur'an is used as inferred evidence – inferred because, of course, there's no specific reference against women leading prayer.[72]

She notes also that weak Hadiths are invoked in justification against the prohibition, such as Ibn Māja's (Hadith scholar, d. 887) proclamation that 'never, ever can a woman lead a man in a prayer'. Other arguments cited include those that came up in my interviews as well: disputes over what constitutes female *'awrah*, claims that women cannot be leaders because they are not endowed with *wilāya* (sovereignty), and female ritual impurity (during menstruation and postnatal discharge).[73] Importantly, these arguments were used not only to explain the wisdom behind the prohibition of female-led prayers (mixed or otherwise, Friday or otherwise) but also to show that women were too impure, incompetent, and unqualified to enter the mosque and touch or even recite the Qur'an. Yet, while women are often treated as too impure to engage in such activities, there are Hadith reports about the Prophet Muhammad praying and reciting the Qur'an while leaning on Aisha's lap when she was menstruating.[74] Not only are weak Hadiths invoked in support of the prohibition but significantly they are used selectively to support a conclusion that has already been made a priori. By doing this, the male scholarly tradition interprets the textual tradition and manipulates it in such a way that it confirms their patriarchal biases and anxieties.

Contemporary views on mixed female-led prayers range from absolute rejection to absolute acceptance, with some scholars supporting them conditionally. The historical debate differentiates between the type of prayer a woman can lead, if at all, such as whether it is the obligatory daily prayer or voluntary prayers, or whether she can lead only women or a mixed congregation. For funeral prayers, some Ḥanafīs allow a woman to pray next to a man. They also discuss where the woman should stand in relation to the congregation – e.g. behind the men if leading men, in the middle of the women if leading women only. The tradition therefore offers a range of opinions and complexities that are ignored in today's debate.

Today, the primary justifications against such prayers are that scholarly consensus prohibits them and that they lack precedent in historical Islam – i.e. no Muslim woman is known to have led a mixed prayer in all of Islam's fourteen-hundred years. Those who support mixed female-led prayers not only argue that Umm Waraqa led her community of women and men, not just her family, in prayer, but they also argue that in order for the prohibition to be Islamic, it must be textually supported. Yet, all historical and contemporary scholars agree that no textual justification in the Qur'an or in the Hadiths exists for the prohibition.

MY RESPONDENTS' JUSTIFICATIONS FOR THE PROHIBITION ON FEMALE-LED PRAYERS

Here, I discuss my respondents' views on the prohibition on mixed-gender, female-led prayer, their explanations for the justifications of the prohibition, and, when relevant, their reactions to historical rationales for the prohibition. The two justifications that my respondents offered were the lack of historical precedent, and female modesty and male concentration (i.e. women should not be or are not allowed to lead men in prayer because of their ability to distract men during prayer, and that Islam upholds female modesty through the segregation of the genders especially during prayer). I discuss these with direct quotes from the interviews, and I conclude with a discussion on the ways in which these explanations and some of the opinions depart from historical scholarly ones and why these departures are significant.

I begin this section with Pamir (65) and Lema (57)'s insights on the subject. The married couple, whom I interviewed together, entered a debate during this portion of the interview, as they did throughout the interview. Lema said that she does not believe female-led prayers are permissible 'because it never happened in the Prophet's time. Plus, men are required to go to the mosque for prayer [and women are not].'

> Pamir: But maybe that was because men were considered to be in charge. But that's not the case today.
>
> Lema: But that comes back to the fact that we don't know the wisdom behind it. That's when you stop and say Allah's will is Allah's will.

Pamir was not convinced: 'It's not clear in my mind – is this in the Qur'an or *Sunnah*?' he asked. Lema told him that the Prophet said women cannot lead mixed prayers. Pamir remained uncertain and asked if the four schools also prohibit it, to which Lema said yes, she thinks so. I asked why they think that some women might want to lead such prayers. Lema replied, 'Just to show that they're equal, or no less than the men or whatever.' Pamir said, 'It's the reality. Women can lead in all other aspects of life, why not in prayers? They're leading big companies, countries – even Muslim countries. So if they can do all that, why can't they lead a group in prayers?' He thus interrogates the ruling on female-led prayer by drawing a parallel between ritual leadership such as in prayer and other forms of leadership, such as political.

The couple agreed that the existing consensus is binding but that if the evidence and reasons for the prohibition were unclear and weak, then 'the prohibition should be lifted'. While the couple did not bring up the question of modesty for women, the notion that historical precedent should determine the Islamic validity of a practice came up frequently during this and almost all of the other interviews.

Female Modesty and Male Sexuality

The most common reason given to support the prohibition was that of an assumed uncontrollable male sex drive. According to Gahez (77, married male, South Asian background), Islam does not permit women to lead mixed prayers – but this prohibition does not indicate their inferiority to men but rather Islam's emphasis on modesty:

> There are reasons for that. It's not that women are in any way inferior to men. The reason is the modesty of women. The general mixing of the sexes is not encouraged in Islam. It is not to denigrate them, but it is to keep their modesty and respect intact… Also, it has not been done during the Prophet's time. And it had not been done several centuries after the Prophet's time. So if we start some new practice, that is called *bid'a*, or innovation. We should not start something that may lead to a problem later on. In Islam, anything that may lead to a problem later on is prohibited as a general guideline… Like drinking and gambling. Not everyone can drink or gamble responsibly. They may be sacrificing their families. The same thing with women leading prayer.

There are several significant points being raised here. First, note that in this response, men's modesty is not mentioned or acknowledged. I will explain and theorise below why this is, as it was a common point in almost all my respondents' perspectives. Second, I did not ask if in his opinion, not being allowed to lead prayers 'denigrates' women, and the fact that he voluntarily argued that it does not suggests that such a denial of leadership *can* be a source of denigration. He does not qualify that it is not to denigrate the men, which means he knows it benefits men. As we will see in many of my other respondents' views, the differences between women and men consistently benefit men.

Scarlet (26, married female, white, convert) was opposed to the prohibition, if it exists at all:

> I don't think it's a clear prohibition. Islam is not black and white. I hear reasons like temptation. Women are viewed as sexual in every way! I've even heard that women can't recite the Qur'an because their voice is soft, but I've heard male recitations that are so beautiful I've found it distracting! I was like oh man, I felt wrong that I found his voice attractive!

She is in favour of women leading mixed-gender prayers:

> I've no idea where they [allow it]! I wish we'd protest mosques because of not letting women lead prayers but I guess women already do that but it's used as an excuse to diminish women's spaces by saying, 'They don't come to the mosque anyway.' I never would have converted to Islam if I had talked to these people in mosques before I converted.

Still, she adds that she is not sure she'd be comfortable praying with men who are not related to her: 'I don't know if I'd feel comfortable praying next to men. My husband okay. I think it's fine to have a private area for women but not be confined to it.' In other words, she wants women to have multiple options, not to be forced to pray in mixed congregations and not to be prohibited from them. Scarlet connects female-led prayers to gender equality: 'I think women who want to lead mixed-gender prayer are making a stand for equality. And also because my understanding was that whoever had the most knowledge of Islam and memorisation of the Qur'an is who leads the prayer. It's not always gonna be a man in every situation.' For her, if the reasons for the prohibition change with time, Scarlet believes the scholarly opinion should change as well:

> The most liberating thing I've heard at the mosque recently is that the scholars that you look up to should be of your time and of your society. Islam in America will look different from Islam in Malaysia. And time, too. Islam today in America looks different from [how] it will in the future. I'm not saying change the core things in the Qur'an, like five pillars, but the way you implement them will change.

When I asked Gahez (77, married male, South Asian background) if he believes such prayers might be acceptable if the barriers that are a part of many mosques today remained in place, he said, 'I don't know if Islam would allow it in that case. I think that as an exception, maybe it will be okay.' That he was uncertain whether Islam would allow a woman to lead a mixed prayer if barriers were in place indicates that he is uncertain about the logic behind the prohibition.

Zalaan (42, married male, South Asian background) stated that he 'would not be upset about it' if he entered a mosque and a woman was leading the prayer, but 'if I was living in a town and there was one mosque where a woman was leading and another with a man leading, I'd go to the one with the man leading. A woman leading would mess up my concentration.' He is aware that female-led prayers take place but does not support them because he views it as 'a personal thing':

> A lot of this stuff you're asking about [Muslim women's marriage to non-Muslims and female-led prayers] happens in Canada. It rarely happens in America, like in just a few spots. There's a lady somewhere in the East Coast who does it. She's an activist… I think it's a personal thing. Like that lady from the East Coast. She's a hardcore activist. Whether she's Muslim or not, an activist is gonna stand for whatever. Because their activism is gonna override any other thing because it's a personal thing.

His statement that 'it's a personal thing' is significant because he is implying that Muslim women who lead prayers are guided not by a sense of justice or by their understanding of Islam but by personal motives, presumed to be selfish. He did not know if such prayers are prohibited in Islamic law, but if they were, he would understand why. Besides male sexuality, other reasons, he speculated, might be 'because historically, women had kids at home, but now you have a lot of women who have no kids. So the reason they said it was prohibited was to make sure women don't leave their kids just to go pray, you know?' However, he does not think about this issue because 'this is totally irrelevant to me, so I don't waste my time thinking about it'. This comment on relevance is important, and I will return to it below.

When I asked Sultan (41, African male, married, convert) if female-led communal prayers were allowed in Islam, he immediately answered, 'Of course not. It's *bid'a*, innovation.' His reason, similar to the others', was that 'when I'm in a *masjid* [mosque] that I consider to be the House of Allah and I'm trying to communicate with my Lord, I'm not gonna be behind a woman that's bending over and showing her behind. That environment doesn't suit my worship.' I asked, 'What if there were a barrier between the genders?' He paused before responding, 'Did the Rasool [Muhammad] do this? Why're we tryina do something that he did not do?' His conclusion was that 'from what I know, only men can be leaders, not just for prayer but for other things, too. And not just any kind of men but he has to be pious. And he has to have the best *tajwīd* [recitation of the Qur'an] in the congregation.'[75] Men can pray in front of women and the bending of the men is not an issue, he stated, because 'women and men are not equal', suggesting that their sex drives are different and women do not worry about distraction during prayer while men do.

Sangin (69, married male, Middle Eastern background) apologetically said that women are not allowed to lead men in prayers and that the imam must always be male:

> I apologize I have to say this. Forgive me, sister. Don't be upset. The more knowledge I give you from this side, the better for you. When I [was] growing up, I realised that men have a strong feeling of sexuality and they do not want to control it. They have a dirty mind… The prayer is a time of concentration… And I want to say, majority of the men – please forgive me – are animals. So please understand that Allah is not wrong when He says women cannot be in front. Second, *Sunnah*. This is painful for me, but it is in the Qur'an when Musa saw those three girls taking the water, and they said, 'You helped us, so we want to introduce you to our father.' And Moses told them, 'I will walk in front, and you are in the back.' That was the lifestyle. It's not because men are more intelligent than women. It's just the *Sunnah*.

For him, then, there are three main reasons why women are not permitted to lead prayers: first, because they must always pray behind men, whereas in traditional Muslim prayer, the imam stands in the front; second, since men apparently have a high sex drive, which they choose not to control, they may therefore be tempted by the women praying in front of them; and third, because men must always be in charge, as demonstrated through the story of Moses, where Moses leads the way for the women (despite being a guest in the women's village). This is why, according to him, female-led prayers are not acceptable even with a barrier between the genders: 'No no no. Women being in the front is not in Islam. Even when I pray at home with my sister, she has to be behind me. I just know Islam says that. Islam is very clear.' In fact, when I first approached Sangin about participating in my study and he agreed, he led me towards the women's area of the mosque where we were to do the interview. As we walked towards the area, he walked in front of me, gently reminding me to stay behind him while he led, since a woman must never be in front of a man or lead a man. He believes men should always be in charge and be the leader – despite their supposed innate inability to control their sexual drives.

Barsalai (31, married female, South Asian background) is open to female-led prayers in mixed congregations if they were to become mainstream, but she is 'uncomfortable' with the idea 'just because it goes against what I was taught'. She is not opposed to the idea and understands why some women might want to lead prayers: perhaps because 'they're qualified, perhaps they have a pleasant voice, trained to recite beautifully, perhaps they're capable of doing it, and it's an honour to lead prayers'. Note here that she believes having a 'pleasant voice' is part of what would qualify a person to lead a prayer. Traditional Islam considers women's voice to be *'awrah*, literally genital, a source of shame and something to be concealed from the opposite sex. This is one of the reasons advanced for prohibiting women from reciting the Qur'an publicly.[76] For Barsalai, leading mixed prayers is prohibited because 'it's out of respect for women and women's bodies. I don't think these reasons are relevant to culture necessarily [i.e. they are Islamic and not merely societal] so if those are the reasons, then that transcends time.' In other words, male and female sexuality is static and these rulings are permanent because they are not tied to cultural norms but to biological facts.

Abigail (39, married female, white) also considers sexuality and modesty rules to be static, connected to biology, and not open to change. She recognises that for some women, the issue of prayer leadership is about equality but she does not agree this is a good way to fight for equality. The mosque 'is a sacred space', and the rules of prayer are about the biological distinctions between women and men. Women should be focused on their families and children, not leading mixed-gender prayers. Because the reasons are biological for her, there is no room for renegotiation on this topic, and even if the scholarly rationales change, she does not believe the scholarly opinion should change to allow women to lead mixed-gender prayer.

Michael (56, married male, white, convert) has prayed behind a woman before but did not want to disclose details.[77] Female-led prayers, he said, 'are just uncomfortable and very distracting. It's so much more comfortable for people otherwise [with a male leading].' He shared that he did his research on this subject before converting to Islam over a decade earlier and 'I couldn't find much evidence to support or oppose it. But I have to say it's practically disallowed.' He acknowledged that this is a struggle for him because:

> the imam has to be the most knowledgeable. And I can remember only one case where a woman was the best reciter in the group… You're gonna have cases where the best reciter is a woman. What do you do in those cases? Is the *salat* [prayer] valid if you choose a poor male reciter instead of a perfect woman reciter? *Salat* is not gonna be accepted.

Michael's statement that prayer leadership is about knowledgeability finds support in legal texts on the subject. Some historical scholars from the Ḥanbalī school held that a woman can lead a mixed-gender prayer if she is the most knowledgeable in the group, the most capable of reciting the Qur'an, or at least better than all the men present.[78] However, she is not to stand in front of the congregation and is required to be as concealed as possible.[79]

Unsurprisingly, most of the women also referenced female modesty and male sexuality to argue against female-led prayers. Aisyah (20, single female, Southeast Asian background) said that she's heard women are not allowed, but she thinks that 'if it's a mom leading her son in prayer, that shouldn't be a big deal'. When I asked her what she thinks the scholars' reasons might have been for the prohibition, she suggested, 'Doesn't it have to do with the male gaze and, like, not staring at a woman for that long? I'm not sure… There's also that interpretation that a woman's voice is *'awrah*. Even though a lot of Muslim girls will choose their husbands based on their voice! So men's voice can be attractive too.' She did not believe that the presumed consensus on this topic is binding on Muslims and suggested that today's scholars should reconsider the prohibition. Her comment that men are not allowed to 'stare at' women for 'that long' is intriguing: during Muslim prayer, one looks down, not at the imam.

Nour (20, single female, Middle Eastern background) regrets that 'there's this idea that all women are good for is a distraction. I mean, that just doesn't sound right.' She initially said that she does not push this issue much when she thinks about it because 'it's not like I'm the one leading the prayer'. But she later added, 'There've been times when I've been like, I have a better recitation than the guy leading, and it's not like a big deal, but I just knew that I could've led better… He was like, "Sorry, I don't make the rule." I know that it's not in the Qur'an, but I am assuming it's in the Hadith, so I guess that makes sense then.' That she believes the idea must be supported by Hadiths because of its prevalence is significant because it indicates what her sources of Islam are: for her, a practice or doctrine is legitimate only if textually supported, and she cannot conceive of the dominance of a legal opinion unless it is textually supported, hence her assumption that it must be in a Hadith and that's why 'it makes sense then'. This idea was popular among the discussants, many of whom stated that if an opinion is based on consensus, then it must be in the Qur'an or Hadiths because the scholars were not authorised to invent rulings outside of these two sources. However, in Nour's case, she begins to doubt her own certainty about the injustice of being denied leading a prayer once she suggests that perhaps the prohibition is in the Hadiths and thus acceptable to her.

Others also believed, and accepted, the reason that women are inherently a source of distraction for men. Wagma (20, single female, South Asian background), for example, recounted an incident at the mosque where women's recitation of the Qur'an at the mosque 'distracted' the men:

> Women are a distraction for males. Like in social gatherings, if a woman passes by, she's like a big distraction… Every month, there's a really good *hifz* [Qur'an memorisation] program at our *masjid* [mosque], and there's a Qur'an night, and there's women with the mic if they want to read the Qur'an. And some of them do, and you can tell it's a distraction for the guys downstairs. I think it's just natural instinct for men to be inclined to that.

She did not elaborate how one can tell that 'it's a distraction for the guys downstairs' or how so. In any case, since women's voice and presence in a worship place distracts men, women should not be allowed to lead mixed prayer – but they can lead other women in prayer. In fact, since Islam is 'really big on separating men and women', women are also 'not supposed to talk out loud in front of men' and 'it's not modest' to lead a prayer or pray in front of men. However, the denial of the right to lead prayer is also potentially a good thing, according to Wagma, because women already have so many responsibilities – 'like family' – that this is a useful relief from another, extra responsibility.

Zala (27, unmarried, racially mixed background) strongly believed that such prayers were categorically prohibited and she does not support them.

While she suspected that 'the traditional thing would be, like, *'awrah*, and male distraction', her initial reason was that 'it kinda makes guys look bad, incompetent', suggesting that female leadership is a threat to male dignity and potential. Like many others, she also invoked women's and men's biologies to rationalise the prohibition: 'I think there's wisdom behind why women pray behind men… There are biological reasons for that. Men and women are biologically different, and we can't deny that. Men have a higher sex drive than women do, and our base desires are completely different. It's an evolutionary procedure…it has to be that way.'

When I asked her if she believes having a barrier in the mosque to separate the genders might change anything, she did not answer the question but responded instead that the question is irrelevant because the prohibition is valid:

> Why're we even talking about this? Where would that make a difference? Why do you want to lead?… I just feel like this is not an issue we should be spending our time and energy challenging, or feeling like we made an advancement if we challenge that. Do we think we're advancing anything by doing certain things, or are we chasing after stuff that aren't even problems? It's a useless battle to fight… What we want and the questions we ask are indicative of what we value as a community. This concerns me where we stand internally. These are like symptoms that lead to certain diseases. I don't care about the question of female-led prayers; I'm interested in the disease.

She does not answer the question of the barriers as a possible way to prevent male temptation if women lead the prayer. Instead, her concern is that the discussion of female-led prayer is irrelevant because as a society, there are far bigger, more important battles to be fought. Because she imagines it to be purposeless and pointless, spending time on it indicates a larger problem in society. She did not explain what this 'larger problem' in society was.

Finally, Diwa (67, married female, South Asian background), believes that the reason there is such strong opposition to female-led prayers is 'because of men's weakness of temptation'. She does not believe that mixed-gender female-led prayers were prohibited and said that she has never been led by a woman in a mixed congregation but that she would 'not mind' such a congregation. Still, she stated that 'I personally don't care [about this topic] because it's not important to me. Prayer is very personal. amina wadud says that it is about equality, but I disagree. It just doesn't matter to me who leads the prayer. We should focus on other things we [Muslims] are behind on.'

According to Malala (37, married female, South Asian background), 'I'm kinda not okay with [women leading mixed-gender prayers] personally. I'm not in favour of barriers but not in favour of leading either. For the reason of being provocative. Even if you don't have your bum in front of someone else's face, it could incite someone's thoughts.' She adds that she believes prayer is 'a very personal thing' and she has no issues with 'women in leadership roles' but 'prayer is a very personal, intimate issue'. Here, female-led prayers are not only immodest and unnecessary but also 'provocative', a source of enticement for men. She, like many other respondents, does not find any connection between leadership generally and prayer leadership. When I asked her why she thinks some Muslim women might want to lead mixed prayers, she said, 'I have no idea. I can't put my head around it.' She vehemently disagrees with prohibiting women from leading other women in prayer: 'I don't know why any school would forbid it! Probably to control women. Equal but same BS.' Although she argues that women's leadership of prayer is about modesty, she believes that if the current consensus were to change to allow women to lead mixed prayer, she would 'absolutely' support it because 'if it is not a very clear black and white in the Qur'an, then it's always up for renegotiation and re-examination'. She is currently 'not sure' if the consensus is binding because 'it seems like the reasonings are misogynistic and I truly feel Islam is not a misogynistic religion'.

Turan (24, single male, South Asian background), who otherwise in the interview argued that 'the Qur'an always takes precedence, whether we like it or not', proposed in this case that the prohibition on female-led prayers remain because 'it has to do with female sexuality' and because 'the consensus of the first three generations of Muslims' is binding. Patang (23, single male, South Asian background) believes that women should not be and are not allowed to lead mixed-gender prayer 'out of respect for men', because women menstruate, and because of the biological distinctions between women and men: 'women give birth, men don't'. But it is not women only who cannot lead prayer; children, too, Patang believes, cannot lead prayers. Since these reasons 'have not changed in today's time', there is no reason to change the ruling. He believes that perhaps the reason Muslim women might want to lead prayers is 'equality. But if they do [get this right], they'll be surpassing men.'

Wadaan (21, unmarried male, of South Asian origin) is certain that Islam prohibits women from leading prayers and there is a justification for it, but he does not know what it is, other than perhaps 'that certain things were given to women, certain things to men'. Significantly, he appears to reject the gender binary, as he qualified his statement with 'not to fall in a gender binary here, but if there was one', it would be the biological distinctions between women and men. While traditionally it is frowned upon in Islam, if he were to come across a congregation led by a woman, he would not frown upon it himself – but he also would not join it. Still, he states that he has never met a woman who wants to lead a prayer and is confident that 'if God intended for women to lead prayer, it would have happened. There were many opportunities, but women never did so.'

The idea that the reasons must be rooted in female modesty and male sexuality – or generally in purity of thoughts – was common even among those who did not hold the position that women cannot or should not lead prayers, commenting that they suspect that would be the explanation. Since the explanation made sense to most of them, few were open to resisting the prohibition on female-led prayers or opening up the conversation so that the consensus can change with time.

Lack of Precedent

Some of the above comments already mention a supposed lack of precedent as the explanation for keeping the prohibition. However, others were more explicit in stating that as the reason, sometimes the sole reason. This part of the discussion includes the more supportive positions towards female-led prayer. This includes those who are either open to changing the prohibition as well as those who do not believe the prohibition is valid. One participant, a married woman, said that she currently believes it is prohibited because it has never happened before, but that she is open to changing her position if she learns that it did take place during the Prophet's time.

Zala's idea, as quoted in the previous section, that 'it makes the guys look bad' was echoed also by Selma (48, married), who said, 'We should leave it to the guys. Islamically, it said that men are supposed to lead the prayer. For me, what's the point of a woman leading prayers? I do believe women can be scholars and give lectures, give *khutba*s [sermons], but to lead the prayer?

Why?' She was certain that the Qur'an and *Sunnah* oppose such prayers, but if not, then, 'We never saw women in the Prophet's time leading prayer. Has any woman ever done it in the Prophet's time?'

Sandara (20, unmarried, South Asian) said, 'I just think it never happened over time. I don't see anything wrong with it [the prohibition]. So I don't think it needs to be changed... I don't understand why women would want to lead men. I just don't get it. Maybe if I met someone and if they could give a valid reason, it'd be something to think about, but I don't think it's necessary.' While she does believe female-led prayers of other women are 'probably not prohibited', she 'find[s] them weird. It's just not the normal thing.' When I asked her if she knew of any examples where women had led prayers, she mentioned she had been in a group with three other women where one of them led the other two in prayer:

> I know of a lady who did it at a church 'cause no one would let her do it in a mosque. I know a friend who did it [for a women-only group], and it was actually funny 'cause we didn't understand that she meant we'd do a congregation together. We thought she meant we'd all just pray individually but at the same time. So she ended up leading the prayer for the two other girls.

That she and the other girls in the group found it 'funny' implies that they had not heard of or considered the possibility of a woman leading anyone in prayer, whether women or men. While the other two girls in the group joined the prayer, Sandara did not because she does not believe a woman is allowed to lead others in prayer, regardless of gender.

The reasons given by Orzala (33, married, white) in support of the prohibition, besides precedent, were not cited by anyone else:

> Prayer is very sacred. The Prophet went up to *jannah* [heaven] and was taught by Jibreel and Ibrahim as about how the prayer was performed. I mean, I've never heard a story that had a woman leading the prayer. I think there's a lot of *nafs* [self-regard] involved in women who demand that position. And I don't really see the value in it at this point. I am a huge proponent of not separating women and men in mosques because Allah and the Prophet didn't decree it. But I think there would be precedent [of female-led prayer] if women were to be leading it. Prayer is

> sacred. I don't think it's casual enough to have women just say, 'Oh, I'm gonna lead it.' I think it's very complex and it'd have to come from a major consensus for me to support it.

This response is especially insightful. Orzala dismisses the importance of female-led prayers and seems to imply that for a woman to want to lead prayer is selfish. The language of prayer not being 'casual enough' for a woman to want to lead it because prayer is 'very sacred' suggests that, for Orzala, women's leadership of prayer has the potential to remove the sacred element from the prayer. However, she reiterated that she does not think such prayers should be prohibited, but merely that no one should be 'fighting *to* lead the prayer; the most humble of scholars usually fight *off* trying to pray. They're like, "No, you lead. No, you lead." So I think that's the etiquette we should approach prayer with, not demanding to lead the prayer.' For her, the prohibition is not the point; the point is how humbly one goes about leading a prayer, since leaders are to be sought after by others rather than be the ones demanding the right to lead. Yet, by this logic, men should be encouraging or inviting women to lead prayer if it is a sign of humility to 'fight off' leading the prayer, just as they are inviting each other to lead to demonstrate their humility. Is it not a sign of arrogance for men to prevent women from leading prayers?

Finally, for Travis (25, unmarried male, white, convert), the reason the prohibition remains relevant is especially because 'mainstream Islam' is opposed to it. He would not pray behind a woman because such a prayer would not be considered valid in the school of thought he follows. The consensus remains binding, he says, because 'I don't know if scholars even have the mechanism for changing' the mainstream position.

Disagreements With the Prohibition

Several respondents disagreed with the prohibition, either because it does not have a Qur'anic foundation, or because it is rooted in false ideas of male and female sexuality, so that it is tied to male ego, or is insulting to men. Sarbaz (28, unmarried male, South Asian background), for example, believes women should be allowed to lead mixed-gender prayers, and he would pray behind a woman if the opportunity arose. He states that women's leadership in prayer 'symbolises bigger issues. The prayer itself is not so important but it symbolises equal level of participation' and he disagrees with the root of the prohibition, which, for him, is 'the idea that men have more carnal instinct than women'. If it is going to remain prohibited, he argues, 'tradition is not a good enough reason'. Samandar (29, unmarried male, South Asian background) similarly believes that since the root of the prohibition lies in the 'patriarchal idea that men are lustful', it should not be honoured today.

Others supporting the practice cited the contemporary context as being different from the one in which the prohibition emerged. Rokhan (39, South Asian male, single) stated that because times have changed:

> the prohibition should not just be reconsidered; it needs to be changed. Because everything I believe about Islam [is that it] should be a religion that is applicable to different historical and social contexts. And I wouldn't be a Muslim if I didn't believe this... I think a lot of the times, Muslims take precedent as the way to determine if something should be allowed or not, but I don't think that's the right way. You need to take cultural and historical contexts into mind and adapt Islam, the values of Islam, to different cultures and time periods. So by definition, you can't use precedence as evidence for anything because no time and no context is the same.

Rokhan believes the reason it is prohibited is probably a lack of historical precedent: 'Probably if you go back to the Prophet, everything was men-led, so you kinda just hold on to that culture. Muslim societies are more male-dominated, so you just stick to that.' Prayer leadership, he suggested, should be 'gender-agnostic. It should be the person with the most knowledge or most senior in age.' Thus, since the explanation for the prohibition on female-led prayer does not make sense for contemporary times where women also enjoy positions of leadership, the prohibition is no longer applicable, and women should be permitted to lead mixed prayers.

Amadou (40, married male, Black) said he thinks Islam allows women to lead communal prayers 'if you're in a place where the most knowledgeable person is a woman', but that 'I'm assuming Islamic law says it has to be a man 'cause I've never seen a woman leading a prayer in any mosque'. When I asked him what he thinks the reasons for the prohibition might be, he said, 'Seeing how the male brain works, I can see why it'd be prohibited. The way we pray, the way we bend. You could easily be distracted when you pray.'

He did not, however, agree with the prohibition, emphatically claiming that he does not think this is a fair reason for the prohibition. He thinks it needs to be revisited, that it is not permanent: 'I think eventually, it'll come out. We're going to eventually have to let women lead prayer. It's just a very slow change.'

Athena (21, single female, convert, of mixed background) also supports female-led prayers and has prayed in a mixed congregation:

> In Paris after the terrorist attack, a Muslim friend told me that there would be a progressive *jum'a* [Friday prayer]. The imam is homosexual, so we had to be very careful about who would get to attend the prayer. So we had to confirm the identity of the person we knew attending… The imam asked me if I wanted to lead the prayer, but I was too nervous. So he led the prayer. I didn't wear the *hijab* while praying. A lot of women didn't, a lot of women did. And we all stood in mixed congregation and prayed together. It was amazing. The Christians, Jews, and atheists didn't have to participate, but some did. This was the first time I feel like I truly experienced Islam. I felt completely comfortable there.

Athena believes that female-led prayers did occur in Islamic history – but that, even so, she does not think Islam allows it now: 'Khadija either led prayers or was a part of a female-led prayer. But I'm not sure if it was Khadija. I just know someone did in the Prophet's time? But I don't think Islam allows it. I personally think it's awesome.' I believe she is referring here to Aisha, not Khadija – the former is reported to have led prayers. She proposed that women want to lead prayers because 'they want to empower themselves. And it should be the person who is most knowledgeable about Islam, so if it happens to be a woman, why not?' When I asked her why she believes the prohibition exists, she said, 'women bending over: I get it from the male perspective. But I feel like if that's the reason, then why not have the genders pray together but horizontally [women on one side, men on the other, as opposed to either gender in front of the other]? And also, why do they think I am not attracted to a man bending over?… I hate the curtain.'

Athena also recognised that prayer leadership was about more than prayer and leadership, connecting it to gender equality, access to God and worship, patriarchal attitudes towards female sexuality, and female empowerment overall. Her statement that she '[hates] the curtain' is a reference to the physical barriers in many mosques that separate the genders such that women are often behind the men.

Adam (21, single male, South Asian origin) did not support the prohibition because he believes it is tied to 'men and their ego'. Whether the consensus should be maintained or not for him 'depends on evidence. If it is in the Qur'an, it's binding. If it's in the *Sunnah*, it's debatable.' His response to whether it should be allowed or not is complicated: on the one hand, the consensus is binding because the legal schools 'usually have good evidence' for their position, but on the other hand, women should be allowed to lead prayers because the prohibition is likely rooted in male ego.

Table 21: General Attitude Towards Female-Led Prayer.

	Single Women	Single Men	Married Women	Married Men	Women Total	Men Total	Total Overall
Support	7	5	5	3	12	8	20
Opposition	2	3	5	7	7	10	17

As table 21 above shows, more Muslim women support female-led prayers – they either believe that women already are permitted in Islam to lead mixed-gender prayer or that the consensus should be changed to permit it. More single women support this practice than any other group in this study. Overall, 12 out of the 20 women participants and 8 out of 20 men support female-led mixed-gender prayers. Single women were the least opposed to it, with 2 out of 10 explicitly arguing that it should not be allowed, and married men the most resistant, with 7 out of 10.

While the contemporary Muslim scholarly community treats female-led prayer as a non-negotiable and dismisses any alternative viewpoints, many of my respondents disagree with the dominant position. To be sure, this topic invited the most backlash from my interlocuters, many of whom dismissed the issue as irrelevant and spoke negatively of women who want to lead prayers. As I discuss in the conclusion of this book in detail, their dismissal seems to be about more than simply not wanting women to lead prayers. Still, many others supported it, connected it to larger issues like women's religious authority and male privilege, and openly expressed disagreement with even their favourite scholars.

FEMALE-LED PRAYER IN THE ISLAMIC LEGAL TRADITION

The conversation on female-led prayer in contemporary Muslim discourse is similar to the one in the historical discourse: it begins with the conclusion – a prohibition – rather than with a question to be explored. Such a method requires new explanations and justifications for the conclusion. Behnam Sadeghi argues that new rationales are given for the preservation of a past juristic consensus, even if the consensus bears no grounding in the Qur'an and/or the *Sunnah*. This thesis finds much support in my research. While past Muslim jurists debated women's leadership in prayer even among women-only congregants, contemporary Muslim Americans are shocked to learn that the scholars may have found issues with women leading other women in prayer. While most of my respondents are certain that the reason the prohibition on female-led prayers in mixed-gender settings makes sense because of Islam's emphasis on modesty, and, according to some, because women's voice is *'awrah*, this is suspect because two legal schools prohibit women from leading other women in prayer as well. According to the Ḥanafī and Māliki positions on the issue, women are not allowed to lead other women in prayer. Ḥanafī law initially permitted it, but later prohibited it – despite, as Sadeghi notes, having the example of Aisha, the Prophet's wife, leading other women in prayer. In the words of the Ḥanafī jurist al-Shaybāni (d. 805), 'We would not like (*lā yu'jibunā*) a woman to lead, but if she does, she must stand in the middle of the row with the women, as Aisha did.'[80] Later, however, he altogether ruled against female leadership of female-only congregants as well, despite having the evidence against him that women had led such prayers during the Prophet's time.[81] Note that here, somehow, a male scholar's dislike of something becomes equated with a prohibition. Other scholars, too, such as al-Taḥāwī, ruled that it is better for women to pray individually than together with a woman leading, but they do not say why. Being a part of the congregation is treated here as a male privilege. Interestingly, later scholars wonder about whether the prayer that Aisha led was with her community or in private.[82]

While little is known about the position of Umm Waraqa when she led prayers in her *dār*, what is interesting about Aisha's prayer leadership is that as she led, she stood among the other women, as opposed to in front of them. As Calderini comments, 'to stress [a woman's] position of equality among other women, some hadiths specify that, instead of placing herself in front of the assembly, she should be in the middle of it'.[83] When men lead prayers, the male imam stands in the first row by himself, and this is also the case with women today who lead other women as well as in communal congregations. That Aisha stood in the same row as the women she was leading is significant: it may mean that no hierarchy exists between the woman leading the prayer and those following her (i.e. all women are equal), but the same hierarchy does and perhaps must exist when men lead (i.e. the man who leads enjoys a higher status than the ones he is leading). Prayer leadership thus becomes exclusively a male privilege, the status of the imam not accessible even to Muhammad's wives. It therefore makes more sense that the schools prohibited female-led prayers – two schools prohibited female-led prayer of other women, and all four for mixed congregations – because of the assumption of women's inferiority relative to men.

The reasons that the historical scholars gave, however, were not unanimous in relating the prohibition back to the uncontrollable male sex drive or to female modesty. Those who rejected sexual attraction as a relevant factor included Ibn al-Humām (Ḥanafī jurist, d. 1457), al-Ḥalabī (Ḥanafī jurist, d. 1549), Abu al-Su'ud (Ḥanafī jurist, d. 1574), and Ibn 'Abidīn (Ḥanafī jurist, d. 1836).[84] Foremost among those who linked the issue to sexuality in the eleventh century was al-Sarakhsī (Ḥanafī jurist, d. 1096), whose justification for support was primarily the Hadith 'keep women behind', which later scholars did not consider seriously because of its uncertain authenticity.[85] Sadeghi shows, however, that the law did not derive from the Hadith, since it was invoked inconsistently. In general, Hadiths were invoked only where they fit with the law, while they were ignored where they did not fit.[86] This is precisely what my respondents and other contemporary Muslims, including religious authorities, do today. Calderini writes that 'not clearly spelt out but implicitly assumed, is the issue of ritual purity (*ṭahāra*) whereby a menstruating woman or one of child-bearing age with any discharge is deemed impure to perform, let alone to lead, religious rituals such as salat (ritual prayer), hajj and fasting during Ramadan, which would consequently be considered as invalid'.[87] Similarly, Sadeghi finds that the prohibition is rooted actually in a 'first-century [AH, that is, seventh century CE] minority view that held that women break prayers due to their transmission of ritual impurity', which explains, Sadeghi argues, why a man's prayer was invalidated when he prayed in the same row as a woman, 'even if the woman praying next to the man is someone to whom he is not sexually attracted such as his grandmother, mother, sister, or daughter'.[88] The origin of the root of the prohibition is significant because it shows yet another way in which a shared attitude towards women guides a conclusive argument about what is permissible and impermissible for them and, more importantly, these arguments and explanations change with time while the dominant conclusion remains the same.

In several significant ways, the conversation today is different from the past. For example, in the past, not all women were a threat to male concentration. Since enslaved women were not believed to distract men from their prayer, they were not subjected to the same rules of prayer in the congregation as free women. This does not mean, however, that enslaved women were permitted to pray alongside men; typically, the jurists expected the rows to be arranged by social hierarchy such that, for instance, free men were in the first rows behind the imam, enslaved men next, children in the third category, followed by enslaved women, and free women in the last rows.[89] These groups were further subcategorised to include intersex individuals, and the debates about leadership specifically also included blind men, enslaved people, and children as imams. Moreover, free women were not the only potential source of distraction: prepubescent male worshippers were also treated as too similar to women to be allowed to pray next to men. None of these points come up when Muslims talk about female-led prayer today. This suggests that the rules of prayer are socially constructed, and the prohibition on women leading prayer is not universal Islamic law, but a custom based on prevalent social norms, which work to women's disadvantage, and these norms have changed and continue to change.

Another way in which contemporary ideas on prayer leadership differ from historical understandings is that none of the participants distinguished between Friday prayers and regular prayers: those who believed it is impermissible said it was not about the time of the day or the day of the week but that women simply are prohibited from leading them, at all times. Similarly, those who believed they should be allowed stated that the time and day was irrelevant. In other words, all prayers are equal. Historically, however, the Friday prayer, which includes a sermon and an abbreviated form of prayer, has been considered more significant. The communal Friday prayer is considered obligatory for men and not for women, despite the historical scholarly disagreement on the specific nuances of the Friday prayer. As Hammer explains, 'Friday prayers have to be performed in a public setting in order to be considered valid, thus making them by their very nature a public performance.'[90] Thus, an important question for historical scholars was whether women can lead the Friday prayer. For my participants, however, this was an unnecessary distinction. Some almost appeared confused that I distinguished between Friday and the other daily prayers. Clearly, the conversation has shifted and the elements of the conversation that were prioritised by past scholars are not as prioritised or even treated as relevant today: again, the rules are socially constructed and are not static.

RESULTS AND DISCUSSION

Much of the data on this topic is presented in this chart below:

Table 22: Muslims' Attitudes Towards Female-Led Prayer.

	Single Women	**Single Men**	**Married Women**	**Married Men**	**Total**
Women are allowed to lead mixed prayers.	0	1	1	0	2
Women are not allowed to lead mixed-gender prayer but they should be allowed.	5	4	2	3	14
Women should not be allowed to lead mixed-gender prayer.	2	3	5	7	17
I don't know what Islam's position is, but I think it should be allowed.	2	0	2	0	4
I don't know anything about this topic.	1	2	0	0	3

As these answers show, only 2 (of the 40) individuals believe that Islam allows women to lead mixed prayer, 14 believe that such prayers should be permissible, whereas 17 support the existing position of impermissibility, 4 do not know the 'Islamic' position but believe it should be allowed regardless of what Islam's position is, and 30 (see table 23) believe that the existing consensus is binding on today's Muslims. Notably, among those who believed that the consensus is binding were individuals who support changing the consensus but maintain that until a new one is established, the current one must be honoured.

Table 23: The consensus on female-led prayer is binding today.

	Single Women	**Single Men**	**Married Women**	**Married Men**	**Total**
Yes	7	6	7	10	30
No	2	2	3	0	7
I don't know	1	2	0	0	3

For reference again, I include here table 2, which documents my respondents' answer to whether scholarly consensus is always binding:

Table 2: The consensus of the scholars is always binding.

Scale	**Single Women (10 total)**	**Single Men (10 total)**	**Married Women (10 total)**	**Married Men (10 total)**	**Total**
1 (completely disagree)	3	2	3	3	11
2	1	6	2	3	12
3 (I'm not sure)	2		1	2	5
4	1		3		4
5 (completely agree)	3	2	1	2	8

Generational views appear to play a role in general attitudes towards female-led prayer. Unlike the other topics, where married men and single women held similar opinions while married women and single men agreed more, in the case of female-led prayer, married men were unanimously against contradicting the existing consensus. Among the married men, even those who believed women *should* be allowed qualified their responses with statements about not contradicting the consensus until scholars arrive at a new one. But there are hints of a generational shift in that only two married women support female-led prayer, while five of the ten unmarried ones do. This holds true for the men as well: only three of the unmarried men believe women should not be allowed to lead prayer. Thus, the opinions on female-led prayer vary across the generations.

Uncontrollable Male Sexual Urges As Justification for the Prohibition

My respondents agree with the past legal tradition on female-led prayers in some ways (e.g. women cannot lead mixed-gender prayers; women's level of attractiveness, age, and social status matters) and depart from it in other ways (e.g, women can lead other women in prayers, the rules apply to all prayers and not just to obligatory or Friday prayers). What explains this inconsistent reliance on, or perception of, the tradition? Those who learned that women were not allowed to lead other women in prayer (i.e. not mixed-gender) in some schools immediately said, 'No, I definitely disagree with that. That makes no sense.' Only one woman (single, 21 year old) believed that the prohibition on female-led prayer of mixed congregation 'makes no sense', while another woman stated that 'it's just not a big deal, but I think it should be allowed'. Many of the remaining participants expressed discomfort with the subject and with the demand of some Muslim women to lead prayers. Their idea is that Muslim women's leadership in prayer is simply not 'relevant' and does not need to be addressed, and the current position does not need to be changed. Thus, I suggest that the reason for the reluctance is the assumption that female-led prayer is irrelevant and does not warrant a discussion or re-evaluation. Since few of the women personally wanted to lead prayers, this was not an important issue for them, despite the impact that the prohibition on their potential to lead prayer has on other aspects of their lives as Muslim women. This is because, as scholars point out, this issue is more than simply about prayer leadership and indicates problems with larger issues of recognising women's leadership, public participation, and access to religious authority more broadly. Ultimately, the discussion on female-led prayer is more ideological than theological, serving and benefiting a patriarchal worldview that relies on incorrect, essentialised ideas of women as limited by their biology while men are privileged by it. In their discussion of gender hierarchy in modern and pre-modern commentaries on the Qur'an, Bauer and Hamza write:

> Modern conservative commentators overwhelmingly believe that the hierarchical verses in the Qur'an refer to innate differences in the sexes, and that spousal roles, and to some extent other social roles, are biologically determined. These interpretations often rely on fixed ideas

> of human nature, in which the sexes' abilities to function in the world are determined biologically. While conservatives claim authenticity by virtue of establishing links with tradition, their own interpretations are inextricably linked to the global influence of modern norms: whereas medieval authors justified their commentaries by claiming women's inferiority to men, modern conservatives often find explanations rooted in science, pseudo-science or 'human nature'.[91]

These essentialist ideas about male and female sexuality are linked to the preservation of a patriarchal world order and social set up that, again, benefits men and views them as the default occupiers of public space. Barbara Stowasser notes that '[for] the medieval theologians, the Qur'an's female images and models both symbolised essential aspects of the Islamic order as they knew it, and also aided them in its preservation'.[92] The essentialist ideas, understood as divinely decreed, immutable differences between the genders, continue to be used in contemporary times in tandem with claims of gender equality.[93] amina wadud has also discussed extensively the Islamic tradition's 'habit of sustaining the normative Muslim as a male'.[94] She writes, 'the major canon of Islamic public discourse and ethical articulation makes the male experience and articulation the norm and the standard measurement for what it means to be human in the public arena', despite women being *khalifah* ('full moral agent') as much as men.[95]

Many of my respondents suggested that the reason some Muslim women might want to lead communal prayers is that 'they just want to compete with men', or 'they just want to show they can do anything men can'. These comments speak more to popular perceptions of feminism – given the common (Muslim and non-Muslim) view of feminists as striving to compete with men – than they do to women's prayer leadership specifically. (Still, it is worth noting that this idea of women's competition with men did not appear in any other topics, such as women's interfaith marriage or female inheritance.) The idea seems to be that the change is motivated by modern Western notions of gender equality, which, according to the understandings of some participants, do not take into account the differences between women and men. No one sufficiently explained, however, what these differences were and how they account for or explain the reasons that men can lead women but women cannot lead men, except that male sexuality is less controllable than female sexuality.

The idea that female-led prayers pose a distraction for men makes many problematic assumptions about women and men. Occasionally, if I sensed that the respondent might be comfortable responding, I asked further questions about their concern for modesty. For instance, when they said that women cannot or should not bend in front of men, I asked how anyone would have a chance to look at or watch another congregant if everyone is bending at the same time. While the imam is ahead of everyone else, presumably she would not be seen by the male congregants because of the rows of women behind her. This generated different responses. Some (women and men) said some variant of, 'I don't know. I would just feel very uncomfortable.' Others said, 'This never happened in the Prophet's time. If it was allowed, it would've happened then.' Some men said, 'I would be distracted if I knew there was a woman praying, even if there were barriers and even if I couldn't see her or the other women.' It appears that the prohibition merely validates common assumptions and anxieties about male sexuality; it privileges male discomfort over the greater implications of female-led prayers, whether prohibited or permitted. The idea that women are unlikely to be attracted to the men (or the voice of the men) leading the prayer is part of a larger socially motivated claim that women are naturally and inherently capable of controlling their urges but men are not.

It is remarkable that the assumption that men cannot concentrate if a woman is leading the prayer, reciting the call to prayer, or giving the *khutbah* (sermon) is treated as a legitimate and Islamically appropriate explanation. The implication is clear: women's worship and women's access to communal places of worship take second place to making sure men maintain their sexual self-control in a sacred space. None of my discussants who supported the prohibitions challenged their own assumptions embedded in their explanations for why female-led prayer was inappropriate or un-Islamic – e.g. why is prayer intimate only when women perform or lead it? Why do only women need privacy during prayer? And why are we trusting with leadership, especially prayer leadership in a sacred space, men who are apparently incapable of self-control and thus cannot be trusted with women anywhere? Although a few did pause to comment that a certain claim or statement of theirs did not make any sense, they maintained their position that they would defer to authorities on these matters and/or that there must be wisdom behind the prohibitions. Ultimately, they are attributing divine value to prohibitions constructed by male scholars who drew their conclusions from patriarchal assumptions about women's worship and male sexuality.

What exactly is it about prayer that makes women's leadership of it a matter of contention? What is it about prayer that makes so many of my respondents insist that female-led prayers are 'irrelevant' for us to talk about? If they are as irrelevant as imagined by some, why is it such a matter of debate and why are many so invested in maintaining the prohibition? Women's leadership of prayer appears to *feel* immodest, and it deprives women of intimacy and privacy, some of my respondents told me. But what is so intimate about prayer that women must not lead it, that women are more entitled to privacy during prayer than men are – and why is this intimateness gendered? There appears to be an assumption in my respondents' comments that every woman prefers bodily privacy during prayer, or that they all understand bodily privacy the same way. But why is privacy gendered? Why is modesty gendered such that it benefits men, views all public spaces as men's territory by default, treats men as the leaders who can have access to the public sphere while women belong to the private sphere? Exploring possible answers to these questions requires theorising the gendering of modesty and privacy and the privatisation of the female body. As Sa'diyya Shaikh contends, the argument against women's leadership of prayer 'is premised on a rather convoluted gendered view of humanity in which a carefully constructed and highly problematic religious universe is created for the moral benefit of men at the expense of women'.[96]

This conversation and these opinions are male-dominated and are coloured by male prejudice. The dominant opinions seldom, if at all, consider women's experiences and women's opinions; there appears to be a severe lack of interest in deep engagement with women who want to or do lead mixed prayers. Recall that the Ḥanafī jurist al-Shaybāni and several other male jurists explicitly stated that 'we' would not like for women to lead even other women in prayer despite there being evidence in support of female-led prayers at least of other women; many unashamedly distinguished between women who are attractive and unattractive, old and young, to discuss which types of women were entitled to access the mosque, and for what reasons. Their personal preferences became laws women were subject to. As Aisha Geissinger, argues, however, this is not simply a reflection of biases that were common in pre-modern times; such attitudes are 'linked to contestations over…interpretive authority', which affect other aspects of women's lives as well.[97] As I discuss toward the end of the chapter, I interpret this as a form of psychic violence against women. Indeed, medieval scholars and jurists even debated whether women are entitled to full access to the mosque, an issue that persists in some parts of Muslim-majority countries around the world where women are still not permitted to attend mosques. The dominant argument was that women could access mosques on the condition that they were not visible to the male worshippers so as not to disrupt the latter. The default here, again, is that men alone are entitled to the public space, and women are mere guests and visitors and must conform to certain norms so that their presence is regulated in ways acceptable to the men. In this framing, women are not full, complete human beings with the ability to worship God freely in the ways men are; they are sexual objects who exist as temptations men must fight in their service of God. This is clearly not a universally male trait, and the assumption that men are incapable of self-control is not only insulting to men but is arguably un-Islamic since fighting one's temptation is a form of *jihad*, personal struggle. Men are not only capable of controlling their gaze and sexual urges, but some also find it unacceptable that this is what they are reduced to. Imam Mohammed Khaleel (d. 2022), for example, writes:

> It is extremely sad to see that some are advocating the sexist argument that a woman's body can be distracting. One would assume that people going to pray would have communication with the Lord as the primary goal. One would also assume that the woman leading the prayers would be dressed in such garb that is solemn as opposed to sexy (of course, if one has a perverted mind, even a nun's habit will be seen as sexy). If it is pointed out that the woman's voice can be attractive, then one wonders about the effect that the male voice has on female worshippers?[98]

Ḥasan al-Turābī (d. 2016) similarly argues, 'When there is a pious woman… she should lead the prayers and whoever is distracted by her beauty should be deemed sick.'[99] Even some pre-modern scholars took issues with forming laws based on such a limited idea of maleness, rejecting the idea of debating whether women could attend mosques or not, for whatever reasons. Ibn 'Arabi (d. 1240), for example, 'analyses men's resistance to the divine decree allowing women to go to mosques as an instance of jealousy (*ghayra*), arguing that personal animus can lead humans to be jealous even of the rulings of God. Only full establishment of the authority of intellect and faith can prevent such feelings of resentment (*haraj*) against God's decree.'[100] For him, men who prevent women from going to the mosque are 'not preventing other men from succumbing to [female] charm' but are themselves 'succumbing to base sentiments of sexual possessiveness'.[101]

While my respondents largely dismiss most pre-modern Islamic ideas on gender and sexuality (male dominance, female subordination, sexual slavery, women's lack of agency, etc.) and hold ideas popular in the broader American contemporary culture, their ideas of female modesty and uncontrollable male sexual desire remain parallel to patriarchal ideas in traditional Islamic, nineteenth-century and even some contemporary European and American ideals. As with patriarchal ideals elsewhere, my American Muslim respondents cannot imagine the reverse situation, and some did not even think it possible: if women cannot lead men in prayer because some men might be sexually aroused by the voice of a woman, what happens when a woman is sexually aroused by the voice of a man when he is leading the prayer? There is an assumption and expectation that women either do not have significant enough sexual urges to be distracted from prayer, or if they do, they must control their urges – at the very least in a sacred space where they should be focusing on God.

It is no secret that, in all patriarchies, the feminine is seen as an intrinsically intimate, private, protected position. Traditional Islamic norms, which many of my respondents and the opponents of female-led prayers uphold, dictate that women, more so than men, exist in such a way that they do not attract any kind of attention to themselves, their bodies, their speech, their presence. This is a form of psychic violence against women: the pressure and obligation to be rendered invisible, to force themselves into invisibleness, the knowledge that she is being reduced entirely to an object of desire for heterosexual males with no input of her own, the pressure to tread in the world carefully believing she is not entitled to it. Shaikh, too, identifies this privileging of a hetero-patriarchal worldview as the default for patriarchal religious anthropology, which is binary and hierarchical: the woman, the feminine, and femaleness are conceptualised as sexual, carnal, irrational, a source of chaos because of which the female must be controlled; this sexualised feminine is the antithesis of the spiritual, the intellect, the rational, all represented by maleness.[102] The irony here is that the default, the rational male, is incapable of self-control and self-discipline, of existing around women in a healthy, secure way. One of the most obvious implications of this problem is the rampant sexual harassment women experience in a patriarchy, the message of which is obvious: a woman subject to this treatment is occupying space in which she does not belong and is therefore attracting attention towards herself for being somewhere where she does not belong. Not only is this kind of treatment disempowering but the necessity of having to seek basic rights, such as access to authority and sacred spaces, distracts women as a collective from achieving their full spiritual potential.

However, in this construction of maleness and femaleness, women are not the only ones who suffer: men, too, are infantilised as incapable of meaningfully and thoughtfully engaging with women without subjecting them to their gaze, and they too are dehumanised by being misrepresented in such limited ways, i.e. as a dangerous threat to women's safety and rights. Essentialising men as incapable of self-control upon seeing women in any public space but especially in a place considered as the House of God, the mosque, allows them to avoid accountability for any harmful behaviour toward women, who are reduced to being objects of male desire. It appears that patriarchy invents a problem – that of women existing in tandem with men, sharing a space with men – and then attempts to resolve it by offering an insecure, questionable, and extremely limited conception of masculinity. The reason men are expected and allowed to control their environments is precisely because of an insecure notion of masculinity. Men do, in fact, have the ability to resist negative behaviour, control themselves, and be better. As bell hooks argues, patriarchy demands of men 'to give up their true self in order to realise the patriarchal ideal' from the time they are young boys, leading to the beginnings of self-betrayal, all in order to 'conform to the acceptable behaviors sexism defines as male'.[103] As she points out, this 'stress of guarding and protecting a false self is harmful to male emotional well-being; it erodes self-esteem'; she gives the example of male depression as a direct consequence of the inability to be whole.[104] Contemporary Muslims who unquestioningly accept claims about male sexuality in order to prevent women from prayer leadership must contend with the harms asserted by these claims. We must also contend with the contradiction in the idea that self-control is a positive ideal on the one hand, while also investing so little in holding men accountable for not working towards it.

In this discourse, in addition to being the silent objects of male desire, women are explicitly feared as a threat to male presence through the language of *fitna*, disruption, chaos. The erasure of women from public spaces becomes essential for male flourishing. The male in this discourse is treated as the universal norm, the default, and sexual differences, perceived or real, benefit him. As Sa'diyya Shaikh points out, 'women's mere presence in a mosque often needs to be explicated, explained, justified, or vilified'.[105] Women are othered to such an extent that they 'are inherently positioned as impostors in the public sacred space' and they '[desacralise] the mosque for male worshippers'.[106]

As shown already, not only is a specific misogynistic heterosexual norm assumed, but women are further treated merely as objects of male desire and fantasy rather than full humans with their own agency. This is especially clear in the aspect of the mosque debate where pre-modern heterosexual male scholars considered whether or not to allow older women, unattractive women, and enslaved people to attend mosques. They concluded in the affirmative due to an assumption that since older and unattractive women could not legitimately be considered an object of sexual desire for the men, they could attend. However, younger women should be discouraged or even prohibited because they were assumed to be more desirable. As amina wadud points out, 'The patriarchal formulations of Islamic law throughout history hold condescending utilitarian perspectives on women. Not only is the female looked down upon, she is treated as an object in shariah discussions, not as a discussant. The woman is a recipient of its decisions, not a decision maker. Decisions made concerning her role in the family and society were made from the perspective of those who did not and could not share her experience and therefore judged on the basis of second-hand perceptions.'[107] Such notions of the body and sexuality are culturally constructed, which is particularly clear from the shift in these understandings: women's bodies and sexuality were not always perceived as a threat to society; women weren't always seen as naturally deserving of more modesty; and men's sexuality was not always seen as stronger than women's – as I discuss below.

For opponents of female-led prayers, women's leadership of prayer becomes a form of sexual immodesty, which is perceived as a threat to the larger society because of an imagined fear of its impact on men. The gendering of privacy and modesty is such that only women need privacy during prayer and only women's modesty requires that they not lead prayer, pray in front of, or even in the vicinity of men, or even show the same body parts that men are permitted to show. Women were historically part of the domestic sphere – they belong in the privacy of their homes – while men are entitled to public spaces. In Islamic history, for instance, while women were integral to the development of the Islamic tradition, their role was generally often limited to serving in private homes or mosques, teaching individual men privately who later became renowned scholars[108] The relegation of women to private spheres and the connection between female modesty and men's supposed inability to display sexual discipline both contribute to women's lack of access to the public sphere. The assumption in historical Muslim discourse has always been that granting women access to the public, allowing them to occupy the same public space as men, will lead to *fitna*. This assumption continues to be an important factor in discussions on gender segregation and women's presence in the public.

The pre-modern Muslim tradition developed an entire concept of excluding women from public space to prevent what they understood would be social chaos. The linking of female-led prayer or women's public performance of worship to notions of modesty is a conceptual matter associated with the general idea of female seclusion but more particular with a specific idea of *hijab* and female dignity. Barabara Stowassser offers an excellent analysis of the development of this concept, noting that the medieval meaning of the term *hijab* – which literally, Qur'anically, refers to seclusion – 'remained conceptual and generic', which 'permitted the debate to remain conceptual rather than get bogged down in the specifics of articles of clothing whose meaning, in any case, was prone to changes both geographic/regional and also chronological'.[109] In her discussion of women's access to the public and the sacred, Hosn Abboud uses the story of Maryam in the Qur'an to make a case for women's equal access to places of worship: 'Maryam's entry into the *mihrab* [prayer niche, or sacred space] coincides with the female's entry into the *ka'ba* [the focal point of prayer for Muslims, where women and men circumambulate together], and Maryam being commanded by the angels to pray in the same space with other male worshipers can be reinterpreted as a license for Muslim women, in present times, to pray in the same space in the mosque.'[110]

This treatment of male and female bodies has a profound impact on women's rights and the continuation of male dominance in the public sphere because it tends to benefit men: men enjoy more expansive freedom outside the home, better access to religious and other forms of leadership, and, as indicated from my respondents' comments, even permission not to control their sexual urges. This same permission is denied to them, one might hope, outside of the mosque or other religious space. The men who admitted to not being able to concentrate on their prayer if they knew a woman was leading the prayer work and operate in mixed-gender settings, but it is exclusively in the mosque setting that they feel safe admitting to being unable to control themselves. Muslim men today work with, lead behind, and work under, the supervision of women. One must ask, therefore, why only in the mosque setting is it that their ideas of women's leadership are considered legitimate and appropriate? Scholars identify this as compartmentalisation. bell hooks notes, for example, that 'patriarchy encourages men to surrender their integrity and to live lives of denial'.[111] This is possible because '[by] learning the arts of compartmentalization, dissimulation, and disassociation, men are able to see themselves as acting with integrity in cases where they are not'.[112] Quoting psychotherapist Scott Peck, hooks writes that 'patriarchal masculinity normalizes male compartmentalization'.[113] Peck gives the example of a religious man going to church on Sunday believing that he loves God and God's creation and fellow human beings but he also 'has no trouble with his company's policy of dumping toxic wastes in the local stream. He can do this because he has religion in one compartment and his business in another.'[114] Similarly, the Muslim male who believes that women and men are at least spiritually equal but simultaneously denies them access to the sacred space he feels inherently entitled to, while likely working with women outside of the mosque, is boxing religion in one compartment, work in another.

Still, if it is men who are incapable of controlling themselves when they see or hear a woman praying or speaking, one has to wonder why women are the ones punished by being denied access to the public instead of restricting men's access to the public? Similarly, if men are the natural leaders, superior to women, why do they lack the capacity for self-control, and why endow men with such a position of leadership if they are incapable of self-control, helpless victims of their libidos? On the one hand, male leadership is a privilege bestowed on men specifically because of their imagined innate superiority in terms of strength, but on the other hand, women are denied the same privilege because of an imagined male weakness in discipline. Why does the woman need to be removed from the man's presence so he can worship God, rather than the man removing himself from a space where he might be a threat to a woman because of his apparent innate inability, or choice, to self-control? As Shaikh notes, 'ironically, even perhaps humorously', these claims about male sexuality 'significantly diminish male humanity'.[115]

In a place of worship, Nina Hoel asks, 'Why are women's bodies the locus of attention?'[116] Indeed, when the congregants are there specifically to worship God, develop a connection with God, enrich their spirituality, why are they instead focusing on women's bodies? The counter response to this question, of course, is that *especially* the sacred space is not to be tainted with any potentially sexually distracting ideas and practices. But one must ask, then, why is it assumed that only women's voice, women's bodies, women's leadership of prayer is distracting and not men's? This is why it is important to recognise that these sexual anxieties are rooted in an ideology that treats female sexuality as a danger to society and the female body as inherently seductive but male sexuality as the default, the norm. This view of sexuality is not isolated and certainly not unique to Muslims. Western, non-Muslim theorists have shown the ways in which culture, particularly in patriarchal societies, regulates and disciplines male and female bodies, and in particular the female body, as a source of shame and as an object for another's gaze. They have also shown the impacts that such treatment of the female body has on other areas of life, such as language and linguistics, philosophy, culture, politics, etc.[117]

By analysing the limitations of this approach to modesty, I do not suggest that modesty and privacy are never desirable or praiseworthy. In fact, meaningful forms of individual privacy can be profoundly beneficial to individuals and societies; and everyone who wants privacy should be granted it. There are, indeed, many important benefits of privacy.[118] However, I am more interested in the pattern of gendering modesty to such an extent that it grants men certain problematic permissions (e.g. lack of sexual discipline) and denies women a seemingly basic right (leadership of prayer). I contend that the distinction between private and public in conversations on leadership and Islam has harmful impacts on society, as feminist scholars have argued for other contexts, as in the famous expression 'the personal is political'. The individual preference for privacy, while valuable, is therefore not separate from the broader issue. Individual choices and preferences do not exist in a vacuum: clearly, with moral value attached to women's modesty in ways that it is not the case for men's modesty, the choice to pray in seclusion, not to lead prayer, and not be seen by men during prayer or in a religious space – these are not simply personal issues. Hammer's argument about amina wadud's leadership of the mixed-gender prayer in 2005 is quite relevant here, as indeed such leadership is about religious authority, representation, and access and not about prayer alone.

Moreover, the charge that this is women's attempt at competing with men also fails to acknowledge the fact that the debate over female-led prayers is not a modern one. Ahmed Elewa and Laury Silvers address this denial in their discussion of 'westoxification', a certain fascination with the West that is 'typically understood to be the uncritical adoption of "Western" or secular modes of thought with its damaging effects on Islamic values'.[119] As they write, 'despite the fact that female-led prayer has been…a topic of discussion since the time of the Prophet, most disapproving responses viewed the performance of the wadud prayer as entirely alien to Islamic values'.[120] As

Hammer points out, a juristic discourse existed on female-led prayers from the ninth century onwards: 'If one were to read juristic discourse and legal opinions as reflections of social realities, then it stands to reason that early Muslim communities and the women within them had questions about the very issues Muslims are discussing today, including those of gender, though they would not have been identified as such.'[121] If anything, as Leila Ahmed argues, 'texts that repeatedly call for the prohibition of certain practices tell us that these were social practices that jurists and scholars deemed worthy of critique without being able to end them'.[122] In other words, these were not non-issues as most of my respondents believe.

As Hoel argues, 'Muslim women's religious leadership in Islam can be seen as a human enactment of moral agency, an expression of gender justice, and responsive to the right to participate as equally enfleshed, sexual, and spiritual subjects in the production of religious meaning and meaning-making.' Muslim women who seek access to prayer leadership are not simply trying to appropriate rights granted to men, as some of my respondents believe, but see such leadership as a part of their moral, spiritual, and religious responsibility, as an expression of gender justice that they recognise as inherent to Islam, and as their right to participation in religious meaning-making.

To be sure, while women are treated in this discourse as beings who ought to flourish only in the privacy of their homes, and whose seclusion is required for upholding social order, women have always served in public spaces – as leaders, as queens, as teachers, as students, as workers. The expectation and ideal clearly are not aligned with the practical realities of Muslim women. Further, no data supporting the legitimacy of the fear of women's leadership of prayer exists, in any religion. There is no evidence that when women lead prayers or when men follow women in prayer, however uncommon the practice might be, *fitna* will necessarily ensue, and the congregation will necessarily become sexually distracted. Many Muslim communities around the world exist where the genders are either not separated during prayer, no physical barriers exist between them in mosques, and/or they can even pray next to each other. In her discussion of racial and ethnic division in American Muslim communities, Jamillah Karim observes, for example, that in the Black-majority mosque she attended while growing up in Atlanta, 'women sat behind the men but still could see and hear the imam' whereas the 'immigrant mosque' separated women and men, and 'women sat downstairs, unable to see the imam, listen[ing] to him from speakers'.[123] Men and women pray together, side by side, at mosques like the Qal'bu Maryam mosque in

California.[124] Toronto's Unity Mosque similarly has women, men, and non-binary Muslims all praying alongside each other, as well as women leading prayers, giving the sermon, and performing the call to prayer.[125] Similar examples exist around the world.

Shifting Perceptions of Male and Female Sexuality

It is paradoxical that women are perceived to be the cause of *fitna* while men are the ones with a dangerously high sexual appetite. Several studies have shown that pre-modern Muslim thinkers in fact did not consistently understand men to have a high sex drive that needs to be contained; on the contrary, women had to be be controlled because of their dangerously high sexual appetite. For instance, in her book *Gendered Morality: Classical Islamic Ethics of the Self, Family, and Society*, Zahra Ayubi discusses the contradictions of traditional Muslim ethics (as a genre) as understood through the works of three major figures: Abu Hamīd Muhammad al-Ghazālī, Jalāl ad-Din Davānī, and Nasīr ad-Dīn Tusī. She finds that medieval Muslim scholars' understandings of morality and ethics are fundamentally gendered – and classed – and necessarily require hierarchical, exclusionary ways of living and being. As an example, femininity and masculinity are constructed such that women are believed to be incapable of controlling their *nafs* (metaphysical soul), therefore requiring men to control them.[126] This is because, the scholars believed, women have a higher sexual appetite than men, which they are unable to contain, and granting them certain sexual and social freedoms would wreak havoc on society. In their ethical teachings, these Muslim scholars insist that the husband is responsible over his wife's *nafs*, that he must make sure to rule over his wife's *nafs*.[127] During prayer, too, women should be secluded from men and ideally not attend mosques or public worship to avoid tempting men.[128] This is because men are inherently more rational than women, hence men's moral duty to control women's *nafs*. Yet, in modern discussions on prayer leadership, it is men who are incapable of controlling their *nafs*, resulting in the ban on women leading them in prayer. The issue is not women's presence during communal prayer or women leading men in prayer. It is the legacy and continuation of a gender hierarchal idea of leadership that legitimates men's power over women.

Pernilla Myrne, too, in her book *Female Sexuality in the Early Medieval Islamic World*, discusses the ways that female sexuality and erotic behavior have been understood historically, as gleaned from eleventh- to thirteenth-century writings by Muslim authors in multiple genres and disciplines, such as in medicine, *fiqh*, and erotology. Relying on a large corpus of literature in different genres (medical, religious-legal, and literary), she highlights attitudes toward pleasure and sexual satisfaction. She shows that women were generally believed to be hypersexual, that women's sexual appetite (*shahwa*) was much stronger than men's – nine times stronger, in some reports, ninety-nine in others.[129] A Hadith report attributed to the Prophet states that 'God created ten parts of *shahwa*, and then made nine parts in women and one part in men.'[130] Shi'ī scholars attribute a similar claim to 'Ali, with an important addition: 'God created ten parts of *shahwa*, and then made nine parts in women and one part in men. Had God not given them bashfulness (ḥayāʾ) in proportion to their appetite, every man would have nine women clinging to him.'[131] Later Shi'ī traditions highlighted women's natural tendency towards *ṣabr*, endurance or patience, which they used to prevent chaos despite their high libido. Since the implication appears to be that God did not endow men with such virtues, the dominant idea of men's inability to control themselves sexually makes sense. This idea is likely borrowed from Greek mythology, where instead of desire, 'pleasure from sex' was measured and debated. As Myrne notes, 'By giving the saying the status as a Prophetic tradition, it became an authoritative saying about female and male libido.'[132] In other words, the non- and extra-Islamic idea of male and female desire became validated by being constructed and imagined as a prophetic statement. The discussion on female sexuality in medieval Islamic literature and scholarship is intimately tied to ancient Greek ideas of female inferiority generally, such as claims about internal genitalia being a sign of inferiority and the first stage toward completion, as compared to men's external genitalia, which were the second and perfect stage.[133]

Similarly, Roshan Iqbal notes the contradictory ways the Muslim tradition has dealt with female and male sex drives.[134] Defining 'sex drive' as 'sexual motivation, including frequency and intensity of sexual desires', she explains that it 'may be measured in numerous ways, including sexual thoughts, fantasies, desired frequency of intercourse, number of partners, and masturbation'.[135] The Muslim legal tradition views women's sex drive as low and men's as high in order to justify men's supposedly 'natural' desires for simultaneous multiple sex partners; in contrast, the non-legal discourse, such as in poetry and medicine, speak of women as hyper-sexed. Notably, as Myrne has also shown, the idea that women are hyper-sexual and have an intensely higher sex drive than men is rooted in the idea that women are closer to nature, an assumption shared by the late Antique and early medieval world broadly.[136] Iqbal argues that 'the idea of a naturally low sex drive is based on an idea that emphasizes traits as biologically innate rather than socially constructed or shaped'.[137] These traits are clearly socially constructed since different genres of the Muslim intellectual tradition treat sexuality differently.

It was not just the philosophers and ethicists discussed in Ayubi's study who thought of women in these ways. Geissinger shows that commentators on the Qur'an also 'link[ed] femaleness to a lack of eloquence, limited intelligence, and weak reasoning abilities'.[138] While this comment is specifically about the exegetes' interpretation of Q. 43:18, which outwardly has nothing to do with gender or women, the point here is to note how far religious patriarchy goes to attribute misogyny to God.[139] Hadiths were constructed and employed to religiously validate the idea of women's inherent inferiority. In her discussion of commentaries on women in the Qur'an, Barbara Stowasser notes that Hadith 'materials on women's inferior nature were accepted and propagated by the consensus ('*ijmā'*) of the learned doctors of law and theology until eighteenth-century premodern reformists began to question their authoritative status. Since the nineteenth century, Islamic modernists have denied the authenticity and doctrinal validity of what they viewed as medieval extraneous interpretative "lore", while re-emphasising the Qur'anic notion of the female's full personhood and moral responsibility.'[140] As Asma Sayeed has shown, early Islamic scholars operated on the principle that 'women's authority in matters of religion was uncertain', and the caliph Umar in particular is reported to have sought male witnesses to corroborate the opinions of women.[141] Some made exceptions if the Hadiths were reported by Muhammad's wives, however.

It is especially interesting that regardless of the view of female sexuality, women end up being restricted and men end up benefiting. On the one hand, in traditional Islamic teachings, men have more sexual freedom than women, and are permitted to have an infinite number of concubines in addition to up to four wives, because of their greater inherent biological need for sex. On the other, women need to be controlled and relegated to the private sphere because they have an uncontrollable sex drive that needs to be regulated – by men. The issue is clearly not about who has a higher or lower sex drive but about whichever attitude will divinely legitimate men's sexual freedom while restricting women's at a given historical moment. It's also significant that these ideas continue to be perpetuated today, as among my participants. These considerations about lower or higher sex drive are then instrumentalised as a rationale for prohibiting women from leading prayer and accessing public spaces. The sacred space becomes sexualised in a way that non-sacred spaces, such as workplaces or educational institutions, are not.

CONCLUSION

The topic of female-led prayer received the most resistance from my respondents. The disrespect and negative judgement of those women who might want to lead mixed-gender prayer, the idea that any woman who wants to or does lead prayer is selfish, the insistence (often with aggressive tones, as some of my respondents began to speak more loudly than before) that this was an irrelevant topic – all indicate that the issue is not merely about female-led prayer. Sometimes, when I would ask a follow-up question, such as, 'Would you support it if there were barriers between the female imam and the congregation?' I did not receive an answer but was asked, 'Why are we even talking about this?' Or 'There should not be a barrier between the imam and the congregation', which is especially interesting because most mosques are gender segregated in a way where there are physical barriers between men and women and the women congregants cannot see the imam. Further, the lack of respect and the dismissal of women who desire to lead prayers suggest that there is something deeper here than a simple dislike of female-led prayer. This is the only topic in which some of my respondents brought up feminism – and rejected it as un-Islamic ('their activism will override anything', 'they want to be like men or whatever', etc., as some said).

That my discussants invoked the need for precedent for the legitimacy of an Islamic position exclusively in their discussion on female-led prayer is striking. First, because that is a primary reason among popular Muslim scholars who oppose it – which might suggest that the lay Muslim community is at least somewhat informed about the debate, although only three of my discussants were aware of wadud's prayer in 2005. Second, because all participants admitted that they did not know much about the topic, and almost all stated that they had never come across anything in Islamic texts that a woman had ever led any prayer, even in women-only settings. Thus, when some of my interviewees responded, 'I've just never heard of or read about a woman doing this', I am struck by their certainty that they have studied this matter, and that the records of women leading prayers would necessarily be highlighted in the sources they read – as we have seen, such records are in fact downplayed or omitted. Moreover, this is the only case in which the question of precedent comes up so prominently. If the lack of precedent is a legitimate reason, then what must they do in the case of child marriage and slave concubinage, for which there is plenty of precedent in that Muslims did historically enslave people and marry children or permit the marriage of children? The argument of the opponents appears to be that in order for a practice to be legitimated today, it has to have been practised by at leat some Muslims in the past, but those same opponents do not use that same standard for the continuation of child marriage and slavery – and for good reasons. Clearly, then, precedent is not the only ground for permissibility while a lack of precedent is viewed as a problem or at least insufficient for claiming permissibility. My point here is twofold: to highlight the inconsistency in the logic being used to prohibit female-led prayers, and to argue that seeking validation from past practices is not a productive source of justification because many immoral practices were considered acceptable in the past. In any case, I have shown plenty of evidence of precedence of women leading mixed prayers or being permitted to lead certain voluntary prayers. The standards of the past therefore cannot always work for the present if we seek an ethical practice of Islam.

Another reason an argument based on the lack of apparent precedent is questionable is that while many Muslims confidently assert that women have never led communal prayers in Islamic history, they do not consider the possibility that the lack of records of female-led prayers is possibly due to the erasure of women's contributions to Islam in the historical writing by men.[142] Nor do they consider the possibility that there are records of women leading prayer, but these are ignored by scholars seeking to maintain the existing prohibition. Interestingly many participants stated that women-led prayers in mixed-gender settings were not acceptable because they had never come across any woman leading a prayer, or at least a mixed prayer, in their research on Islam, despite having told me earlier that they did not feel qualified to answer these questions from Islam's perspective, but would do so according to their general understanding of Islam. One must ask, then, now that women have definitely led mixed-gender prayers, for how long can it be argued that the action is unprecedented?

Contemporary Muslim scholars who oppose female-led prayers in mixed-gender congregations often engage with the issue in ways that do not address the deeper questions at play in the historical legal discourse. They merely provide the legal opinions of the jurists who engaged this question, as though the consensus is simply the established opinion of the historical jurists, and they themselves have no active role in the construction of the tradition. Among these detractors, there appears to be little concern for the reasons behind the prohibition. When Zaid Shakir explains, for instance, that the Ḥanafī, Shāfi'ī, and Ḥanbalī schools allow female-led prayers 'if certain conditions prevail', there is no discussion on what these conditions might be, or of the possibility that these conditions may change, or even, ultimately, of the relevance of the point of 'if certain conditions prevail'.[143] Why, for instance, must a woman who leads even her household in prayer be more qualified than any man around in order to be able to lead? Why do similar restrictions not apply to male leaders of prayer, particularly when even male children are permitted to lead prayers?

Possible answers to these questions are related to broader notions of authority – in particular, the gendering of authority – and the exclusion of women from the process of lawmaking, including on decisions about women. This becomes important because of the assumption that a woman leading communal prayers would create sexual thoughts in the male congregants, which is the most popular argument that my participants offered against female-led prayers in support of the prohibition. This argument was less prominent in the earlier Islamic sources, which instead spoke of female inferiority and male superiority to explain the prohibition. Since such language is no longer acceptable and is certainly not a valid justification for the prohibition today, new reasons are being offered to support the prohibition.

It therefore makes more sense, I suggest, to explain the reluctance to re-evaluate the prohibition on female-led prayer as rooted in maintaining gender inequality by any means necessary. That is, if the position presumed to be 'Islamic' is not supported by the Qur'an or the Hadiths, then the consensus of the scholars becomes a critical source, even if there were scholars whose juristic opinion disrupted the consensus. If the consensus does not exist or there are alternative opinions, then the issue can be ignored on grounds of irrelevance. Thus, as Sadeghi's study also illustrates, though it focuses on jurists, lay Muslims in their approach to female-led prayer are more interested in justifying the existing law rather than deriving 'new' laws. In other words, the effort appears to be to maintain the historical juristic position, regardless of what the texts (Qur'an and Hadiths) might or might not say on the issue, and to justify maintaining that position by offering new explanations.

Conclusion to Section 2

This section focused on two topics for which contemporary views are largely in line with historical scholarly views. The questions of female-led prayer and women's interfaith marriage are non-negotiable according to the scholarly elite. According to some lay Muslims, they are negotiable, but with female-led prayer significantly less so than interfaith marriage. This negotiation is a process mediated by the personal (direct or indirect) impact that the prohibitions on female-led prayer and women's interfaith marriage have on the individuals who support them. For instance, since Muslim women are the ones who experience the consequences of the injunction against marriage to non-Muslim men, their experiences with these prohibitions need to be considered in any discussions on these debates. Similarly, since most women did not want to lead prayers, they did not perceive the topic as relevant even if other women wanted the right.

As in the case of women's marriage to non-Muslims, scholarly authorities represent female-led prayers as an ossified element of the Islamic tradition – despite claims by the same scholars that the tradition is nuanced, complex, and diverse. These scholars are correct that the tradition is nuanced and diverse – and it is especially so in the question of female-led prayers: Shakir himself acknowledges that there were scholars in Islamic history who permitted unrestricted female leadership in prayer, but he, like other opponents of the practice, dismisses those scholars' opinions as being in the minority and therefore inapplicable. He also claims that those opinions emerged due to a misunderstanding of the Hadiths about women leading prayers.[1]

My respondents do not think of female-led prayer and women's interfaith marriage as equally negotiable; they do not support both in the same ways. The majority of my participants agree that the reasons for the prohibition of women's interreligious marriages do not make sense but they nonetheless maintain that it was prohibited; they also emphasise that they think Muslim men should not marry non-Muslim women. Yet, they invoked the same ideas of female modesty and uncontrollable male sexual urges as those put forward by pre-modern Islamic scholars to support the prohibition on female-led prayers, and few supported female-led prayers in mixed settings.

Before the research, I had assumed that my participants would view neither of these issues as relevant, urgent, or pressing and therefore they would not see them as open to renegotiation. I further assumed they would claim this to be the reason that the consensus should remain binding in these issues, unlike the consensus on the other issues (child marriage, slave concubinage). The issues of interfaith marriage and female-led prayer do not pose a perceptible threat to women's rights or dignity in the same ways that slavery or child marriage do, as is commonly argued in rejection of the latter two. As my respondent Sandara suggested, these topics are not openly or widely discussed; they do not 'come up in conversations in the community' – but this is a matter of politics. As I have explained in the introduction, a part of my argument is precisely that issues that affect predominantly women are not considered urgent enough to warrant a re-examination, despite their impact on women's lives today. In other words, 'no one talks about it' because it is not perceived to be a relevant and important enough topic to be addressed more openly. But they are discussed widely online, whether through Muslim preachers preaching against them or lay Muslims asking about them in online forums.

I contend that these issues are relevant and urgent. Popular perceptions of relevance and urgency are motivated by social norms, politics, and in this case, also by patriarchal assumptions and dictates. Muslim women's marriage to non-Muslim men is a reality, as is Muslim women's demand for leadership in prayer, even as more Muslim women find themselves contemplating interfaith marriage than they do leading prayers. Although my female participants largely did not themselves want to lead prayers and some considered it irrelevant, the issue received most of its limited support from women, as the charts above show. That these conversations are not taking place widely enough for the lay Muslim community to acknowledge their relevance reflects a silence born of stigma.

The gendered nature of authority is crucial to this discussion. As many of my respondents pointed out, the fact that women are not allowed to lead prayer is not 'oppressive' (Adam) or 'morally repugnant' (Rokhan), although both of these individuals personally support female-led prayers in mixed settings. I want to briefly address here the gendered element of these claims. Only 2 of the 40 participants named a woman (Yasmin Mogahed) when asked if they knew any Muslim female scholars – and Mogahed does not in fact meet the definition they gave of Muslim scholars (i.e. someone who has studied at a seminary for years and attained expertise on *sharīʿa* and *fiqh*). One participant listed primarily the wives or other associates of his favourite male scholars and asked for a definition of 'scholar' after I asked him if he knew any women scholars. That the discussants named exclusively male scholars (among whom are individuals who also did not fit their explicit definition, such as Nouman Ali Khan) is important because it shapes their notion of which issues can change with time and which historical consensuses can be challenged by scholars today: would the group of scholars who would 'gather' to debate historical positions on issues such as women's marriage to non-Muslims include women? If so, which women?

I would argue that interfaith marriages are viewed as theologically problematic only insofar as they concern Muslim women because Islam has traditionally been interpreted by men, issuing guidelines and mandating laws that have real implications for women. As An-Naʿim points out, 'men [tend] to juggle religious, ethnic, and modern rules favourable to their own interests'.[2] His point finds subtle, implicit support in my study. As the respondents' attitudes towards female-led prayer and women's marriage to non-Muslims show, for many of them an issue that bears no relevance to men does not need to be re-evaluated. As feminist scholars have argued, there is a need to consider women's experiences a legitimate and acceptable source of law.[3]

However, the difference between female-led prayers and interfaith marriage, and child marriage and sexual slavery is that the rulings on the former two issues are assumed to be based in women's innate nature. Because they are thought to be linked to women's biology (whether women's submission to men in marriage and hence the prohibition on interfaith marriage, or female sexuality as tempting for men and thus the prohibition on mixed female-led prayer), they are treated as so essentially Islamic that they cannot be modified with time, even if the context changes. While women's bodies are used to defend or oppose a certain practice, the larger issue, I believe, is of privilege: when an issue is not directly, personally applicable to a group or individual and it does not have an immediate, direct negative impact on them, they are less likely – and even unlikely – to want it changed. Even many of the women and men who had supported women's interfaith marriage argued that this was not a relevant issue. Among the women, only those who had either led a prayer, knew (of) women who had led prayers, or recognised the issue as related to women's rights more generally supported such prayers.

Conclusion: The Politics of Negotiation and Relevance

Two comments that two of my respondents made sum up a major conclusion of this study. The first comment reflects my respondents' hesitation to continue sharing their opinions once they realised the inconsistencies in their attitudes towards change, tradition, and gender in Islam. The second comment illustrates the complex relationship of my respondents with those individuals who are in positions of authority over them: all of Islam is negotiable if a group of scholars agree that a change in an existing consensus is necessary.

When I asked Orzala (33, married female, white) what, in her opinion, counts as a legitimate reason for changing a historically established position, she said:

> I want to say social norms, but is that really good enough? As a society, as a Muslim, is that really a good enough impetus for change where we're following the example of a society we live in? Shouldn't we be questioning our ethics and morals and setting precedence for others? Why should slavery be wrong just because it's illegal in the US?

She paused for several moments before adding:

> That's a really good question. I'd love to ask a *sheikh* [scholar] that question... Scholars aren't asking these kinds of questions. I don't know what to say. I think we should all be asking ourselves that question. Should we as Muslims really only be allowing or disallowing things *after* everyone else has reflected on them? I mean, are we just saying no to child marriage today just because it would make Muslims and Islam look backward if we didn't?

This insight is valuable. It highlights the inconsistent ways in which 'context' is invoked as an explanation or justification for modifying a scholarly consensus. When Muslims explain that slavery and child marriage are unacceptable because 'times have changed' or 'context has changed', what is the context that they imagine? And why are changes relating to how we view gender and sexuality not considered to be a relevant sociocultural context as well? Will Muslim women be allowed to lead communal prayers and marry men of their choice from other faiths only when Muslims universally think that the rest of the world views Islam as backward because of these restrictions on women? Will interfaith marriage and female-led prayers become acceptable for today's Muslims only if followers of other religions permit them first? After all, some sub-groups within several world religions have, to varying extents, accepted female-led prayers and women's interfaith marriage. How useful, then, is the idea that 'social norms have changed' only for child marriage and slavery? What might a change in context look like in order for Muslims to predominantly accept female-led prayers and women's interfaith marriage as Islamically acceptable?

The second comment is by Turan (24, single male, South Asian background). When he explained that the criteria for changing historical positions of consensus are simply a change in time and context, I asked him why he does not believe that the prohibitions on female-led prayer and women's interfaith marriage may also need to be contextualised. He responded:

> That's actually a very good question... The scholars can come together to form a new *ijmāʿ* [scholarly consensus], I don't have a problem with that. But the problem is that...a lot of the scholars themselves agree with the *ijmāʿ* that's reached them... I'll also add that if there was a particular issue that existed at the time of the Prophet or three genera-

> tions after him, and there is *ijmāʿ* on that, we should follow that, just because the Qur'an raises the status of that generation by explicitly saying that 'We're pleased with them and they're pleased with us.' If a new issue comes up, like Muslims have never been under occupation before, like colonialism… I do personally think the *ʿulama* [scholars of Islam] have the right and authority to do another *ijmāʿ*.

Note that he places great emphasis on scholarly consensus. For him, it appears, the ultimate source of a prohibition or even permission is scholarly consensus, since even if the Qur'an may suggest one particular view, the Qur'an is subject to interpretation, and the interpretation of the scholars is the most correct interpretation. He also recognises that most scholars themselves accept some of the gendered prohibitions as non-negotiable.

Several other respondents shared the belief that they may change their opinions on female-led prayer and women's interfaith marriage if new consensuses emerge on these issues. This thought further illustrates the adaptability and flexibility of the Islamic tradition according to these respondents. However, given the fact that all respondents named only men when asked which scholars they follow whose understandings of Islam they trust, I am sceptical about whether any women would be included as a part of this hypothetical new consensus they might support. While they did name women, they did so in response specifically to my question, 'Are any female scholars among those you follow?' or 'Do you know any female scholars?' Since it is primarily women for whom these particular 'non-negotiables' are relevant and significant, the absence of women in the gathering of scholars needed to arrive at a new consensus will merely reinforce the existing consensus. Concerns specific to women are not viewed as relevant enough to undergo change simply because of a change in a context. Moreover, the scholarly consensus as presented to a popular Muslim audience will continue to ignore disagreements, as we saw in the chapter on female-led prayers, where much scholarly disagreement exists, but is excluded from guidance given to Muslims at large. Instead, this guidance claims a consensus which doesn't actually exist.

However, there are unclear meanings about the term 'consensus' and its place in Islam. The chart below illustrates the important discrepancy between my respondents' initial idea of whether consensus is binding (not open to change, obligatory on Muslims to follow and apply at all times) and their response to the same question about consensus on specific issues.

Table 24: Is *ijmāʿ* (or scholarly consensus) binding on Muslims?

Scale 1-5 (1 being completely disagree)	**Initial Response: Islam generally**	**Slavery***	**Child marriage**	**Female-led prayer (mixed-gender)**	**Women's interfaith marriage**	**Female inher-itance**
Yes, agree (4–5)	12	9	3	30	15	20
No, disagree (1–2)	23	24	25	7	18	17
Not sure/I don't know/ Depends (3)	5	6	9	3	7	3

**Recall that one respondent declined to answer most of the questions on slavery.*

The fact that these numbers diverge is significant because it shows that my respondents are thinking critically about whether and when scholarly opinion matters. Moreover, as each of the respective chapters discuss, it is also interesting that despite believing that scholarly consensus is binding on issues like female inheritance (20) and female-led prayers (30), there was a clear disagreement with this consensus. Finally, while only 12 people believed consensus is binding generally, that number increased in the case of female inheritance, female-led prayer, and women's interfaith marriage but decreased for child marriage and slavery. This further supports my argument that these attitudes are rooted in an idea of gendered topics as irrelevant issues.

In all the issues of this study, we learn that Muslims are negotiating their understandings of the tradition and of change. Muslims seek to preserve the Islamic tradition as sincerely as possible, while also acknowledging the need to respond to contemporary struggles and realities. When asked what counts as a legitimate reason to modify or change historical positions of consensus, all respondents referenced a shift in context and time. They agreed that Islam and Islamic law are flexible, as illustrated by their question, 'Which Islamic law?' (in questions regarding Islamic law's position on slavery and child marriage). They all also agreed that a position, however much it is based in consensus, can change with time, context, or a shift in social norms. In other words, consensus is not always binding. But they did not agree on what 'context' refers to and whether a specific issue I discussed with them indeed needs to be re-evaluated today.

When asked why they do not support female-led prayers or women's interfaith marriage – or, if they supported these but were aware that their position does not reflect the majority view, why they think other Muslims do not – almost all participants explained that this was because 'these aren't [or are not considered to be] relevant or urgent matters'. And yet, female interfaith marriage is taking place, sometimes out of necessity. Why does this issue not qualify as relevant enough to be adapted? I conclude that relevance is dictated by patriarchal norms and gender hierarchy, such that issues considered to be women's concerns are not viewed as relevant enough to be revisited. Feminist struggles for religious and ritual authority do not seem urgent to my respondents. However, this does not explain why the majority of my participants willingly supported equal inheritance laws for sons and daughters, since female inheritance, too, is an explicitly gendered issue, despite a seemingly clear Qur'anic text about unequal inheritance for daughters. The answers to these questions, then, are deeply nuanced. Not only did 22 of the 40 respondents explicitly disagree that a daughter's share should be half that of a son's, but single women almost unanimously disagree with the prohibition on women's interfaith marriage. The fairer conclusions, then, are that first, my discussants' opinions do not reflect the scholarly position in any of the five cases under study and second, lived reality and personal interest or privilege act as important motivators for the desire for change – or for maintaining the status quo.

The point to be emphasised here is, both lay Muslims and those whom they deem authoritative display a pattern in their attitude towards change: both demonstrate reluctance to modify a 'historically established' position if the issue involves gender. As I have discussed in the previous chapters, my informants' opinions are more complex because some of these issues have an acknowledged impact on their daily lives, such as interfaith marriage. Female-led prayer, however, many insisted, is an irrelevant issue and therefore does not need to be re-evaluated. When I asked them why they did not consider these issues to be relevant, many responded that these prohibitions are 'not oppressive', like child marriage and slavery. Slavery and child marriage infringe on an individual's basic human right to autonomy, it appears, and are therefore unacceptable. Prayer leadership is not seen as a right but as an exclusively male responsibility. Yet, while inheritance laws are connected to assumptions of exclusive male responsibility, single men largely want those laws changed. No one rationale, then, explains why some issues are negotiable and others are not. It is precisely this unevenness that helps us to imagine

Islam as a rhizome. While it seems inconsistent, disparate, incoherent, the tradition and its practice in fact allow for a weaving of different parts of Islam to make it whole in ways that make sense to individuals.

THE POLITICS OF RELEVANCE, A GENDERED APPROACH TO CHANGE, AND RESISTANCE TO FEMINISM

If the predominant rationale for change is the assumption that some issues are urgent and need to be addressed because of the negative impact they have on society, we must ask for whom are they urgent and upon whom do they have a negative impact? On the one hand, opponents of women's interfaith marriage argue that the prohibition can change as long as scholars decide it needs to be changed; on the other hand, they imagine only men as scholars of Islam, and some acknowledge that most male scholars might not consider this a relevant enough issue to revisit. As the views of most of the single women demonstrate, interfaith marriage *is* a relevant concern – to them. The prohibition has an impact on their lives, limiting their marital options. Single men do not support granting women the right to marry men of their choice because more options for Muslim women may mean fewer options for them; increasing the pool of eligible husbands for Muslim women would mean facing more male competition. Some married women do not support such marriages because, as some of them pointed out, they were able to find a Muslim man to marry, and therefore, other women can too. The married men who support women's interfaith marriage explained that they do not care who their own daughters marry as long as they are responsible, good men who treat their daughters well.

I believe this conception of 'relevance' is connected to a larger academic trend in which feminist scholarship is marginalised and treated as irrelevant and unrelatable. This connection is not explicit, however: lay Muslims are not, in most cases, reading academic scholarship on gender issues and applying those findings into their lives, but rather, I suggest, lay Muslims and academic scholars of Islam are both exhibiting a similar subconscious preference for patriarchal tendencies. Kecia Ali discusses the politics of citation, in a forthcoming book about the gender politics of academic Islamic Studies.[1] As she describes it, 'There's [gender] bias in classroom evaluations, hiring, invitations to deliver papers, Wikipedia coverage, inclusion in edited volumes, and, especially relevant to professional status, citations.'[2] One expression of this is that 'male scholars more often fail to cite or substantively engage work by women and nonbinary scholars in a much greater proportion than women and nonbinary scholars fail to engage that scholarship'.[3] In her essay 'The Omnipresent Muslim Male Scholar', she surveys the bibliographies and notes of several books on Islam and finds that women are hardly, if at all, being cited in those works. Others have called this issue out as well. For example, in his review essay of Shahab Ahmed's *What Is Islam? The Importance of Being Islamic*, Michael Pregill points out that Ahmad makes almost no mention of gender as a point of analysis.[4]

I argue that this bias against gender- and/or feminism-centric scholarship exists due to an outright rejection of gender concerns. The reluctance to engage Islamic feminism and the works of feminist scholars who specialise in gender and Islam stems from the assumption that gender bears no relevance in most scholarship about Islam, a notion shared among non-Islam specialists in other academic fields and disciplines as well.[5] Many male scholars of Islam see gender as irrelevant to their work. Considering the wider implications of the tendency to marginalise feminist works on the Qur'an, I ask how such a reluctance to acknowledge feminist scholarship influences assumptions on what counts as an authentic and authoritative interpretations of the Qur'an, and about Islam more broadly.

Specialists on Islam are, of course, not alone in their failure to recognise women's and especially feminist scholarship. A similar, prominent example from outside Islamic Studies is that of Pierre Bourdieu, who, in *Masculine Domination* (2001 in English, 1998 in French), fails to cite or recognise the works of feminist theorists. Bourdieu also portrays feminists as 'being better suited to making artistic, rather than scientific, contributions to analyses of masculine domination'.[6] Catherine Lutz, who has researched this phenomenon, conducted a study in 1990 involving citation rates of sociocultural anthropology literature published from 1977–86. Lutz searched 'the citation lists of the 452 articles published [in four journals] …' and 446 articles of a single gender author were surveyed.[7] Notably, the '446 articles had a total of 11,642 citations: 8661 to males, 1932 to females (excluding self-citations).' This is despite the high rates of journal article and book writing by women.[8] Other research has shown that women are more likely to cite other women, men more likely to cite other men.[9] Maria do Mar Pereira, whose research explores the epistemic status of feminist scholarship and interrogates the boundaries of 'proper' academic knowledge, highlights the ways in which feminist works are referenced selectively and skeptically because of negative preconceptions about their epistemic merits, though often without an explicit rejection of feminist principles. Pereira's fieldwork illustrates that 'some non-feminist scholars' reactions to references to gender are framed saliently on the basis of a distinction between research about gender that can produce credible knowledge, and research that is too dogmatic and political...and therefore academically unacceptable'.[10] Since feminist studies are an interdisciplinary field, the dismissive attitude towards feminism transfers over to the areas in which the research is being conducted, including Islamic Studies. As Lutz points out, while it may be claimed that 'female anthropologists' frequent focus on gender explains the lower citation rates of women by men', this is not a plausible claim: studies show that when women enunciate ideas, the field (in her case anthropology, but generally applicable to any field) does not take notice until and unless men enunciate similar ideas.[11] At play here is the patriarchal 'view of the male as universal person and female as marked, gendered, partial person', replicated 'in academic work by the failure of those who focus on aspects of men's lives (on hunting, religion, politics, warfare, or colonial culture, for instance) to consider the work of feminism relevant to their own'.[12]

The refusal to acknowledge women's scholarship informs notions of expertise, which becomes effectively a masculine preserve. Outside of academia, this dismissal is reflected in the rejection of women's authority, as expressed in all-male or male-dominated panels in conferences on Islam (where women are often accepted as scholars and teachers only for women-only audiences).[13] In practice, this refusal also has consequences in the lived experiences of women and others affected negatively by exclusionary interpretations of texts. One of my findings highlights this: my respondents on the one hand acknowledge that positions of consensus can change with time when scholars agree to a change, but on the other hand, perceive only men as scholarly authorities – and few of these see gendered issues like female-led prayers and women's interfaith marriage as relevant enough to deserve a change. While my own research focuses on lay Muslims' engagements with when and whether change is acceptable in 'Islam', scholars have already pointed out the gendered pattern of this change. Ayesha Chaudhry, for example, in *Domestic Violence and the Islamic Tradition*, questions the construction of the 'Islamic tradition', which seems to be flexible and diverse in virtually all ways except in interpretations of Qur'anic verses that support gender hierarchy. She states: 'I had believed in the myth of the "Islamic tradition," of the greatness of its scholars, their nobility and relentless pursuit of justice, their ability to challenge and fight an oppressive status quo. This was the framing story when Muslim scholars spoke of racial and economic distinctions, so why was this not true for gender distensions?'[14] Abdullahi Ahmed An-Na'im has described colonialism's role in relegating only issues relating to gender – what the colonialists identified as 'personal' matters, such as marriage, divorce, custody of children, and inheritance – to customary practice, including *sharīʿa* principles, while civil codes were instituted to 'govern matters of property, commercial and criminal law, and regulate various aspects of the public administration of the state'.[15] Finally, Shahab Ahmed, in *What Is Islam?*, briefly notes the common tendency among Muslims to seek reform on questions of social hierarchy (e.g. forbidding slavery and declaring it un-Islamic) but avoiding, or denying altogether, re-interpretations and reforms of gender hierarchy.[16]

Modern conservative scholars, Bauer and Hamza note, simultaneously argue for gender equality while continuing to draw from the pre-modern tradition's views on gender inequality.[17] Indeed, religious authority is intimately connected to a desire to maintain gender hierarchy. I also suggest that the reason for the dismissal of gender in social change is connected to male privilege: as Bauer and Hamza note, 'As in the medieval period, the scholars putting forth these views often benefit directly from them: they have a vested interest in upholding a tradition of which they claim to be the sole authentic curators.'[18]

Whether gendered and sexual matters are 'relevant' and therefore open to revision due to necessity is a matter of privilege, I argue. While my respondents suggest that they are open to changing any position of consensus if the collective of scholars decides on doing so, what they seem not to realise is that the majority of the scholars the Muslim American community turns to for their knowledge of Islam are men who enjoy the privileges bestowed upon them by historical traditional Islam, including their right to leadership of mixed-gender prayer, marriage to non-Muslims, and higher shares of inheritance, all of which are denied to women in this version of Islam. Privilege is at the center of this negotiation with change.

The politics of relevance, clearly gendered and manifest in questions of privilege, affect perceptions of feminist interpretations and gender concerns beyond academia as well. Other suggested reasons for the mainstream community's unwillingness to engage feminist interpretations of Islam include Muslim feminists' presumed tendency to depart from 'the Islamic tradition', an abstract term that evades any particular meaning. However, this claim lacks credibility because not only are the boundaries of the 'Islamic tradition' unclear, but also because non-feminist male scholars and leaders who have often 'departed' from the tradition continue to be held in high esteem. Lamia Shehadeh's study of Muslim leaders and scholars highlights the tendency of these individuals to retweak the 'tradition' in order to project their own oscillating, inconsistent perceptions of gender onto Islam. For instance:

> [In Pakistan,] Al-Mawdudi, after vehemently opposing women's participation in politics and arguing for their incompetence, promptly reversed himself and fully supported the candidacy of Fatimah al-Jinnah for the presidency. [In Iran,] Khomeini, after decrying voting rights for women as un-Islamic in 1963, went on to solicit their votes for an Islamic republic, declaring the vote 'religious, Islamic, and a divine duty.' Al-Ghannoushi changed his stand on the segregation of women and their minimal education when he discovered the importance of the role they could play for the Islamic Tendency Movement in the realms of public relations and the propagation of the Islamic message… The private life of Zaynab al-Ghazali differed drastically from her public stand on the role of women in society and at home.[19]

Such inconsistencies in attitudes towards women's rights and roles are motivated not by what is acceptable in 'Islam' but by the political and personal motives in play at any given moment in history.

Shehadeh observes that while all of the fundamentalists in her work approach the Islamic tradition as a flexible and dynamic construct in matters where they want to see change, in accordance with their political motives, they deny that same flexibility to questions of gender: 'none of these methods was applied to any matter relating to gender relations or women's rights', with the thinkers 'claiming such relations to be God's divine will and, therefore, not subject to change'.[20] Unclear references to Islam and God's divine will, largely imagined and constructed to fit specific ideological tendencies such as those of gender hierarchy, also contribute to the broader reluctance to engage Muslim feminist scholarship.

Why, though, as Shehadeh asks, does this fear of accepting gender equality exist? While my main point is that feminist research, arguments, and modes of analyses are perceived as irrelevant, it is also true that feminist interpretations pose a threat to the patriarchal legacy, to a tradition (such as the Islamic tradition) presumed to be rooted in gender hierarchy. Rumee

Ahmed, in his discussion on this issue points out that 'though feminists may offer traditionally grounded legal alternatives to patriarchal, hetero-normative laws, they nonetheless face resistance from scholars espousing patriarchal heteronormative theologies, based on which reform is rebuffed'.[21] Discussing the refusal of the *'ulama*, for whom gender egalitarianism is no virtuous ideal, to take feminist critiques seriously, Ahmed argues that:

> It would appear that this scorn for gender egalitarianism has deep historical roots. The ulama historically promoted, and for the most part continue to promote, a hierarchical model of gender relations in which men are accorded 'a degree' over women in terms of rights and responsibilities. This hierarchy is what Ayesha S. Chaudhry calls an 'idealized cosmology,' and it describes the theological presuppositions about the God–human relationship that informs how law is created and discussed. So long as jurists presume a patriarchal idealized cosmology, in which men and women are fundamentally unequal, gender-egalitarian Islamic legal reforms will be stymied.[22]

The idea that there is resistance to engage feminism is supported by much other research on the general resistance to gender equality.[23] One might argue that this does not sound true for many academics who, at least outwardly, support feminist works and are conscious of structural gender injustices. In that case, internalised patriarchy whereby one unintentionally plays a role in supporting patriarchal standards might explain their subconscious bias. Such subconscious perpetuation of patriarchal standards indicates the profundity of the problem.

Ahmed's theory that feminist critiques pose a threat to the patriarchal ideals of Muslim scholars finds support in the teachings of the Muslim male teachers of Islam featured in this book, such as Yasir Qadhi. Qadhi, like many other scholars and teachers as well as lay Muslims, imagines the Islamic tradition, or Islam generally, as a system founded on the agreements of 'all scholars' – though apparently only the scholars of an undefined, ambiguous past. As I have disused earlier, while Qadhi agrees that the 'basic principles' of Islam should never be changed, there is no clarity on what these basic principles are. In fact, in his lecture on change and modernity, he claims on the one hand that Islam is a flexible religion that recognises the need for change when necessary, but on the other, cites gender issues (same-sex relations and female-led mixed-gender prayers) as those which are among 'the basic principles' of Islam that absolutely cannot change with time because 'all' scholars have decided this.[24] For him, clearly, the gender hierarchy established by earlier Muslim scholars is a fundamental part of Islam.

In her discussion on the resistance that Islamic feminism faces from various groups – categorised into Muslim traditionalists, Islamic fundamentalists, and secular fundamentalists – Ziba Mir-Hosseini writes that:

> Though adhering to very different ideologies and scholarly traditions and following very different agendas, all these opponents of the feminist project in Islam share one thing – an essentialist and nonhistorical understanding of Islam and Islamic law. They fail to recognise that assumptions and laws about gender in Islam – as in any other religion – are socially constructed and thus historically changing and open to negotiation. They resist readings of Islamic law that treat it like any other system of law and disguise their resistance by mystification and misrepresentation.[25]

That Muslim feminists in particular are denied engagement, and thus credibility, is also often attributed to the claim that Muslim feminists do not display piety – as determined by their clothing style, perhaps, most notably by the refusal of some Muslim feminists to don the *hijab*. Submission on this point is often taken as essential proof of their 'proper' knowledge of Islam.[26] Others reject Islamic feminism because, they say, Muslim feminists lack the necessary 'authentic' training in 'Islamic culture and religious sciences' and are thus not well equipped with the correct methodology to study and interpret the Qur'an.[27] Yet others claim that the 'feminist solution' to the problem of gendered oppression is 'not Islamic'.[28] However, such claims carelessly place the responsibility for Muslim feminists' supposed 'invalidity' on the feminists themselves; that is, Muslim feminists are blamed for not being taken seriously. The contexts of the unwillingness to engage Muslim feminist thought, specifically as it relates to the relationship between gender and authority, are ignored. That is, Muslim feminists are told that in order to be accepted as legitimate authority figures, they must conform to the gendered notions of piety and knowledgeability that they seek to challenge in the first place.

Moreover, not only are men not held to the same standards of piety, knowledge, and training, but all women are not consistently expected to be trained religiously. As I discussed earlier, some of my respondents named

Yasmin Mogahed as a scholar of Islam, but she has no training in Islamic Studies, either in the Western academy or in a traditional Muslim seminary, despite being a teacher at one. Nonetheless, her teachings, her aura, her tone are all inspiring for my discussants who mentioned her. Not all scholars are ranked equally – education, training, perceptions of their expertise, assumptions of their piety based on how they dress (if women), and their ethics are all taken into account. Nouman Ali Khan may be trained as a scholar, many claimed, but his ethics are questionable and un-Islamic and therefore he should not be relied on as a source of Islam.

The irrelevance that is attributed to gender broadly also manifests in lay Muslims' understanding of Islam and gender. The results of my study show that according to nearly all of the participants, change is necessary and Islamically acceptable when 'context' changes – and, often, what counts as a valid context for change is also a matter of the personal impact of the historical issue in question. The majority, for example, considered female-led prayers an 'irrelevant' issue that does not need to even be discussed; single women largely suggested that women be allowed to marry non-Muslim men; and most of the participants believed that female inheritance laws be revised – different responses from the various groups for different, personal, reasons. I conclude from my conversations with my discussants overall that what is negotiable is determined by its impact on an individual's life and by a gendered perception of relevance. Re-interpretations that threaten the patriarchal, hierarchal relations between women and men, however they are manifested (e.g. in marriage or female leadership), are generally considered non-negotiable. In other words, the tradition is imagined to be inherently patriarchal, and the foundation of it is a hierarchical gender model; without this gendered hierarchy, it seems, Islam might stop existing. While such an interpretaion might seem like an exaggeration, the language often used by both traditionalist Muslim scholars and lay Muslims includes terms like 'essence of Islam' and 'foundation of Islam', which to me clearly indicates that they see gender hierarchy as so integral to Islam that without it, Islam may begin to fall apart.

MAJOR FINDINGS AND CONCLUSIONS

My findings have significant implications, not just for Muslims but also for other religious communities today. They raise questions of privilege, authority, lived reality, and the definitions and assumptions of 'need' and 'community'.

Generation, gender, marital status, and lived reality were significant factors in my respondents' views. All categories (married, unmarried, men, women) opposed child marriage and sexual slavery. Married men and unmarried women supported women's interfaith marriage. More women than men supported mixed female-led prayers, the topic that faced the most resistance to change, while also being the topic my respondents viewed as the least important and urgent. An equal number of married men supported or opposed equal inheritance rights for their sons and daughter. However, the number of married men who agreed with equal inheritance rights (4 out of 10) for their own daughters was lower than for all the other categories of person (7 for single women, 5 for single men, and 5 for married women); and the number of men that opposed the statement (4 out of 10) was the highest among the categories of person (1 for single women, 2 for single men, and 2 for married women). These results suggest that the tradition is currently undergoing, and has always undergone, change – and while this is generational, it is also gendered. Almost all participants agreed that slavery is immoral according to contemporary norms and unacceptable according to contemporary ideas of Islam, and almost all believed that child marriage, or any marriage without the consent of the marrying parties, was today and always has been un-Islamic. On the other three issues, however, gender and generation played important roles.

These uneven ideas about change, sometimes gendered and other times generational, can be explained through a rhizomatic approach to the Islamic tradition. The rhizomatic approach entails a negotiation with the tradition, a negotiation from which the negotiator receives some benefit, whether as an individual or a part of a larger group. Thus, when most of my discussants argued that Islam either never allowed slavery in the first place or that it was historically acceptable globally, but is certainly not acceptable ('Islamic') today, they understand Islam to allow them to select which source is useful to them for a given topic. In this case, they relied on an interpretation of Islam that views all humans as equal, as well as allowing them to believe that Islam is a reasonable religion that accommodates social change and norms. Since slavery is universally officially considered unacceptable and illegal, it benefits not Muslims individually but their communities and Islam as a whole to consider slavery un-Islamic (e.g. because of the damage to Islam's reputation that would result from not taking this position). Similarly, when they explained that female-led mixed prayers are un-Islamic and should not be permitted, they relied on a different source to justify their position: certainly not the Qur'an or even Hadiths, but scholarly consensus, socialised ideas of male and female sexualities, and personal preferences. Moreover, the rhizomatic model allows not just for different genders but also different generations of Muslims to disagree with each other, since, again, their sources of Islam shift on a case-by-case basis. As Michael Muhammad Knight writes, 'Islam also belongs to the minor, marginal, and condemned; as much as… modern states and transnational forces desire a hegemonic, monolithic, self-contained, and historically consistent Islam, the tradition remains disordered and capable of unpredictable connections both within and beyond its borders, which themselves remain in motion.'[29] The tradition, Islam as a whole, simply does not exist without the active participation of my respondents and other lay Muslims everywhere in constructing it.

The inconsistent appeal to the multiple sources of Islam, lived reality, or to fears for the reputation of Islam is especially interesting in the case of slavery. Some respondents qualified their answers to questions on this topic with statements like, as long as slavery is done 'the Islamic' way or 'correctly' or 'as long as one (the enslaver) follows the rules'. Yet, no opponents of interfaith marriage and female-led prayers qualified their statements in similar terms – that is, they did not argue that once those conditions under which interfaith marriage or female-led prayers are believed to be prohibited are no longer present, the prohibition does not apply. Similarly, no one suggested that the prohibition is only applicable in certain circumstances.

Additionally, the role of the *'ulama* (Islamic scholars, whether contemporary or historical) is significant and is both idealistic and practical. On the one hand, my discussants disagreed with scholarly positions in multiple cases – sexual slavery, child marriage, and even female inheritance; on the other, on female-led prayer and women's interfaith marriage, most believe that the current consensus must remain as it is until scholars arrive at a new agreement. In other words, only on the issues of female-led prayer and women's marriage to non-Muslims, the issues that some explicitly viewed as 'irrelevant' because they are not 'oppressive', do they seek scholarly permission to change their views. Significantly, as I have discussed earlier, none of the single women believed women's marriage to non-Muslims is permissible currently, but most of them did support changing the prohibition to allow them to marry non-Muslims if they need to. That even the respondents to whom the issue is most pertinent personally believe any changes to the existing consensus must be validated by scholars points to the level of respect for and reliance on scholarly authority. They did not, however, need scholarly permission to hold the positions they did on child marriage and slavery, or female inheritance, because their positions on these issues seemed to make sense and therefore did not need scholars' approval. Clearly, then, scholars' authority is not simply defined and articulated but radically transformed in the contemporary Muslim American imagination because it is unevenly invoked and relied upon. Muslims do not uncritically consume what Muslim scholars and preachers teach about Islam but actively disagree with them and express those disagreements – although when they disagree and why depends on their personal investment in a given issue.

There is also a discrepancy between what scholars assume lay Muslims believe, want, and need, and what lay Muslims in fact believe. While the Muslim scholarly community renders the explicitly gendered issues in this study (female-led prayer, women's marriage to non-Muslims, and female inheritance laws) non-negotiable, some of my respondents perceive them as negotiable because of their own lived experiences. The scholarly elite is often out of touch with the reality of the people they claim or aspire to represent and reach. Here, we see that the relationship between lay Muslims and those whom they consider authoritative shows that the two groups rely on each other in complex ways: lay Muslims do not unconditionally rely on Muslim scholars for the 'correct' interpretations of Islam but critically evaluate the interpretations given to them to make sense of them themselves.

We also learn a great deal about lay Muslims' assumptions about Islam from this study: that Islam is a clear religion with clear texts that offer clear answers to questions they have; that Islam, in the seventh century, already gave women all the rights they could possibly need, and even as reality changes, new rights for women (e.g. prayer leadership) are not necessary unless they are a question of urgency; that Islam is a rational religion, and to justify this rationality, lay Muslims offer creative explanations to support their positions, however much they might depart from dominant scholarly positions – these explanations might include why a certain scholarly position is or is not still applicable. Such explanations lack logical consistency, to such an extent that even the meaning of the term 'Islam' changes depending on the specific topic, but this makes sense if we imagine Islam as a rhizome.

Significantly, my findings – the statistics combined with the interviews and the reviews of literature on the topics – suggest that a 'mainstream' Islam simply does not exist. Not only do scholars, other figures of authority, and lay Muslims constantly disagree with each other, lay Muslims themselves disagree with each other depending on the specific issues in question. They do not hold the same opinions on any of the topics studied here. They do not even understand what some might view as an essential basic of Islam the same way: the *Sunnah*, the practice of the Prophet. Muhammad's role in their perceptions is different as well: the moral and intellectual justification for change involves imagining what the Prophet Muhammad would have endorsed and rejected. This process requires perceiving Muhammad as the ideal for all times and all places, which entails projecting onto him contemporary values and ideals. For instance, as discussed in chapter 1, most of my respondents eagerly identified Muhammad as a feminist even if hesitant to self-identify as such. But here, too, my respondents are not unthinkingly borrowing from Muhammad's *Sunnah*: they engage critically and negotiate accordingly when to emulate his actions, and make decisions based on what feels and is right according to their ethical norms.

I have interrogated meanings of 'Islam' in order to explore the ways in which change occurs and is ascribed to Islam, and to describe the negotiation process that contemporary Muslims are involved in when deciding on the negotiables and non-negotiables of Islam. Focusing on the ways in which contemporary Muslim Americans depart from historical consensus, I show that consensus is not, in fact, always binding. This study demonstrates that the pattern in which change occurs is highly complex and layered; it is gendered, generational, and personal. It is gendered such that explicitly gendered topics, such as female-led prayer and women's marriage to non-Muslims, are viewed as non-negotiable because they are not 'relevant' and not 'oppressive'. According to this approach to change and Islam, the historical Islamic tradition is founded on a gender hierarchy that is perceived as essential to the survival of Islam. Change is also, however, based on one's generation and age in complicated ways: older women and men in my study did not consistently endorse or resist a change. Generation sometimes confers privilege: recall married women's opposition to women's interfaith marriage since they are already married, and single Muslims' support for egalitarian inheritance laws. Ultimately, the decisive factor in motivating calls for change is lived reality. Individual or groups who experience disadvantage on the basis of the existing rules are the most likely to call for the consensus to shift.

These findings paint an optimistic picture of the future of the Islamic tradition – indeed, of any tradition. That change is inconsistent is not new information. What is hopeful is the role that lay people, ordinary practioners, play in the development and sustenance of a tradition. And they do this consciously and subconsciously, both cooperating with those on whom they bestow authority and diverging from them. Significantly, as human values globally change, so do religious practitioners' relationship with their religion, not just the present but also the past, as the past is re-imagined to make sense of the religion's relevance in the present. This book's findings on the roles of gender, generation, and lived reality in the push for change are important for the future of Islam. Since Muslims are unlikely to argue that Islam is an unjust religion, the finding that there is a connection between the preservation of male privilege and resistance to change may serve as an important motivator for them to work toward interrogating any unjust practices and understandings of Islam. As this book has shown, acknowledging Islam as a rhizome – and Muslims' relationship with it as rhizomatic – are productive ways of appreciating not only the nuances of this change but any discrepancies that arise in the process of change as well.

Acknowledgements

This book would not be possible without the love and support of many, many people I am lucky to call mentors, friends, and colleagues. I am grateful finally to have the opportunity to recognise some of them publicly, though I worry I will leave out many. In no particular order, except the niblings, who must of course always be thanked first, I'd like to recognise the following people.

Foremost I want to thank my niblings, my nieces and nephews – Shehzad, Kushmala, Aimal, Aria, and Zain – who fill my life with immeasurable joy I had not known before they came into my life. Thank you for your brilliance, curiosity, observations, and questions about Islam and society (and most importantly, about patriarchy), which inspire me to push boundaries. May this book give you peace of mind knowing that traditions simply cannot exist without you, and that traditions that harm you and others must be modified or discarded. You deserve the beauty that God has blessed the universe with. You deserve unconditional love and joy. Remember: God is so much grander, so much more profound, than the rules and regulations you are taught.

To my siblings for their love, for expressing faith in me when I faced obstacles and could go no further. Nazish, I love you. You are my rock. I'm so incredibly lucky to have you as a sister, as a friend since forever, as family, as everything. Anjum, Neelum, and Ziaullah, I'm so excited about where we're headed, about where our relationship is going!

This book is the final product of my doctoral dissertation, which was completed and defended in 2018. I am grateful to my committee members – Drs. Hina Azam, Kecia Ali, Karen Bauer, Mounira Charrad, Faegheh Shirazi, and John Traphagan – who not only agreed to work with me but also challenged my ideas and conclusions and pushed me beyond my own limitations.

This book is my proudest achievement yet, and it would not have been possible without them. It's not often that I like to read my own writing (it's usually about sad stuff – who wants to read sad stuff all the time?), but I was thrilled to read various drafts of this book, although that's probably because of my exceptional editor at Oneworld, Rida Vaquas, but we'll get to that in just a bit.

Kecia Ali and Karen Bauer have remained good friends and mentors. Kecia, thank you for your wisdom; I have a 'WWKD' motto for my own students – what would Kecia do – when I face something I think you'd handle with care in a way that does not come as naturally to me as it does to you. You've taught me to be careful with my words because they have impact.

Karen, I am grateful for how far our friendship has come. I've grown to be a better person, a more thoughtful person, a better scholar and educator, because of your impact, because you trusted me and took me on as a mentee. Our WhatsApp voice notes are always a source of joy and comfort for me.

Special thanks to my respondents in Austin, TX, whose participation in this research made this book possible. Thank you for your time and commitment to this project, for your vulnerability, for your questions. Without you, this book would not be possible and also not necessary. I hope that one of the things you got out of our interviews was that your practice of Islam, your relationship with Islam, matters, whatever it is.

To Devin Stewart. Always to Devin Stewart. I tell people that I am in Islamic Studies because of Devin Stewart. Thank you for challenging me, for exposing me to ideas I had never heard before I took your classes. Thank you for your patience with me and for the resources you provided as I struggled through this newfound knowledge, a beautiful, incredible Islam that was completely different from what I was used to. My life is better because I took your classes and because you nurtured my personal, spiritual, and intellectual growth. Thank you for still being a mentor to me.

I'm also grateful for the mentorship of Abdullahi Ahmed An-Na'im, who continues to guide me. Thank you for being one of the first people to invest in me by hiring me as a research assistant, for having faith in me, and for encouraging me to explore different pathways of existing.

To my community at Ithaca College for supporting me in all ways. I served as a Diversity Scholar at Ithaca College in the Women's and Gender Studies program in 2017–18, where Carla Golden not only took me on as a mentee then but has continued to be a friend and mentor since I left. Thank you, Carla. I'm also thankful for Harriet Malinowitz and Asma Barlas, whose conversations and friendship sustained me during my nine months in cold,

cold Ithaca. I was also fortunate to be part of a writing group that met weekly. Tremendous thanks to my writing partners there – Ashley Hall, Iokepa Casumbal-Salazar, and Shobhana Xavier – for their support and conversations as I finished up my dissertation while working with them. I am deeply saddened by the untimely and unacceptable loss of an incredible mentor, Sue-Je Gage, whose guidance, wisdom, and support gave me the strength to get through my dissertation year. I continue to use some of her life advice today. In the Ithaca local Muslim community, Saba Hathaway became a close friend whose friendship has remained meaningful and important to me.

At the University of Texas at Austin, Kristen Brustad's unwavering support and confidence in me helped me thrive as a young student and now a scholar. It was Kristen who first introduced me to the idea of a rhizome, which later became the backbone of this book, when I was describing my research findings to her. She gave me the language for my findings. It was also Kristen who, when I mentioned to her in passing once that I had a job interview coming up, said, 'Be yourself.' I had until that point repeatedly been told not to be myself, because few people think of graduate students as wise and intelligent enough to know when to be themselves. So, Kristen, I went and I be'd myself, and I have thrived since. Thank you for letting me know that was an option, that I did not have to erase myself to have an impact, to be who I want to be, that I could achieve what I want without compromising my worth. I have never loved myself more.

I want to also thank the International Institute of Islamic Thought (IIIT) for supporting this project when it was in the dissertation stages. I received short-term summer research grants that helped me focus on writing some of the chapters of this book. Special thanks to Saulat Parvez at IIIT whose face always, always brings a light to my heart whenever I see her.

To my writing partners, of one time or another during the last several years – Jamila Davey (my peace!), Hannah Nabi, Karen Bray, Shobhana Xavier, Katie Roseau, Sarah Gardner, Bryan Whitfield, and Sara Ronis. I don't just have writing buddies in these people but also deep, intimate friendships that allow us to air our grievances about all things life and work, which helps me to make it through the week. Thank you for your friendships and the light you bring to my life. Thank you for being parts of my community of care and love.

To the Muslim feminists and womanists and other gender-egalitarian-minded folks who are a major source of inspiration for me, for every project I take on. amina wadud, thank you for fighting a *jihad* that made it so much easier for me and many others like me to continue on the same path. Juliane Hammer, thank you for your deep friendship and mentorship, for your love and support, for all of our conversations beyond Islam and justice. Yasmin Amin, where would this book be without you? Thank you for always answering my calls, for being there when I have needed a reference in an emergency, for sharing your wisdom and skills with me, for sitting down for hours at a time with me to work through a difficult text. Ziba Mir-Hosseini, Sa'diyya Shaikh, Zahra Ayubi, Omaima Abou-Bakr, Ayesha Chaudhry, Roshan Iqbal, Aysha Hidayatullah, Carolyn Baugh, Elliott Bazzano, Saadia Yacoob, Zaid Adhami, Ali Mian, Shabana Mir, Asifa Quraishi-Landes, Mahdi Tourage, Michael Muhammad Knight, and Laury Silvers – thank you for your continued love and care, and, to the older generation in this list, for making the fight towards peace and justice easier for the rest of us.

To my Pashtun sisters in the academy, Kiran Nazir Ahmed and Anila Daulatzai: you make it less lonely being me. Kiran, I miss our chai and *kakoorri*-filled hangouts. Anila, it's amazing that two people who have never met in person can love and trust each other this much. Thank you especially for your culturally informed guidance! You get it.

In Macon, I'm grateful for my Taekwondo community. Thank you for adding tremendous joy and new forms of challenges to my life these last few years. I am a better me for having taken up martial arts. Thanks also to the Women's Interfaith Alliance of Central Georgia, especially Flo Martin, Shazia Akbar, and Laura Ilan. There is beautiful and meaningful interfaith and peacebuilding work happening on the ground all over the world, led by women, and the WIA is one such space.

To Zeb Rocklin, thank you for your care and support during the writing of this book, for reading my book contract alongside me, carefully and closely, and offering suggestions, for reading drafts of some of my chapters and asking insightful and relevant – and good, very good – questions. For believing in me and reminding me of my worth when I faltered. For helping me become a much, much better version of myself. For helping me internalise the idea that 'the world needs more Shehnaz'. Look where your confidence in me brought me! I told you I know stuff!

To the Columbus Roberts Department of Religion at Mercer: I am fortunate to have the unwavering support of every member of my department, especially my current chair, Bryan Whitfield, and my former chair, Richard Wilson. The department and the college have also supported my research financially. I do not take this support for granted. I wish everyone, especially junior faculty and researchers, could have such a supportive and healthy environment to thrive in.

Also at Mercer, I am infinitely grateful for the friendship and mentorship of Chinekwu Obidoa, Natalie Bourdon, Matt Harper, Kathy Kloepper, Alana Alvarez, Evey Wilson, Tom Bullington, Doug Thompson, Rachel Schaff, Jason Smith, Rachael Goodman, Sahar Hasim, Deneen Senasi, Jacqueline Pinkowitz, Kristen Bailey – working with and being with you all has been a complete joy. How fortunate I am to have colleagues who are also close friends! Chichi, thank you for knowing exactly what to say to lift up my spirits and give me confidence when I need it most, in all areas of my life.

A few more friends deserve to be thanked because their love these last three to four years has been necessary for me to complete this book and to thrive as a human, especially in a global pandemic. Hiba Alkhadra, Neda Momeni, Pam Davis, Sabina Khan-Ibarra, Sahil Warsi, Papa and Yasmin Diallo-Turk and their wonderful children, Banafsheh Madaninejad, Courtney and Phil Dorrol, Fatima Nidali, Hina Din, Jessica Gardner, Jumanah Hassan, Samina Hussain, Kathleen Tran, Faiza Rahman, Ambereeen Shaffie, Jessica Thompson, Michael Thompson, Lisa Thompson, David and Laura Ilan, Courtney Talley, Amanda Rogers, Nida Kazim, Bea Benhalim, Alan Howard, Zahra Khan (for FITNA and good trouble!), Daanish Fruqi, Homayra Ziad, Josh Shahryar, Melanie Magidow, and Fathima Mahmood.

Deep gratitude to Oneworld Publications for trusting me with this book, for eagerly supporting its publication, and for giving me the best editors an author could ask for! Rida, thank you for sharing your brilliance with me, for your patience as I attempted to meet all our deadlines – sometimes unsuccessfully – for catching serious errors that I know the patriarchy would not have let go if they'd not been corrected. You've made this process so much easier than I thought it would be. I'm also grateful to my copy editor at Oneworld, Jon Walker, whose excellent editing skills had me accepting pretty much all suggested changes!

Thanks also to the anonymous reviewers who read the book proposal and the manuscript for challenging me in productive ways, for asking important questions, and for making helpful suggestions. All have made this book stronger and better. I wish every author such helpful and generous reviewers.

And finally, but certainly not least, my parents. Words definitely fail me here. The sacrifices you have made, which you should never have had to make, the struggles you have fought, the people and privileges you have lost, for defying everything to accommodate my passions. They will never go unnoticed. May all the good that comes out of this book and from my life and my legacies benefit you in this life and the next, *aameen*.

And this feels weird, but I also want to thank the people on YouTube who post 'calming, deep focus' music for productivity purposes. I wrote much of this book while having that music on. It works, people. It really works.

I am certain I have forgotten many important people to thank. I hope to be forgiven for that oversight, as well as for any errors in this book. Of course, all errors are my own, but all good things are by God's grace.

Bibliography

SACRED, LEGAL, AND ARABIC SOURCES

Translations from sacred and legal sources in Arabic are my own unless otherwise noted. However, sometimes I also drew upon the translations of the Qur'an from sources that offer multiple translations of the Qur'an by different translators, such as the website https://corpus.quran.com/translation.jsp (accessed March 27, 2024). For those Arabic sources where I consulted the English translations, I have identified them.

Abū Ṭālib, Imām 'Ali Ibn. *Peak of Eloquence, Nahjul Balāgha*, ed. Yasin T. Al-Jibouri. Elmhurst, NY: Tahrike Tasile Quran, 1984.

Bin Anas, Mālik. *Al-Muwaṭṭa', the Royal Moroccan Edition: The Recension of Yaḥyā Ibn Yaḥyā al-Laythī*, ed. and trans. Mohammad Fadel and Connell Monette. Cambridge, MA: Harvard Islamic Legal Studies Program, 2019.

Ibn 'Āshūr, Muḥammad al-Ṭāhir. *Treatise on Maqaṣid al-Shariah*, trans. and annotated Mohamed El-Tahir El-Mesawi. London and Washington, D.C.: The International Institute of Islamic Thought, 2006.

— *Al-Tahrīr wa al-Tanwīr*, Part 2, Book 1. Tunis: Dār al-Tūnisiyyah al-Nashr, 1984.

Bint al-Shāṭi'[Aisha Abd al-Rahman]. *Tarājim Sayyidāt Bait al-Nubuwwa.* Cairo: Dār al-Rayyān Li-l-Turāth, first edn, 1987.

— *Wives of the Prophet*, trans. Matti Moosa and D. Nicholas Ranson. Piscataway, NJ: Gorgias Press, 2006.

Al-Bukhārī, Muhammad b. Ismā'il. *Sahih al-Bukhari*. [Online]. https://sunnah.com/bukhari. Accessed March 25, 2024.

Ibn Kathīr, *Tafsīr al-Qur'ān*, ed. Sāmī bin Muḥammad al-Salāmah. 10 vols. Riyadh: Dār Ṭayibba, 2007.

Ibn Mājah, Abū 'Abd Allah Muḥammad ibn Yazīd. *Sunan ibn Majah*. [Online]. https://sunnah.com/ibnmajah. Accessed March 25, 2024.

Al-Qarāfī, Aḥmad Ibn Idrīs. *al-Dhakhīrah fī furū' al-Mālikīyah*. Beirut: Dār al-Gharb al-Islāmī, 1994.

Ibn Qudāmah, ʿAbd Allāh ibn Aḥmad ibn Muḥammad. *Kitāb Al-Mughnī*, vol. 6. Beirut: Dār Iḥyā' al-Turāth al-'Arabī, 1985.

The Qur'anic Arabic Corpus. English Translation. [Online]. https://corpus.quran.com/translation.jsp (accessed March 29, 2024).

Al-Qurṭubī, Abū ʿAbd Allāh Muḥammad ibn Aḥmad al-Anṣārī. *Al-Jāmiʿ li-aḥkām al-Qurʾān,* ed. ʿAbd Allāh b. ʿAbd al-Ḥasan al-Turkī, 20 vols. Beirut: Muʾassasāt al-Risālah, no date.

— *Tafsīr al-Qurṭubī: The General Judgements of the Qur'an and Clarification of What It Contains of the Sunnah and Āyahs of Discrimination*, trans. Aisha Bewley, 6 vols. Bradford: Diwan Press, 2018.

Qutb, Sayyid. *Fī Ẓilāl al-Qur'ān*, 6 vols. Cairo: Dār al-Shurūq, 1972. Available online at https://archive.org/details/ThilalQuran/delalquraan1/ (accessed March 28, 2024).

Ibn Rushd, Abū l-Walīd Muhammad bin ʾAḥmad. *Bidāyat al-Mujtahid*, vol. 1. Beirut, Dār al-Ma'rifah 1986.

— *The Distinguished Jurist's Primer*, trans. Imran Ahsan Khan Nyazee, 2 vols. Center for Muslim Contribution to Civilization. No place of publication given except 'UK': Garnet Press, 2000.

Al-Shāfi'ī, Abū 'Abdullāh Muhammad ibn Idrīs. *Kitāb al-Umm*, ed. Mahmūd Matrajī, vol. 7. Manṣūra: Dār al-Wafā', 2001.

Al-Ṭabarī, Abū Jaʿfar Muhammad ibn Jarīr. *Jāmi' al-Bayān 'an Ta'wīl āy al-Qurʾān*. Cairo: Dār al-Hijr, 2001.

— *The History of al-Ṭabarī*, vol. 39: Biographies of the Prophet's Companions and Their Successors, trans. Ella Landau-Tasseron. New York: State University of New York, 1998.

Ibn Taymiyya, Taqī al-Dīn Abu al-'Abbās. *Majmū' Fatāwā*, 32 vols. Riyadh: Maṭā bi' al-Riyāḍ, 1961.

Al-Wāḥidī, Alī ibn Ahmad. *Asbāb al-Nuzūl*. Amman, Jordan: Royal Aal al-Bayt Institute for Islamic Thought, 2008.

SECONDARY LITERATURE

Abboud, Hosn. *Mary in the Qur'an: A Literary Reading*. London: Routledge, 2014.

Abou El-Fadl, Khaled. *Speaking in God's Name: Islamic Law, Authority and Women*. Oxford: Oneworld Publications, 2001.

— *Reasoning with God: Reclaiming Shari'ah in the Modern Age*. Lanham, MD: Rowman & Littlefield, 2014.

— (May 1, 2016). 'FATWA: On Christian Men Marrying Muslim Women (Updated)'. *The Search for Beauty: on beauty and reason in Islam*. [Online]. https://www.searchforbeauty.org/2016/05/01/on-christian-men-marrying-muslimwomen-updated/ (Accessed December 20, 2017).

Abu Zayd, Nasr. *Reformation of Islamic Thought: A Critical Historical Analysis*. Amsterdam: Amsterdam University Press, 2006.

— 'The Status of Women between Qur'an and Fiqh'. In *Gender and Equality in Muslim Family Law*, eds Mir-Hosseini, *et al*., 2013, pp. 153–68.

Adkins, Brent and Hinlicky, Paul R. *Rethinking Philosophy and Theology with Deleuze: A New Cartography*. London: Bloomsbury, 2014.

Afsaruddin, Asma (2014). Qur'anic Ethics of Partnership and Gender: The Concept of Wilaya in Qur'an 9:71. [Online]. http://www.cilecenter.org/en/wpcontent/uploads/2014/11/Recommended-ArticleEnglish-Quranic-Ethics-of-Partnership-and-Gender.pdf. *CILE Journal*, (Spring 2014), pp. 30–41. (Accessed December 20, 2017).

Ahmad, Atif. *The Fatigue of the Shari'a*. New York: Palgrave Macmillan, 2012.

Ahmed An-Na'im, Abdullahi (ed.), *Inter-religious Marriages among Muslims: Negotiating Religious and Social Identity in Family and Community*. New Delhi: Global Media Publications, 2005.

Ahmed, Leila. *Women and Gender in Islam: Historical Roots of a Modern Debate*. New Haven: Yale University Press, 1992.

Ahmed, Rumee. *Narratives of Islamic Legal Theory*. Oxford: Oxford University Press, 2012.

Aini, Noryamin (2008). 'Inter-Religious Marriage from Socio-Historical Islamic Perspectives'. *BYU Law Review*, 2008 (3), pp. 669–705.

Ali, Kecia. 'Money, Sex, and Power: The Contractual Nature of Marriage in Islamic Jurisprudence of the Formative Period'. Ph.D. diss., Duke University, 2002.

— 'Progressive Muslims and Islamic Jurisprudence: The Necessity for Critical Engagement with Marriage and Divorce Law'. In *Progressive Muslims: On Justice, Gender, and Pluralism*, ed. Omid Safi. Oxford: Oneworld Publications, 2003, pp. 163–89.

— *Marriage and Slavery in Early Islam*. Cambridge, MA: Harvard University Press, 2010.

— *The Lives of Muhammad*. Cambridge, MA: Harvard University Press, 2016.

— (2017). 'Concubinage and Consent'. *International Journal of Middle Eastern Studies*, 49 (1), pp. 148–52.

— *Sexual Ethics and Islam: Feminist Reflections on Qur'an, Hadith, and Jurisprudence*, second edn. London: Oneworld Publications, 2017.

Allen, Anita L. and Mack, Erin (1991). 'How Privacy Got Its Gender'. *Northern Illinois University Law Review*, 441, pp. 441–78.

Amin, Yasmin. 'Umm Salama and Her Hadith'. Master's diss., American University in Cairo, 2011.

— 'Wives of the Prophet'. In *The Oxford Encyclopedia of Islam and Women*, ed. Natana J. DeLong-Bas. Oxford: Oxford University Press, 2013, pp. 426–9.

— 'Age is just a number or is it? ʿA'isha's age between Ḥadīth and History'. Unpublished paper delivered at the Third Annual Conference of the British Association for Islamic Studies (BRAIS), London, 11–12 April 2016.

Anchassi, Omar (2001). 'Status Distinctions and Sartorial Difference: Slavery, Sexual Ethics, and the Social Logic of Veiling in Islamic Law'. *Islamic Law and Society*, 28 (3), pp. 125–55.

Asad, Talal (2009). 'The Idea of an Anthropology of Islam'. *Qui Parle*, 17 (2), pp. 1–30. Originally published in 1986.

Azam, Hina. *Sexual Violation in Islamic Law: Substance, Evidence, and Procedure*. Cambridge: Cambridge University Press, 2015.

Azzam, Leena. 'The regulation of interfaith marriages in Islamic legal discourse'. Ph.D. diss., American University in Cairo, 2015.

Bano, Masooda and Kalmbach, Hilary (eds). *Women, Leadership and Mosques: Changes in Contemporary Islamic Authority*. Leiden: Brill, 2012.

Barlas, Asma. *Believing Women in Islam: Unreading Patriarchal Interpretations of the Qur'ān*. Austin: University of Texas Press, 2002.

Bauer, Karen. *Gender Hierarchy in the Qur'ān: Medieval Interpretations, Modern Responses*. Cambridge: Cambridge University Press, 2015.

Bauer, Karen and Hamza, Feras (eds). *An Anthology of Qur'anic Commentaries, Volume II: On Women*. New York: Oxford University Press, 2021.

Baugh, Carolyn (2009). 'An Exploration of the Juristic Consensus (Ijmā') on Compulsion in the Marriages of Minors'. *Comparative Islamic Studies*, 5 (1), pp. 33–92.

Bennett, Clinton. *Muslim Women of Power: Gender, Politics, and Culture in Islam*. London: Continuum, 2010.

Berkey, Jonathan Porter. *Popular Preaching and Religious Authority in the Medieval Islamic Near East*. Seattle: University of Washington Press, 2001.

— *The Formation of Islam: Religion and Society in the Near East, 600–1800*. Cambridge: Cambridge University Press, 2003.

Brockopp, Jonathan. *Early Mālikī Law: Ibn 'Abd Al-Ḥakam and His Major Compendium of Jurisprudence*. Leiden: Brill, 2000.

Brooks, Ann (2006). 'Gendering Knowledge'. *Theory, Culture & Society*, 23 (2–3), pp. 211–14.

Brown, Anna (November 19, 2021). 'Growing share of childless adults in U.S. don't expect to ever have children'. *Pew Research Center*. [Online]. https://www.pewresearch.org/short-reads/2021/11/19/growing-share-of-childless-adults-in-u-s-dont-expect-to-ever-have-children/ (Accessed February 20, 2024).

Buisson, Johanna. 'Interfaith Marriage for Muslim Women: This Day are Things Good and Pure Made Lawful Unto You'. *CrossCurrents*, 66 (4), pp. 430–49.

Calderini, Simonetta (2008). 'Islam and Diversity: Alternative Voices within Contemporary Islam'. *New Blackfriars*, 89 (1021), pp. 324–36.

— (2009). 'Contextualising Arguments about Female Ritual Leadership in Classical Islamic Sources'. *Comparative Islamic Studies*, 5 (1), pp. 5–32.

— *Women as Imams: Classical Islamic Sources and Modern Debates on Leading Prayer*. London: Bloomsbury Publishing, 2022.

Carbajal, Alberto Fernández. *Queer Muslim Diasporas in Contemporary Literature and Film*. Manchester: Manchester University Press, 2019.

Chaudhry, Ayesha S. *Domestic Violence and the Islamic Tradition*. Oxford: Oxford University Press, 2014.

— 'Producing Gender-Egalitarian Islamic Law: A Case Study of Guardianship (Wilayah) in Prophetic Practice'. In *Men in Charge? Rethinking Authority in Muslim Legal Tradition*, eds Ziba Mir-Hosseini, Mulki Al-Sharmani and Jana Rumminger. London: Oneworld Publications, 2015, pp. 88–105.

Cila, Jorida and Lalonde, Richard N. (2014). 'Personal Openness Toward Interfaith Dating and Marriage among Muslim Young Adults: The Role of Religiosity, Cultural Identity, and Family Connectedness'. *Group Processes & Intergroup Relations*, 17 (3), pp. 357–70.

Clarence-Smith, William Gervase. *Islam and the Abolition of Slavery*. Oxford: Oxford University Press, 2006.

Connel, R. W. (2005). 'Change among the Gatekeepers: Men, Masculinities, and Gender Equality in the Global Arena'. *Signs*, 30 (3), pp. 1801–25.

Cooke, Miriam. *Women Claim Islam: Creating Islamic Feminism through Literature*. New York: Routledge, 2001.

Deleuze, Gilles and Guattari, Félix. *On the Line*. Cambridge, MA: Semiotext(e), MIT Press, Foreign Agents series, 1983.

— *A Thousand Plateaus*. Minneapolis: University of Minnesota Press, 1987.

Eickelman, Dale F. and Piscatori, James (eds). *Muslim Travellers: Pilgrimage, Migration and the Religious Imagination*. London: Routledge, 1990.

Elewa, Ahmed and Silvers, Laury (2010–11). '"I am one of the people": A Survey and Analysis of Legal Arguments on Woman-led Prayer in Islam'. *Journal of Law and Religion*, 26 (1), pp. 141–71.

Freamon, Bernard K. *Possessed by the Right Hand: The Problem of Slavery in Islamic Law and Muslim Cultures*. Studies in Global Slavery, vol. 8. Leiden: Brill, 2019.

Frechet, Denise. 'Toward a Post-Phallic Science'. In *(En)gendering Knowledge: Feminists in Academe*, eds Joan Hartman and Ellen Messer-Davidow. Knoxville: University of Tennessee Press, 1991, pp. 205–21.

Friedmann, Yohanan. *Tolerance and Coercion in Islam*. Cambridge: Cambridge University Press, 2003.

Geissinger, Aisha. *Gender and Muslim Constructions of Exegetical Authority: A Rereading ofthe Classical Genre of Qur'an Commentary*. Leiden: Brill, 2015.

Grewal, Zareena. *Islam Is a Foreign Country: American Muslims and the Global Crisis of Authority*. New York: New York University Press, 2014.

Gumport, Patricia J. *Academic Pathfinders: Knowledge Creation and Feminist Scholarship*. Westport: Greenwood Publishing Group, 2002.

Al-Ḥaddād, Ṭāhir. *Muslim Women in Law and Society: Annotated Translation of Al-Tahir Al-Haddad*, trans. Ronak Husni and Daniel Newman. London: Routledge, 2007.

Haddad, Yvonne Yazbeck, and Esposito, John L. (eds). *Islam, Gender, and Social Change*. New York: Oxford University Press, 1998.

Haddad, Yvonne Yazbeck, Smith, Jane, I. and Moore, Kathleen M. 'Gender and the Family'. In *Muslim Women in America: The Challenge of Islamic Identity Today*. New York: Oxford University Press, 2006, pp. 81–100.

Hallaq, Wael (1992). 'Beyond Tradition'. *Journal of Islamic Studies*, 3 (2), pp. 172–202.

— *Authority, Continuity, and Change in Islamic Law*. Cambridge: Cambridge University Press, 2001.

— 'Can the Sharīʿa be Restored?' In *Islamic Law and the Challenges of Modernity*, eds Yvonne Haddad and Barbara Stowasser. Walnut Creek, CA: AltaMira Press, 2004, pp. 21–53.

— *An Introduction to Islamic Law*. Cambridge: Cambridge University Press, 2009.

Hammer, Juliane. *American Muslim Women, Religious Authority, and Activism More Than a Prayer*. Austin: University of Texas Press, 2012.

Haqqani, Shehnaz (2023). 'The Qur'an on Muslim Women's Marriage to Non-Muslims: Premodern Exegetical Strategies, Contradictions, and Assumptions'. *Journal of Qur'anic Studies* 25 (1), pp. 36–78.

Harding, Sandra. *The Science Question in Feminism*. Ithaca: Cornell University Press, 1986.

Hasan, Ahmad. *The Doctrine of Ijmāʿ in Islam*. Islamabad: Islamic Research Institute, 1978.

Hidayatullah, Aysha A. (2010) 'Māriya the Copt: Gender, Sex, and Heritage in the Legacy of Muhammad's *Umm Walad*'. *Islam and Christian-Muslim Relations*, 21 (3), pp. 221–43.

— *Feminist Edges of the Qur'an*. Oxford: Oxford University Press, 2014

Hoel, Nina (2013). 'Sexualising the Sacred, Sacralising Sexuality: An Analysis of Public Responses to Muslim Women's Religious Leadership in the Context of a Cape Town Mosque'. *Journal for the Study of Religion*, 26 (2), pp. 26–41.

hooks, bell. *The Will to Change: Men, Masculinity, and Love*. New York: Washington Square Books, 2004.

Ibrahim, Ahmed Fekry. 'Takhayyur and Talfīq'. *The Oxford Encyclopedia of Islamic Law*. [Online]. http://www.oxfordislamicstudies.com/article/opr/t349/e0082 (Accessed February 13, 2024).

— *Pragmatism in Islamic Law: A Social and Intellectual History*. Syracuse, NY: Syracuse University Press, 2017.

Iqbal, Roshan. *Marital and Sexual Ethics in Islamic Law: Rethinking Temporary Marriage*. Lanham, MD: Rowman & Littlefield, 2023.

Iqtidar, Humeira (2016). 'Redefining 'Tradition' in Political Thought'. *European Journal of Political Theory*, 15, pp. 424–44.

Irigaray, Luce. *This Sex Which Is Not One*. Ithaca: Cornell University Press, 1985.

Islam, Zahidul (2014). 'Interfaith marriage in Islam and present situation'. *Global Journal of Politics and Law Research*, 2 (1), pp. 36–47.

Jackson, Sherman A. *Islam and the Blackamerican: Looking toward the Third Resurrection*. New York: Oxford University Press, 2005.

Jeenah, Naeem. '"A degree above…" The Emergence of Islamic Feminisms in South Africa in the 1990s'. Master's diss., University of the Witwatersrand, 2001.

Jones, Stephen. 'Knowledge, Tradition and Authority in British Islamic Theology'. In *Religion and Knowledge: Sociological Perspectives*, eds Mathew Guest and Elisabeth Arweck. Farnham: Ashgate, 2012, pp. 133–47.

Karakaya, Ayse Elmali. 'Being Married to a Non-Muslim Husband: Religious Identity in Muslim Women's Interfaith Marriage'. In *Research in the Social Scientific Study of Religion, Volume 31: A Diversity of Paradigms*, eds Ralph W. Hood and Sariya Cheruvallil-Contractor. Leiden: Brill, 2020, pp. 388–410.

— (2022). Interfaith Marriage in Islam: Classical Islamic Resources and Contemporary Debates on Muslim Women's Interfaith Marriages. [Online]. https://www.mdpi.com/2077-1444/13/8/726. *Religions*, 13 (8), 726. (Accessed February 29, 2024).

Karim, Jamillah. *American Muslim Women: Negotiating Race, Class, and Gender within the Ummah*. New York: New York University Press, 2009.

Katila, Saija and Meriläinen, Susan (1999). 'A Serious Researcher or Just Another Nice Girl?: Doing Gender in a Male-Dominated Scientific Community'. *Gender Work and Organization*, 6 (3), pp. 163–73.

Katz, Marion. *Prayer in Islamic Thought and Practice*. Cambridge: Cambridge University Press, 2013.

Keddie, Nikki R. and Baron, Beth. *Women in Middle Eastern History: Shifting Boundaries in Sex and Gender*. New Haven: Yale University Press, 1991.

Khabeer, Su'ad Abdul. *Muslim Cool: Race, Religion, and Hip Hop in the United States*. New York: New York University Press, 2016.

Knight, Michael Muhammad. *Sufi Deleuze: Secretions of Islamic Atheism*. New York: Fordham University Press, 2023.

Kramer, Gudrun and Schmidtke, Sabine (eds). *Speaking for Islam: Religious Authorities in Muslim Societies*. Leiden: Brill, 2006.

Kugle, Scott. 'The Reception of the Qur'an in the LGBTQ Muslim Community'. In *Communities of the Qur'an: Dialogue, Debate and Diversity in the 21st Century*, eds Emran El-Badawi and Paula Sanders. London: Oneworld Publications, 2019, pp. 98–134.

Kurmila, Nina. 'The Indonesian Muslim Feminist Reinterpretation of Inheritance'. In *Islam in Indonesia: Contrasting Images and Interpretations*, ed. Kees van Dijk Jajat Burhanudin. Amsterdam: Amsterdam University Press, 2013, pp. 109–22.

LaCapra, Dominick. *Rethinking Intellectual History: Texts, Contexts, Language*. Ithaca: Cornell University Press, 1983.

Lamrabet, Asra (January 18, 2013). 'What Does the Qur'an Say About the Interfaith Marriage?', *Asra Lamrabet.* [Online]. http://asma-lamrabet.com/articles/what-does-the-qur-an-say-about-the-interfaith-marriage/ (Accessed March 17, 2024).

Makdisi, George (1979). 'The Significance of the Sunni Schools of Law in Islamic Religious History'. *International Journal of Middle East Studies*, 10 (1), pp. 1–8.

Martin, Emily (1991). 'The Egg and the Sperm: How Science Has Constructed a Romance Based on Stereotypical Male Female Roles'. *Signs*, 16 (3), pp. 485–501.

Masud, Muhammad Khalid (1985). 'The Sources of the Māliki Doctrine of Ijbar'. *Islamic Studies*, 24 (2), pp. 215–53.

Mernissi, Fatima. *The Veil and the Male Elite: A Feminist Interpretation of Women's Rights in Islam*. New York: Basic Books, 1991.

Mir-Hosseini, Ziba. *Marriage on Trial: Islamic Family Law in Iran and Morocco*. London and New York: I.B. Tauris, 2011 [1993].

— *Islam and Gender: The Religious Debate in Contemporary Iran*. Princeton: Princeton University Press, 1999.

— 'Islamic Family Law and Social Practice: Anthropological Reflections on the Terms of the Debate'. In *Family, Law and Religion: Debates in the Muslim World and Europe and their Implications for Co-operation and Dialogue*, ed. Siegfried Hass. Vienna: Austrian Association for the Middle East Hammer-Purgstall, 2009, pp. 37–48.

— 'Justice, Equality and Muslim Family Laws: New Ideas, New Prospects'. In *Gender and Equality in Muslim Family Law: Justice and Ethics in the Islamic Legal Tradition*, eds Ziba Mir-Hosseini, Kari Vogt, Lena Larson, *et al.* London and New York: I.B. Tauris, 2013, pp. 7–34.

— *Journeys Toward Gender Equality in Islam*. London: Oneworld Publications, 2022.

Mir-Hosseini, Ziba, Al-Sharmani, Mulki and Ruminger, Jana (eds). *Men in Charge? Rethinking Authority in Muslim Legal Tradition.* London: Oneworld Publications, 2015.

Mirza, Younus. 'Remembering the Umm al-Walad Ibn Kathir's Treatise on the Sale of the Concubine'. In *Concubines and Courtesans: Women and Slavery in Islamic History,* eds. Matthew S. Gordon and Kathryn A. Hain. Oxford: Oxford University Press, 2017, pp. 297–322.

Moghissi, Haideh. *Feminism and Islamic Fundamentalism: The Limits of Postmodern Analysis*. London: Zed Books, 1999.

Motzki, Harald. 'Child Marriage in Seventeenth-Century Palestine'. In *Islamic Legal Interpretation: Muftis and Their Fatwas*, eds Muhammad Khalid Masud, Brinkley Morris Messick and David Stephan Powers. Karachi: Oxford University Press, 2005, pp. 129–40.

Mubarak, Hadia. *Rebellious Wives, Neglectful Husbands: Controversies in Modern Qur'anic Commentaries*. New York: Oxford University Press, 2022.

Mulia, Siti Musdah. 'Promoting Gender Equity Through Interreligious Marriage: Empowering Indonesian Women'. In *Muslim Non-Muslim Marriage: Political and Cultural Contestations in Southeast Asia*, eds Gavin Jones, CheeHeng Leng and Maznah Mohamad. Singapore: ISEAS publishing, 2009, pp. 255–82.

Nagel, Caroline. 'Introduction'. In *Geographies of Muslim Women: Gender, Religion, and Space*, eds Ghazi Walid Falah and Caroline Nagel. New York and London: The Guilford Press, 2005, pp. 1–15.

Nightingale, Virginia (ed.). *The Handbook of Media Audiences*. Malden: Wiley Blackwell, 2011.

Nouri, Melody (September 12, 2018). The Power of Influence: Traditional Celebrity vs Social Media Influencer. [Online]. https://scholarcommons.scu.edu/cgi/viewcontent.cgi?article=1032&context=engl_176. *Advanced Writing: Pop Culture Intersections*, 32. (Accessed 14 February, 2024).

Owoahene-Acheampong, Stephen (2020). 'Contemporary Zongo Communities in Accra Interfaith Marriages: The Case of Muslims and Christians in Accra'. *African Studies Quarterly*, 19 (1), pp. 23–40.

Peek, Lori (2006). 'The United States'. *Encyclopedia of Women and Islamic Cultures*, vol. 3: Family, Body, Sexuality and Health, ed. Suad Joseph. Leiden: Brill, pp. 264-67.

Pereira, Maria do Mar (2012). '"Feminist theory is Proper Knowledge, But…": The Status of Feminist Scholarship in the Academy'. *Feminist Theory*, 13 (3), pp. 283–303.

Plaskow, *Judith. Standing Again at Sinai: Judaism from a Feminist Perspective*. New York: Harper San Francisco, 1991.

Qadhi, Yasir (uploaded December 13, 2013, but dated December 7, 2013 in the title). 'Looking Back as We Look Forward'. YouTube video. [Online]. https://www.youtube.com/watch?v=jJmrPh2sRuw (Accessed February 14, 2024).

Al-Qaraḍāwi, Yusuf. *The Lawful and the Prohibited in Islam*. Plainfield, IN: American Trust Publications, 1994.

Quraishi-Landes, Asifa. 'A Meditation on Mahr, Modernity, and Muslim Marriage Contract Law'. In *Feminism, Law, and Religion*, eds Marie Failinger, Elizabeth Schlitz and Susan Stable.London: Routledge, 2016, pp. 173–95.

Rapoport, Yossef. *Marriage, Money and Divorce in Medieval Islamic Society*. Cambridge: Cambridge University Press, 2005.

Rawls, John. *Political Liberalism*. New York: Columbia University Press, 1996.

Reinhart, Kevin (1983). 'Islamic Law as Islamic Ethics'. *Journal of Islamic Ethics*, 11 (2), pp. 186–203.

Rhouni, Raja. *Secular and Islamic Feminist Critiques in the Work of Fatima Mernissi*. Leiden: Brill, 2010.

Robinson, Lynn and McGuire, Mike (2010). 'The Rhizome and the Tree: Changing Metaphors for Information Organization'. *Journal of Documentation*, 66 (4), pp. 604–13.

Roded, Ruth (2012). 'Islamic and Jewish Religious Feminism: Similarities, Parallels and Interactions'. *Religion Compass*, 6 (4), pp. 213–24.

— *Women in Islamic Biographical Collections: From Ibn Sa'd to Who's Who*. Piscataway, NJ: Gorgias Press, 2018.

Rosdiana, Ahmad Bahtiar. 'Preferences of Children's Religious Interfaith Marriages: Case Study in the International Conference on Religion and Peace', *Justicia Islamica: Jurnal Kajian Hukum dan Sosial*, 17.2, 2020, pp. 205–22.

Rosenthal, Franz. *Knowledge Triumphant the Concept of Knowledge in Medieval Islam*. Leiden: Brill, 2007.

Sadeghi, Behnam. *The Logic of Law Making in Islam: Women and Prayer in the Legal Tradition*. Cambridge: Cambridge University Press, 2013.

Salaymeh, Lena. *The Beginnings of Islamic Law: Late Antique Islamicate Legal Traditions*. Cambridge: Cambridge University Press, 2016.

Savant, Sara Bowen. *The New Muslims of Post-Conquest Iran: Tradition, Memory, and Conversion*. Cambridge: Cambridge University Press, 2015.

Sayeed, Asma. *Women and the Transmission of Religious Knowledge in Islam*. Cambridge: Cambridge University Press, 2013.

Shaikh, Sa'diyya. 'A Tafsir of Praxis: Gender, Marital Violence, and Resistance in a South African Muslim Community'. In *Violence Against Women in Contemporary World Religions: Roots and Cures*, eds Dan Maguire and Sa'diyya Shaikh. Ohio: The Pilgrim Press, 2007, pp. 66–89.

— *Sufi Narratives of Intimacy: Ibn 'Arabī, Gender, and Sexuality*. Chapel Hill: University of North Carolina Press, 2012.

Shaikh, Sa'diyya and Seedat, Fatima (eds). *The Women's Khutbah Book*. New Haven: Yale University Press, 2022.

Sharafeldin, Marwa. 'Egyptian Women's Rights NGOs: Personal Status Law Reform between Islamic and International Human Rights Law'. In *Gender and Equality in Muslim Family Law*, eds Mir-Hosseini, *et al.*, pp. 57–80.

— 'Islamic Law Meets Human Rights: Reformulating Qiwamah and Wilayah for Personal Status Law Reform Advocacy in Egypt'. In Mir-Hosseini, *et al.* (eds), *Men in Charge?: Rethinking Authority in Muslim Legal Tradition*. London: Oneworld Publications, 2015, pp. 163–96.

Shehadeh, Lamia. *The Idea of Women Under Fundamentalist Islam*. Gainesville: University Press of Florida, 2007.

Silvers, Laury (2008). 'In the Book We Have Left Out Nothing: The Ethical Problem of the Existence of Verse 4:34 in The Qur'an'. *Comparative Islamic Studies*, 2 (2), pp. 171–80.

Smith, Jane I. *Muslims, Christians, and the Challenge of Interfaith Dialogue*. Oxford: Oxford University Press, 2007.

Spellberg, Denise A. *Politics, Gender, and the Islamic Past: The Legacy of 'A'isha Bint Abi Bakr*. New York: Columbia University Press, 1994.

Stowasser, Barbara Freyer. *Women in the Qur'an, Traditions, and Interpretation*. Oxford: Oxford University Press, 1994.

Syed, Mohammad Ali. *The Position of Women in Islam: A Progressive View*. New York: State University of New York Press, 2004.

Tabbaa, Yasser. *Constructions of Power and Piety in Medieval Aleppo*. University Park: Pennsylvania State University Press, 1997.

Todd, Douglas (May 30, 2012). 'Muslim Women in a Marriage Bond'. *Vancouver Sun*. [Online]. http://vancouversun.com/news/staff-blogs/muslim-women-in-a-marriage-bind. (Accessed December 20, 2017).

Todd, May. *Gilles Deleuze: An Introduction*. Cambridge: Cambridge University Press, 2005.

Tucker, Judith. *In the House of the Law: Gender and Islamic Law in Ottoman Syria and Palestine*. Los Angeles: University of California Press, 1998.

— *Women, Family, and Gender in Islamic Law*. Cambridge: Cambridge University Press, 2008.

Tutt, Daniel (December 1, 2015). Deleuzian Theology and the Immanence of the Act of Being. [Online]. https://www.researchgate.net/publication/332655382_Deleuzian_Theology_and_the_Immanence_of_the_Act_of_Being. *SCTIW Review*. (Accessed March 25, 2024).

'U.S. Muslims Concerned About Their Place in Society, but Continue to Believe in the American Dream: Identity Assimilation, and Community'. *Pew Research Center: Religion & Public Life*. [Online]. July 26, 2017, http://www.pewforum.org/2017/07/26/identity-assimilation-and-community/ (accessed December 20, 2017).

Vishanoff, David R. *The Formation of Islamic Hermeneutics: How Sunni Legal Theorists Imagined a Revealed Law*. New Haven: American Oriental Society, 2011.

wadud, amina. *Qur'an and Woman: Rereading the Sacred Text from a Woman's Perspective*, second edn. Oxford: Oxford University Press, 1999.

— *Inside the Gender Jihad: Women's Reform in Islam*. Oxford: Oneworld Publications, 2006.

Weisberg, Dvora E. *Levirate Marriage and the Family in Ancient Judaism*. Waltham, MA: Brandeis University Press, 2009.

Witztum, Joseph. 'Q. 4:24 Revisited' (2009). *Islamic Law and Society* 16 (1), 1–33.

Al-Yousuf, Heather (2006). 'Negotiating Faith and Identity in Muslim–Christian Marriages in Britain'. *Islam and Christian-Muslim Relations*. 17 (3), pp. 317–29.

Youssef, Olfa. *The Perplexity of a Muslim Woman: Over Inheritance, Marriage, and Homosexuality*. New York: Lexington Books, 2017.

Yuskaev, Timur, and Stark, Harvey. 'The American 'ulam' and the public sphere'. In *Routledge Handbook of Islam in the West*, ed. Roberto Tottoli. London: Routledge, 2022, pp. 357–73.

Endnotes

INTRODUCTION

1 amina wadud's prayer and responses to it will be discussed in chapter 6 of this book. For now, however, see [Author unknown], 'Woman Leads Controversial US Prayer', *Al Jazeera* [online], March 19, 2005, https://www.aljazeera.com/archive/2005/03/200849145527855944.html (accessed March 2, 2018). In December 2017, a Muslim woman in India, Jamida Beevi, led a mixed-gender Friday prayer and faced backlash as well, even receiving death threats: Amrit Dhillon, 'Muslim woman receives death threats after leading prayers in Kerala', The *Guardian* [online], January 30, 2018, https://www.theguardian.com/world/2018/jan/30/muslim-woman-receives-death-threats-leading-prayers-kerala-india (accessed February 12, 2024).

2 ISIS, the Islamic State of Iraq and Syria, refers to an extremist group that emerged in Iraq and Syria in 2004. It is also known as the Islamic State and ISIL, the Islamic State of Iraq and Levant. For an example of the response by Muslims, see 'Open Letter to Dr. Ibrahim Awwad Al-Badri, Alias "Abu Bakr Al-Baghdadi", And to the Fighters and Followers of the Self-Declared "Islamic State"', *The Royal Islamic Strategic Studies Centre* [online], https://rissc.jo/wp-content/uploads/2019/04/Letter_to_Baghdadi-EN.pdf created September 19, 2014 (accessed March 14, 2024).

3 I consider all the unmarried (single) participants as being of a younger generation than the married participants. With the exception of one 39-year-old, all other unmarried respondents were under 30 years of age.

4 See 'Muslim Population by State 2024', *World Population Review* [online], https://worldpopulationreview.com/state-rankings/muslim-population-by-state (accessed February 12, 2024).

5 E.g. Kecia Ali, *Marriage and Slavery in Early Islam* (Cambridge, MA.: Harvard University Press, 2010); Hina Azam, *Sexual Violation in Islamic Law: Substance, Evidence, and Procedure*, Cambridge Studies in Islamic Civilization (Cambridge: Cambridge University Press, 2015); Olfa Youssef, *The Perplexity of a Muslim Woman: Over Inheritance, Marriage, and Homosexuality* (Lanham, MD: Lexington Books, 2017).

6 Talal Asad, 'The Idea of an Anthropology of Islam', *Qui Parle*, 17.2, 2009, pp. 20–21.

7 Zareena Grewal, *Islam Is a Foreign Country: American Muslims and the Global Crisis of Authority* (New York: New York University Press, 2014).

8 Karen Bauer, *Gender Hierarchy in the Qur'ān: Medieval Interpretations, Modern Responses*, Cambridge Studies in Islamic Civilization (Cambridge: Cambridge University Press, 2015), p. 12.

9 Walid Saleh, *The Formation of the Classical 'Tafsir' Tradition: The Qur'anic Commentary of Al-Tha'labi D. 427/1035* (Leiden: Brill, 2004); Bauer, *Gender Hierarchy in the Qur'ān.*

10 Nevin Reda and Yasmin Amin (eds), *Islamic Interpretive Tradition and Gender Justice: Processes of Canonization, Subversion, and Change* (McGill-Queen's University Press, 2020).

11 E.g. Aisha Geissinger, *Gender and Muslim Constructions of Exegetical Authority: A Rereading of the Classical Genre of Qur'an Commentary* (Leiden: Brill, 2015).

12 E.g. Sandra Harding, *The Science Question in Feminism* (Ithaca: Cornell University Press, 1986), especially ch. 4.

13 See, for example, Denise Frechet, 'Toward a Post-Phallic Science', in *(En)gendering Knowledge: Feminists in Academe*, eds Joan Hartman and Ellen Messer-Davidow (Knoxville: University of Tennessee Press, 1991), pp. 205–21 at p. 205.

14 E.g. Ann Sterling, *Sexing the Body: Gender Politics and the Construction of Sexuality* (New York: Basic Books, 2000).

15 'Feminist Philosophy of Biology', *Stanford Encyclopedia of Philosophy* [online], June 2011, https://plato.stanford.edu/entries/feminist-philosophy-biology/#MotEpiPerMet (accessed February 12, 2024).

16 Emily Martin, 'The Egg and the Sperm: How Science Has Constructed a Romance Based on Stereotypical Male Female Roles', *Signs*, 16.3, 1991, pp. 485–501.

17 Ibid., pp. 486–7.

18 E.g. Muhammad Qasim Zaman, *The Ulama in Contemporary Islam: Custodians of Change* (Princeton: Princeton University Press, 2002); Bauer, *Gender Hierarchy in the Qur'ān*; Behnam Sadeghi, *The Logic of Law Making in Islam: Women and Prayer in the Legal Tradition* (Cambridge: Cambridge University Press, 2013).

19 Ziba Mir-Hosseini, *Islam and Gender: The Religious Debate in Contemporary Iran* (Princeton: Princeton University Press, 1999).

20 See ch. 4 of Ayesha Chaudhry, *Domestic Violence and the Islamic Tradition* (New York: Oxford University Press, 2014) in particular.

21 Bauer, *Gender Hierarchy in the Qur'ān.*

22 Hadia Mubarak, *Rebellious Wives, Neglectful Husbands: Controversies in Modern Qur'anic Commentaries* (New York: Oxford University Press, 2022).

23 I am not, however, convinced by Mubarak's argument about this diversity. While the scholars she studies do disagree in many ways, I believe that diversity of opinions would include statements that reject male hierarchy altogether, such as in polygyny and divorce – e.g. none of the scholars she studies read Qur'anic verses on polygyny collectively to conclude that it is prohibited, not merely discouraged, or at least question who the intended audience of the polygyny verses are. In my interview with her on her book, we discuss this question, and she offers examples of scholars (not mentioned in the book) who do argue, for instance, that polygyny is prohibited. See our discussion at Shehnaz Haqqani, 'Hadia Mubarak, *Rebellious Wives, Neglectful*

Husbands: Controversies in Modern Qur'anic Commentaries', *New Books Network* [online], February 17, 2023, https://newbooksnetwork.com/rebellious-wives-neglectful-husbands (accessed February 12, 2024).

24 Karen Bauer and Feras Hamza (eds), *An Anthology of Qur'anic Commentaries, Volume II: On Women* (New York: Oxford University Press, 2021).

25 E.g. Hina Azam, *Sexual Violations in Islamic Law*, esp. pp. 80-1; Keica Ali, *Sexual Ethics and Islam: Feminist Reflections on Qur'an, Hadith, and Jurisprudence* (London: Oneworld Publication, 2016); and Chaudhry, *Domestic Violence and the Islamic Tradition.*

26 Leila Ahmed, *Women and Gender in Islam: Historical Roots of a Modern Debate* (New Haven: Yale University Press, 1992), p. 86.

27 Dominick LaCapra, *Rethinking Intellectual History: Texts, Contexts, Language* (Cornell University Press, 1983), p. 14.

28 An important note about Hadiths is that they are classified into three major categories: authentic or sound, which means they have a reliable chain of transmission and a reliable text; good, referring to those with a reliable text but unreliable chain of transmission; and weak, those with an unreliable chain and unreliable text. Muslim scholars are discouraged from using weak Hadiths as a source for a legal opinion, but nonetheless weak Hadiths are commonly relied upon, as we'll see in examples in this book.

29 Abū l-Walīd Muḥammad bin ʾAḥmad Ibn Rushd, *The Distinguished Jurist's Primer*, trans. Imran Ahsan Khan Nyazee, Center for Muslim Contribution to Civilization, 2 vols (No place of publication given except 'UK': Garnet Press, 2000). The second volume of the book, which is most relevant to my research (i.e. it deals with questions of marriage, divorce, and slavery), is available online at: https://islamfuture.files.wordpress.com/2011/05/the-distinguished-jurist-s-primer-vol-ii.pdf (accessed February 14, 2024).

30 Taqī al-Dīn Abu al-'Abbās Ibn Taymiyya, *Majmū' Fatāwā*, vol. 32 (Riyadh: Maṭābi' al-Riyāḍ, 1961), pp. 181–5. Available online at: http://library.islamweb.net/newlibrary/display_book.php?idfrom=5378&idto=5378&bk_no=22&ID=3238 (accessed March 16, 2024); ʿAbd Allāh ibn Aḥmad ibn Muḥammad ibn Qudāmah, *Kitāb al-Mughnī*, vol. 6 (Ihyar al-Turāth al-'Arabi, 1985). Available online at: http://library.islamweb.net/newlibrary/display_book.php?bk_no=15&ID=&idfrom=4273&idto=4275&bookid=15&startno=0 (accessed March 16, 2024).

31 I recognise that Nouman Ali Khan (informally known as NAK) has been accused of sexual misconduct and spiritual abuse. At the time that I began this research in 2016, the allegations were not yet public, and many of my respondents relied on him for Islamic knowledge. I have chosen to keep his name in this book to capture the larger point about religious authority.

32 Hadiths are categorised as authentic (legitimate chain and content), good (authenticity not established but still a good message so considered reliable), and weak (not reliable because of a questionable chain and/or content). However, Sunnis and Shi'is don't use the same measures to test reliability or even the same sources for their Hadiths – e.g., whether Muhammad must be in the chain or not, which of Muhammad's Companions can be in the chain, and so on.

33 I have given Salim a second, different pseudonym elsewhere in this book to avoid prejudicing readers against him in his answers.

CHAPTER 1

1 Gilles Deleuze and Félix Guattari, *On the Line*, Foreign Agents series (Cambridge, MA: Semiotext(e), MIT Press, 1983).
2 Lyn Robinson and Mike McGuire, 'The Rhizome and the Tree: Changing Metaphors for Information Organization', *Journal of Documentation*, 66.4, 2010, pp. 604–13 at p. 607.
3 Karen Bauer, *Gender Hierarchy in the Qur'ān*, pp. 5–6.
4 Talal Asad, 'The Idea of an Anthropology of Islam', p. 20.
5 Ibid.
6 Zareena Grewal, *Islam Is a Foreign Country: American Muslims and the Global Crisis of Authority* (New York: New York University Press, 2014), p. 36.
7 Ibid., p. 36.
8 Ibid., p. 200.
9 Ibid.
10 Chaudhry, *Domestic Violence and the Islamic Tradition*, p. 7.
11 Su'ad Abdul Khabeer, *Muslim Cool: Race, Religion, and Hip Hop in the United States* (New York: New York University Press, 2016), p. 2.
12 Ibid.
13 Ibid., p. 165.
14 Ibid., p. 160.
15 Sherman Jackson, *Islam and the Blackamerican: Looking toward the Third Resurrect*ion (New York: Oxford University Press, 2005).
16 Jamilla Karim, *American Muslim Women: Negotiating Race, Class, and Gender within the Ummah* (New York: New York University Press, 2009).
17 Sara Savant, *The New Muslims of Post-Conquest Iran: Tradition, Memory, and Conversion* (Cambridge: Cambridge University Press), p. 4.
18 Alberto Fernández Carbajal, *Queer Muslim Diasporas in Contemporary Literature and Film* (Manchester: Manchester University Press, 2019); Daniel Tutt, Deleuzian Theology and the Immanence of the Act of Being [online], https://www.researchgate.net/publication/332655382_Deleuzian_Theology_and_the_Immanence_of_the_Act_of_Being, *SCTIW Review*, December 1, 2015, pp. 1–9 (accessed March 25, 2024); Michael Muhammad Knight, *Sufi Deleuze: Secretions of Islamic Atheism* (New York: Fordham University Press, 2023).
19 Michael Muhammad Knight, *Sufi Deleuze*, p. 15.
20 Ibid.
21 Ibid.
22 Ibid., p. 16.
23 Ibid., p. 50.
24 Ibid., p. 51.
25 Ibid., p. 93.
26 Ibid., p. 121.
27 Ibid., p. 16.
28 E.g. Fatima Mernissi, *The Veil and the Male Elite: A Feminist Interpretation of Women's Rights in Islam* (New York: Basic Books, 1991); Ahmed, *Women and Gender in Islam*.
29 Sa'diyya Shaikh, 'A Tafsir of Praxis: Gender, Marital Violence, and Resistance in a South African Muslim Community', in *Violence Against Women in Contemporary World Religions: Roots and Cures*, eds Dan Maguire and Sa'diyya Shaikh

(Cleveland: The Pilgrim Press), pp. 66–89; Juliane Hammer, *American Muslim Women, Religious Authority, and Activism: More Than a Prayer* (Austin: University of Texas Press, 2012).

30 Scott Kugle, 'The Reception of the Qur'an in the LGBTQ Muslim Community', in *Communities of the Qur'an: Dialogue, Debate and Diversity in the 21st Century*, eds Emran Elbadawi and Paula Sanders (London: Oneworld Publications, 2019), pp. 98–134.

31 Ibid., p. 101.

32 I recognise Gilles Deleuze's Islamophobic attitudes towards Muslims and Islam. Michael Muhammad Knight addresses some of Deleuze's anti-Muslim and orientalist prejudices in the Introduction of *Sufi Deleuze*. Of course, I reject all forms of Islamophobia and other prejudices. I have chosen nonetheless to cite him here because the language I am using in this chapter is deeply influenced by Deleuze and Guattari, and credit must be given, even if to a scholar who chose to remain wilfully ignorant of Islam and bigoted toward Muslims.

33 Quoted in Robinson and McGuire. 'The Rhizome and the Tree', p. 606.

34 E.g. the BBC's 'Have Your Say' column on female-led prayer in Islam: 'Should Women Lead Muslim Prayers?', *BBC News* [online], March 24, 2005, http://news.bbc.co.uk/1/hi/talking_point/4369681.stm (accessed February 13, 2024). For a detailed discussion on female-led prayer, see ch. 6 of this book.

35 Quoted in Todd May, *Gilles Deleuze: An Introduction* (Cambridge: Cambridge University Press, 2005), p. 133.

36 Ibid., p. 133.

37 Ibid., 133-4.

38 Gilles Deleuze and Felix Guattari, *A Thousand Plateaus: Capitalism and Schizophrenia*, trans. Brian Massumi (Minneapolis: University of Minnesota Press, 1987), p. 7.

39 Ibid., p. 8.

40 Ibid., p. 9.

41 Brent Adkins and Paul Hinlicky, *Rethinking Philosophy and Theology with Deleuze: A New Cartography* (London: Bloomsbury, 2014), p. 73.

42 Deleuze and Guattari, *A Thousand Plateaus*, p. 12.

43 Ibid., p. 20.

44 May, *Gilles Deleuze: An Introduction*, p. 165.

45 Ibid.

46 Robinson and McGuire, 'The Rhizome and the Tree', p. 607.

47 Deleuze and Guattari, *A Thousand Plateaus*, p. 21.

48 David Vishanoff, *The Formation of Islamic Hermeneutics: How Sunni Legal Theorists Imagined a Revealed Law* (New Haven: American Oriental Society, 2011), p. 278.

49 Sara Savant, *The New Muslims of Post-Conquest Iran*, p. 128.

50 Ibid.

51 Ibid., p. 13. For more on 'picking and choosing' in the exegetical tradition, see Saleh, *The Formation of the Classical 'Tafsir' Tradition.*

52 E.g. Saleh, *The Formation of the Classical 'Tafsir' Tradition*, p. 62.

53 While medieval Muslim jurists did not coin the term *takhayyur*, Ahmed Fekry Ibrahim argues that post-classical Islamic law made increasing use of this principle, which later, modern scholars rely on heavily in their quest for Islamic reform. See

his *Pragmatism in Islamic Law: A Social and Intellectual History* (Syracuse, NY: Syracuse University Press, 2017).

54 Wael Hallaq, 'Can the Sharī'a be Restored?', in *Islamic Law and the Challenges of Modernity*, eds Yvonne Haddad and Barbara Stowasser (Walnut Creek, CA: AltaMira, 2004), pp. 21–53.

55 Ibrahim, *Pragmatism in Islamic Law*, p. 8.

56 Ibid., p. 3.

57 Ibid., p. 12.

58 Ibid., p. 195.

59 Ibid., p. 3.

60 Ibid., p. 63.

61 Ibid., p. 64.

62 Ibrahim, p. 64.

63 Ahmed Fekry Ibrahim, 'Takhayyur and Talfīq', *The Oxford Encyclopedia of Islamic Law* [online], March 18, 2017 at http://www.oxfordislamicstudies.com/article/opr/t349/e0082 (accessed February 13, 2024).

64 Ibrahim, *Pragmatism*, p. 179.

65 Wael Hallaq, 'Can the Sharī'a be Restored?', in *Islamic Law and the Challenges of Modernity*, ed. Yvonne Haddad and Barbara Stowasser (Walnut Creek, CA: AltaMira, 2004), pp. 21–53.

66 Ibrahim, 'Takhayyur and Talfīq'.

67 Ibrahim, *Pragmatism*, p. 105.

68 Ibrahim, 'Takhayyur and Talfīq'.

69 Wael Hallaq, *An Introduction to Islamic Law* (Cambridge: Cambridge University Press, 2009), p. 117.

70 Ibid.

71 Ibn 'Āshūr, *Treatise on Maqaṣid al-Shariah*, trans. and annotated by Mohamed El-Tahir El-Mesawi (London and Washington, D.C.: The International Institute of Islamic Thought, 2006), p. 118. Available online at: https://ia600407.us.archive.org/20/items/TreatiseOnMaqasidAlShariah/Treatise%20on%20Maqasid%20al-Shari'ah.pdf (accessed February 13, 2024).

72 Ibn 'Āshūr, *Treatise*, p. 146.

73 Ibid., p. 147.

74 Ibrahim, 'Takhayyur and Talfīq'.

75 Ibrahim, 'Takhayyur and Talfīq'.

76 Judith Tucker, *In the House of the Law: Gender and Islamic Law in Ottoman Syria and Palestine* (Los Angeles: University of California Press, 1998), p. 84.

77 Ibid., p. 180.

78 Yossef Rapoport, *Marriage, Money and Divorce in Medieval Islamic Society* (Cambridge: Cambridge University Press, 2005). For more on Muslim women's use of Islamic courts to seek divorce, in both modern and pre-modern times, see: Mohamad Abdun Nasir, 'Islamic Law and Paradox of Domination and Resistance: Women's Judicial Divorce in Lombok, Indonesia', *Asian Journal of Social Science*, 44.1–2, 2016, pp. 78-103; Susan Hirsch, *Pronouncing and Persevering: Gender and the Discourses of Disputing in an African Islamic Court* (Chicago: University of Chicago Press, 1998).

79 Humeira Iqtidar, 'Redefining "Tradition" in Political Thought', *European Journal of Political Theory*, 15, 2016, p. 426.

80 Cited in ibid., p. 428.
81 Ibid., p. 428.
82 Ibid.
83 Ibid.
84 Muhammad Qasim Zaman, *The Ulama in Contemporary Islam*: *Custodians of Change* (Princeton: Princeton University Press, 2002). See especially the first chapter.
85 Ibid., p. 28.
86 Chaudhry, *Domestic Violence*, p. 7.
87 Cited in Wael Hallaq, 'Beyond Tradition', *Journal of Islamic Studies*, 3.2, 1992, pp. 172–202 at p. 174.
88 E.g. as claimed by mainstream Muslim authorities, including Yasir Qadhi, and by my respondents.
89 For more on influencers, see Melody Nouri, The Power of Influence: Traditional Celebrity vs Social Media Influencer [online], https://scholarcommons.scu.edu/cgi/viewcontent.cgi?article=1032&context=engl_176 *Advanced Writing: Pop Culture Intersections*, 32, 2018 (accessed 14 February, 2024).
90 See, for example, Timur Yuskaev and Harvey Stark, 'The American "ulama" and the Public Sphere', in *Routledge Handbook of Islam in the West*, ed. Roberto Tottoli (London: Routledge, 2022), pp. 357–73.
91 For more on this, see Zaman, *The 'Ulama in Contemporary Islam*; Zareena Grewal, *Islam is a Foreign Country: American Muslims and the Global Crisis of Authority* (New York: New York University Press, 2014).
92 Yasir Qadhi, 'Looking Back as We Look Forward', YouTube video [online], uploaded December 13, 2013, but dated December 7, 2013 in the title, https://www.youtube.com/watch?v=jJmrPh2sRuw (accessed February 14, 2024).
93 Ibid., 45:08–45:50.
94 Ibid., 34:14–34:38.
95 Ibid., 39:12–39:56.
96 Ibid., 43:50–44:22.
97 Ibid., 45:08–45:50.
98 Ibid., 46:04–46:40
99 Ibid., 49:14–49:41
100 Abu Thawr and al-Ṭabarī's opinions on this matter are mentioned in Ibn Rushd, *The Distinguished Jurist's Primer*, vol. 1, p. 161. Available online at: https://islamfuture.files.wordpress.com/2011/05/the-distinguished-jurist-s-primer-vol-i.pdf (accessed February 14, 2024). For a detailed discussion on the multiplicity of opinions on female-led prayer, see ch. 6 of this book.
101 Yasir Qadhi, *Looking Back as We Look Forward*, 49:13–49:30.
102 'Ustaadha Yasmin Mogahed', *AlMaghrib Institute* [online], http://almaghrib.org/instructors/yasmin-mogahed#profile (accessed February 14, 2024).
103 'Biography', *Free Quran Education* [online], http://www.nakcollection.com/naks-biography.html (accessed February 14, 2024)
104 *Bayyinah* [online], https://www.bayyinah.com/ (accessed December 27, 2017).
105 I discuss Mogahed's engagement with tradition and female-led prayer in ch. 6, and Khan's discussion on sexual slavery in ch. 3 of this book.
106 Grewal, *Islam is a Foreign Country*, p. 265.
107 Zaman, *The Ulama in Contemporary Islam*, p. 189.

108 Ziba Mir-Hosseini, *Journeys Toward Gender Equality in Islam* (London: Oneworld Publications, 2022). In this book, which consists of interviews with other Muslim intellectuals, Abdullahi Ahmed An-Naʿim is the one scholar who disagrees about highlighting the difference between *sharīʿa* and *fiqh*.

109 Ziba Mir-Hosseini, 'Islamic Family Law and Social Practice: Anthropological Reflections on the Terms of the Debate', in *Family, Law and Religion: Debates in the Muslim World and Europe and their Implications for Co-operation and Dialogue*, ed. Siegfried Hass (Vienna: Austrian Association for the Middle East Hammer-Purgstall, 2009), pp. 37–48 at p. 23.

110 Ibid., p. 42.

111 Khaled Abou El Fadl, *Reasoning with God: Reclaiming Shariʿah in the Modern Age* (Lanham, MD: Rowman & Littlefield, 2014), p. xl.

112 The exact number of schools of thought is unknown, but it ranges from dozens to hundreds. See George Makdisi, 'The Significance of the Sunni Schools of Law in Islamic Religious History', *International Journal of Middle East Studies*, 10.1, 1979, pp. 1–8; Lena Salaymeh, *The Beginnings of Islamic Law Late Antique Islamicate Legal Traditions* (Cambridge: Cambridge University Press, 2016, p. 152.

113 Abou El Fadl, *Reasoning with God*, p. xli.

114 Marwa Sharfaldein, 'Egyptian Women's Rights NGOs: Personal Status Law Reform between Islamic and International Human Rights Law', in *Gender and Equality in Muslim Family Law: Justice and Ethics in the Islamic Legal Tradition*, eds Ziba Mir-Hosseini, Kari Vogt, Lena Larsen, *et al.* (London and New York: I.B. Tauris, 2013), pp. 57–80 at p. 62.

115 Ibid., p. 62.

116 Ibid.

117 My respondents are not alone in their unclear meanings of 'Islam' and related terms. For a detailed critical discussion of these terms and other relevant ones – e.g. *Sunnah*, *sharīʿa*, *fiqh*, Islam – see Kevin Reinhart, 'Islamic Law as Islamic Ethics', *Journal of Islamic Ethics*, 11.2, 1983, pp. 186–203.

118 Imam Mālik b. Anas, *Al-Muwaṭṭa'*, ed. and trans. Mohammad Fadel and Connell Monette (Cambridge, MA: Harvard Islamic Legal Studies Program, 2019), p. 16.

119 Ibid., p. 18.

120 Ibid., p. 18.

121 Carolyn Baugh, 'An Exploration of the Juristic Consensus (*Ijmāʿ*) on Compulsion in the Marriages of Minors', *Comparative Islamic Studies*, 5.1, 2009, pp. 33–92.

122 The Qur'anic reference she makes here is to Q. 2:170, which reads, 'And when it is said to them, "Follow what God has revealed," they say, "Rather, we will follow that which we found our forefathers doing"; and Q. 5:104, 'When it is said to them, "Come to what God has revealed to the Messenger," they say, "Sufficient for us is that upon which we found our forefathers" even though their forefathers knew nothing, nor were they guided.'

123 This statement is a reference to Qur'anic verse 3:36, which includes the statement: 'And the male is not like the female.' In Q. 3:35-36, the mother of Mary and wife of 'Imrān dedicates her unborn child to the services of God, seemingly expecting a male child. When she gives birth to a daughter, she appears to be disappointed and says, 'My Sustainer! I have given birth to a girl!' Q. 3:36 responds to her disappointment with 'and God fully knew what she had delivered – and the male is not like the female.'

124 Kecia Ali, *Sexual Ethics and Islam: Feminist Reflections on Qur'an, Hadith, and Jurisprudence* (London: Oneworld Publications, 2016), p. 195.

CHAPTER 2

1 Ibn Rushd, *The Distinguished Jurist's Primer*, vol. 2, p. 9. https://islamfuture.files.wordpress.com/2011/05/the-distinguished-jurist-s-primer-vol-ii.pdf.

2 The Arabic *lam* can mean 'not' or 'not yet'.

3 'Verse 65:4 English Translation', *The Qur'anic Arabic Corpus* [online], http://corpus.quran.com/translation.jsp?chapter=65&verse=4 (accessed December 22, 2017). Mohsin Khan parenthetical note in original.

4 'Surah al-An'am 6:1-10', *Towards Understanding the Quran* [online], http://www.islamicstudies.info/tafheem.php?sura=65 (accessed December 22, 2017).

5 Ibid.

6 'Child Marriage in Islam', *IslamWeb*. [online], June 24, 2004, http://www.islamweb.net/emainpage/index.php?page=showfatwa&Option=Fatwald&Id=88089 (accessed December 22, 2017).

7 Ibid.

8 Yasmin Amin, 'Revisiting the Issue of Minor Marriages Multidisciplinary Ijtihād on Contemporary Ethical Problems' in Reda and Amin (eds), *Islamic Interpretive Tradition*, pp. 314–63 at p. 330.

9 Ibid.

10 Ibid., p. 333.

11 Ibid., p. 333.

12 Abu Dawud, *Sunan Abi Dawud, K. al-Nikāḥ*, Book 12, Hadith Number 48. Available online at: https://sunnah.com/abudawud:2093 (accessed March 26, 2024).

13 See Ayesha Chaudhry, 'Producing Gender-Egalitarian Islamic Law: A Case Study of Guardianship (Wilayah) in Prophetic Practice', in *Men in Charge?*, eds Ziba Mir-Hosseini, Mulki Al-Sharmani and Jana Rumminger (London: Oneworld Publications, 2015), pp. 88–105.

14 The complete version of this Hadith reads: 'A widow has more right concerning herself than her guardian, and a virgin should be consulted [*al-ayyimu awlā binafsihā min waliyyiha wa al-bikru tusta'maru fī nafisha*]. It was said: "O Messenger of Allah, a virgin may be too shy to speak." He said: "[In that case] her consent is her silence [*idhnuhā sukūtuhā*].'"

15 Muḥammad al-Bukhārī, *Sahih al-Bukhari, K. al-Ikrāh* (*The Book of Coercion*), trans. Muhammad Muhsin Khan, vol. 9 (Riyādh: Dārussalām, 1997), Hadith no. 6945, p. 89; also Hadith no. 6969 in *K. al- Ḥīl* (*The Book of Tricks*), p. 74. Available online at: https://futureislam.files.wordpress.com/2012/11/sahih-al-bukhari-volume-9-ahadith-6861-7563.pdf (accessed March 26, 2024). Many other Hadith reports exist about the requirement of consent in the marriage of virgins (previously unmarried women) and married women (divorced or widowed women), such as Hadith 6968 on p. 90 and Hadith 6946 on p. 89 of same source. Sunan Ibn Mājah, Book 9, Hadith 27 also reports that neither virgin nor previously married women can be married without their consent. See https://sunnah.com/ibnmajah:1871 (accessed March 26, 2024).

16 Ibn Mājah, *Sunan Ibn Mājah* Book 9, *K. al-Nikāḥ* (*The Book of Marriage*), Hadith 30. Available online at: https://sunnah.com/ibnmajah:1874 (accessed March 26, 2024).
17 Ali, *Marriage and Slavery in Early Islam*, p. 41.
18 Ibid.
19 Ibn Rushd, *The Distinguished Jurist's Primer*, vol. 2, p. 5. https://islamfuture.files.wordpress.com/2011/05/the-distinguished-jurist-s-primer-vol-ii.pdf.
20 Al-Bukhārī, *Sahih al-Bukhari,* vol. 7, Book 62, Number 64.
21 Ali, *Marriage and Slavery in Early Islam*, p. 35.
22 Ibid.
23 Ibid., p. 36.
24 For a detailed discussion of Muhammad's marriage to Aisha and modern debates about her age and the justification of the marriage, see Kecia Ali, *The Lives of Muhammad* (Boston: Harvard University Press, 2016), ch. 4. See, also, Ali, *Sexual Ethics and Islam*, ch. 8.
25 Yasmin Amin, 'Age is just a number or is it? ʿA'isha's age between Ḥadīth and History' (unpublished paper delivered at the Third Annual Conference of the British Association for Islamic Studies (BRAIS), London, 11–12 April 2016).
26 Ali, *Sexual Ethics and Islam*, p. 175.
27 Yasmin Amin, 'Revisiting the Issue of Minor Marriages', p. 318.
28 Ibid., p. 321.
29 Jasser Auda, 'How Old Was Aisha When She Married the Prophet (S)?', *Official Website: Dr. Jasser Auda*, March 1, 2017, https://www.jasserauda.net/old-aisha-married-prophet-s/?lang=en (accessed February 14, 2024).
30 Joshua Little, 'The Hadith of 'Aisha's Marital Age: A Study in the Evolution of Early Islamic Historical Memory', D.Phil. diss., University of Oxford, 2022, A version is available online at: https://islamicorigins.com/the-unabridged-version-of-my-phd-thesis/ (accessed June 10, 2023).
31 Harald Motzki, 'Child Marriage in Seventeenth-Century Palestine', in *Islamic Legal Interpretation: Muftis and Their Fatwas*, eds Muhammad Khalid Masud, Brinkley Morris Messick and David Stephan Powers (Cambridge, MA: Harvard University Press, 1996), pp. 129–40 at p. 135.
32 Ibid., p. 138.
33 Baugh, 'An Exploration of the Juristic Consensus (*Ijmāʿ*)', p. 54.
34 Ibid.
35 Ibid.
36 Ibid.
37 It appears that there were no regulations, unless it resulted in the death of the young bride. The rule that consummation should only take place after puberty was not always followed, often with tragic consequences for the bride. See, for example, Allan Christelow, *Muslim Law Courts and the French Colonial State in Algeria* (Princeton: Princeton University Press, 2014).
38 Baugh, 'An Exploration of the Juristic Consensus (*Ijmāʿ*)', pp. 38–9. Also, Ibn Ḥazm (d. 1072) posits later on that the marriage of prepubescent males is invalid because the marriage of prepubescent girls is a result not of *ijmāʿ* but of *Sunnah*: girls can be married without their consent because of Aisha's marriage to the Prophet. See ibid., p. 62.

39 Ibid., p. 62.
40 As cited in Baugh, 'An Exploration of the Juristic Consensus (*Ijmāʿ*)', p. 36.
41 Ibid., pp. 37, 51.
42 Baugh, 'An Exploration of the Juristic Consensus (*Ijmāʿ*)', p. 61.
43 Ibn Rushd, *The Distinguished Jurist's Primer* vol. 2, p. 3. https://islamfuture.files.wordpress.com/2011/05/the-distinguished-jurist-s-primer-vol-ii.pdf
44 Baugh, 'An Exploration of the Juristic Consensus (*Ijmāʿ*)', p. 51.
45 Ibn Rushd, *The Distinguished Jurist's Primer* vol. 2, p.4.
46 Ibid.
47 Ibid., p. 6.
48 Sarah Eltantawi, 'Between Strict Constructionist Shariah and Protecting Young Girls in Nigeria: The Case of Child Marriage (ijbār)', in *Women's Rights and Religious Law: Domestic and International Perspectives*, eds Fareda and Lisa Fishbayn Joffe Banda (London: Routledge, 2016), pp. 91–107 at. p. 96. For more on *rushd*, see Baugh, 'An Exploration of the Juristic Consensus (*Ijmāʿ*)', p. 66 onwards; for a discussion on the meaning of *bāligh*, see ibid., p. 68.
49 Baugh, 'An Exploration of the Juristic Consensus (*Ijmāʿ*)', p. 39.
50 Muhammad Khalid Masud, 'The Sources of the Maliki Doctrine of Ijbar', *Islamic Studies*, 24.2, 1985, pp. 215–53 at p. 218.
51 Ibid.
52 Ibid., p. 219.
53 Ibid.
54 Ibid.
55 Ibn Rushd, *The Distinguished Jurist's Primer* vol. 2, p. 7.
56 Ibid., p. 9.
57 On poverty being a reason, see Masud, 'The Sources of the Maliki Doctrine of Ijbar', p. 221.
58 'Authoritative' here refers to Muslim-majority nations' policy changes regarding child marriage as well as the opinions of popular religious scholars, such as Yasir Qadhi and others whom my discussants referenced frequently in our discussion.
59 E.g. in Pakistan, the clergy – the Council of Islamic Ideology – declared Pakistan's effort to increase the minimum age for marriage from 16 to 19 'blasphemous'. See Faras Ghani, 'Pakistan failure to outlaw child marriage sparks outrage', *Al Jazeera* [online], January 19, 2016, http://www.aljazeera.com/news/2016/01/pakistan-child-marriage-160118062004700.html; http://www.loc.gov/law/foreign-news/article/pakistan-child-marriage-bill-withdrawn/ (accessed 14 February, 2024).
60 'Pakistan: Sindh Province Assembly Passes Child Marriage Restraint Bill', *Library of Congress* [online], May 23, 2014, https://www.loc.gov/item/global-legal-monitor/2014-05-23/pakistan-sindh-provincial-assembly-passes-child-marriage-restraint-bill/ (accessed March 16, 2024).
61 'Pakistan: Child Marriage Bill Withdrawn', *Library of Congress* [online], Jan 25, 2016, https://www.loc.gov/item/global-legal-monitor/2016-01-25/pakistan-child-marriage-bill-withdrawn/ (accessed March 16, 2024).
62 'Addressing Muhammad (PBUH)'s Marriage to Aisha', YouTube video [online], April 17, 2011. https://www.youtube.com/watch?v=StISnUEVkaM, 0:22–1:06 (accessed December 27, 2017).

63 'Why did Prophet Muhammad marry Aishah at a young age? - Q&A - Sh. Dr. Yasir Qadhi', YouTube video [online], July 30, 2015, https://www.youtube.com/watch?v=1GMwR1gmZ6M, 0:21–1:21 (accessed December 27, 2017).

64 Ibid.

65 Ibid.

66 Nouman Ali Khan, 'Forced Marriages - That's Messed Up', YouTube video [online], December 28, 2015, https://www.youtube.com/watch?v=UbeoJX2Fo2w (accessed December 22, 2017).

67 Mohammad Ali Syed, *The Position of Women in Islam* (New York: SUNY Press, 2004), p. 40.

68 Ibid., p. 41.

69 Ibid.

70 Child marriage is in fact not illegal in the United States. The minimum age for marriage varies across all the US states, ranging from 14 to 17. Forty-four of fifty states allow children to marry with parental consent. See, for example, Kaya Van Roost, Miranda Horn and Alissa Koski,'Child Marriage or Statutory Rape? A Comparison of Law and Practice Across the United States', *Journal of Adolescent Health*, 70.3, 2022, pp. 72–7. Available online at: https://www.sciencedirect.com/science/article/pii/S1054139X21005528. See also Fraidy Reiss, 'America's Child-Marriage Problem', *New York Times* [online], October 13, 2015, https://www.nytimes.com/2015/10/14/opinion/americas-child-marriage-problem.html (accessed February 15, 2024); Nurith Aizenman, 'The Loopholes that Allow Child Marriage in the U.S', *NPR* [online], August 30, 2017, https://www.npr.org/sections/goatsandsoda/2017/08/30/547072368/a-look-at-the-loopholes-that-allow-child-marriage-in-the-u-s (accessed February 15, 2024); 'Why Does the U.S. Have So Many Child Brides?', *BBC News* [online], October 23, 2017, http://www.bbc.com/news/av/world-us-canada-41727495/why-does-the-us-have-so-many-child-brides (accessed December 21, 2017).

71 *Astaghfirullah*, literally 'I seek forgiveness from Allah', is an Islamic expression one recites as a form of quick repentance for saying or thinking something considered Islamically unacceptable.

72 Many respondents asked throughout the interview what I thought or if I knew whether a certain practice was Islamically acceptable or 'what does Islam say on this?' I would let them know that I am happy to share my own knowledge after the interview was over so as not to affect their answers in any way, and we sometimes did revisit the topic.

73 Yasir Qadhi, 'Looking Back as We Look Forward', 18:00–18:16.

74 Syed, *The Position of Women in Islam*, p. 174.

75 Ibid., p. 175.

76 Baugh, 'An Exploration of the Juristic Consensus (*Ijmāʿ*)', p. 39.

77 Also see, for example, Lynn Welchman, '*Qiwāmah* and *Wilāyah* as Legal Postulates in Muslim Family Laws', in *Men in Charge?*, eds Mir-Hosseini, *et al.*, pp. 133–62, where she discusses the ways that pre-modern ideas of marriage and gender inequality continue to shape Muslims' perceptions of marriage in practice as gleaned from marital laws.

78 Baugh, 'An Exploration of the Juristic Consensus (*Ijmāʿ*)', p. 42.

79 Ibid.

80 Eltantawi, 'Between Strict Constructionist Shariah and Protecting Young Girls in Nigeria', p. 91.
81 Ibid., p. 103.

CHAPTER 3

1 Ali, *Sexual Ethics and Islam*, p. 61.
2 While Q. 4:24 seems to suggest that marriage with already married women among 'those whom [the men's] right hands possess' is permissible, jurists historically categorically forbade men from marrying their female slaves who were already married. They debated, however, whether sexual contact with married enslaved women was permissible.
3 As cited in Ali, *Marriage and Slavery in Early Islam*, pp. 12–14.
4 E.g. Asifa Quraishi-Landes, 'A Meditation on Mahr, Modernity, and Muslim Marriage Contract Law', in *Feminism, Law, and Religion*, eds Marie Failinger, Elizabeth Schlitz, and Susan Stable (London: Routledge, 2016), pp. 173–95. See, also, Nehad Khanfar, 'What Your Right Hand Possesses: The Islamic legal concept of 'Mulk al-yameen' between Family Law and the Law on War and Slavery' (unpublished paper delivered at the British Association for Islamic Studies (BRAIS), Chester, 11–13 April 2017). Khanfar argues that the Qur'anic phrase refers not to female slaves but to the wives of the Muslims newly converted to Islam (i.e. their wives or spouses from before Islam).
5 Quraishi-Landes, 'A Meditation on Mahr, Modernity, and Muslim Marriage Contract Law', p. 178.
6 Ibid., p. 179.
7 Jonathan Brockopp, *Early Mālikī Law: Ibn 'Abd Al-Ḥakam and His Major Compendium of Jurisprudence* (Leiden: Brill, 2000), p. 133. Meccan verses are those that were revealed before Muhammad's migration from Mecca to Medina in 622 CE; Medinan verses are post-migration.
8 Ibn Rushd, *The Distinguished Jurist's Primer*, vol. 2, p. 475. https://islamfuture.files.wordpress.com/2011/05/the-distinguished-jurist-s-primer-vol-ii.pdf
9 Ibid, p. 476.
10 Younus Mirza, 'Remembering the Umm al-Walad Ibn Kathir's Treatise on the Sale of the Concubine', in *Concubines and Courtesans: Women and Slavery in Islamic History*, eds Matthew S. Gordon and Kathryn A. Hain (New York: Oxford University Press, 2017), pp. 297–322 at p. 297.
11 Ibid., p. 300.
12 Ibid., p. 301.
13 Ibid.
14 Ibid., p. 302.
15 Bint al-Shāṭi' [Aisha Abd al-Rahman], *Wives of the Prophet*, trans. Matti Moosa and D. Nicholas Ranson (New Jersey: Gorgias Press, 2006), p. 206.
16 Ibid., p. 203.
17 Bint al-Shāṭi' [Aisha Abd al-Rahman], *Tarājim Sayyidāt Bait al-Nubuwwa* (Cairo: Dār al-Rayyan Li-l-Turāth, first edn, 1987), p. 396.

18 Bint al-Shāṭi', *Wives of the Prophet*, p. 208. For the original Arabic, see Bint al-Shāṭi, *Tarājim Sayyidāt Bait al-Nubuwwa*, p. 402.
19 Bint al-Shāṭi', *Wives of the Prophet*, p. 206.
20 Ibid., pp. 207–8.
21 Aysha Hidayatullah, 'Māriya the Copt: Gender, Sex, and Heritage in the Legacy of Muhammad's *Umm Walad*', *Islam and Christian–Muslim Relations*, 21.3, 2010, pp. 221–42 at p. 221.
22 Ibid, pp. 225–6.
23 Ibid.
24 Ibid., p. 229.
25 For more examples of modern revision of Māriya's status in relation to Muhammad, see Kecia Ali, *Sexual Ethics and Islam*, pp. 57–8.
26 Hidayatullah, 'Māriya the Copt', p. 229.
27 Ibid.
28 Ali, *The Lives of Muhammad*, p. 186.
29 Muhammad famously allotted different days to each of his wives, which Muslims believe was intended to ensure all his wives received equal attention from him.
30 As cited in Hidayatullah, 'Māriya the Copt', p. 227.
31 Bint al-Shāṭi, *Wives of the Prophet*, p. 81. According to the Sunni tradition, Muhammad's favourite wife was Aisha, something about which Aisha often boasts in Hadiths, claiming that her co-wives were jealous of Muhammad's love for her.
32 Yasir Qadih, 'Seerah of the Prophet Muhammad 97 - Maria the Copt & Death of Ibrahim', YouTube video [online], uploaded Dec 6, 2014, but dated November 19, 2014 in the title, https://www.youtube.com/watch?v=lvBgwrl-UC0#t=54m, 55:42–56:24 (accessed December 20, 2017).
33 Hidayatullah, 'Māriya the Copt', pp. 221–2.
34 Ibid., p. 222.
35 Yasmin Amin, 'Wives of the Prophet', in *The Oxford Encyclopedia of Islam and Women*, ed. Natana J. DeLong-Bas (Oxford: Oxford University Press, 2013), pp. 426–9 at p. 428.
36 Ibid., p. 428.
37 Yasir Qadhi, 'Slavery, Sex-slave and Sex-maid in Islam', YouTube video [online], December 6, 2014, https://www.youtube.com/watch?v=AEa-cM2lS_E, 1:05–1:31 (accessed December 20, 2017).
38 Ibid., 2:30–3:03.
39 Islam is not, in fact, the only or first religion to deal with slavery and its ethics. Among other religions, Judaism, too, has a complex legal system and a long history that addresses the question of slavery, including definitions, who could be enslaved, different types of slavery, and rules surrounding treatment of the enslaved. See, for example, David M. Cobin, 'A Brief Look at the Jewish Law of Manumission - Freedom: Beyond the United States', *Chicago-Kent Law Review*, 70.3, 1995, *Symposium on the Law of Freedom, Part II: Freedom: Beyond the United States*, pp. 1339–48. Available online at: https://scholarship.kentlaw.iit.edu/cklawreview/vol70/iss3/13 (accessed February 16, 2024). For a more detailed discussion on slavery and Judaism, see Catherin Hezser, *Jewish Slavery in Antiquity* (New York: Oxford University Press, 2005).
40 Yasir Qadhi, 'Slavery, Sex-slave and Sex-maid in Islam', 3:24–3:34.
41 Ibid., 6:34–6:47.

42 Ibid., 6:52–7:00.
43 Ibid., 7:57–8:32. Qur'anic verse 24:33: 'Do not compel your slave girls to prostitution, if they desire chastity, to seek [thereby] the temporary interests of worldly life.'
44 Qadhi, 'Slavery, Sex-slave and Sex-maid in Islam', 9:34–10:17.
45 Ibid., 10:33–10:37.
46 Ibid., 10:38–10:57.
47 Ibid., 12:48–12:53.
48 Nouman Ali Khan, 'What "right hand possess" (slave woman, POW) really means', YouTube video [online], September 19, 2011, https://www.youtube.com/watch?v=L1_ikJRVnM8, 1:38–2:42 (accessed December 20, 2017).
49 Ibid., 0:23–2:45.
50 Hina Azam, *Sexual Violation in Islamic Law*, p. 172.
51 Ali, *Marriage and Slavery in Early Islam*, p. 39.
52 Ibid., p. 40.
53 Bernard Freamon, *Possessed by the Right Hand: The Problem of Slavery in Islamic Law and Muslim Cultures*, Studies in Global Slavery, vol. 8 (Leiden: Brill), p. 468.
54 Ibid., pp. 511–15.
55 Ibid., pp. 273–4.
56 Ibid., p. 459.
57 Ibid., p. 460.
58 Khaled Abou El Fadl, *Reasoning with God*, p. 118.
59 This Hadith is found in the Sunni collection in Sahih Muslim, Book 27 in 'The Book of Oaths', Hadith 64. The Arabic word for 'slave' in this Hadith, however, is *khādim* which generally means 'servant'. Available online at: https://sunnah.com/muslim/27 (accessed March 16, 2024).
60 This verse does not exist in the Qur'an.
61 Imam Ali ibn Abū Ṭālib, *Peak of Eloquence, Nahjul Balāgha*, ed. Yasin T. Al-Jibouri (Elmhurst, NY: Tahrike Tasile Quran, 1984), p. 278. Available online at: http://www.duas.org/pdfs/Nahjul-Balagha.pdf (accessed December 20, 2017).
62 49:13: 'O humankind, indeed We have created you from male and female and made you peoples and tribes that you may know one another. Indeed, the most noble of you in the sight of Allah is the most righteous of you.' 4:1: 'O humankind, fear your Creator, who created you from one soul and created from it its mate and dispersed from both of them many men and women. And fear Allah, through whom you ask one another, and the wombs.'
63 Although I have not been able to track down this story, it is irrelevant to me whether it is true or not. What I find significant is that for Travis, this is relevant and informs his position on slavery and Islam.
64 Freamon, *Possessed by the Right Hand*, p. 3.
65 Ibid., p. 244
66 What I mean by this question is whether the historical scholarly consensus that a male is entitled to have sexual relations with his female slaves is binding or not. That is, are today's Muslims allowed to disagree with – or even prohibit – the idea of having sex with (i.e. raping) one's female slaves.
67 Quraishi-Landes, 'A Meditation on Mahr, Modernity, and Muslim Marriage Contract Law', p. 178.
68 Ibid.
69 Ibid., p. 185.

70 Ibid., p. 187.
71 Bauer, *Gender Hierarchy in the Qur'ān*, p. 260.
72 As cited in Kecia Ali, 'Concubinage and Consent', *International Journal of Middle Eastern Studies*, 49.1, 2017, pp. 148–152 at p. 148.
73 Ali, 'Concubinage and Consent', p. 149.
74 Ibid.
75 Freamon, *Possessed by the Right Hand*, p. 97.
76 Ibid., p. 96.

CHAPTER 4

1 E.g. Asma Barlas, *Believing Women in Islam: Unreading Patriarchal Interpretations of the Qur'ān* (Austin: University of Texas Press, 2002), p. 170.
2 Mufti Menk, 'Woman Gets Half Share of Men Islamic Inheritance' [sic], YouTube video [online], October 8, 2016, https://www.youtube.com/watch?v=KnPAIpR0jTo, 0:23–1:10 (accessed December 27, 2017).
3 4:11–12 reads in full: 'God directs you as regards your children's (Inheritance): to the male, a portion equal to that of two females: if only daughters, two or more, their share is two-thirds of the inheritance; if only one, her share is a half. For parents, a sixth share of the inheritance to each, if the deceased left children; if no children, and the parents are the (only) heirs, the mother has a third; if the deceased left brothers (or sisters) the mother has a sixth. Ye know not whether your parents or your children are nearest to you in benefit. These are settled portions ordained by Allah; and Allah is All-knowing, All-wise. In what your wives leave, your share is a half, if they leave no child; but if they leave a child, ye get a fourth, after payment of legacies and debts. In what ye leave, their share is a fourth, if ye leave no child; but if ye leave a child, they get an eighth, after payment of legacies and debts. If the man or woman whose inheritance is in question, has left neither ascendants nor descendants, but has left a brother or a sister, each one of the two gets a sixth; but if more than two, they share in a third; after payment of legacies and debts; so that no loss is caused (to any one). Thus is it ordained by Allah; and Allah is All-knowing, Most Forbearing.'
4 E.g. Sayyid Quṭb, *Fī Ẓilāl al-Qur'ān*, vol. 1 (Cairo: Dār al-Shurūq, 1972), p. 558. Available online at: https://ia801300.us.archive.org/2/items/ThilalQuran/delalquraan1.pdf (accessed March 28, 2024). See also the English translation of his *tafsīr*: Sayyid Quṭb, *In the Shade of the Qur'an: Fī Ẓilāl al-Qur'ān*, ed. and trans. Adil Salahi, vol. 3 (Leicester: The Islamic Foundation, 2004), pp. 5–6. Available online at: https://tafsirzilal.files.wordpress.com/2012/06/an-nisa-eng.pdf (accessed March 25, 2024).
5 Ziba Mir-Hosseini, 'Justice, Equality and Muslim Family Laws: New Ideas, New Prospects', in *Gender and Equality in Muslim Family Law*, eds Mir-Hosseini, *et al.*, pp. 7–34 at p. 11. For more such reasons that historical male scholars offered to explain the innate inferiority of women and Qur'an's treatment of them, see Asma Lamrabet, 'An Egalitarian Reading of the Concepts of *Khilāfah*, *Wilāyah*, and *Qiwāmah*' in *Men in Charge?*, eds Mir-Hosseini, *et al.*, pp. 65–87 at p. 80.
6 Mir-Hosseini, 'Justice, Equality and Muslim Family Laws', p. 11.

7 amina wadud, *Qur'an and Woman: Rereading the Sacred Text from a Woman's Perspective*, second edn (New York: Oxford University Press, 1999), p. 70.
8 For a detailed discussion on this, see Bauer, *Gender Hierarchy in the Qur'ān*, especially p. 189.
9 As discussed and quoted in ibid., p. 459.
10 As quoted in Olfa Youssef, *The Perplexity of a Muslim Woman*, p. 33.
11 As cited in Mernissi, *The Veil and the Male Elite*, p. 122. Also see al-Tabarī's *tafsīr* on verse 4:11: Abū Jaʿfar Muḥammad ibn Jarīr al-Ṭabarī, *Jāmiʿ al-Bayān ʿan Taʾwīl āy al-Qurʾān*, vol. 6 (Cairo: Dār al-Hijr, 2001), p. 458. Available online in Arabic at: http://www.esinislam.com/Quran-And-Tafseer-PDF/Tafseer-At-Tabari-6.pdf (accessed March 26, 2024).
12 Mernissi, *The Veil and the Male Elite*, p. 120.
13 Ibid.
14 Ibid.
15 Ibid.
16 Ibn Rushd, *The Distinguished Jurist's Primer*, vol. 2, p. 413.
17 Ibid.
18 Youssef, *The Perplexity of a Muslim Woman*, ch. 1.
19 On Indonesian Muslim feminists' interpretations of inheritance in Islam, see Nina Kurmila, 'The Indonesian Muslim Feminist Reinterpretation of Inheritance', in *Islam in Indonesia: Contrasting Images and Interpretations*, eds Jajat Burhanudin and Kees van Dijk (Amsterdam: Amsterdam University Press, 2013), pp. 109–22 at pp. 115–19.
20 See e.g. Ahmed Nadhif, 'Tunisian president calls for gender equality in inheritance law', *Al-Monitor: The Pulse of the Middle East* [online], August 21, 2017, https://www.al-monitor.com/pulse/originals/2017/08/equality-in-inheritance-raises-controversy-in-tunisia.html (accessed December 27, 2017); Ruth Sherlock, 'As Tunisia Weighs Women's Rights Proposal, Some of the Staunchest Opponents Are Women', *NPR* [online], August 17, 2017, https://www.npr.org/sections/parallels/2017/08/17/544123358/as-tunisia-weighs-womens-rights-proposal-some-of-the-staunchest-opponents-are-wo (accessed December 27, 2017).
21 Ṭāhir al-Ḥaddād, *Muslim Women in Law and Society: Annotated Translation of Al-Tahir Al-Haddad*, trans. Ronak Husni and Daniel Newman (London: Routledge, 2007), p. 46.
22 Ibid., p. 47.
23 Ibid.
24 Ibid., p. 48.
25 Nasr Abu Zayd, 'The Status of Women Between the Qur'an and Fiqh', in *Gender and Equality in Muslim Family Law*, eds Mir-Hosseini, *et al.*, pp. 153–68 at p. 162. Available online at: https://www.rwi.uzh.ch/dam/jcr:7d59a884-d169-44d5-8eec-b5f9fc498c71/Abu-Zayd%20StatusofWomen2013.pdf (accessed December 27, 2017).
26 Abu Zayd, 'The Status of Women', p. 161.
27 Ibid., p. 162.
28 Youssef, *The Perplexity of a Muslim Woman*, p. 31.
29 Ibid.
30 Ibid.
31 Ibid., p. 32.

32 Ibid.
33 Ibid., p. 34.
34 Kurmila, 'The Indonesian Muslim Feminist Reinterpretation of Inheritance', p. 116.
35 Shaikh, 'A Tafsir of Praxis', p. 70.
36 Youssef, *The Perplexity of a Muslim Woman*, p. 34.
37 'The World's Muslims: Religion, Politics and Society: Chapter 4: Women in Society', *Pew Research Center* [online], April 30, 2013, http://www.pewforum.org/2013/04/30/the-worlds-muslims-religion-politics-society-women-in-society/ (accessed December 27, 2017).
38 Ibid.
39 Ibid.

CONCLUSION TO SECTION 1

1 E.g. Zaid Shakir, 'ISIS, Sex Slaves and Islam'. *New Islamic Directions* [online], August 14, 2015, https://www.newislamicdirections.com/new_nid/note/isis_sex_slaves_and_islam (accessed February 17, 2024).
2 Khaled Abou El Fadl, *Reasoning with God*, p. 38.

SECTION 2

1 On this point, see, for example, the work of Yusuf al-Qaradawi, who considers women's marriage to non-Muslims impermissible, but he also writes that 'Nothing is haram except what is prohibited by a sound and explicit *nass* from the Law-Giver, Allah.' In a footnote, the translator adds, '*Nass* denotes either a verse of the Qur'an or a clear, authentic, and explicit sunnah (practice or saying) of Prophet Muhammad.' See Qaradawi's *The Lawful and the Prohibited*, trans. K. al-Hilbawi, M. Siddiqi, and S. Shukri (Cairo: Al Falah Foundation, 2001), p. 6.

CHAPTER 5

1 Al-Qaradawi, p. 203; Khaled Abou El-Fadl, 'FATWA: On Christian Men Marrying Muslim Women (Updated)', *The Search for Beauty: on beauty and reason in Islam* [online], May 1, 2016, https://www.searchforbeauty.org/2016/05/01/on-christian-men-marrying-muslim-women-updated/ (accessed March 26, 2024).
2 Ali, *Sexual Ethics and Islam*, p. 21.
3 Even scholars otherwise recognised as gender egalitarian, such as Khaled Abou El Fadl, hesitate to challenge the claim of prohibition because it is 'unanimously' agreed upon. See Abou El Fadl, 'FATWA: On Christian Men Marrying Muslim Women (Updated)'. For the mainstream dominant position on the matter, see Al-Qaradawi, *The Lawful and the Prohibited*, p. 203. I discuss other opponents in detail below.

4 See, for example, 'Why a Muslim woman can't marry a non Muslim?', *Dar Al-ifta Al-Misriyyah* [online], July 31, 2013, https://www.dar-alifta.org/en/fatwa/details/6167/why-a-muslim-woman-can%E2%80%99t-marry-a-non-muslim (accessed March 17, 2024).

5 Akbar Ahmed, *Jinnah, Pakistan and Islamic Identity: The Search for Saladin* (London: Routledge, 1997), p. 52.

6 Yvonne Yazbeck Haddad, Jane I. Smith, Kathleen M. Moore, 'Gender and Family', in *Muslim Women in America: The Challenge of Islamic Identity Today* (New York: Oxford University Press, 2006), pp. 81–100 at p. 86; Douglas Todd, 'Muslim Women in a Marriage Bond', *Vancouver Sun* [online,], May 30, 2012, http://vancouversun.com/news/staff-blogs/muslim-women-in-a-marriage-bind (accessed December 20, 2017).

7 'U.S. Muslims Concerned About Their Place in Society, but Continue to Believe in the American Dream: Identity Assimilation, and Community', *Pew Research Center: Religion & Public Life* [online], July 26, 2017, http://www.pewforum.org/2017/07/26/identity-assimilation-and-community/ (accessed December 20, 2017).

8 I also moderate a Facebook group exclusively for Muslim women in interfaith marriages and relationships; as of May 2023, the group has over 230 members and continues to grow weekly.

9 Yohanan Friedmann, *Tolerance and Coercion in Islam* (Cambridge: Cambridge University Press, 2003), pp. 160–93.

10 Kecia Ali, *Sexual Ethics and Islam*, pp. 14–22.

11 Mohammed Gamal Abdelnour's 'The Islamic Theology of Interfaith Marriages: between Theology, Law, and Individual *Itjihad, Interreligious Relations: Occasional Papers of the Studies in Inter-Religious Relations in Plural Societies Programme*, 17, June 2020.

12 In Friedmann, *Tolerance and Coercion*.

13 Alex Leeman, 'Interfaith Marriage in Islam: An Examination of the Legal Theory Behind the Traditional and Reformist Positions', *Indiana Law Journal*, 84.2, 2009, pp. 743–72.

14 Abdelnour, 'The Islamic Theology of Interfaith Marriages'.

15 Johanna Buisson, 'Interfaith Marriage for Muslim Women: This Day are Things Good and Pure Made Lawful Unto You', *CrossCurrents*, 66.4, 2016, pp. 430–49.

16 Leena Azzam, 'The regulation of interfaith marriages in Islamic legal discourse', Ph.D. diss., American University in Cairo, 2015).

17 Abdullahi Ahmed An-Na'im (ed.), *Inter-religious Marriages Among Muslims: Negotiating Religious and Social Identity in Family and Community* (New Delhi: Global Media Publications, 2005); Haifaa Jawad and Ayse Elmali-Karakaya, 'Interfaith Marriages in Islam from a Woman's Perspective: Turkish Women's Interfaith Marriage Practices in the United Kingdom', *Journal of Muslim Minority Affairs*, 40.1, 2020, pp. 128–47; Heather Al-Yousuf, 'Negotiating Faith and Identity in Muslim–Christian Marriages in Britain', *Islam and Christian–Muslim Relations*, 17.3, 2006, pp. 317–29.

18 Jawad and Elmali-Karakaya, 'Interfaith Marriages in Islam from a Woman's Perspective'.

19 Shehnaz Haqqani, 'The Qur'an on Muslim Women's Marriage to Non-Muslims: Premodern Exegetical Strategies, Contradictions, and Assumptions', *Journal of Qur'anic Studies*, 25.1, 2023, pp. 36–78.

20 Naomi Schaefer Riley, *'Til Faith Do Us Part: How Interfaith Marriage is Transforming America* (New York: Oxford University Press, 2013).
21 Ibid., p. 147.
22 Ibid., p. 150.
23 'America's Changing Religious Landscape: Chapter 2: Religious Switching and Intermarriage', *Pew Research Center* [online], May 12, 2015, http://www.pewforum.org/2015/05/12/chapter-2-religious-switching-and-intermarriage/ (accessed February 19, 2024).
24 Riley, *'Til Faith Do Us Part*,, p. 158.
25 Ibid., p. 160.
26 Ibid., p. 33.
27 Ibid.
28 Ibid.
29 Masood A. Baderin, *International Human Rights and Islamic Law* (Oxford: Oxford University Press, 2003), p. 144.
30 Jane I. Smith, *Muslims, Christians, and the Challenge of Interfaith Dialogue* (Oxford: Oxford University Press, 2007), p. 58.
31 Ibid., p. 58.
32 E.g. Syma Mohammed, 'Why British Muslim Women Struggle to find a Marriage Partner', The *Guardian* [online], January 18, 2012, https://www.theguardian.com/commentisfree/belief/2012/jan/18/british-muslim-women-marriage-struggle (accessed November 2, 2017); Hena Zuberi, 'The Muslim Marriage Crisis', *Muslim Matters* [online], September 27, 2013, https://muslimmatters.org/2013/09/27/muslim-marriage-crisis/ (accessed November 2, 2017).
33 Lori Peek, 'The United States', in *Encyclopedia of Women and Islamic Cultures, vol. 3: Family, Body, Sexuality and Health*, ed. Suad Joseph (Leiden: Brill, 2006), pp. 264–7 at p. 267.
34 Ibid.
35 Todd, 'Muslim Women in a Marriage Bond'.
36 Jorida Cila and Richard N. Lalonde, 'Personal Openness Toward Interfaith Dating and Marriage among Muslim Young Adults: The Role of Religiosity, Cultural Identity, and Family Connectedness', *Group Processes & Intergroup Relations*, 17.3, 2014, pp. 357–70.
37 Ibid, p. 359.
38 Stephen Owoahene-Acheampong, 'Contemporary Zongo Communities in Accra Interfaith Marriages: The Case of Muslims and Christians in Accra', *African Studies Quarterly*, 19.1, 2020, pp. 23–40 at p. 30.
39 Ibid., p. 32.
40 Dvora E. Weisberg, *Levirate Marriage and the Family in Ancient Judaism* (Waltham, MA: Brandeis University Press, 2009), p. xcvii.
41 Parts of this section were originally published elsewhere, in Haqqani, 'The Qur'an on Muslim Women's Marriage to Non-Muslims'.
42 The Qur'anic term in these verses is never 'Muslim' – it is either 'believer' (*mu'min*) or *kum* (pl. 'you', the presumably Muslim audience of the Qur'an). However, I use the term 'Muslim' because it is implied, and because 'believer' could include at least Christians and Jews, but that would not make sense in some of these verses as these believers are sometimes also identified as People of the Book in the Qur'an.

43 Yohanan Friedmann identifies this as the chronological order of the three verses. See his *Tolerance and Coercion in Islam* (Cambridge: Cambridge University Press, 2003), pp. 160–93. at p. 161. The order seems to be correct according to Behnam Sadeghi's presentation of Mehdi Bazargan's – and his own modified – chronology of the Qur'an, wherein Q. 2:221 falls in Block 183 (of 194) and Group 21 (of 22), 60:10 in Block 184 and Group 22, and 5:4 in Block 194 and Group 22. See Behnam Sadeghi, 'The Chronology of the Qurān: A Stylometric Research Program', *Arabica*, 58.3–4, 2011, pp. 210–99 at p. 234.

44 This translation is my own.

45 In this chapter, I translate *mu'min* as a believer of monotheism ('believer' for short), *mushrik* as 'polytheist' or someone who associates other deities with the one God Islamic monotheism is founded on, and – when relevant in other verses – *kāfir* as someone who wilfully denies the oneness of God, therefore 'denier'. *Kāfir* is often translated as 'disbeliever', a polemical term by which is meant holding the wrong belief or a belief different from the specific community's.

46 This translation is my own.

47 The term *muḥṣanāt* has received considerable attention in both classical and modern scholarship on the Qur'an. It appears in Q. 5:5 and Q. 4:24 and is interpreted differently in both. In Q. 4:24, *muḥṣanāt* is generally understood to mean married women. Joseph Witztum states that Harald Motzki (1986) challenges this meaning, noting that other verses in the Qur'an recommend marrying *muḥṣanāt* and even see them as the ideal candidates for marriage. A thorough discussion of this term is not relevant to the focus of this study, as I want to show that contemporary scholars understand this word differently from historical ones. But for a detailed, critical discussion on the meanings of *muḥṣanāt*, see Witztum, 'Q. 4:24 Revisited', *Islamic Law and Society*, 16.1 (2009), pp. 1–33.

48 As cited in Abdelnour, 'The Islamic Theology of Interfaith Marriages', p. 9.

49 Ibid., p. 9.

50 Ibid.

51 Ibid.

52 Ali, *Sexual Ethics and Islam*, p. 21.

53 Q. 5:6 reads: O believers! When you rise up for prayer, wash your faces and your hands up to the elbows, wipe your heads, and wash your feet to the ankles. And if you are in a state of full impurity, then take a full bath. But if you are ill, on a journey, or have relieved yourselves, or have been intimate with your wives and cannot find water, then purify yourselves with clean earth by wiping your faces and hands. It is not God's Will to burden you, but to purify you and complete His favour upon you, so perhaps you will be grateful.

54 A discussion of the application of the story of the people of Lot to female homosexuality is outside the scope of this study, although I take it as axiomatic that it is a well-known claim that same-sex desire and sexual activity is Qur'anically prohibited according to the current dominant narrative in Muslim-majority contexts. Often, the story of Lot is invoked as justification for the claim. Among the exegetes studied in this book, as one example (the latest of the traditionalist exegetes here), see Sayyid Quṭb's discussion on the story of Lot's people in Q. 7:80–81 (Quṭb, *Fī Ẓilāl al-Qur'ān*, vol. 3, p. 1315). Quṭb applies the story to male and female sexual nature more generally, claiming that women and men are naturally created for one another and either gender's preference for anything else is a deviation from nature,

or perversion (*al-inḥirāf*). According to Q. 7:80–81, *And ... Lot when he said to his people, 'Do you commit an indecency that has never been committed before among the worlds? Indeed, you approach men with lustful desire instead of women. You are a transgressing people.*' Other passages related to this story are Q. 11:77–82 and Q. 26:160–73.

55 Haqqani, 'The Qur'an on Muslim Women's Marriage to Non-Muslims'.

56 See, for example, Buisson, 'Interfaith Marriage for Muslim Women'; Azzam, 'The regulation of interfaith marriages in Islamic legal discourse'; Ayse Elmali Karakaya, Interfaith Marriage in Islam: Classical Islamic Resources and Contemporary Debates on Muslim Women's Interfaith Marriages [online], https://www.mdpi.com/2077-1444/13/8/726 *Religions*, 13:8, 2022, 726 (accessed February 29, 2024).

57 Abū Jaʿfar Muhammad ibn Jarīr al-Ṭabarī, *The History of al-Ṭabarī*, vol. 39: Biographies of the Prophet's Companions and Their Successors, trans. Ella Landau-Tasseron (New York: State University of New York), 1998, p. 13.

58 Ibid.

59 Claims stating that Zaynab was prohibited sexual access to her husband (but still not divorced) in order to pressure him to convert are unfounded because Zaynab was pregnant at the time of her death. It is more likely that this claim was added to Zaynab's biography later because the evidence that is provided in this source is Q. 60:10 (see e.g. al-Ṭabarī, *History*, vol. 39, p. 16 and note 57).

60 I am not suggesting that the story of Zaynab as presented in the literature is necessarily historically accurate. That there are discrepancies and contradictions in the various accounts is sufficient reason to question at least some of the details about it. However, I also am not convinced that Zaynab must have absolutely and immediately divorced her husband simply because of Q. 2:221, partly due to a lack of evidence of such an act and partly because literally applying scripture to one's life is not always as simple as it might appear. I thus propose that Q. 2:221 complicates any literal, simplistic readings and assumptions about Muslim-*mushrik* marriages.

61 'Ali ibn Aḥmad al-Wāḥidī, *Asbāb al-Nuzūl* (Amman, Jordan: Royal Aal al-Bayt Institute for Islamic Thought, 2008), p. 221.

62 Al-Ṭabarī, *Jāmiʿ al-Bayān ʻan Taʾwīl āy al-Qurʾān*, vol. 3 (Cairo: Dār al-Hijr, 2001), p. 711.

63 Ibid.

64 Ibid.

65 Ibid., p. 715.

66 Ibn Kathīr, *Tafsīr*, vol. 1, p. 583.

67 Al-Ṭabarī, *Jāmiʿal-bayān*, vol. 3, p. 716.

68 Ibid. Here, it is relevant to reiterate that individual Hadith reports are classified as authentic or sound (reliable chain of transmission and reliable text), good (reliable text but unreliable chain of transmission), and weak (unreliable chain and text).

69 Abū ʿAbd Allāh Muḥammad al-Qurṭubī, *Tafsīr al-Qurṭubī: The General Judgements of the Qurʾan and Clarification of What It Contains of the Sunnah and* Ayahs *of Discrimination*, trans. Aisha Bewley, vol. 1. Bradford: Diwan Press, 2018, p. 388.

70 Ibid., p. 390.

71 Ibid., p. 392.

72 Ibid., p. 397.

73 Ibid., p. 395.

74 Ibid., p. 399.

75 Ibid., p. 581.
76 Quṭb, *Fī Ẓilāl al-Qur'ān*, vol. 1, p. 240. Available online at: https://ia801300.us.archive.org/2/items/ThilalQuran/delalquraan1.pdf (accessed March 28, 2024).
77 Ibid., p. 241.
78 Ibid., p. 241.
79 Ibid., pp. 234–6. He writes, for example, that both the mother's and children's mental health is sacrificed (*yaḍḥā bi'l-siḥḥat al-nafsiyya*) merely in exchange for an increase in a family's income. He scolds Western societies for allowing children, the most precious of earth's resources (*aghlā dhakhīrah*) to be raised without a mother's love and attention by pressuring women to work. See ibid. for a detailed explanation of the important role mothers play in their children's life, and which for Quṭb is the reason why women are not permitted to marry non-Muslims.
80 Asma Lamrabet, 'What Does the Qur'an Say About the Interfaith Marriage?', *Asma Lamrabet* [online], January 18, 2013, http://asma-lamrabet.com/articles/what-does-the-qur-an-say-about-the-interfaith-marriage/ (accessed December 20, 2017).
81 Ibid.
82 Asma Afsaruddin makes a similar argument in 'Qur'anic Ethics of Partnership and Gender: The Concept of Wilāya in Qur'an 9:71', *CILE Journal* (Spr. 2014), pp. 30–41 at p. 33. Available online at: https://www.cilecenter.org/sites/default/files/pdfs/Recommended-Article-English-Quranic-Ethics-of-Partnership-and-Gender.pdf (accessed December 20, 2017).
83 Lamrabet, 'What Does the Qur'an Say?'
84 Ibn 'Abbās, *Tanwīr*, p. 663.
85 Al-Wāhidī, *Asbāb al-Nuzūl*, p. 154.
86 Ibn 'Abbās, *Tanwīr*, p. 664.
87 Al-Ṭabarī, *Jāmi ʿal-bayān*, vol. 22, p. 581.
88 Abū ʿAbd Allāh Muḥammad Al-Qurṭubī, *Al-Jāmiʿ li-aḥkām al-Qurʾān,* ed. Abd Allāh b. ʿAbd al-Ḥasan al-Turkī, vol. 20 (Beirut: Muʾassasāt al-Risālah, no date), p. 411.
89 Ibid.
90 Ibid., p. 418.
91 Quṭb, *Fī Ẓilāl al-Qur'ān*, vol. 6, p. 3546. Available online at: link: https://ia601300.us.archive.org/2/items/ThilalQuran/delalquraan6.pdf (accessed March 28, 2024).
92 Ibid., p. 3546.
93 Ibn ʿAbbās, *Tanwīr al-miqbās*, p. 113.
94 E.g. Maududi, *Tafhīm al-Qur'an.*
95 Ali, *Sexual Ethics and Islam*, p. 16.
96 Al-Qurṭubī, *Al-Jāmiʿ*, vol. 7, p. 32.
97 Ibn Kathīr, *Tafsīr al-Qurʾān*, ed. Sāmī bin Muḥammad al-Salāmah, vol. 1 (Riyadh: Dār Tayyiba, 2007), p. 105.
98 Quṭb, *Fī Ẓilāl al-Qur'ān*, vol. 2, p. 848. Available online at: https://ia601300.us.archive.org/2/items/ThilalQuran/delalquraan2.pdf (accessed March 28, 2024).
99 Ibid.
100 Ibid.
101 Initially noted by Asma Lamrabet, 'What Does the Qur'an Say?'. I verified it in Ibn 'Āshūr's *tafsīr* of Q. 5:5, where he recognises that the prohibition stems from *ijmā'*. According to Ibn 'Āshūr, in his exegesis of Q. 2:222, 'This verse [2:221] prohibits a Muslim man's marriage to a *mushrik* woman… As for Muslim women's marriage to

People of the Book, the text is silent on it' (w*a naṣṣ hādhihī al-āyah* [2:222] *taḥrīm tazawwaj al-muslim al-mar'a al-mushrikah...wa ammā...tazwīj al-muslimāt al-rajul al-kitābī fa al-ayah sakitah 'anhu*). He goes on to add that the part of the verse that reads 'and do not marry your daughters to the *mushrikīn* until they believe' forbids Muslim women's marriage to the *mushrik*, but the verse does not address Muslim women's marriage to the People of the Book, and therefore, the prohibition is a result of consensus (*wa qawluhu wa lā tunkiḥū al-mushrikīna ḥattā yu'minu taḥrīm li al-ttazwīj al-muslimah min al-mushrik...fa al-āyah lam tata'arradh li-hukm tazwij al-muslimah min al-kāfir al-kitābī fa yakunu dalīl taḥrīm dhālik illa al-ijmā'...*). For details, see Ibn 'Āshūr, *al-Tahrīr wa al-Tanwīr*, Part 2, Book 1 (Tunis: Dār al-Tūnisiyyah al-Nashr: 1984), p. 362.

102 Ali, *Sexual Ethics and Islam*, p. 15.

103 Buisson and Lamrabet make this observation as well. See Buisson, 'Interfaith Marriage for Muslim Women', and Lamrabet, 'What Does the Qur'an Say?'.

104 Buisson, 'Interfaith Marriage for Muslim Women', p. 433; Lamrabet, 'What Does the Qur'an Say?'.

105 For example, Behnam Sadeghi shows precisely this – that in the discussion of women's prayer leadership, Muslim scholars operated on the premise that it was prohibited, and then sought evidence to support that claim, evidence that might come from scripture, jurisprudence, or social customs and norms. See his *The Logic of Law Making*: *Women and Prayer in the Legal Tradition* (Cambridge: Cambridge University Press, 2013).

106 Al-Qurṭubī, *Tafsīr al-Qurṭubī*, vol. 1, p. 399.

107 Ibid., p. 402.

108 Quṭb, *Fī Ẓilāl al-Qur'ān*, vol. 2, p. 848. Available online at: https://ia601300.us.archive.org/2/items/ThilalQuran/delalquraan2.pdf (accessed March 28, 2024).

109 Ibn Taymiyya's *Majmū' Fatāwā* states that the majority of the scholars agreed that a child's religion is that of the Muslim parent's because Islam is exalted and nothing to be exalted above it (*al-Islām ya'lu wa-lā yu'la 'alayhi*) (vol. 10, p. 437). Additionally, in his discussion on intercourse with Zoroastrian females who are taken as captives, al-Shāfi'ī writes that Muslims are not permitted to have sexual intercourse with her if both of her parents are Zoroastrians; this is because the child's religion is believed to be the parents' religion. However, if one of her parents – whether the father or the mother – is a Muslim, then the child, too, is considered a Muslim, and the Muslim captors can have sex with her. See Abū 'Abdullāh Muḥammad ibn Idrīs al-Shāfi'ī, *Kitāb al-Umm*, ed. Mahmūd Matrajī, vol. 7 (Manṣūra: Dār al-Wafā', 2001), pp. 670–5.

110 Qutb, Al-Baqarah (https://tafsirzilal.files.wordpress.com/2012/06/al-baqarah-eng.pdf), p. 297.

111 Some verses in the Qur'an, such as 5:73, consider belief in the Trinity a form of *kufr* (denial, disbelief). The relevant portion of Q. 5:73 reads, 'They have certainly committed *kufr* who say, "God is the third of three."'

112 This is a particularly interesting claim because Islam, like most other religions, endorses the notion that children inherit the faith of their fathers. This position appears to be a primarily modern edict issued by Muslim states that the father's religion dictates the children's. In religious discourse, it is not entirely clear that Islam is hereditary; it appears as though it has to be embraced by an individual her or himself.

113 Cited also in Siti Musdah Mulia, 'Promoting Gender Equity Through Interreligious Marriage', in *Muslim-Non-Muslim Marriage: Political and Cultural Contestations in Southeast Asia*, eds Gavin Jones, *et al.* (Singapore: ISEAS publishing, 2009), pp. 255–82 at p. 267.
114 Muhammad did not, in fact, ask any of his three daughters who were married to *mushrik*s (polytheists) to leave their husbands.
115 There is also, of course, the question of chastity in the West given high rates of premarital sex. Still, preachers who permit interfaith marriages to men consistently qualify the permission by emphasising that it is only 'chaste women' among the People of the Book that Muslim men can marry.
116 Some parts of this section were originally published in Haqqani, 'The Qur'an on Muslim Women's Marriage to Non-Muslims'.
117 Taha Jabir Alalwani's *fatwa*, as discussed and cited in Ali, *Sexual Ethics and Islam,* p. 17.
118 Ali, *Sexual Ethics and Islam,* p. 17.
119 'Why a Muslim woman can't marry a non Muslim?', *Dar Al-ifta Al-Misriyyah.*
120 Ibid.
121 Ibid.
122 Zahidul Islam, 'Interfaith Marriage in Islam and Present Situation', *Global Journal of Politics and Law Research*, 2.1, 2014, pp. 36–47 at p. 40.
123 Ibid., p. 41.
124 Ibid, p. 45.
125 Ibid., p. 41.
126 'Tunisian President: Allow Women to Marry Non-Muslims, Inherit Equally', *Al Bawaba: The Loop* [online], August 16, 2017, https://www.albawaba.com/loop/tunisian-president-allow-women-marry-non-muslims-inherit-equally-1010572 (accessed December 20, 2017).
127 E.g. ibid.
128 Habib Toumi, 'Tunisia wades into controversy amid calls for equality', *Gulf News* [online], August 15, 2017, http://gulfnews.com/news/mena/tunisia/tunisia-wades-into-controversy-amid-calls-for-equality-1.2074823 (accessed December 20, 2017).
129 Junaid Jahangir, 'Muslim Women Can Marry Outside The Faith', *The Huffington Post* [online], March 21, 2017, http://www.huffingtonpost.ca/junaid-jahangir/muslim-women-marriage_b_15472982.html (accessed December 20, 2017).
130 *Lamppost Education Initiative* [online], https://www.lamppostproductions.com/ (accessed December 20, 2017).
131 The note of the talk as forthcoming is at: '"Why Muslim women can't marry non-Muslim men?" Shaykh Abdullah Ali'', *Lamppost Education Initiative* [online], http://mye-mail.constantcontact.com/Why-can-t-Muslim-women-marry-non-Muslim-men--Shaykh-Abdullah-Ali-.html?soid=1102236409107&aid=1WTP8uTGAh0 (accessed December 20, 2017).
132 Shaykh Abdullah Ali, 'Why Muslim women can't marry non-Muslim men', *Lamppost Education Initiative* [online], March 25, 2017, https://lamppostedu.org/marriage-non-muslims/ (accessed March 17, 2024).
133 Ibid., 9:04–11:40.
134 Ibid., 28:56–29:29.

135 Thanks to Nahida Nisa for raising this point in a private conversation about the subject.

136 Shaykh Abdullah Ali, 'Why Muslim Women …', 22:32–23:06.

137 Ibid., 24:18–26:26.

138 See, for example, Aysha Hidayatullah on Māriyya the Copt and her status as a wife or concubine of the Prophet: 'Māriyya the Copt', p. 221; and Yasmin Amin on Rayḥāna, a Jewish concubine of the Prophet: 'sources disagree about her status and whether or not she converted to Islam or remained a Jewess'. See Yasmin Amin, 'Wives of the Prophet' in *The Oxford Encyclopaedia of Islam and Women*, ed. Natana J. DeLong-Bas, vol. 2, pp. 426–30 at p. 427.

139 I am aware that this could be a slippery slope. I do not suggest that it is clear which Qur'anic verses are merely historically situated and inapplicable in other contexts. I believe the argument of historical situatedness versus the universal applicability of a given Qur'anic verse or injunction is a case-by-case situation that should be up to scholarly and communal discussions.

140 Feisal Abdul Rauf, *Moving the Mountain: Beyond Ground Zero to a New Vision of Islam in America* (New York: Simon & Schuster, 2012), p. 131.

141 Ibid., p. 133.

142 Ibid.

143 Ibid.

144 'Can Muslim Women Marry Non-Muslim Men?'

145 'Imam Khaleel Mohammed's Defense'.

146 Abou El Fadl, 'FATWA: On Christian Men Marrying Muslim Women (Updated)'.

147 Ibid.

148 For example, an article on a popular website, 'Why a Muslim Woman is not Allowed to Marry a Non-Muslim Man', *IslamOnline* [online], [undated], https://fiqh.islamonline.net/en/why-a-muslim-woman-is-not-allowed-to-marry-a-non-muslim-man/ (accessed March 17, 2024) attempts to explain why a Muslim woman is prohibited from marrying a non-Muslim but a Muslim man can do so.

149 Haqqani, 'The Qur'an on Muslim Women's Marriage to Non-Muslims'.

150 This section deals primarily with the pre-modern legal discussion on the relationship between slavery and marriage. I chose not to include this in the section dealing with pre-modern interpretations of interfaith-marriage-related verses because that discussion is devoted strictly to Qur'anic interpretations and not to interfaith marriage in pre-modern Islamic legal discourse.

151 Ibn Taymiyya, *Majmū' Fatāwā*, vol. 32, pp. 181–5. Also available online at: http://library.islamweb.net/newlibrary/display_book.php?idfrom=5378&idto=5378&bk_no=22&ID=3238 (accessed March 16, 2024).

152 Chaudhry, *Domestic Violence and the Islamic Tradition*, p. 196.

153 For a detailed explanation on this, see Azam, *Sexual Violation in Islamic Law*, esp. p. 34.

154 Ibid., p. 85.

155 Ali, *Marriage and Slavery in Early Islam*, ch. 1 in particular.

156 Ali, *Sexual Ethics and Islam*, p. 14.

157 Ibn Taymiyya, *Majmū' Fatāwā*, vol. 32, pp. 184–5.

158 Friedmann, *Tolerance and Coercion*, p. 162.

159 Ibid, p. 163.

160 Ibid.

161 Friedmann, *Tolerance and Coercion*, p. 161–2.
162 *Yarith al-Muslim al-kāfir wa lā yarith al-kāfir al-Muslim bi-fadhli al-Islāmi kamā natazawwaj nisā'uhum wa lā yatazawwajūna nisā'ana*. Ahmad Ibn Idrīs al-Qarāfī, *Al-Dhakhīrah* (Beirut: Dār al-Gharb al-Islāmī, 1994). Available online at: http://library.islamweb.net/newlibrary/display_book.php?bk_no=92&ID=&idfrom=1841&idto=2114&bookid=92&startno=3 (accessed March 16, 2024).
163 Aḥmad ibn Qudāmah, *Kitāb al-Mughnī*, vol. 6 (Beirut: Dār Iḥyā' al-Turāth al-'Arabī, 1985), p. 246. Available online at: http://library.islamweb.net/newlibrary/display_book.php?bk_no=15&ID=&idfrom=4273&idto=4275&bookid=15&startno=0 (accessed March 16, 2024).
164 Ibn Taymiyya, *Majmū' Fatāwā*, vol. 32. Available online at: http://library.islamweb.net/newlibrary/display_book.php?idfrom=5378&idto=5378&bk_no=22&ID=3238 (accessed February 20, 2024),
165 Friedmann, *Tolerance and Coercion*, p. 163.
166 Ibid.
167 Ibid.
168 See, for example, Lynn Welchman, 'Qiwamah and Wilayah as Legal Postulates in Muslim Family Laws' and Marwa Sharfeldin, 'Islamic Law Meets Human Rights', both in *Men in Charge?*, eds Mir-Hosseini, *et al*, pp. 132–62 and pp. 163–96 respectively.
169 Ali, *Marriage and Slavery in Early Islam*, pp. 16–17.
170 Ibid., p. 25.
171 Azzam, 'The regulation of interfaith marriages in Islamic legal discourse', pp. 31–3.
172 Ibid., p. 8.
173 See, for example, Mir-Hosseini *et al.* (eds), *Men in Charge?*; Ziba Mir Hosseini, Mulki Al-Sharmani, Jane Rumminger, *et al.* (eds), *Justice and Beauty in Muslim Marriage: Towards Egalitarian Ethics and Laws* (London: Oneworld Publications, 2022).
174 Every chapter in Mir-Hosseini, *et al.*, *Justice and Beauty in Marriage* imagines ethics at the centre of marriage in its reconceptualisation of marriage in Islam.
175 Mir-Hosseini, *et al.*, 'Introduction', in *Men in Charge?*, pp. 1–12 at p. 2.
176 Ibid., pp. 2–3.
177 It should be mentioned that the conscious choice to not have children is discouraged in Islam, but those Muslim adults who remain voluntarily childless are part of a larger global population making this choice. See Anna Brown, 'Growing share of childless adults in U.S. don't expect to ever have children', *Pew Research Center* [online], November 19, 2021, https://www.pewresearch.org/short-reads/2021/11/19/growing-share-of-childless-adults-in-u-s-dont-expect-to-ever-have-children/ (accessed February 20, 2024). Islam encourages having children, and in a Hadith report, the Prophet Muhammad even reportedly forbade a man from marrying an infertile woman (*Sunan al-Nasā'ī*, vol. 4, Book 26, Hadith 3229, available online at: https://sunnah.com/nasai:3227 (accessed March 17, 2024)), which is questionable given that only one of Muhammad's wives bore him any children. Still, the scholarly consensus is that marrying an infertile woman is discouraged but not prohibited.
178 E.g. An-Na'im, *Inter-religious Marriages among Muslims*.
179 Noryamin Aini, 'Inter-Religious Marriage from Socio-Historical Islamic Perspectives', *BYU Law Review*, 2008.3, 2008, pp. 669–705 at p. 688.
180 Ibid., p. 688.

181 Ahmad Bahtiar Rosdiana, 'Preferences of Children's Religious Interfaith Marriages: Case Study in the International Conference on Religion and Peace', *Justicia Islamica: Jurnal Kajian Hukum dan Sosial*, 17.2, 2020, pp. 214–20.

182 In Ireland, for example, while Civil Law historically dictated that children in a mixed marriage must follow the father's religion, the Catholic Church insisted that children in such marriages should be raised Catholics regardless of the father's faith. In 1950, the issue of Catholic supremacy in a mixed marriage came to the forefront in a high-profile case involving a Catholic wife and a Protestant husband, when the latter reneged on his promise that their children would be raised as Catholic. See David Jameson, *The Tilson Case Church and State in 1950s' Ireland* (Cork: Cork University Press, 2023).

183 Jawad and Elmali-Karakaya, 'Interfaith Marriages in Islam from a Woman's Perspective', p. 16.

184 Ibid., p. 11.

185 That some non-Muslim husbands renege on their original agreement should not be treated as something that only Muslim women married to non-Muslim men deal with. In Facebook groups devoted to interfaith couples, such as one for Muslim–Christian couples, Christian women frequently raise concerns about their Muslim husbands going back on their word and raising their children differently from what both partners had initially agreed upon, or even later requiring their wife to convert to Islam. Other non-Muslim women comment to express similar worries. See, for example, the Facebook group 'Muslim Christian Interfaith Families (MCIF). Home', *Facebook* [online], https://www.facebook.com/groups/538114869892668 (accessed March 18, 2024).

186 Heather al-Yousuf, 'Negotiating Faith and Identity in Muslim–Christian Marriages', p. 328.

187 Ibid., p. 320. I should note here that in al-Yousuf's study, only 20% of the 230 couples involved a Muslim woman marrying a non-Muslim.

188 Ibid., p. 319.

189 Ayse Elmali-Karakaya, 'Being Married to a Non-Muslim Husband: Religious Identity in Muslim Women's Interfaith Marriage', in *Research in the Social Scientific Study of Religion, Volume 31: A Diversity of Paradigms,* eds Ralph W. Hood and Sariya Cheruvallil-Contractor (Leiden: Brill, 2020), pp. 388–410 at p. 407.

190 Nearly all of my respondents in this new research group interviewed so far find it 'ridiculous' that the prevailing assumption is that women will abandon their own faith and will do what their husband says. Many ask, in fact, why the Muslim community does not criticise or correct men who are controlling and dominant in marriage and instead enables them to remain that way. In other words, my respondents wonder why the community does not step up to raise men who would not force or control their wives to be like them or to not have a say in how their children are raised and instead forbid women from marrying outside because 'men tend to be controlling'.

191 Elmali-Karakaya, 'Being Married to a Non-Muslim Husband', p. 36.

CHAPTER 6

1 Luce Irigaray, *This Sex Which Is Not One* (Ithaca: Cornell University Press), p. 20.

2 Simonetta Calderini, *Women as Imams: Classical Islamic Sources and Modern Debates on Leading Prayer* (New York: I.B.Taurus, 2021), p. 60.
3 Traditional Muslim prayer involves standing, sitting, and bending throughout. This becomes relevant when women's bodies are viewed as sources of sexual attraction for men and this understanding is used to prevent women from leading mixed-gender prayer because women bending down in the presence of men is considered immodest.
4 Juliane Hammer, *American Muslim Women, Religious Authority, and Activism: More Than a Prayer* (Austin: University of Texas Press, 2012); Sadeghi, *The Logic of Law Making in Islam*; Sa'diyya Shaikh, *Sufi Narratives of Intimacy* (Chapel Hill: University of North Carolina Press, 2012); Calderini, *Women as Imams*; Sa'diyya Shaikh and Fatima Seedat (eds), *The Women's Khutbah Book* (New Haven: Yale University Press, 2022).
5 Hammer, *American Muslim Women, Religious Authority, and Activism.*
6 Sadeghi, *The Logic of Law Making in Islam.*
7 Calderini, *Women as Imams.*
8 Shaikh, *Sufi Narratives of Intimacy.*
9 Shaikh and Seedat, *The Women's Khutbah Book*, p. 7.
10 Ibid., p. 3.
11 Ibid., p. 4.
12 Ibid., p. 207.
13 Respectively, Hammer, *American Muslim Women, Religious Authority, and Activism*; Elewa and Silvers '"I am one of the people": A Survey and Analysis of Legal Arguments on Woman-Led Prayer in Islam', *Journal of Law and Religion*, 26.1, 2010–11, pp. 141–72, and Reda, 'The Islamic Basis of Female-led Prayer', *Islamic Research Foundation International, Inc.* [online], http://www.irfi.org/articles/articles_351_400/islamic_basis_for_femaleled.htm (accessed March 18, 2024).
14 As defined in Zaid Shakir, 'An Examination of the Issue of Female Prayer Leadership', *Islamic Research Foundation International, Inc.* [online], https://www.irfi.org/articles/articles_351_400/an_examination_of_the_issue_of_f.htm (accessed March 18, 2024).
15 Shakir, 'An Examination'.
16 As quoted in Shaikh, *Sufi Narratives of Intimacy*, p. 91.
17 Reda, 'The Islamic Basis of Female-led Prayer'.
18 As defined in Zaid Shakir, 'An Examination'.
19 Details in Hammer, *American Muslim Women*, p. 80.
20 Discussion in ibid., p. 79.
21 Simonetta Calderini, 'Classical Sources on the Permissibility of Female Imams: An analysis of Some Hadiths about Umm Waraqa', in *Sources and Approaches Across Near Eastern Disciplines*, eds Verena Klemm, *et al.* (Leuven: Peters, 2013); Simonetta Calderini, 'Contextualising Arguments about Female Ritual Leadership in Classical Islamic Sources', *Comparative Islamic Studies*, 5.1, 2009, pp. 5–32.
22 Calderini, *Women as Imams*, p. 98.
23 Ibid., p. 101.
24 Ibid., pp. 99–106.
25 'A Collection of Fatwas and Legal Opinion on the Issue of: Women Leading Prayers', *The Assembly of Muslim Jurists of America* [online], April 5, 2005, https://www.scribd.com/document/7125605/Fatwas-and-Legal-Opinions-on-Women-Leading-Prayers

(accessed March 24, 2024). Note that this collection is no longer available from the AMJA site (https://www.amjaonline.org/), so the link here is to an archived version of the original posted elsewhere.

26 Calderini, *Women as Imams*, p. 13.

27 Yasmin Mogahed, 'A Woman's Reflection on Leading Prayer', *Yasmin Mogahed* [online], http://www.yasminmogahed.com/2010/12/19/a-woman%E2%80%99s-reflection-on-leading-prayer/ (accessed March 18, 2024).

28 Ibid.

29 Ibid.

30 Ibid.

31 'Women's Rights in Islam: Can a Woman lead prayer [sic]', *Alsiraj Official Website* [online], https://www.alsiraj.net/English/misc/women/html/page23.html (accessed March 18, 2024).

32 Ibid.

33 Ibid.

34 Ibid.

35 E.g. 'When she is praying, whispers come to her about sexual matters', *Islam Question & Answer* [online], August 1, 2019, https://islamqa.info/en/answers/88106/when-she-is-praying-whispers-come-to-her-about-sexual-matters (accessed July 19, 2023).

36 Yasir Qadhi, 'Looking Back as We Look Forward'.

37 Ibid., 45:08–45:50.

38 Ibid., 49:13–49:30.

39 Ibn Rushd, *Bidāyat al-Mujtahid*, vol. 1 (Beirut: Dār al-Ma'rifah, 1986), p. 145.

40 Al-Nawawī, *Al-Majmū': Sharḥ al-Muhadhdhab lil-Shīrāzī,* ed. Muḥammad al-Muṭī'ī, vol. 4 (Jeddah: al-Irshad, [n.d.]), p. 152. Available online at: http://ia802700.us.archive.org/27/items/FP3865/magm04.pdf (accessed December 20, 2017).

41 Khaled Abou El-Fadl, 'Fatwa: On Women Leading Prayer', *The Search for Beauty: on beauty and reason in Islam* [online], April 5, 2010, http://www.scholarofthe-house.org/onwolepr.html (accessed March 18, 2024).

42 Ibid.

43 MomentMag, 'Why Amina Wadud Led a Mixed-Gender Muslim Prayer', YouTube video [online], May 16, 2013, https://youtu.be/E_flQbtI1U4?si=bgnMkyRyg4HDEfWq, 05:12–05:39 (accessed March 26, 2024).

44 amina wadud, *Inside the Gender Jihad: Women's Reform in Islam* (Oxford: Oneworld Publications, 2006), p. 176.

45 For example, Jonathan Brown, who shows that no textual evidence, from either the Qur'an or Sunnah, exists that prohibits women from leading mixed congregations, in *Misquoting Muhammad: The Challenge and Choices of Interpreting the Prophet's Legacy* (London: Oneworld Publications, 2015), p. 190.

46 As reported by Ibn Mājah in *Ibn Ḥajar al-ʿAsqalānī* vol. 1, Book 2 (*K. al-Ṣalāh*, 'The Book of Prayers'), Hadith 409 available online at: https://sunnah.com/bulugh/2/319 (accessed March 26, 2024). Note that the source reports immediately after the Hadith, 'Its chain of narrators is Wahin (extremely weak)'.

47 Even contemporary scholars acknowledge this Hadith as weak. See, for example, 'Woman Acting as Imam in Prayer', *Islam Online*, https://fiqh.islamonline.net/en/woman-acting-as-imam-in-prayer/ (accessed February 21, 2024).

48 wadud, *Inside the Gender Jihad*, pp. 168–9.
49 Ibid., p. 168.
50 Ibid., p. 29. For a more detailed discussion of the tawhidic paradigm, see ch. 2 of the same work.
51 Marion Katz, *Prayer in Islamic Thought and Practice* (Cambridge: Cambridge University Press, 2013), p. 179. For the veiling of enslaved women and conflicting ideas of whether they were to cover their breasts and hair and whether the the rules of not covering applied to concubines or married enslaved women, see Omar Anchassi, 'Status Distinctions and Sartorial Difference: Slavery, Sexual Ethics, and the Social Logic of Veiling in Islamic Law', *Islamic Law and Society*, 28.3, 2001, pp. 125–55.
52 To be very clear, I consider the classical jurists' logic abhorrent and unacceptable and do not believe slavery should exist at all. My purpose here is to question their logic and not to advocate for the enslavement of anyone.
53 Sadeghi, *The Logic of Law Making in Islam,* footnote on p. 59. See also Bauer and Hamza, *An Anthology of Qur'anic Commentaries, Volume II*, p. 473: in his commentary on the veiling verses, Hūd writes that the verse refers only to free women because the caliph Umar hit an enslaved girl who was covering her hair and whom he accused of 'imitating' free women. Umar's slave girls are described as serving men 'with their heads uncovered, their breasts quivering and their anklets showing'. Anchassi also discusses twenty-nine versions of the report in which 'Umar reproaches an enslaved woman for covering. See 'Status Distinctions and Sartorial Difference', pp. 130–9.
54 Marion Katz, *Women in the Mosque* (New York: Columbia University Press, 2014), p. 23.
55 As quoted in ibid., p. 35.
56 As quoted in ibid., p. 46.
57 Calderini, *Women as Imams*, pp. 71–2.
58 Ibid.
59 Shaikh and Seedat, *The Women's Khutbah Book*, p. 11.
60 Simonetta Calderini, 'Citing the Past to Address the Present: Authorities and Unexpected Interlocutors on Female Leadership of Salat' (lecture delivered in the Spring 2014 series, sponsored by Ali Vural Ak Center for Global Islamic Studies, George Mason University, April 24, 2014). See the notice and event video at *Abusulayman Center for Global Islamic Studies, George Mason University* [online], http://islamicstudiescenter.gmu.edu/events/3944 (accessed December 22, 2017).
61 Ibid., 01:08–01:27.
62 'A Collection of Fatwas and Legal Opinion on the Issue of: Women Leading Prayers', cited in Calderini, *Women as Imams*, p. 13.
63 Calderini, 'Citing the Past', 05:00–05:10.
64 Calderini, *Women as Imams*, p. 53.
65 Ibid., p. 54.
66 Ibid., p. 118.
67 Ibid. Calderini does not elaborate on this claim, and some sources dismiss it, arguing that *if* Nafisa led such a prayer, it would have been privately. To me, it is significant nonetheless, whether it was a private or a public funeral prayer.
68 Ibid., p. 106.
69 Ibid., p. 107.
70 Ibid., p. 97.

71 Ibid., p. 106.

72 Calderini, 'Citing the Past', 07:45–09:07. She discusses the reasonings further in ch. 5 of *Women as Imams*.

73 Calderini, 'Citing the Past', 09:10–10:33.

74 See, for example, Muḥammad b. Ismāʿī l al-Bukhārī, *Sahih al-Bukhari*, vol. 1, Book 6, *K. al- Ḥaiḍ* ('Book of Menstruation'), Hadith 4. Available online at: https://sunnah.com/bukhari:297 (accessed March 26, 2024).

75 *Tajwīd* refers to the art of reciting the Qur'an, which involves following a set of rules.

76 While women's voice is not considered *'awrah* 'in principle', it is not supposed to be 'alluring', as stated on a popular *fatwa*-generating website: 'Is a Woman's Voice 'Awrah?', *Islam Question & Answer* [online], May 2, 2002, https://islamqa.info/en/answers/26304/is-a-womans-voice-awrah (accessed February 21, 2024). Others claim that a woman's voice should be kept as private as possible because it can lead to temptation: 'Is a woman's voice considered as her awrah?', *IslamQA* [online], https://islamqa.org/hanafi/askimam/127637/is-a-womans-voice-considered-as-her-awrah/ (accessed February 21, 2024). In 2013, when Tahera Ahmad, a Muslim American woman reciter of the Qur'an and a chaplain, became the first woman to recite the Qur'an at the opening of the fiftieth annual Islamic Society of North America (ISNA) convention, the reaction was mixed, including much harassment from Muslims to the point that the video had to be removed from *YouTube*. See 'Ramadan 2014 – The Quran and the Recitation', *patheos* [online], July 9, 2014, https://www.patheos.com/blogs/altmuslim/2014/07/ramadan-2014-the-quran-and-the-recitation/ (accessed February 21, 2024). Further, the app Qariah was created in response to the exclusion of women reciters of the Qur'an from most popular Qur'an websites and apps. It exclusively curates Muslim women reciters of the Qur'an. The app's FAQ expects disapproval and addresses the question of the female voice: 'Frequently asked questions: Who are Qariahs and what does the Figh say about it?', *Qariah APP* [online], https://www.qariah.app/faq/ (accessed February 21, 2024) Thus, that women's voice is part of her *'awrah* is a widely held historical position, although less controversial in contemporary times. For instance, in the 1990s, *Radio Islam*, a Johannesburg Muslim radio station in South Africa, refused to allow any women broadcasters because the woman's voice is part of her *'awrah*. The station claimed that their choice not to allow any women to present on the radio 'represent[ed] the views of [the Muslim] community in not allowing women's voices to be heard' (quoted in Naeem Jeenah, '"A degree above…" The Emergence of Islamic Feminisms in South Africa in the 1990s', Master's diss., University of the Witwatersrand, 2001, pp. 47–8. See also Jay Yeo, 'Is a Woman's Voice 'Awra?: Gendered Muslim Voices in Twentieth-Century Egypt', Master's diss., University of Carolina Chapel Hill, 2018.

77 The interview with Michael took place on the phone while he was at home. When I asked him if he might be willing and comfortable to share more about the prayer he performed behind a female imam, he laughed and said, 'No.'

78 Katz, *Prayer in Islamic Thought*, p. 181.

79 Ibid.

80 As cited in Sadeghi, *The Logic of Law Making in Islam*, p. 78.

81 Ibid.

82 See note 51 in Barbara Freyer Stowasser, *Women in the Qur'an, Traditions, and Interpretation* (New York: Oxford University Press, 1994), p. 180.

83 Calderini, 'Islam and Diversity: Alternative Voices within Contemporary Islam', *New Blackfriars*, 89.1021, 2008, pp. 324–36 at p. 328.
84 Sadeghi, *The Logic of Law Making in Islam*, pp. 60–1.
85 Ibid., pp. 56–65 but esp. p. 58.
86 Ibid., p. 64.
87 Calderini, 'Islam and Diversity'.
88 Sadeghi, *The Logic of Law Making in Islam*, p. 64.
89 Whether enslaved men can lead prayers was a topic of debate among the jurists, allowed by some and prohibited by others. See Calderini, *Women as Imams*, p. 38. In fact, Ahmed Elewa and Laury Silvers note that precisely one of the reasons that Abu Thawr supported women's right to lead prayers unconditionally was that he argued that 'the legal deficiency inherent in being a male slave is greater than that in being a free woman'. And since enslaved men are permitted to lead free men in prayer, free women should be as well. See their '"I am one of the people": A Survey and Analysis of Legal Arguments on Woman-Led Prayer in Islam', *Journal of Law and Religion*, 26.1, 2010–11, pp. 141–72 at p. 157.
90 Hammer, *American Muslim Women*, p. 130.
91 Bauer and Hamza, *An Anthology of Qur'anic Commentaries, Volume II*, p. 18.
92 Barbar Stowasser, *Women in the Qur'an*, p. 8.
93 Ibid., pp. 37–8.
94 wadud, *Inside the Gender Jihad*, p. 182.
95 Ibid., p. 183.
96 Shaikh, *Sufi Narratives of Intimacy*, p. 7.
97 Geissinger, *Gender and Muslim Constructions of Exegetical Authority*, p. 50.
98 Mohammed, Khaleel, 'Female-led prayer', *The Message of Islam For People Who Think* [online], April 10, 2005, www.forpeoplewhothink.org/ (accessed February 23, 2024).
99 As cited in Noor Siddiqui, 'Female Imams', *Noor Siddiqui* [online], May 12, 2016, https://noorsiddiqui.com/female-imams/ (accessed April 16, 2023).
100 As cited in Marion Katz, *Women in the Mosque*, p. 41.
101 Ibid..
102 Shaikh, *Sufi Narratives of Intimacy*, p. 8.
103 bell hooks, *The Will to Change: Men, Masculinity, and Love* (New York: Washington Square Press, 2004), p. 153.
104 Ibid., p. 157.
105 Shaikh, *Sufi Narratives of Intimacy*, p. 8.
106 Ibid.
107 wadud, *Inside the Gender Jihad*, p. 96.
108 Ruth Roded, *Women in Islamic Biographical Collections: From Ibn Sa'd to Who's Who* (Piscataway, NJ: Gorgias Press, 2018), pp. 82–9.
109 Stowasser, *Women in the Qur'an*, p. 93.
110 Hosn Abboud, *Mary in the Qur'an: A Literary Reading* (London: Routledge, 2014), p. 154.
111 hooks, *The Will to Change*, p. 156.
112 Ibid.
113 As quoted in ibid.
114 As quoted in ibid.
115 Shaikh, *Sufi Narratives of Intimacy*, p. 8.

116 Nina Hoel, 'Sexualising the Sacred, Sacralising Sexuality: An Analysis of Public Responses to Muslim Women's Religious Leadership in the Context of a Cape Town Mosque', *Journal for the Study of Religion*, 26.2, 2013, pp. 26–41 at p. 33. Available online at: http://www.scielo.org.za/pdf/jsr/v26n2/03.pdf (accessed February 23, 2024).

117 See, for example, Kathleen Lennon, 'Feminist Perspectives on the Body', *Stanford Encyclopedia of Philosophy Archive: Fall 2019 Edition* [online], published June 28, 2010, revised August 2, 2019, https://plato.stanford.edu/archives/fall2019/entries/feminist-body/ (accessed February 23, 2024). See also Luce Irigaray, *Speculum of the Other Woman* (Ithaca: Cornell University Press, 1989); Luce Irigaray, *This Sex Which Is Not One* (Ithaca: Cornell University Press, 1985); and Genevieve Lloyd, *The Man of Reason: 'Male' and 'Female' in Western Philosophy* (Minneapolis: University of Minnesota Press, 1993).

118 Anita L. Allen and Erin Mack, 'How Privacy Got Its Gender', Northern Illinois University Law Review, 441, 1991, pp. 441–78 at p. 445. Available via *Faculty Scholarship at Penn Carey Law* [online], 1309, https://scholarship.law.upenn.edu/faculty_scholarship/1309/ (accessed February 23, 2024).

119 Ahmed Elewa and Laury Silvers, '"I am one of the people"', p. 9.

120 Ibid.

121 Hammer, *American Muslim Women*, p. 81.

122 Cited in ibid.

123 Karim, *American Muslim Women*, p. 8.

124 For more information about this mosque, see *Qual'bu Maryam Women's Justice Center* [online], https://qalbumaryam.weebly.com/ (accessed February 23, 2024).

125 Davide Mastracci, 'What It's Like To Pray At A Queer-Inclusive Mosque', *Buzzfeed News* [online], April 4, 2017, https://www.buzzfeed.com/davidemastracci/toronto-lgbt-unity-mosque (accessed February 23, 2024).

126 Zahra Ayubi, *Gendered Morality: Classical Islamic Ethics of the Self, Family, and Society* (New York: Columbia University Press, 2019), e.g. pp. 73, 82, 85, 92, 139.

127 Ibid., p. 143.

128 Ibid., p. 93.

129 Pernilla Myrne, *Female Sexuality in the Early Medieval Islamic World: Gender and Sex in Arabic Literature* (London: Bloomsbury Publishing, 2021), pp. 57–8.

130 Ibid.

131 As cited in ibid., p. 58.

132 Ibid.

133 Myrne, *Female Sexuality*, 48.

134 Roshan Iqbal, *Marital and Sexual Ethics in Islamic Law: Rethinking Temporary Marriage* (Lanham, MD: Rowman & Littlefield, 2023), p. 143.

135 Ibid.

136 Myrne, *Female Sexuality*, p. 8.

137 Iqbal, *Marital and Sexual Ethics in Islamic Law*, p. 143.

138 Geissinger, *Gender and Muslim Constructions of Exegetical Authority*, p. 50.

139 Q. 43:18 reads: 'Do they assign to God one who grows up amidst ornaments and is not well-versed in the art of disputation?'

140 Barabara Stowasser, *Women in the Qur'an*, p. 28.

141 Asma Sayeed, 'Gender and Legal Authority', p. 130.

142 E.g. Asma Sayeed, *Women and the Transmission of Religious Knowledge in Islam* (Cambridge: Cambridge University Press, 2013).
143 Shakir, 'An Examination', p. 5.

CONCLUSION TO SECTION 2

1 Shakir, 'An Examination of the Issue of Female Prayer Leadership'.
2 An-Na'im, *Inter-religious Marriages Among Muslims*, p. 36.
3 Sa'diyya Shaikh, 'A Tafsir of Praxis', p. 70.

CONCLUSION: THE POLITICS OF NEGOTIATION AND RELEVANCE

1 Kecia Ali, *The Woman Question in Islamic Studies* (Princeton: Princeton University Press, 2024). See also Kecia Ali and Lolo Serrano, 'The Person of the Author: Constructing Gendered Scholars in Religious Studies Book Reviews', *Journal of the American Academy of Religion*, 90.3, 2022, pp. 554–78.
2 Kecia Ali, 'The Politics of Citation', *Gender Avenger* [online], May 31, 2019, https://www.genderavenger.com/blog/politics-of-citation (accessed May 20, 2023).
3 Rich Barlow, 'Kecia Ali to Examine Gender Bias in Academia', *BU Today* [online], July 15, 2020, https://www.bu.edu/articles/2020/kecia-ali-examines-gender-bias-in-academia/ (accessed June 10, 2023).
4 Shahab Ali, What Is Islam? The Importance of Being Islamic (Princeton: Princeton University Press, 2016); review essay by Michael Pregill, 'I Hear Islam Singing: Shahab Ahmed's What Is Islam? The Importance of Being Islamic', *Harvard Theological Review*, 110, 2017, pp. 149–65 at p. 164 on omission of gender.
5 I share this concern with other scholars, such as Maria do Mar Pereira in her '"Feminist Theory is Proper Knowledge, But…": The Status of Feminist Scholarship in the Academy', *Feminist Theory*, 13.3, 2012, pp. 283–303, esp. p. 286. See also Saija Katila and Susan Meriläinen, 'A Serious Researcher or Just Another Nice Girl?: Doing Gender in a Male-Dominated Scientific Community', *Gender Work and Organization*, 6.3, 1999, pp. 163–73.
6 As cited in Do Mar Pereira, '"Feminist Theory is Proper Knowledge, But…"', p. 295.
7 Catherine Lutz, 'The Erasure of Women's Writing in Sociocultural Anthropology', *American Ethnologist*, 17, 1990, pp. 611–27 at p. 619.
8 Ibid., p. 622.
9 Marianne Ferber, 'Citations: Are They an Objective Measure of Scholarly Merit?', *Signs: Journal of Women in Culture and Society*, 11.2, 1986, pp. 381–9 at p. 382.
10 Do Mar Pereira, '"Feminist theory is Proper Knowledge, But…"', p. 289.
11 Lutz, 'The Erasure of Women's Writing', p. 621.
12 Ibid., p. 622.

13 See, for example, Nur Laura Caskey, 'Muslim Women Speakers: Whatta Mashallah', *patheos* [online], February 28, 2013, http://www.patheos.com/blogs/mmw/2013/02/muslim-women-speakers-whatta-mashallah/ (accessed February 24, 2024).
14 Chaudhry, *Domestic Violence and the Islamic Tradition*, pp. 8–9.
15 An-Na'im, *Inter-religious Marriages Among Muslims*, p. 24.
16 Ahmed, *What Is Islam?*, p. 513.
17 Bauer and Hamza, *An Anthology of Qur'anic Commentaries, Volume II*, p. 17.
18 Ibid., p. 18.
19 Lamia Shehadeh, *The Idea of Women Under Fundamentalist Islam* (Gainesville: University Press of Florida, 2007), p. 235. Here, the author is reviewing prominent Muslim male political and religious leaders – whom she identifies as fundamentalists – in various Muslim-majority countries who have exploited women's rights in support for their political agendas, sometimes contradicting their own teachings 'when it is to their advantage to do so', p.23. The book devotes a chapter to each such figure, e.g. the Pakistani Abu al-'A'la al-Mawdudi (d. 1979), the Iranian Ayatollah Khomeini (d. 1989), and the Tunisian Rachid al-Ghannoushi (b. 1941). The author includes one woman in her study, Egyptian Zaynab al-Ghazali (d. 2005), whom she identifies as 'the most prominent female Islamic fundamentalist and activist', p. 7.
20 Ibid., p. 228.
21 Rumee Ahmed, 'Islamic Law and Theology', in *The Oxford Handbook of Islamic Law*, eds Anver Emon and Rumee Ahmed (Oxford: Oxford University Press, 2018), pp. 105–32 at p. 126.
22 Ibid.
23 E.g. R. W. Connell, 'Change among the Gatekeepers: Men, Masculinities, and Gender Equality in the Global Arena', *Signs*, 30.3, 2005, pp. 1801–25.
24 Yasir Qadhi, 'Looking Back as We Look Forward', 49:13–49:30.
25 Ziba Mir-Hosseini, 'Muslim Women's Quest for Equality: Between Islamic Law and Feminism', *Critical Inquiry*, 32.4, 2006, pp. 629–45 at p. 241.
26 See, for example, Mohammad Akram Nadwi, *Al-Muḥaddithāt: The Women Scholars in Islam* (London: Interface Publications, 2007), where Nadwi pits contemporary Muslim feminists against historical Muslim women on whom he projects a patriarchal, limited idea of piety and religiosity; see also Aysha Hidayatullah, 'Our living Hagar', in *A Jihad for Justice: Honoring the Work and Life of Amina Wadud*, eds Kecia Ali, Juliane Hammer, and Laury Silvers (Boston: OpenBU, 2012), pp. 217–24 at p. 217; wadud, *Inside the Gender Jihad* also discusses authority and legitimacy, and accusations of forfeiting 'Islamic legitimacy' and 'going against "Islam"', p.21.
27 E.g. Hasan Maḥmūd 'Abd al-Laṭīf Al-Shāfi'ī, 'The Movement for Feminist Interpretation of the Qur'an and Religion and its Threat to the Arabic Language and Tradition', *Dialogic.ws: Reforming Discourse, Promoting Dialogue* [online], June 2011, https://dialogicws.files.wordpress.com/2011/06/feminist-hermeneutics_shafii.pdf (accessed February 24, 2024).
28 M. Akram Nadwi, 'Islam and Feminism', *YouTube* video [online], December 30, 2016, https://www.youtube.com/watch?v=Ihun2G2GgrQ (accessed February 24, 2024).
29 Knight, *Sufi Deleuze*, p. 121.

Index

Abboud, Hosn 289
Abd al-Rahman, Aisha (Bint al-Shaṭi) 117–8
Abd al-Razzāq 108
Abd al-Wahhāb 46
Abdelnour Gamal 175
Abdul Khabeer, Su'ad 33
Abdul Rauf, Feisal, 225–6
Abou El Fadl, Khaled 54–5, 125, 168, 253
Abu Zayd, Nasr Hamid 148
Ahmed, Akbar 175
Ahmed, Leila 12, 292
Ahmed, Rumee 312–3
Ahmed, Shahab 309, 311
Aisha bint Abi Bakr 119–21,
  and child marriage to Muhammad 72, 75–7, 79, 85–96, 106–7
  and prayer leadership 257, 276–7
al-ʿAlāylī, ʿAbd Allāh 183
Ali, Abdullah 223, 224
Ali, Kecia 10
  and interfaith marriage 174, 175, 184, 194–5, 230
  and Muhammad's marriage to Aisha 76
  and the politics of citation 308–9
  and sexual slavery 114, 123–4, 138, 140,
Amin, Yasmin 9, 74, 76–77
An-Naʿim, Abdhullahi Ahmed 301, 311, 322
arborescent model 37–8
Asad, Talal 7–8, 31
Assembly of Muslim Jurists of America (AMJA)
  and female-led prayer 248–9
ʿazl (withdrawal) 140
ʿawrah 255–6, 258, 265
Auda, Jasser 77
Azam, Hina 229–230
Azzam, Leena 176, 233
Ayubi, Zahra 293

Baderin, Mashood 177–8
Baugh, Carolyn 79, 80, 107
Bauer, Karen 8, 11, 30, 40–1, 139, 281, 311
Bint al-Shaṭi, *see* Aisha Abd al-Rahman
Bourdieu, Pierre 309
Brockopp, Jonathan 115
Buisson, Johanna 176, 195

Calderini, Simonetta 242, 243, 244, 247, 248–9, 255–9, 277
Carbajal, Alberto Fernández 35
Chaudhry, Ayesha 11, 32, 47, 228, 310–1, 313
child marriage 81–2

and Aisha's marriage to Muhammad 72, 75–7, 79, 84, 85–96, 106
and consent 72, 73–4, 77–82, 85
and consummation 72, 73–4, 76, 77–8, 82
and Hadith 74–7, 106
and historical context 84, 85
and legal schools +
and the Qur'an 73–4
Cila, Jorida 179
compartmentalization 289–90
concubinage 112, 117–121, 133, 138

dār (community or household) 246–7
Deleuze, Gilles 29, 37–9
dhimmi (non-Muslim granted legal protections) 193, 230, 232
al-Dihlawī, Shah Walī Ullah 46
discursive tradition 7–8, 31
divorce (*ṭalāq*) 45, 73, 201, 233, 311
Do Mar Preira, Maria 309–10

Essebsi, Mohamed Beji Caid, 222–3
Eltantawi, Sarah 80, 108
emancipatory piety 141
Esposito, John 48
al-Fāruqi, Ismail 118–9
al-Fawzan, Shaykh Saleh 125

female body
as source of social chaos 289–91
female inheritance
in Hadith 1490
in the Qur'an 68, 143, 144–5, 148–50
and contemporary Muslim attitudes 150–161, 163–6
and exegetical tradition (*tafsīr*) 144–7, 148–150
and legal schools 147
and male obligation to provide for family 144, 145, 150–62, 164, 165
and modern scholarly support for equal inheritance 147–48
female-led mixed-gender prayer 51–52, 171
and centering male consensus and experience 244, 253, 282–4
and consensus of scholars as justification of prohibition 248, 251–3, 259
and female religious authority 243–5, 258, 281
and female modesty 260, 261, 265, 283–4
as *fitna* 245, 248, 287–9, 292
and gendered access to sacred space 244–5, 247, 255–6, 274–5, 281, 283–4
and Hadith 242, 246–8, 250–1, 253–4, 276–7
and lack of scriptural evidence for prohibition 242–4, 248, 253–4, 259, 284
and male sexuality 251, 255, 260, 261, 264–8, 277, 281–4
and precedents for the practice 246, 247–8, 257–9, 297
and pre-modern legal tradition 266, 276–9, 284, 291–2
and prophetic approval for the practice 246–7
and ritual impurity 256, 258–9, 277
and the validity of prayers 252, 277
and wadud's prayer leadership 1–2, 243–5
and female leadership 260, 268, 272–3, 281, 286. 292
see also female-led prayer
female-led prayer
and female-only congregants 246–7, 252
see also female-led mixed-gender prayer

feminism 9–10, 19, 31, 37, 45, 61–62, 244, 249, 282, 307, 308–15
fiqh (Islamic jurisprudence) 54–6, 148
fitna (disruption, temptation) see female-led mixed-gender prayer
Freamon, Bernard 124–5, 141
Friedmann, Yohanan 175, 230–1

Geissinger, Aisha 284, 295
gender
and construction of knowledge 9–10
and biological essentialism 68, 145, 265, 268, 269, 281–2, 295, 301
and the politics of relevance 311–2, 315, 317
and religious authority 9, 244–5, 301, 307, 311
gender hierarchy in Islamic tradition, 145, 148, 195–6, 228–9, 232–4, 253–4, 259, 293, 313, 315
and resistance to change 8–9, 12, 31, 51, 53, 171, 172, 174, 229, 257, 281–3, 301, 308–15
gender segregation 28, 251, 253, 254–6, 282, 288–289
and age 255–6
and female attractiveness 255–6, 281, 284, 285, 288
and social status 254–5
and women's access to mosques 255, 284–291
and sacred space 244–5, 247, 255–6, 274–5, 281, 283–4
see also female-led mixed-gender prayer; mosques; public space
Ghazala al-Haruriyya 257–8
Ghazizadeh, Muhammad 139
Grewal, Zareena 8, 32, 53
Guattari Félix 29, 37–9

al-Ḥaddād, Ṭāhir 148
Hadith 85
and child marriage 75–7
and female consent in marriage 80, 106
Ḥafṣa b. Umar 119
Hallaq, Wael 41, 48
Hamdani, Hassan 178–9
Hammer, Juliane 36–7, 243–4, 291–2
Hamza, Feras 11, 281, 311
Haykal, Muhammad Husayn 118–9
Hidayatullah, Aysha 118
hijab 289
Hisham b. Urwa 77
historical context
and Qur'anic exegesis 11, 148, 149–150, 226, 228
and renegotiation of scholarly consensus 4, 82, 84, 101–5, 107, 163–6, 228, 306
Hoel, Nina 290–1, 292
hooks, bell 287, 289–90
ḥudūd (punishments derived from the Qur'an) 108

Ibn ʿAbd al-Barr 255
Ibn ʿArabi 246, 285
Ibn ʿĀshūr, Muhammad al-Ṭāhir 44, 149, 194
Ibn Ḥanbal 230
Ibn Ḥazm 79
Ibn Kathīr 185–6, 188–9, 191, 194,
Ibn al-Mundhir 79
Ibn Qudāmah 18, 79, 231
Ibn Rushd (d. 1198) 6, 18, 73, 194–5,
and consent and child marriage 79–80, 81
and female inheritance 147
and female-led prayer 252
Ibn Taymiyya 18, 231
Ibrahim, Ahmed Fekry 41, 42
ijbār (compulsion in marriage) 81, 82, 108
ijmāʿ (consensus) 51–2, 305–6, 317, 319

and child marriage 77, 79, 85
and female-led mixed gender prayer 51–2
and whether Muslims see it as binding 85, 101–5,136–140, 167–8
inheritance law 145–6, 231;
and change 43, 147, 148, 163–6
and war booty 145–6
women as inheritance 146
see also female inheritance
ijtihād (independent reasoning, legal reasoning) 42, 43–4
iktifā' (sufficiency) 183
Iqbal, Roshan 294–5
Iqtidar, Humera 46
interfaith marriage 175, 176–7, 179, 301
and abrogation 186–9, 191
and child raising 177, 179–180, 189, 197–8
and contemporary Muslim perspectives 200, 202–7, 207–12, 212–7, 218–20
and Hadith 187–8, 190–1
and a husband's authority (*qiwāmah*) over his wife 174, 197
and the invalidation of marriage to *mushrik*s and *kāfir*s 185–6, 190–2,
and lack of marriageable Muslim men 177, 178, 208, 234, 235
Muslim women's interfaith marriage in practice 174–5, 176, 178–9, 185–6, 235–8
and the permissibility of Muslim men's marriage to 'People of the Book' 182–4, 189, 192–4, 196–7, 224
and prohibition of Muslim marriage to polytheists 173–4, 180–1, 185–190, 195–8,
and prohibition of Muslim women's interfaith marriage 173–4, 180–1, 186–190, 194–6, 198, 220–8
and the Qur'an 147–50, 173–4, 180–4
and raising children 189, 235, 236, 237–8
and scholarly patriarchal assumptions 174, 176, 183–4
and *tafsīr* (exegetical tradition) 184–6, 186–194
see also *kitābīs*
Islam, Zahidul 223–4
Islamic feminism 61–2; see also, *feminism*
Islamic law 5,
and accommodating change 41–44, 45, 147, 227–8
and human equality 44, 54, 141–2, 233–4, 316
and sociohistorical context 12, 106, 147–150
see also *ijmā'* (consensus); inheritance law; legal reasoning; legal schools
Islamic tradition
and change 3–4, 6, 7, 10–1, 40–1, 47–8, 77, 84, 233–4, 242, 301, 303–6
defined 5, 30, 32
and memory 34, 40
and colonialist/orientalist lenses 46–7, 48, 311
and rhizomatic model 29–30, 35–6, 39–40, 69, 110, 121, 124, 142, 168, 172, 316–7, 320
Sunni Islamic tradition 172
ittibā' al-hawā' (following one's whims) 42

Jackson, Sherman 33
Jahangir, Junaid 223
kafala (sponsorship) 125

Karim, Jamillah 34, 292–3
Katz, Marion 255
Khan, Nouman Ali 52–3, 301, 315
  and child marriage 83–4
  and sexual slavery 122–3
Khansa b. Khidhām 75, 106
khilāf (valid disagreement) 44–5
khutbah (sermon) 244–5
kitābīs (*ahl al-kitāb*; 'People of the Book') 173–4, 230, 231
  see also interfaith marriage
Knight, Michael Muhammad
  and Deleuzian Islamic theology 35–6, 317
Kugle, Scott 37

Lalonde, Richard 179
Lamrabet, Asma 189–190, 195
Leeman, Alex 175
legal pluralism 41–4, 45
legal reasoning, see *ijtihad; takhayyur; talfī; taqlīd; tarjīh; tatabbu' al-rukhaṣ*
legal schools
  and child marriage 75–6, 77–82, 85
  and female consent in marriage 79–80, 106
  and female inheritance 147
  and female-led mixed gender prayer 266, 276–9, 284, 291–2
  and *ijbār* 81
  and sexual slavery 115–117, 123–4, 135, 136, 138, 140
  and slavery 113
  and women's mosque attendance 255
  see also *ijmā'* (consensus); inheritance law; Islamic law; legal reasoning
Little, Joshua 77
Lutz, Catherine 309, 310

male sexuality 251, 255, 260, 261, 264–8, 277, 281–4
marriage
  and female consent 73–4, 75–6, 79–81
  and free/slave status 114–5, 180–1, 186–7
  and Islamic legal doctrines 43, 74, 77–8, 123, 138, 229–230
  as a type of enslavement (*riqq*) 230–1, 232–4
  see also child marriage; *ijbār*; interfaith marriage; marriage contract
marriage contract (*nikāḥ*) 123, 138, 229–230
  and female sexuality as a commodity 229–230
maqāṣid al-sharī'a (objectives of the *sharī'a*) 44
Māriya the Copt (Māriya Qibṭiyya) 112, 116, 117–120
Martin, Emily 10
Maryam 289
maṣlaḥa (welfare of society) 43–4
  and social change 43–4
Masud, Muhammad Khalid 80–1, 82
Maududi, Abul Ala 312
  and child marriage 73–4
May, Todd 38–9
milk al-bud'a' (contract of sexual ownership) 123
Mernissi, Fatima 146, 164
Mir-Hosseini, Ziba 10, 54, 145, 233–4, 314
Mirza, Younis 116
modern Islamic legal systems
  and reform 41, 42, 43
modesty
  and gender 283–8, 291
Mogahed, Yasmin 52–3, 249–50, 301, 315
Mohammed, Imam Khaleel 226, 285
Moosa, Matti 117–8
mosques

and women's access 255, 284–291
see also gender segregation; public space
mu'adhdhin (person performing the call to prayer) 247
Mubarak, Hadia 11
muḥsan (chaste) 193, 195–6,
mushrik (polytheist) 173, 180–2, 185–6, 187–190, 194, 195–6
Myrne, Pernilla 293–5

Nafīsa bin al-Hassan 257
nikāḥ, *see* marriage contract

patriarchal worldview 286
and male privilege 281–7, 301, 311, 319–20
and masculinities 244, 287, 290
and psychic violence against women 284–6
see also gender; gender hierarchy in Islamic tradition
Peck, Scott 290
Peek, Lori 178
People of the Book, see *kitābī*s; interfaith marriage
polygyny 43
popular preachers 48–9
see also Yasir Qadhi; Nouman Ali Khan; Yasmin Mogahed
prayer leadership
and male privilege 248, 251, 253, 254, 276, 277, 293
see also female-led prayer; female-led mixed-gender prayers
Pregill, Michael 309
public space
and women's access 281–5
see also gender segregation; mosques

Qadhi, Yasir 49, 120
and child marriage 83
and female-led prayer 251–2
and slavery 121–2
and unchangeable 'fundamentals' of Islam 50–5, 251–2, 313–4
al-Qaraḍāwi, Yusuf 250–1
qiwāmah (male authority/leadership) 176, 233
Quraishi-Landes, Asifa 115, 135–6, 138
Qur'an
and child marriage 73–4
and female inheritance 68, 143, 144–5, 148–50
and its silence on female-led mixed gender prayer 242–3
and interfaith marriage 147–50, 173–4, 180–4
and slavery 113–5
al-Qurṭubī, Aḥmad 188, 190, 191, 192
Quṭb, Sayyid 189, 192, 194, 196–8

Rabb, Intisar 140
Rayhāna bint Zayd 120
Reda, Nevin 9, 246–7
rhizomatic model 38–39
see also and Islamic tradition
Riley, Naomi 176–7
rushd (intellectual maturity) 74
and emancipation 80

Sabians 193
Sadeghi, Behnam 12, 244, 248, 276, 277
Saleh, Walid 8
Savant, Sara 34, 40
Sayeed, Asma 295
scholarly consensus, see *ijmā'*
Seedat, Fatima 244–5, 256
sermon, see *khutbah*
sex drive 293–5
sexual slavery 112, 113
and legal tradition 115–117, 123–4, 135, 136, 138, 140

and the Qur'an 113–5, 133
and *Sunnah* 112
sexuality
and shifting gendered perspectives 293–6
see also sex drive; female-led mixed gendered prayer; gender segregation; male sexuality; modesty
Shaikh, Sa'diyya 36–7, 162, 244–5, 256, 284
Shakir, Zaid 168, 245–8, 299–300
shahwa (sexual appetite) 294
sharī'a 5, 44, 56–8
and its distinction from *fiqh* 54–5
al-Shaybāni 276, 284
Shehadeh, Lamia 312
shirk (polytheism) see *mushrik*
Sjadzali, Munawir 148
slavery 2, 113, 316
and modern impermissibility 43, 111, 113, 124–5, 139
and contemporary Muslim American perceptions 120, 121–5, 136–140, 141–2, 167–8
and exegetical tradition (*tafsīr*) 113
and historical permissibility according to legal schools 113
and the Qur'an 113–5
see also marriage; marriage contract; sexual slavery
Smith, Jane I. 178
Stowasser, Barbara 282, 289
stratigraphy 8,
and Qur'anic exegesis 40–1
Sunnah 5
and Aisha's marriage to Muhammad 89–96
and concubinage 112
and the rhizomatic model 72, 168
and contemporary Muslim perspectives 89–96, 99, 106–7, 168, 319
surriyya (concubine, bondswoman) *see* concubinage
Syed, Mohammad Ali 85, 107

al-Ṭabarī, 51, 145–6, 187–8, 190–1, 246, 252
tafsīr (exegesis; Qur'anic interpretation) 40–1, 227
and the biases of exegetes 184, 195, 196, 198, 228, 229 281–2
and calls for reinterpretation 148, 149–150, 161, 227–8
and female inheritance 144–7, 148–150
and interfaith marriage 184–6, 186–194
and lived experience 36–37, 161–2, 164, 165, 169, 245
and slavery 113
takhayyur (picking and choosing) 41
talfīq (combing of two doctrines), see *tatabbu' al-rukhaṣ*
taqlīd (conformity of legal opinion) 46
tarjīh (preponderance) 41, 42,
tatabbu' al-rukhaṣ (pursuing the dispensations) 42
and *talfīq* 43
traditionalist scholars 4, 10–1, 314, 315
Treaty of Ḥudaybiyya 190, 191, 192
Tucker, Judith 45
al-Turābi, Ḥasan 194, 285
Tutt, Daniel 35

Umar b. al-Khaṭṭāb 114, 116–7, 187–8, 228, 231
Umm Kajja 146
umm al-walad 115–7, 118
Umm Salama 196, 257
Umm Waraqa 246–8, 257

Vishanoff, David 40

wadud, amina 145
  and the normative status of Muslim male experience 282
  and prayer leadership 1–2, 253–4
  on Q. 4:34 145
  and tawhidic paradigm 254
  and woman as object of legal discourse 288
al-Wāḥidī, Ibn ʿAbbās, 192–3,
Weisberg, Dvora 179

Youssef, Olfa 148–9, 162

Zaman, Muhammad Qasim 47, 53
Zayd b. Ḥāritha al-Kalbi 68
Zaynab bint Muhammad 185–6, 191, 192
Zaynab bint Jahsh 121
Zoroastrians 187
Zulaykha al-Qaraziya 121

About the Author

© Evey Wilson Wetherbee

Dr. Shehnaz Haqqani is an assistant professor at Mercer University and specialises in Islam, with a focus on gender and sexuality. She is a host of the podcast *New Books Network* and runs a YouTube channel called "What the Patriarchy?!"